# THE AMERICAN NEWSROOM

# THE AMERICAN NEWSROOM

## A History, 1920–1960

Will Mari

UNIVERSITY OF MISSOURI PRESS
Columbia

**The volumes of this series are made possible with the generous support of the University of Missouri School of Journalism.**


University of Missouri Press, Columbia, Missouri 65211
Printed and bound in the United States of America
 First paperback printing, 2023.

Library of Congress Cataloging-in-Publication Data

Names: Mari, Will (William) author.
Title: The American newsroom : a history, 1920-1960 / by Will Mari.
Description: Columbia : University of Missouri Press, 2021. | Series: Journalism in perspective | Includes bibliographical references and index.
Identifiers: LCCN 2021003563 (print) | LCCN 2021003564 (ebook) | ISBN 9780826222329 (hardcover) | ISBN 9780826222961 (paperback) | ISBN 9780826274595 (ebook)
Subjects: LCSH: Press--United States--History--20th century. | Journalism--United States--History--20th century. | Newspaper publishing--United States--History--20th century.
Classification: LCC PN4867 .M335 2021 (print) | LCC PN4867 (ebook) | DDC 071/.30904--dc23
LC record available at https://lccn.loc.gov/2021003563
LC ebook record available at https://lccn.loc.gov/2021003564

∞™ This paper meets the requirements of the American National Standard for Permanence of Paper for Printed Library Materials, Z39.48, 1984.

Typefaces: Caslon and Museo Sans

## Journalism in Perspective: Continuities and Disruptions

Tim P. Vos and Yong Volz, Series Editors

---

Journalism is a central institution in the social, cultural, and political life of communities, nations, and the world. Citizens and leaders rely on the news, information, and analysis that journalists produce, curate, and distribute each day. Their work must be understood in the context of journalism's institutional features, including its roles, ethics, operations, and boundaries. These features are themselves the product of a history emerging through periods of stability and change. The volumes in this series span the history of journalism, and advance thoughtful and theoretically-driven arguments for how journalism can best negotiate the currents of change.

*For Dr. Ruth Moon,*
*for being the best co-adventurer, partner and spouse I could ever ask for.*

# Contents

# Illustrations

# Acknowledgments

Every book goes on a journey, and this one is no exception. I need to start by thanking Gary Kass, my first acquisitions editor at the University of Missouri Press, who saw me present parts of my book project in its very early stages and invited me to submit the manuscript. His guidance through the review process was invaluable. He "found" the book before it was really a book. Thank you, Gary.

I should next thank the Press's editor in chief, Andrew Davidson, for taking over for Gary and shepherding me through the editorial board's review process. Andrew's gracious encouragement helped me navigate the book's final revisions. Mary Conley's organization, editing, and guidance during the book's final steps to press were also critical. Her keen sense of the book's argument enhanced the final product. Robin Rennison and Deanna Davis and their marketing squad shepherded the book into the wider academic and journalistic worlds. The people who copyedited (especially Dr. du Quenoy!), indexed, and designed the book ensured that it would be an enjoyable reading experience as well as an informative one. Without the team at the University of Missouri Press, the book would look much different (and not as good). Thank you, all.

Tim Vos, as the series editor, advocated for the book from our first coffee meeting at the AEJMC conference in Washington, DC, back in August 2017. Tim pushed me to incorporate a more holistic sense of theory and helped me to deepen the book's utility for journalism studies scholars, as well as for my fellow media historians.

A very early end-to-end reader of the book was my dissertation adviser at the University of Washington, Richard Kielbowicz. He and the rest of my wonderful committee—Randal Beam, David Domke, Doug Underwood, and Richard Johnson—encouraged my wide-ranging idea for a new history of the American newsroom in the twentieth century and guided me through the various pitfalls of doing media history on such an ambitious topic.

Other friends and colleagues helped me through the book-writing and revision process, including Clint Bryan, Joe McQueen, Renee Bourdeaux, and Chrystal Helmcke at Northwest University. Seattle friends Betty Winfield, Tom and Linda Ackerman, Ken and Frances Knutzen, Geoff and Ashley Van Dragt, Lindsey Meeks, Matt Bellinger, Jason Gilmore, Miles Coleman, and Shin Lee took the time to talk through various aspects of the project, give me honest feedback, and generally encouraged me on the way.

My colleagues at the Manship School at Louisiana State University deserve a special thank you, too. These include Erin Coyle, now at Temple University, and the late Martin Johnson, our dean. Martin recruited me to the Manship School, and I will remain grateful for the supportive Manship community he fostered. Teri Finneman at AEJMC connected me to the History Division there and mentored me through the leadership ranks. Thank you, Teri, for your own leadership, encouragement, and advice as I made career transitions.

Librarians and archivists made this project possible. In my case, the UW Libraries Interlibrary Loan crew under Jennifer Rossie worked wonders, moving dozens and dozens of volumes of rarely transferred material from across the country, extracting them from storage stacks, scanning materials, and checking on the location of others. Nearly every footnote reflects their cheerful aid. Jessica Albano, the subject librarian at the UW for journalism, has more than earned recognition for her creative assistance with finding sources. At LSU, our Manship librarian, Rebecca Kelley, helped me with last-minute searches, as did Jacob Fontenot, in his capacity as head of the ILL department.

The NewsGuild-Communications Workers of America, the Society of Professional Journalists, the staff at *Editor & Publisher*, the UW Press, and the staff at the National Archives granted permission to use images, helped me locate sources, funded trips, and were generally supportive. The Bridges Center for Labor History at the UW funded crucial travel to conduct research at the National Archives. Sarah Pulliam Bailey and Jason Bailey—themselves courageous journalists—helped me to navigate Washington, DC, and deserve thanks as well.

To my writing group, the Notion Club, and all my friends there, especially Elise, Kevin, Nick, Carrie, Sammy, Hannah, and Casey—thank you. Chris and Natasha Lim and their family extended their hospitality for many years to keep me sane and supported from the beginning of this project. My family also supported me during graduate school and beyond.

A final thank you is due to my wife, colleague and co-adventurer, Dr. Ruth Moon, to whom this book is dedicated. May God bless your work, and our work together.

I love you!

*Deo gratias.*

Will Mari
Baton Rouge, Louisiana
Nov. 21, 2020

# Note on Sources

This study draws on a variety of primary-source documents, including trade publications, memoirs, textbooks, archival material, and contemporary research from early journalism studies researchers. The driving goal with both source selection and methodology was to tell the story (but also to complicate the story) of the typical news worker in the typical newsroom. A representative sample was constructed, detailed below, that accounted for challenges of access and completeness of print runs over the period in question. This sample also attempted to address some of the built-in biases of the authors by triangulating perspectives. If, for example, an issue or issues of a trade publication addressed a trend in the newsroom (like, say, the use of mobile telephones for reporting), I looked for corroborating evidence of this trend in a memoir, textbooks, or correspondence in archival material. And since some of the contemporary observations of the newsroom were often written by editors or other "bosses," I sought out rank-and-file perspectives. I am aware that these were sometimes heavily filtered through personal experiences, but my goal was to examine newsroom work culture from several internal perspectives. This was done in order to best recreate as many of the subtle interactions within it as possible (barring actually being present and conducting an ethnography). While not ethnographic history, strictly speaking, this study borrows from some of the elements of this approach, including its holistic focus on the lived environment and a focus on subaltern voices. More properly a social history, or social history applied to media history, it uses theory to inform, but not drive, an inductive interpretation of historical evidence.

Related to concerns over how best to balance the points of view of those in power with those less empowered is the matter of geography. The gravitational pull of New York City in American journalistic culture was quite pronounced throughout the twentieth century. Some of the biggest, most well-resourced, -trained, -staffed, and -led newspapers were based there, and the city's influence casts a long shadow over media history research. This is, of course, quite acceptable if a researcher is looking at the New York region or its influence specifically. But in an attempt to create a more balanced national case study, I attempted to privilege sources where possible that were *not* based in New York. In many cases this desire to not focus on New York was limited by how key journalistic organizations were based in the city, had key members who hailed from there, or held events there that were covered by the trade press. It was often possible, however, to look beyond New York for parallel examples in other urban centers important for the development of newsroom culture. These include cities such as Chicago, St. Louis, Washington, DC, Los Angeles, and San Francisco, where, for example, important chapters of the American Newspaper Guild (ANG) formed independently of New York.

## SOURCES[1]

Trade publications show debates among news workers about best practices in the field.[2] They also show power relationships. Most were written for and by editors or others in positions of authority in the newsroom. When reporters were present, their senior status or collaboration with newsroom bosses meant that they may not have represented the majority views of lesser-empowered peers. Some trade publications, however, sought a more middle road or even advocated on behalf of more ordinary news workers. Of the trade publications examined, the American Society of Newspaper Editors' *Problems of Journalism* (its annual proceedings), the Associated Press Managing Editors' *Red Book* (its annual proceedings), and *Editor & Publisher* (published as a weekly newspaper) fell into a broadly pro-publisher camp.[3] The publications of the ASNE and APME included discussions of members' management problems, such as hiring, firing, budgeting, interactions with local and national governments, and issues of distribution and sales. *Editor & Publisher* covered the industry's developments more broadly, including ownership moves, mergers, technology adoption, newsroom renovation, construction, and other national trends.

The *Quill*, published as a monthly magazine by Sigma Delta Chi (later the Society of Professional Journalists), was at first focused on collegiate journalism (through the 1910s), but by the 1920s it had expanded its coverage to focus on how its young members were faring as reporters and junior-level reporters. While often in favor of management initiatives, its stories and editorials also included contrarian perspectives, including critiques of how employers treated employees. The *Guild Reporter*, being the official organ of the American Newspaper Guild, was, of course, pro-union and generally anti-management in tone and coverage. It focused on strikes, the news of local chapters, and national trends that affected labor law. Finally, the *Journalism Quarterly* (formerly *Journalism Bulletin* for its first few years of existence, 1924–1927), contained the work of early journalism studies scholars, who in many cases were reporters-turned-journalism professors. These authors usually took a painfully neutral tone, usually avoiding direct commentary and conducting and interpreting surveys of news workers and college journalism students.

Whenever possible, existing indices were consulted when searching for topics of interest to the newsroom, including firing, hiring, technology, unionization, relationships between different types of news workers, and interactions with managers. The *Journalism Quarterly* (1924 through 1960) and the volumes of the *Red Book* of the APME (launched in 1948 and examined through 1960) were covered by thorough, published indices. A working index was constructed from skimming the content pages of the ASNE's *Problems* (from 1923 through 1960). Relevant articles were read for discussions or research pertaining to newsroom life.

In some cases, however, it was necessary to create a representative sample covering 1920 to 1960.[4] Issues that were examined were skimmed closely for any items, photos, or text related to newsroom life. Articles or elements that were related to newsroom life were then read more carefully, and, in many cases, scanned with a smartphone's or microfilm reader's camera when possible, identified with date, title, and other temporal tags, and described in source notes arranged chronologically. With the *Guild Reporter*, every first issue of the month was examined from 1934 (its inaugural issue) through 1960.[5] For every five years, this was alternated, so the second issue of the month was examined. With the *Quill*, every available issue from 1917 through 1960 was read. Many of the earliest issues of the *Quill* had to be specially requested through interlibrary loan from DePauw University or the University of Oregon. With *Editor & Publisher*, the most exhaustively utilized source for this study (with more than 400 pages alone of notes, or 157,000 words' worth, taken on more than 40 volumes of material), a system of volume sampling was used in which every other volume was inspected. There were often several volumes per year, especially as the magazine expanded.

Bound volumes from 1919 to 1947 were requested in batches of three to five volumes from the University of Oregon's Knight Library; bound volumes from the UW Libraries were available from 1948 through 1960. Additional issues in the 1960s were also looked at, for context. Due to the wide-ranging nature of the information in each issue, and its cartoons, photographs, and illustrations, bound volumes were found by this researcher to be superior to microfilm because they allowed for a more thorough skimming. The first and third issues, and then the second and fourth issues, were examined on an alternating five-year basis. This accounted for most major historical events, including those of the Great Depression and World War II. If adjacent articles continued discussions, the narrative thread was continued and issues were occasionally read in addition to the regularly sampled sequence.

A list of journalism textbooks was assembled for this study based on previous research, but also on lists constructed by Perry Parks, Joseph Mirando, Linda Steiner, and Chalet Seidel.[6] A representative set of autobiographical material, collated from Warren Price's and Roland and Isabel Wolseley's bibliographies, was also utilized.[7] Memoirs and textbooks are challenging sources. As one media historian has noted, they are "often produced by atypically successful journalists who worked for large newspapers." That excludes those who worked for smaller newspapers or those who had less successful and more prosaic careers.

But memoirs can still be representative because "these reporters or editors likely would be more influential in shaping the field later than the typical news worker." These sources captured ideas of "how journalists should act, how they should think, and where they should go to accomplish their work." As sources, "occupational autobiographies offer the historian other advantages: the illumination of the institutional, social, communal, and personal context of a worker's life."[8] Especially if the memoirists worked in a wide variety of publications, their narratives can illuminate a number of different kinds of newsrooms and occupational experiences. As Linda Steiner has also noted, "Autobiographies are needed to understand 'how workers felt about their work . . . whether they resented changes, [or] whether they challenged 'standards.'"[9] They capture underrepresented voices, too, if read carefully, as Calvin Hall has shown.[10] For example, the desire for autonomy emerges as an enduring value for news workers, and one more successfully realized in the newsrooms at the end of the era under consideration. This could be seen in the numbers of journalism memoirs, which spiked in the era from 1930 to 1960. While written about earlier generations of news workers, the fact that so many authors felt triumphant is telling.

Textbooks, with their idealistic portrayals of news workers, their organizations, and their values, show a more static, but still helpful, contrast to

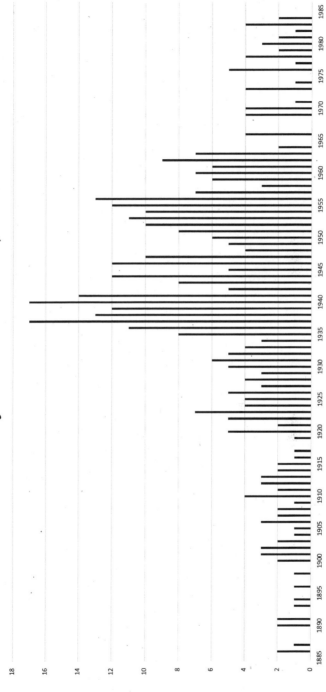


Figure 1. This graph shows the average number of journalism memoirs published from the late nineteenth century through the late twentieth. Created by the author.[11]

memoirs. Textbooks illustrate, sometimes literally, how newsroom norms have been filtered down through generations of journalists. As long as they are read concurrently with trade literature, memoirs, and archival material, they can perform an important triangulating service for the media historian. For a later book project, I also read a representative sample of *Editor & Publisher*, the *Quill*, *Columbia Journalism Review*, and other trade publications through the end of the century.[12]

Finally, this researcher made a weeklong trip in May 2015 to the National Archives at College Park, Maryland, with funding from the UW's Harry Bridges Center for Labor Studies. There, I was able to examine the wartime records of the National Labor Relations Board (renamed the National War Labor Board). These consisted of reports reviewed by the Daily Newspaper Printing and Publishing Commission based in Chicago and composed of representatives from organized labor, the newspaper publishing industry, and more neutral representatives, including its chairman, Robert K. Burns, a professor at the University of Chicago. While I had been specifically searching for legal depositions or other court-produced testimonies from news workers, I encountered the reports of the Commission and the War Labor Board. Some of these reports were important for the chapter on unionization in the newsroom and helped to serve as an additional verification on the salary data reported by (and to) the federal government during the era. A brief follow-up trip to the National Archives-Pacific Northwest Region, based in Seattle, and conversations with the archivists based there convinced me that there may yet be surviving accounts in various regional centers of the National Archives (NA). These accounts may contain depositions describing newsroom life and conflicts with bosses, specifically pertaining to hours and salaries. Hunting them down is beyond the current scope of this study, but would be helpful for any follow-up studies by myself or other scholars. The Northwest branch of the NA did help confirm how the various regional centers of the National War Labor Board operated, and how its agents and the agents of the peacetime National Labor Relations Board conducted investigations, oversaw elections of labor representatives, and generally intervened in labor disputes between publishers and news workers. The intervention of the federal government through this entity, especially after the war, helped lead to a kind of working détente between the two groups.

# THE AMERICAN NEWSROOM

## CHAPTER 1

# Introduction

## The Newsroom

THE MOST IMPORTANT centering place in American journalism remains the "newsroom," the messy, fraught heart of a vocational community that has grown up in and around the occupation since the middle of the nineteenth century. This storied gathering spot for news workers endures as "a symbolic space of human labor that both challenges and reinforces preconceived notions regarding newswork."[1] It is a space journalists have engaged with, been changed by, and, in their turn, have shaped.[2] But it did not emerge from some primordial past. It was not just a place, either.

The modern newsroom as we know it, or came to know it, emerged after World War I through the 1950s and then came to full bloom during journalism's "high modernism" period. It is a relatively recent innovation. This period has been described by Daniel Hallin as a kind of occupational apogee of American journalism in the twentieth century.[3] The newsroom in this era was where journalists gathered together, fostering a *relational newsroom culture*, where values and routines were learned from peers and the terms of work negotiated with superiors.[4] Journalism existed before newsrooms, to be clear. And it may exist after. But the newsrooms' historical form matters today if we are to understand where present-day journalism came from and where it may be going next.

In midcentury American newsrooms, workers faced publishers and bosses and formed impressions of their audiences through conversations with colleagues and rivals alike. In the process, they developed an ecosystem of relationships with their peers, managers, and sources, as well as with the public, which has imaginatively placed journalists in newsroom spaces through portrayals on stage, in radio, television and TV productions, and in novels. As an occupational phenomenon, the "newsroom" is a place for the social organization of information collection, processing, and dissemination. Its physical layout has defined occupational turf within news organizations. Where a news worker labored within these spaces has mattered. The newsroom's relational roles have defined an occupational identity, and so we should begin by looking at its social history. It has been described as a kind of steady state, a received space that is intrinsically associated with journalism, rather than as a creature of unique circumstances and possibly rare when considering the history of journalism in its totality. This project attempts to extend the historical conceptualization of the newsroom in the past as a metaphorical, relational space.

The individual, routine-level and organizational forces at work in the production of news within the context of the newsroom offer rich research terrain, and the sources that discuss them a rich set of data for an exploration of the push-pull pressures that fuel change over time.[5] This project is interested in how reporters formed a unique *newsroom culture* internally while interacting with one another and with other people outside of their occupational community. By working together, in a collaborative fashion that also left room for autonomy, they made the newsroom a principal site for socialization processes that created and perpetuated a shared occupational community. To tease out this presumption, this study focuses on the daily, experiential nature of journalistic work.

### THE NEWSROOM AS MORE THAN METAPHOR

At the outset it is important conceptualize what "the newsroom" meant for journalism and journalists in the mid-twentieth century in the United States. First, it was—and, in many ways still remains—despite significant disruption, a site of connection and a shared place for collective occupational meaning. Newsrooms, both individually and as a collection of spaces, are locations where inertia, tradition, debate, and contestation formed the heart of journalism's culture.

News workers' past personal formations and their individual experiences inevitably influenced their understanding of themselves and their roles, being "durably inscribed in the body and in belief." These "durable depositions" have lingering power and tend to reinforce themselves or avoid conditions where they are challenged too much or too forcefully.[6] And yet it is important to think of the limitations of theorizing the newsroom in this way: newsrooms and news workers had other, outside influences.[7]

Because historians, and, by extension, media historians, tend to eschew explanatory theories and are more focused on description and narrative, it is important to think about the usefulness of theory at all in this kind of project. Theory here helps the historian understand the processes and power differentials at work in newsrooms. These were not egalitarian spaces, and were historically not particularly kind to women and individuals from minority backgrounds. They could be divided by class, too, and often physically manifested these differences. To take just one example, editors at larger daily newspapers tended to have more office space, set aside from the main newsroom floor, than their employees. These private places could, it was true, be earned only after years of service as rank-and-file reporters, but privilege pervaded this process, and the allocation of power tended to be uneven in even motivated and well-run newsrooms. Ultimately, however, all the parts and members of a newsroom formed (and continue to form) a "work zone," an arena for negotiated professional autonomy. This autonomy was and is complemented, confirmed, and sometimes contested through the active self-policing and reinforcement of values. Through acts of internal surveillance, workplace culture helps to construct an occupation's sense of self and what it considers important for its membership. How workers behave outside of the room also indicates the institution's far-reaching influence.

The newsroom is, in these various senses, a metaphorical space. It is, however, not *just* an imagined or perceived space, in the vein of George Lakoff and Mark Johnson, but also often a real one with felt consequences, as with the metaphorical "wall" between business and news operations.[8] The newsroom-as-metaphor still endures as a powerfully alive allegory for news workers and their relationships to each other and to journalism, culturally situated but in our case located in the United States in the twentieth century. What then, is a newsroom, if it is all three of these things: a part of a collective space for new workers, a flexible metaphor, or vehicle for the social life of journalism? This book is an attempt to provide a history of this relational construct, or concept.

At some level, the interaction between different kinds of news workers creates newsroom relationships. This is not to say that where two or more news workers were or are gathered, that there is a newsroom, as with places of spiritual gathering, but it *is* helpful to think of "the newsroom" as both a physical space *and* a symbolic one, a pragmatic place and an idea, especially when examining the history of American journalism. Newsrooms included buildings with specific affordances (telephone lines, air conditioning, electricity, typewriters, desks, pencils) that were built into these spaces and designed to encourage news work. While bound in space and time, they were and are *relationally* constructed spaces that were and are negotiated, contingent, and deeply embedded with human connections. This study looks not, then, at the physical building of the newsroom alone (though it does feature prominently as a kind of character), and so it is not, in that sense, an *architectural* history. It is, rather, a history of the social life of the newsroom and of the relationships existing in/around that place. The newsroom, then, for our purposes, can be described as the ultimate twentieth-century site of journalistic labor: but it is more than a building. Again, it is a durable, transferable, flexible idea. Much like how journalists in the 1920s created idealized newsrooms for training young reporters, with fictionalized characters and spaces, they also thought of their newsrooms as bigger than the sum of their bricks.[9]

So, while the building spaces are evocative, this study focuses on the *relationships in the newsroom*, and outside of it, these grounded connections that were fraught and rife with racial, class, and gendered disparities but were also romanticized and made nostalgic. When news workers such as reporters and editors talked about "the newsroom," it was shorthand for the relational world encompassed by this space.

To summarize, the theoretical intervention this book employs includes thick descriptions of the kinds of news workers and their hierarchies, of the tools and unions and other material "things" of their newsroom life worlds, to refocus on the portable, transitional, evolving, and flexible nature of the newsroom. In this way conceptions of "the newsroom" concretize some of the nebulousness of the occupation's identity. As a transportable space, one that is metaphorical-physical and relational-real, it is a *little* like "the office" and its various evolutions, but a lot less like the laboratory, the factory, the firehouse, the hospital, the police station, or other occupational spaces—these are more intimately tied up with occupational identifiers and are physically necessary. In contrast, the newsroom has not always existed in journalism and may not be necessary for the profession in the future; at the same time, for the journalism of the present, it has been absolutely critical as an incubator, a shelter, a clarion call, a resource center and, above all, a centering place where journalism's identity as we know it has been forged.

## THE HISTORY OF AMERICAN NEWSROOM CULTURE AS THE HISTORY OF JOURNALISM IN THE UNITED STATES

Professionalization via the newsroom's relational ecosystem set the stage for first the industrialized, then the corporatized newsroom of the twentieth century. Understanding this overarching narrative is crucial to understanding journalism's return today to its original state of nature, that of smaller, more mobile, more ideological news organizations whose connections with space and place are more fragile and less entrenched.

In Michael Stamm's transnational economic history of paper manufacturing by the *Chicago Tribune* in the twentieth century, he points out that newspaper publishers had become mass-producing industrial tycoons in their own right, producing ephemeral products more akin to milk than steel but nonetheless requiring massive investments of resources and infrastructure: "Though rarely considered as such, the printed newspaper was, like the automobile, a product of industrial capitalism."[10] My examination of newsrooms of the 1920s through the 1950s in this study similarly shows how the driving personal, relational, and institutional forces of interpersonal relationships greatly shaped, and were shaped by, these industrial processes, which led to a more fully advertising-reliant, national news ecosystem by the 1960s that was stridently—if this is the right word—nonpartisan. Matthew Pressman's *On Press*, as well as the work of Kevin Lerner and others, shows that this led to an awkward, criticized middle ground, one that still aimed at objectivity but of course fell far short from achieving this goal.[11] Journalistic authority was derived, then, through a combination of complex industrial, capitalistic, corporate, and institutional forces, with ramifications down through our own era, when tech companies act as publishers of data and purveyors of news.[12] But before all that, knowledge production, newspapers, manufacturing, and urbanization went hand-in-hand in American history.[13]

I hope that my own contribution to this conversation on the continued relevance of newsrooms, even as they disappear, reform, shrink, and shift, is to show how the very middle-class aspirations of news workers—rank-and-file reporters and lower-ranking editors—helped to pave the way for the rest of the century's journalism culture, formed, with all its flaws, in the newsroom environment. Moving from their scrappy, blue-collar, self-taught roots to the college-trained, theoretically apolitical people they portrayed themselves to be (an interpretive community, as Barbie Zelizer has described them), American news *workers* became *journalists* as we perceive them in the occupation-shaping decades of the midcentury.[14] In the United Kingdom, as Meryl Aldridge has shown, a similar process was underway.[15]

This period, lasting from the extreme economic boom of the 1920s through the profound bust of the 1930s to the global conflagration of World War II to the early Cold War, has occasionally been dismissed—in my opinion, ironically—as a time of stability, a long-ago golden age of American newsroom history. Quite to the contrary, this same era witnessed the rise of the salaried reporter, the coming-of-age of journalism schools, the birth of newsroom unionization, and the adoption of critical technologies like the car and radio. It was a dynamic period in media history, not a sleepy one.

## THE AMERICAN NEWSROOM IN FURTHER HISTORICAL CONTEXT

Newsrooms have acted as the sites of "news manufacture" in the United States since the early twentieth century.[16] Their cultures are identified with the act of doing journalistic work and the human interactions necessary to accomplish discrete media work tasks—they are centers of work *coordination*. Examining the relationships formed and forged in newsrooms (for example how ideas of "professional" behavior worked themselves out in conflicts with business and management personnel) and how hierarchies developed between different kinds of news workers can help us understand how newsrooms also became centers of *control* over that news-making work. Relational work was what defined newsrooms as such. As C. W. Anderson has pointed out, the genealogical ethnography of these spaces greatly nuances their historicity. It does so by looking beyond isolated work practices and moving into an examination of values and beliefs, situating these in real historical context with contingent realities.[17]

Coordination and control, as well as unionization and technology adoption, constructed the work culture of twentieth-century newsrooms.[18] These emerged during an era characterized by the rise of a manufacturing economy in the United States, fueled by ideas of Taylorism and "efficiency" at the turn of the century.[19] They were organized to reflect certain social values but formed their own, inner occupational societies, as well as their own way of controlling journalistic work, or modulating the control of that work, from within. The "more systematic management" of newspapers in the early twentieth century impressed observers; for example, Alfred M. Lee. Lee, an early media sociologist, believed that the growth of specialized positions like rewrite staff and copy editors within newsrooms reflected how they were becoming more and more like "an automobile manufacturer's assembly line."

Newsrooms had changed from highly idiosyncratic offices run by charismatic editors and a cadre of printers to nerve centers for news-producing factories. In this way, "news-handling" was more complex than ever by the time Lee completed his exhaustive survey of the newspaper industry in 1937.[20] Staff organization had been undergoing differentiation for a generation, since at least the 1880s and the introduction of telegraphy, typewriters, and telephones. This led to the decline of "rugged individualism" and the growth of a more "impersonal," team-produced journalism.[21] Large newspaper newsrooms (operating in cities with a circulation of one hundred thousand or more) appeared with the explosive growth of American cities, sharing "a common set of values—industrial capitalism, specialization of labor, geographic concentration, and an intricate and specialized economic structure" with their surrounding urban environments.[22]

This study explores how *the newsroom as a relational space* evolved during a formative moment for American journalism and its workers, from the 1920s through the 1950s and the ascendancy of broadcast journalism. It examines the effect of that evolution on news workers and their work *in* the newsroom space, evoking what it meant for them to work together as part of an industrial organization. This includes the sights and smells and sounds of a busy, bustling workplace. It was a place designed to produce a daily product, but also one that left room for creativity and autonomy.

### NEWSROOMS AS SITES OF OCCUPATIONAL CHANGE

The ideas behind this book have been inspired by Hanno Hardt and Bonnie Brennen's *Newsworkers*, by Warren Breed's analysis of newsroom culture and its unspoken norms, by Randal Beam's application of the power-relations approach to the study of the professions, and by Nikki Usher's work on the importance of space and place in journalism.[23] This project is centered on the lived experiences of reporters and editors, and how they sought to construct their agency and autonomy. Another inspiration for this project is Ted Curtis Smythe's classic research into the working lives of reporters.[24] Examining the last third of the nineteenth century, Smythe outlined the trials and travails of regular reporters facing totalitarian bosses and equipped with few resources. His study is, however, in need of an extension that takes its ground-level, social history of news workers past the first decade of the twentieth century. Smythe's work previewed the seminal scholarship of Herbert J. Gans, Gaye Tuchman, and other newsroom ethnographers of the 1970s and 1980s.

American media history is often divided into familiar eras. This has especially been true when looking at the history of newspapers and their related spaces and technologies. From the colonial to the revolutionary press, the party press of the early Republic, the penny and abolitionist press of the antebellum era, to the rise of the mass-market daily around the turn of the twentieth century, there is a familiar theme of progress. Perhaps a step back or two occurs, but eventually journalism triumphs and things are righted.

Of course, that is a gross simplification, and since the 1970s this progressive interpretation has become necessarily more nuanced or upended entirely. But one further presumption seems to linger, namely, that of a long, somewhat stagnant era from World War I through the early Cold War, prior to Watergate. While some authors have interrogated this premise, such as the aforementioned Smythe, the newsrooms of journalism's industrial era deserve more nuance, not less. The contemporaries of these institutions certainly found them interesting, problematic, and vibrant—Warren Breed was not alone in his curiosity about social structures within newspapers in the 1950s, nor was Lee in the 1930s. This book builds on their work, telling a story that highlights how newsrooms were critically important to the emergence of an increasingly white-collar, professionalized occupation. In short, the newsrooms of the 1920s through the 1950s birthed modern journalism.[25]

Focusing on the experiences of news workers at larger, daily metropolitan newspaper newsrooms of a certain size, distributed by region (across the West Coast, Midwest, South, and East Coast), and seeking a set of representative newspapers bound this study more effectively than an exhaustive study of all newspapers, including weekly newspapers, magazines, and early radio and TV stations. Furthermore, a study that emphasizes non-New York newsrooms avoids a bias toward New York-based news organizations. Journalism studies scholars such as Karin Wahl-Jorgensen have warned against relying exclusively on studies of the latter, as they were created under unique conditions and had special privileges. These included access to capital, culture, and a workforce that many more typical newsrooms and news workers did not possess.[26] It should also be emphasized at the outset that this is a study of the *American* newsroom experience. Comparative studies of newsrooms in Europe, particularly in the United Kingdom and Canada, are beyond the scope of this present work, but are of course excellent in their own right.[27] Historically situated journalistic and newsroom cultures arise in different contexts.[28] And they continue to have importance in those contexts, as a collection of essays on "media houses," edited by Staffan Ericson and Kristina Riegert, has shown.[29]

At the same time, taken as a whole, the United States is an ideal case study, due to its formative role in global journalistic traditions, its number and location of newsrooms, its number of news workers, and its pioneering role in technology development and adoption. More complex newspaper newsrooms during the era from 1920 to 1960 also had enough differentiation among staff to illustrate larger trends in American journalism, such as the growth of middle management, unionization, and the proliferating use of telephones, cars, and other technologies.

### SITUATING PAST AND CURRENT STUDIES OF NEWSROOMS

Media historians have long grappled with the proper role of theory, as noted above. Media or journalism history in particular has struggled with how best to incorporate interpretative concepts, including elements of the still-ongoing "cultural turn" in the humanities and social sciences. The field has tended to suffer from a sort of myopic, and Whiggish, tendency, in which "great men" and institutions have received more than their fair share of attention. While this has faded, starting in the 1970s, media historians have been accused of being out of step with larger trends in historical scholarship. As James Carey has argued, the continual challenge for our field has been how to do systematic analysis. Recent work reflecting on the state of media history and on future directions for the field has brought media historians to a healthier place, however. They are now creatively applying theories of social construction, temporality, power, culture, and textual criticism, expanding the idea of a "text" (as other allied fields have done) to their subjects.[30] This makes for richer and more relevant conversations with other scholars, including other historians. In addition, the cultural and now the material turns are at work in media history thanks to a closer alliance of media history and journalism studies.[31] Media historians see the value of actively engaging with journalism studies writ large, including some of the field's best scholars.[32] A particularly promising trend involves journalism studies researchers, for their part, recognizing the value of media history.

This means bringing understandings of *past* path dependencies, or paths that-could-have-been, to bear to journalism studies, especially in regard to technology development and adoption.[33] The American experiences with technology, entrepreneurship, and government interventions, or the lack thereof, mean that this is a complex tale. Historians of technology and journalism in this vein, including Brian Creech and Susan Keith, along with Florence Le Cam and Juliette De Maeyer, have explored the in situ development of technology tools. The study of constitutive choices regarding adoption of technology should be at the heart of any history of the newsroom, as it is uniquely dependent on such tools for its work. I explore this more in the chapter on the use of the telephone, car, and radio, to extend the reach and culture of news work outside the newsroom's physical spaces.

This project relies on iterative primary-source research, including memoirs, trade journals, textbooks, and archival material. Details on these sources and the methodology used to explicate them can be found in the notes in each chapter. These are supplemented by an understanding of spatial theory as applied to newsroom spaces, as well as a consideration of newsroom ethnographies throughout. The primary sources consulted—memoirs, trade journals, the first generation of journalism studies research, government reports, textbooks, and archival material—are supplemented with diverse visual material that illustrates how workers defined their jobs and shaped their ideas of success and status. A longer reflection on the challenges associated with the use of these various sources, particularly memoirs and trade publications, can be found in the essay at the front of the book that introduces the rest of the study ("Note on Sources"). In short, they are occasionally difficult to work with due to their penchant for romanticization and mythologization—their perspective is grounded in the experience of elites, and often white, male voices dominate. But with that in mind, they provide a helpful window into the thinking and value systems of news workers during this era.

It should also be noted at the beginning of this study that it is not an analysis of press criticism. There has been critical work on this front done by scholars such as Sam Lebovic, Robert W. McChesney, Ben Scott, Victor Pickard and others; moreover, in their own time, Walter Lippmann, Oswald Garrison Villard, Will Irvin, and A. J. Liebling all aimed erudite and thorough criticism at their peers.[34] While this is not a major focus for this project, however, a couple of points are in order in this regard. First, working journalists usually either ignored (or reacted mostly negatively, when they did react at all) to this kind of criticism (most notoriously to the Hutchins Commission, but also, later, to the Kerner Commission).[35]

Second, most news workers in the mid-twentieth century were not totally oblivious to outside critiques, of course, to be clear, but their work-life worlds—encompassed by their newsroom culture—were perhaps more self-contained than we understand, looking back from our vantage point more than a half century later. While *Editor & Publisher* and the *Quill* reacted to the Hutchins Commission's findings and disagreed with them, more or less, most of the "outside" press criticism of the era did not seem to filter down to the level of the rank-and-file reporter and editor. As Kevin Barnhurst has discussed in a seminal look at journalistic mythologies, "news turns out to be a knowledge system, its content expressing *practitioner* ideas about what is knowable and its audiences interacting in the production of a particular kind of knowledge in culture" (emphasis mine).[36]

### NEWSROOMS BY OTHER NAMES: THE IMPORTANCE OF SPACE AND PLACE

It is critical to situate the study of the newsroom in contextualized places and times, in this case, newspaper offices and relationships. Also sometimes spelled as two words ("news rooms") or called "city rooms" (as in the "city desk") or news "bureaus," newsrooms in the decades since the end of the nineteenth century had gone from being "cyclonic attics with desks gerrymandered into disorderly clusters by sulphurous editors" to "modern . . . as regimented as a real estate office."[37] Agency was negotiated, and contested, in the working world of the newsroom.[38] John Nerone and Kevin Barnhurst, in their high-level review of newspaper types and the American newsroom as a center of journalistic work in the twentieth century, call the "resulting professional newspaper" of the 1920s through the 1950s "a reporter's newspaper."[39] They note several key developments in the formation of the twentieth-century version of the newsroom. The first was the division of mechanical from editorial labor. As mechanical workers unionized, there was a distinct break between typesetters and other production workers and reporters: the latter were no longer trained first as the former. This had the further effect of pushing news workers, when the option came, to pursue higher education, with college becoming a common route into journalism. The second way the newsroom formed as its own space was through the separation of advertising and news. This development was heightened by the growth of a distinct group of more independent, better equipped, and better organized reporters.[40] This "wall" of separation of the business from news operations of newspapers also served as a useful metaphor for newspaper publishers keen on showcasing their product: the stories produced by their editorial staffs.[41]

The legacy of the influential newsroom ethnographies of the late 1960s, 1970s, and 1980s, including those by Gans, Tuchman, and Fishman, reverberates today in the work of scholars such as Nikki Usher, Peter Gade, and others.[42] The older newsroom ethnographers were themselves heavily influenced by the theory of the social construction of reality, organizational theory, and contemporary critiques of the ideology of professionalism.[43] In this regard, their thinking was especially affected by Peter L. Berger and Thomas Luckmann's *Social Construction of Reality* and Thomas Kuhn's *Structure of Scientific Revolutions*.[44] These scholars helped newsroom ethnographers conceive of newsroom spaces as constructed of self-governing norms and priorities, much like Warren Breed had found a generation before.[45] I share the interest of media sociologists in how inter- and intraprofessional competition has shaped journalism, especially in how ideas of professionalism were formed by its practitioners in newsrooms. Specifically, I am curious as to the "where" and "when" of this process. And as newsrooms become more distributed, smaller, more mobile, and less all in one "place" today, as scholars such as Usher have pointed out, it is worth revisiting these spaces, if only to know more about how modern American journalism was shaped by them.

### A NOTE ABOUT "SPACE"

A more explicit application of spatial theory is evident today in the journalism studies literature on newsrooms. Based on the approach of the influential French spatial theorist Henri Lefebvre, newsrooms may be thought of as conceived (produced), perceived (imagined), and lived (manifested) places. While Lefebvre does not specifically mention newsrooms, his approach can be applied to better understanding this space. And indeed, researchers such as Usher and Akhteruz Zaman use his conceptualizations for their work. Usher, for example, demonstrates her indebtedness to Lefebvre when she identifies newsroom spaces as *absolute*, *relative*, and *relational.*

Since newsrooms are spaces built for and by news workers, it is particularly important to think of them as relative and relational. As Usher describes it, "relative space is a way to discuss how people relate to the objects, the social relationships formed, and the cultural meaning extracted" there. Relational space is people-defined and perceived, and both conceptions, along with ideas of absolute space, are at work in parallel ways.[46] Zaman uses the work of Doreen Massey, another critically important spatial theorist, to help explain the idea of relational space for journalists. It is the product of interactions and part of an ongoing production that is never quite finished.[47] In Zaman's words, "news is produced through practices, multiple realities, and trajectories of news . . . [;] the space engendered in news work is always in the making and eternally unfinished."[48] News workers have existed in a continual state of change, both at the occupational and organizational levels, throughout their history. As Massey herself argued, "the spatial is integral to the production of history . . . just as the temporal is to geography."[49]

When regarding Lefebvre's conceived, perceived, and lived spaces as manifested in U.S. newsrooms within the context of media history, several factors are important to consider. At a basic level, reporters socialized one another into their distinctive roles in the newsroom in all three spaces. Newsrooms were built places, and thus conceived with particular purposes (i.e., news production, displays of publisher power) in mind. They were perceived places—written about extensively in memoirs and trade literature—and left an indelible social impression on news workers. They were lived spaces, too, in that reporters created products that were consumed and shared by other newsroom peers and by members of their audience.[50]

American, French, and British spatial theorists therefore have much to say about the *relational* nature of the newsroom.[51] For example, inspired by this approach, Aurora Wallace examined the *exterior* of New York City newspaper buildings for their statements about the beliefs and values of their funders, that is, publishers.[52]

Spatial theory helps media historians understand how organizational-level influences were manifested on (and by) news workers in newsrooms during the period in question, and continue to be today. Granted, the role of newsrooms is still fluctuating. Scholars such as Pablo J. Boczkowski, C. W. Anderson, Karin Wahl-Jorgensen, and David Ryfe have called for examinations of news ecosystems and journalism production beyond newsrooms.[53] Newsrooms are not, of course, the only place news gets produced, and it is important to study the postindustrial newsroom as it becomes a collection of distributed workplaces and spaces.[54] But understanding the function of these individual organizations is still critical to understanding journalism and journalistic culture in historical and current contexts, and perhaps more important than ever as news organizations continue in their struggle to innovate and survive.[55]

A number of scholars have engaged with this topic on another front, connecting "media houses" to ideas of space and place and thus to architecture studies. One exemplary collection of studies has encouraged researchers "to think [of] architecture and media *together*, and to think about their links *historically*" (italics in original).[56] In non-US contexts, a media "house" is a building dedicated to media work, including the centering space of the newsroom, but also its various support facilities, and is often used to describe not just both newspaper and magazine headquarters but also broadcasting and internet-news focused organizations. The tension for architectural historians (at least those who do research on media history) can be found in the idea of "centers," or the role of media organizations' physical manifestations in a digital age. Do they still have meaning in a time of digitized dispersal?

Harkening back to an older debate, one introduced by Canadian media theorist Harold Innis and his "distinction between time-biased and spaced-biased media of communication," Staffan and Riegert argue that such centers do indeed have special meaning and symbolism, even in our more distributed age. Staffan and Riegert are thus concerned with the complications of buildings and their resilient purposes, in the face of massive changes to our information societies.[57] With regard to media history, Stamm (in his excellent history of the *Chicago Tribune* and its tree-harvesting and production networks) makes great use of Innis's questions about the materiality of economic history, in how newspapers are intrinsically steeped in both "the real" (i.e., their use of trees to make paper, or today, the use of powerplants to generate electricity to keep server farms and thus "the cloud" working) *and* the symbolic.

"Twentieth-century newspapers were not just outlets for news but also [the] material products of industrial capitalism manufactured by business firms organized like those in other mass production industries," Stamm writes. "Producing a printed daily newspaper . . . was a process of both creating public information through the work of journalists and mass-producing a consumer good through the labor of hundreds and even thousands of skilled and unskilled workers, forming networks stretching from the forest to the delivery person."[58] As early as the first half of the twentieth century, which is the focus of this book, the American newsroom was composed of a series of physical and representational spaces, with "the newsroom" (and occupational discourse about it) a kind of container for a broader concept. In referring to the newsroom or speaking of their time in that physical space, many news workers referred to the news industry, to each other, to their mission, or to their collective sense of identity and history.

## THE LEGACY OF THE NEWSROOM'S OCCUPATIONAL COMMUNITY

This study conceives of "the newsroom" as an active place of social construction of roles, norms, and practices. News workers sometimes proactively built this space, aware of what they were doing. In other cases, they adopted older practices and retooled them more or less unconsciously to their needs. But at no time was the newsroom a static, single site or simply a place of work. Newsrooms embodied the aspirations of generations of workers and helped to shape an occupation. While other office spaces, or components of office spaces, such as the cubicle, have reflected larger trends in American firms, newsrooms were and are special.[59]

Newsrooms were crucial formational spaces for new news workers. They provided advancement opportunities for veteran news workers. Their arrangement empowered publishers and owners and occasionally disempowered more rank-and-file staff. But these same structures allowed workers to push back and carve out some autonomy of their own. The newsroom inspired what is arguably the first group of middle-class, creative white-collar workers to successfully unionize.[60] It stirred and stirs such nostalgia that journalism as practiced during the twentieth century in the United States is, indeed, synonymous with the newsroom.

#### RACIAL EXCLUSION FROM PRIMARILY WHITE NEWSROOMS

It should be noted from the outset that Black journalists, and minority journalists of other nonwhite ethnicities, were often discouraged or simply barred from pursuing careers in white newsrooms, or in some cases, prevented from even visiting or otherwise collaborating with them. In 1964 the American Newspaper Guild (ANG, or simply Guild) estimated that only forty-five Black reporters, copy editors, photographers, or other newsroom staff were working in white newsrooms.[61] The American Society of Newspaper Editors (ASNE) would only admit its first Black member, John Sengstacke of the *Chicago Daily Defender*, to membership in 1965, using criteria that largely excluded African American editors based on arbitrary definitions of circulation. These had been so construed as to deny membership to publishers of weekly newspapers (many Black newspapers were published weekly).[62]

To be clear, "mainstream" metro newsrooms were often closed to Black journalists, with few exceptions, and the factors and influences that were involved in the active construction of these barriers were real and racist in nature. Black journalists were of course able to influence the national discourse on race and make an indelible impact on the nation, with their fearless reporting and advocacy. Their story deserves more and more complex retellings. At least one scholar has found that the Black press has nuanced connections to the Black churches, labor unions, and technology, to name just a few areas for future exploration.[63] While a holistic history of the Black press and its storied newsrooms in Los Angeles, Chicago, Pittsburgh, Baltimore, and New York, among other cities, is beyond the scope of this study (and needs to be written), no otherwise holistic history of the modern American (mostly white) newsroom, sadly, would be complete without mentioning the reasons for racial exclusion and segregation.

But as was the case in a variety of other mostly white institutions, even during the midcentury, racial barriers were becoming more and more costly to maintain. This was partially due to the activism of the excluded Black press, but also partially due to the Cold War and the ways that the Soviet Union (correctly) pointed out our hypocrisy as a country. As explored by Mary Dudziak and Thomas Borstelmann, this global context was key for the broader civil rights struggle.[64] In the United States, white publishers beyond the big cities of the north and northeast were eventually moved to *begin* integrating their newsrooms, often painfully and reluctantly, by this outside pressure but also by other, internal motivations. The Guild, for example, helped in this push for change, as did some journalism schools, professional associations such as the ASNE (in time, at least) and, again, the Black press itself.

That meant that a courageous handful of Black reporters, columnists, and correspondents were actively able to break the color barrier at the end of this period, in the 1950s and 1960s, including Austin Scott, William Raspberry, Carl Rowan, and Philippa Schuyler; at the same time, some white journalists and editors, such as David Halberstam and Norman Isaacs, were becoming more aware of their role in the exclusion of Black reporters and editors and worked to rectify that. In the chapters that follow, I include discussions about the specific challenges Black and minority journalists faced when encountering white newsroom spaces. In doing so, I highlight the important work of scholars who study this issue, including scholars of color or others who have devoted considerable time and attention to the study of race in journalism, such as D'Weston Haywood, Gerald Horne, Jinx Broussard, Fred Carroll, Calvin Hall, and Gwyneth Mellinger. Their research into the barriers faced by Black journalists both in breaking into white newsrooms and remaining there if they succeeded in getting hired, is vital to understanding the racist legacies baked into our journalistic systems.[65] Black journalists' stories of struggle are a significant counterpoint to nostalgic recollections or reconstructions of newsroom life during the mid-twentieth century by white journalists: while an important institution, the newsroom was also a deeply problematic place with an unfair balance of power weighted toward white communities and interests, often at the expense of Black people.

### BRIEF OVERVIEW OF CHAPTERS

To present the newsroom as a space, place, and site of occupational identity formation, as well as an information processing, production, and dissemination factory, requires a look at the various groups and subgroups of workers within that space, following the classic newsroom sociologies of the twentieth century, but now with the benefit of knowing the end-stage development of corporatized journalism by the end of the century. What follows, then, is a *relational* and *institutional* history of the newsroom's various communities of work. Thinking of news workers as arranged—as they did—into distinct kinds of rough-but-unequal peer groups and of *the newsroom as the milieu* in which they worked, is helpful. The interconnectedness of these groups is emphasized throughout this book, even as a pastiche of perspectives is brought to bear on various aspects of newsroom life and work.

The first two chapters examine the "near peers" of the reporter, which included copy boys and girls, photographers, rewrite staff, and copy editors. Whereas copy boys and girls and photographers were thought to have less power and autonomy in the newsroom than reporters, they were crucial workers on their own terms. The former—acting much as interns would later—helped to circulate copy throughout the newsroom, freeing up reporters to do their jobs and generally providing a reserve workforce that smoothed over the imperfections of the newsroom's often idiosyncratic functions. Photographers provided the increasingly critical visual element that helped newspapers compete first with magazines and the radio, and later with TV. Their interactions with each other, their bosses, and reporters reflect larger intra- and internewsroom tensions.

In contrast, rewrite staff and copy editors were nominally more powerful than reporters. Both groups controlled important parts of the news-production process in the newsroom. Reporters often aspired to the rewrite desk, or spent time on it in the latter part of their careers. They also routinely opposed copy editors' decisions. The parallel work worlds of these groups show how newsroom personnel were well aware of the various subcultures within their workspace, and how they learned to navigate these cultures over time as the newsroom transitioned to a more white-collar institution.

The next two chapters look at the role of the reporter via newsroom relationships. Beginning with the cub, "leg man," and general-assignment (GA) reporters, their internal stratification revealed a "junior" and "senior" status that was reflected in both pay and power. Senior reporters, who included veteran beat reporters and columnists, had more autonomy and were at the top of the newspaper's hierarchy in the newsgathering process. Newsroom norms both reflected and were changed by these "peer-to-peer" interactions. Unspoken norms, competition, and collaboration all had their say in these relationships. Unionization, technology adoption, and the wider social forces affecting the American workplace also influenced newsrooms and their workers, and both junior and senior reporters considered themselves increasingly white collar and professionalized by midcentury.

The middle chapter focuses on the power of newsroom "bosses" over both the news-production and newsgathering processes. The interactions of managing, city, and other midlevel editors in the newsroom saw this power decrease over time as reporters unionized and as newsrooms developed human resources departments. Editors in chief also shared power with a growing group of middle managers, who acted more like junior section editors. As they became less autocratic, their power over reporters and newsroom support personnel became shared and more corporately controlled from above. In this, newsrooms reflected other white-collar business firms, while retaining at least some elements of independence.

The two final chapters then look at the role of technology adoption and unionization in the disruption of newsroom culture and work routines. The telephone and car created whole new groups of workers, notably rewrite and leg men, and again helped print newsrooms to compete with new journalistic forms (radio and television). Newsrooms reoriented their newsgathering and news-production processes around mobile reporting technology. News workers reskilled or multiskilled, learning how to best incorporate practices such as phoning in stories, updating editions throughout the day, and reporting stories as they happened, pioneering techniques later adopted by radio and TV newsroom workers.

In parallel, unionization shifted power away from editors and owners and back toward workers, pushing the long-term professional project of these workers in unexpected directions. While the unionization of the American newsroom was neither as total nor as radical as some in the industrial union movement hoped, postwar prosperity allowed a détente between owners, editors, and their workers. The newsrooms encountered by Gans, Tuchman, and others were spaces that had been shaped by these twin forces of technology adoption and unionization. They were *relationally* conceived as newsrooms and the physical spaces and their tools were manifestations of these underlying influences. "Newsrooms" had become truly complex social structures that attracted the attention of sociologists.

The conclusion summarizes these trends and reflects on the twin relational and physical natures of the newsroom space, as well as on its continuing importance to American journalism. It concludes with a meditation on the long-term prospects of whatever "the newsroom" may be in the future. An appendix on the economic context for the newsroom's move from a blue-collar gathering place to an aspirational white-collar, professionalized space follows, including a table describing salary trends from about 1920 through 1960. As noted earlier, a description of the primary sources, including a discussion of some of the challenges of working with the large collections of professional trade literature, memoir material, textbooks, government documents, and archival material used, is located in the book's front matter.

## CHAPTER 2

# Copy Boys and Girls and Photographers

> **Perhaps, too, you will understand something of the thrill and excitement that every newspaperman feels about his job. For no matter what that job may be, he knows that it is part of the swift daily drama that takes place in the few breath-taking hours between the time news happens and the time you read about it. Whether he is an editor, reporter . . . cameraman, [or] copy boy . . . he is proud to be able to say, "I work on a newspaper!"**
>
> —Henry B. Lent, "*I Work on a Newspaper*" (1948)

IN A TYPICAL newsroom in middle America in the middle of the century, in the middle of the day, one would likely have noticed a number of empty desks, depending on the kind of newspaper you were visiting (an afternoon paper versus a morning paper). Piles of paper would linger in dusty corners. Phones might ring unanswered, but there would still be the clatter of typewriters and wire copy being printed by teletype. Most of the reporters would be out, on assignments, or just about to return, leaving the space populated by other workers, including copy editors, rewrite staff, and, noticeably, copy boys. This latter group would still be busy running copy, errands, or both, and are the subject of this chapter.

Taken together, newsrooms are and were complex communities of news workers collaborating and competing to produce the news.[1] From the 1920s through the 1950s and beyond, these communities grouped themselves into specific categories and formed "near peers" to the centering figure of the reporter, supporting and supervising the latter. This dynamic *relational* ecosystem of editorial workers was composed of many varieties of writers and editors.

The "newsroom" was occupational code, in this sense, for a culture of work critical for identity formation. Beginning with those who had less power vis-à-vis reporters in and out of the newsroom over the newsgathering

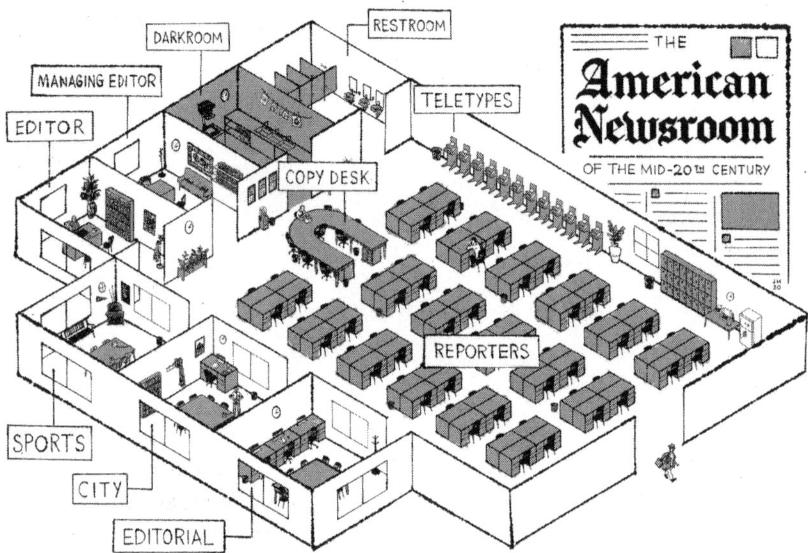


Figure 2. In this illustration, a typical midcentury newsroom is recreated based on news workers' contemporary accounts (including memoirs), for a large, daily metropolitan newspaper with a circulation of about 150,000 to 200,000. A few reporters and editors are placed in the various spaces for scale, but the newsroom could easily accommodate between seventy-five and one hundred workers at peak periods. Created by Jeremiah Moon, 2020.

process, this chapter examines those lower-status news workers referred to as "copy boys" and girls, along with the sometimes-renegade supporting cast of photographers. They operated within and outside of a physical space, one that is important to consider in any historical look at newsroom work culture(s).

### THE COPY STAFF

Copy boys, sometimes called "office boys" or "clerks," intuited newsroom culture from their position as entry-level news workers. To be a copy boy was to be an aspiring reporter, and so in the hierarchy of the newsroom they represented one of the few groups that looked up to, and not down or across to, reporters. While the term was used for young men, women in the uber-masculine culture of newsrooms were also occasionally welcomed, though they faced sexism and harassment outside of the "women's pages." In newsroom culture, only librarians could be considered less influential.[2] Pay, job security, and future prospects were all rated according to what the copy staff might get if they made the coveted jump to "cub" reporter. Copy boys (and in very few cases girls) physically conveyed "copy through the stages of editing and did other routine office work such as distributing proofs, getting clips from the reference library and bringing in food for reporters and editors who are too busy to take time out to eat," observed a contemporary.[3] In this latter duty, as the newsroom's "traditional food bearer," they fetched sandwiches and coffee for reporters when the latter were stuck at their desks trying to meet deadlines.[4] Drawn by the "glamour attached to newspaper work," these mostly high-school graduates "considered themselves fortunate to have gained entrance to a newspaper office in any capacity," noted another observer.[5]

Becoming accustomed to the work could be a challenge, and it took time for a newly hired copy boy to get acclimated, but most did so quickly, being pulled inexorably into the newsroom's routines. The daily, rushing maelstrom of journalistic labor helped. After an initial period of bewilderment, overwhelmed "by the rush of the place, by the calls of 'Boy!' emanating from distant corners of the city room, a new copy boy gradually becomes oriented, [and] learns the routine of the job." Moving among the various departments of the paper, beyond the newsroom itself, and encountering all kinds of staff members, from cub reporters not much further along than themselves to the managing editor and the chief of the copydesk, copy boys were ideally positioned to soak up the many unstated norms of the newsroom. It may have taken up two years of everyday "heel and toe work," but, "far from becoming robotized and doing his work mechanically," a copy boy "beg[an] to feel the news pulse of the paper. He anticipate[d] the needs of editors by studying their personal habits. He d[id]n't have to be told what brand of cigarettes the assistant makeup editor smokes."[6] Before the advent of internships and more formal newsroom-hiring procedures, this process was the most traditional route into the journalism field. In time, however, the internship model would dominate.

Copy boys could be called upon to write copy to fill in holes on a news page or hunt down information for breaking news stories. "Senior boys," once they had proven their competence, could write short reports for less-pressing beats, such as church news, or tackle the occasional obituary.[7] These opportunities were relatively rare, but accumulated over time. Most young staffers (and with few exceptions, they were in their early twenties or younger, sometimes as young as fifteen or sixteen) advanced based on a honed attention to detail, a good memory, and, of course, moving copy around the newsroom and through the newspaper "plant." Into the early 1950s, a copy boy had "a better opportunity than any nonwriting member of a newspaper staff to observe newspaper functions, the foibles of writing men, and other things that will be of inestimable value as he progresses in the writing profession."[8] True, already by the 1930s self-educated copy staffers were facing competition for entry-level reporter jobs from the rising tide of college graduates. It was still a steady springboard for many, however. A key quality-of-life difference existed between those who lived at home and worked at the paper part-time, supported by their families and in some cases still finishing high school, and those who were away from home and who did not have such support. Buying a suit could precipitate an economic crisis, and "cigarette and lunch money make dire incursions into his bankroll," wrote one sympathetic peer.[9] The occasional tip and even some light freelancing might help augment the low pay.

### COPY STAFF, REPORTERS, AND NEWSROOM CULTURE

By the 1920s the most trusted source of new reporters was found in this copy boy/girl system, despite its uneven application in newsrooms.[10] In reality, cub reporters and copy boys were only a few steps apart, in terms of their responsibilities and work tasks. Copy boys existed in a kind of in-between status, as they waited for openings in the cub reporter positions above them.[11] Sometimes a copy boy would be given the chance to become a photographer if there were no openings on the news side. This was regarded as less than ideal, as the status of photographers was improving only slowly in the newsroom.[12] But the reverse could also be true: copy boys could start out exclusively in the photo department. Sammy Schulman, a news photographer who later achieved fame covering the Second World War, was hired as a copy boy at age seventeen, in 1920, for the *New York American*. After a while, he applied and got a copy position with International News Photo, in the same building as the *American*, at nine dollars a week.[13]

Perhaps one of the better-known former copy boys in American journalism, Arthur Gelb, who went on to become the managing editor of the *New York Times*, recounted some of the social divides keeping copy boys from fraternizing too closely with reporters and others. Gelb got his start at the *Times* as a night-shift copy boy in May 1944, while on a wartime hiatus from college.[14] Usually, he noted, outside the newsroom, "a wide gulf existed between reporters and copyboys," with few exceptions.[15] Some of this could be explained by age; since reporters often socialized at bars, and most teenagers were not old enough to enter, that relationship could only begin after the copy boy had become a cub, if not later. Work as a copy boy could lead to an intermediate position, such as a clerk, and then to reporter. This aspiration motivated Gelb and his fellow copy boys, and, starting with the war, copy girls.[16] Until their promotions, however, lower-ranking copy staff would sometimes warm a wooden bench, waiting to be sent on errands in the newsroom. Gelb recounts how when Wilson L. Fairbanks, the *Times*' intimidating telegraph editor, shouted "copy!," the next boy in line for an assignment would rise "like a private saluting a four-star general. Orders would be muttered, and if a mission was not completed with speed and exactitude, his accusing stare was enough to make a grown newspaperman tremble."[17] But there was stratification even within this world. Gelb, for instance, found himself promoted to desk clerk for Fairbanks, which at the *Times* was a kind of stationary office boy.[18]

By the late 1930s many larger and even some smaller newspapers began to organize what had long been an informal arrangement. The ANG's influence had trickled down to affect the status of newsboys, who were sometimes given standardized weekly wages like other news workers. As with all other members of the newsroom, however, the prolonged Depression threatened job security. One estimate claimed that as many as ten thousand copy boys and girls, as well as cub reporters, were waiting for promotion across the country in 1930.[19] Despite these adverse conditions, the *New York Daily News* ran its copy boys through an in-house "school," starting in 1935. This produced some 124 graduates through 1941, 23 of whom were subsequently dismissed for various reasons. Copy boys would start at twenty-one dollars a week and end as junior reporters at twenty-five to fifty-five dollars, with a top scale of sixty to seventy-five each week, based on experience, service, and ability (for a detailed look at salaries for the era compared to other occupations, see the relevant chart in this book in the chapter on unionization). For four days a week, the program's members would learn the ropes by shadowing reporters or photographers on the beat, running photographic plates back to the newsroom, or writing short stories or parts of stories, before gradually being allowed to do more on their own.[20] In 1941 copy boys and girls at the small Binghamton, New York, *Press* attended a "two-year beginner's school to train workers in the editorial department." Focused on copy boys and girls under twenty-three who had finished high school, it did not take "married girls of any age,

[or] persons obviously deficient in personality, appearance, poise and good manners." After passing a health inspection supposedly patterned after that given to aspiring Marines, and a series of written tests, a copy boy or girl in the program would make twelve dollars a week to start and then fourteen after six months, with raises thereafter up to twenty-five. After arriving on the staff through all these hurdles, the new recruit would do the varied tasks associated with such work, everything from running copy to taking down phone numbers, retrieving lunches, running errands, sorting mail, typing, helping the reference library staff, and even transmitting copy through the newsroom's pneumatic tube system.[21]

During the war copy boys increasingly yielded to copy girls, too, as young men of draft age available for work in journalism became rare. They were often the youngest staff members and thus most likely to be drafted. A national survey showed forty-nine unfilled positions on newspapers of more than one hundred thousand circulation across the country in 1943.[22] The *New York Daily News*, with its in-house program, sought out girls due to wartime shortages. Bill Shand, the city editor, found that "copy girls can go through the same mill as copy boys and emerge as good newspaper men." Anne Grosvenor, who started as a copy girl making sixteen dollars a week, pioneered the process, covering police headquarters as part of the initiation ritual of life as a cub before her promotion to reporter.[23] Later a successful Washington, DC, correspondent for *Newsweek*, Grosvenor's contemporary, Ann Cottrell, began as a "try-out clip desk, copy girl" at twenty dollars a week and rose through the ranks at the Richmond *Times-Dispatch*.[24]

Grosvenor and Cottrell were hardly alone. The war brought other changes. Returning veterans, some of whom had left positions as copy boys, had matured and acquired new skills during their military service. Finding positions for them more suitable to their new status was a challenge, and filtered down to the ranks of copy boys and girls.[25] By 1948 the *Detroit Free Press* had developed a six-month internal training program, which included opportunities for copy staff to gradually make the transition to cub reporter, practicing rewriting using "intra-office phones," shadowing experienced reporters on various beats, and then focusing on work for the police beat or being moved to the copydesk for up to three and a half years. This program was designed for copy boys whose Guild contract guaranteed them a trial period on the editorial desk.[26] Similarly, other papers sought to smooth the path to work as reporters.

### THE EMERGENCE OF THE INTERNSHIP AND THE SLOW PHASEOUT OF THE COPY BOY/GIRL SYSTEM

Copy boys and girls, however lowly they were in the newsroom's hierarchy, could and did speak as a group. As early as 1921, copy boys complained that they were not being given enough mentorship by reporters and others.[27] A generation later, a cartoon from January 1949 shows a suit-clad copy boy standing with hand on hip, and his other hand on a table, telling a reporter (or editor), "Don't yell 'Copy Boy' and then keep me waiting; we have a union, too!". While this image and others like it gently satirized niche union groups in the newsroom, as well as federal regulation of underage workers in the news industry, there was a serious point to it.[28] Workers had more rights than before. At the same time, other cartoons from the 1950s depict copy boys as still very much at the bottom of the newsroom's social stratum.

"Don't yell 'Copy Boy' and then keep me waiting; we have a union too!"

Figure 3. "The Fourth Estate," *Editor & Publisher*, January 15, 1949, 32. This image played on the postwar assertiveness of the American Newspaper Guild.

Conditions could be harsh. At the *Los Angeles Examiner*, new copy boys were hazed. Ordered to "call the roll" in the newsroom by reporters or senior copy boys, staff members would shout out, "present," and keep the charade going in hopes that an editor or publisher would pass through. Eventually, this ritual backfired, when a senior editor did, in fact, show up and demanded an explanation for the shenanigans.[29] Other hazing rituals were less kind, including profanity-laced tirades or withholding of wages. Editors who were too harsh toward copy boys and girls, however, would occasionally receive pushback from reporters sympathetic toward copy staff.

There was already nostalgia for the copy boy by the end of the 1950s, as seen in the continued regard for his (and increasingly, postwar, her) plight, romanticized in retrospect.[30] This happened as college internships and campus papers began to supplement and then eventually largely replace the copy boy/girl route into the newsroom. The transition to a more modern "internship" model for copy boys and girls took place over a generation, and then only gradually. Offering college credit, or opening entry-level jobs only to current college students, was one way these newer programs differed from older, more ad hoc recruiting practices.

By the end of the 1950s, Gannett was advertising such a program for some its New England-based members' newspapers, including the Hartford (Connecticut) *Times*, the Albany *Knickerbocker News*, and the *Niagara Falls Gazette*. A paid "training program," it invited journalism graduates to "learn about the opportunities in (1) the newsroom, (2) the circulation department, (3) the advertising department, or (4) the business office."[31] Donald Dow Webb, a staff member at the Akron, Ohio, *Beacon Journal*, suggested that copy boys be invited to more actively shadow the staff, including attending their weekly meetings, so "these young men are introduced to the actual policy-making forces operating today's metropolitan newspapers."[32] In the face of competition from other newsrooms and other lines of related work, including public relations, treating copy boys and girls as a more integral part of the workforce helped retain them. Webb argued that "when copy boys are invited to sit in on the staff meetings, they see [that] today's newsman DOES have job satisfaction. This is because reporting DOES provide challenge, opportunity, creativity, recognition, respect."[33]

A changing newspaper work culture during the postwar period was also affecting the hiring process, and the training expected, for copy boys and girls. Hiring young men and women as copy boys (still sometimes called "office boys" or "office girls") was considered by some managing editors as

BOY!
George Thune
"Finally got back with my coffee, eh? . . . Here's tomorrow's headline: Ace Copy Boy Believed Missing; Returns To Office, Finds Post Vacant."


Figure 4. George Thune, "Boy!" *Editor & Publisher*, August 25, 1956, 66. Thune's fear-infused depiction of the interaction between an editor and a copy boy was not typical. More common were paternalistic or teasing observations.

part of a holistic process of forming a staff. Norman Shaw, associate editor of the *Cleveland Press* and a former managing editor for the same paper, described how his paper's staff of fourteen office boys and girls (eleven and three, respectively) engaged in "chasing proofs, sorting copy, and menial jobs of that kind" for six to eight months.

These staffers had been hired "with the promise that, if they make good, they will get a reporting and writing job, or a job in whatever branch of the business they are interested in," after their trial period of between three months to a year was up. Rotated through the various editorial departments (everything from the police beat to the society or women's page), the library, and the "finance department," the goal was to "find out from the heads of those departments how good these people are." This allowed the staff to judge who they felt was competent and who "we can weed out early."[34]

The ANG approved of this system, especially since these copy or office boys and girls were paid above the union's minimum. Starting pay was thirty-two dollars a week (the Guild's minimum in Cleveland at this time was twenty-five to twenty-seven; first-year reporters, by comparison, made a minimum of forty dollars, and during their second year, fifty). In addition to their other duties, they attended training classes on Wednesday afternoons, with guest speakers from the editorial and mechanical sides of the paper; an hour-and-a-half Monday night class was led by a "chief editorial writer," with ten in each class and six sessions before new students were admitted.[35] Shaw's staff hired an average of one copy boy or girl a month, with very stiff competition for the remaining open positions (he claimed there were up to two thousand applicants a year). Six a year usually made it through the initial training period before being assigned to the police beat, with three surviving that latter process ("survive" being Shaw's word), so three needed to be placed each year. This matched the paper's regular staff vacancies, since its editorial staff consisted of 165 people. The process emphasized the hiring of idea-creating, alert, aggressive, and critical people, who could transcend the routine.[36]

The debate at the end of the 1950s revolved around whether copy boys and girls were still getting legitimate shots at becoming reporters. The system itself was open to criticism, with college as the increasingly preferred entry path into the newsroom. One copy boy in Ithaca, New York, in a letter to the editor of *Editor & Publisher*, deplored his working conditions and noted that his and his peers' pay ranged from thirty-five dollars to forty-seven fifty. With college degrees but unpromising job prospects, they were in a "system" that was "basically a pathetic exploitation of ignorance."[37] Other letter writers called for better treatment of college-educated copy boys, while claiming that those "who had been educated in college were useless for a year because they don't know the routine . . . news sources" or have "news judgment."[38] Regardless, the position of copy boy or girl at this stage was too entrenched in newsroom culture to really fade for another generation.

## PHOTOGRAPHERS

As newspapers became more visually oriented early in the twentieth century, and photographs of even prosaic news events more common (and more easily reproduced), there was an increasing demand for those with the skill and technology to take them. Photographers gradually became one of the truest near peers of the reporter in the newsroom during this era. Printing photos for publication had been done before the 1920s, but really become common by the end of that decade. Though initially regarded as less-sophisticated, image-hunting sidekicks to reporters, photographers gradually came into their own in the newsroom's vocational community. Their transition mirrors broader changes in that community, as well as the increasing acceptance of newspaper photographers as news workers on par with print reporters. As new, rival newsrooms (especially those creating radio and then TV news broadcasts) emerged by the 1950s, the print newsroom embraced the skills and experiences of photographers further, claiming them as their own in the relational ecosystem of work that formed the newsroom.

Contemporary observers of newspaper photographers, sometimes colloquially referred to as "cameramen" or "lensmen," among other nicknames, noted that they were proud of their rough reputations. While it had been "the custom of newspaper reporters to assume a superior attitude toward the photographer," noted Stanley Walker, a New York-based editor, in 1934, the photographers thought of themselves as "the liveliest and most patient of newspaper men."[39] They had to be, to endure the many hours of waiting associated with news coverage, the mechanical breakdowns of their cameras, angry sources smashing their lenses or crushing their cameras, the tricky processes connected with the development of their film (in which one small mistake could mean ruined work), and all manner of other indignities. With their own, more individualistic, even "wolfish," approach to journalism, photographers were "as jealous of each other as the competing ladies at a gladioli exhibit" and enjoyed comparing their work with each other. Tensions existed between reporters and photographers. Some reporters went so far as to refrain from calling photographers "newspaper men" and even from eating with them. Though these more extreme practices were fading by the 1930s, Walker called for faster integration of the two groups.[40] It should be noted that Walker, and other contemporaries, such as Jack Price (whose contributions will be explored more below), were steeped in a nostalgic tradition that valued bonhomie and tradition. But writing as they were during this transitional period, when photographers were finally gaining some respect in the newsroom, their perspectives remain valuable today.

Morton Sontheimer, reflecting on photographers as a group a few years later, described how "from the slovenly Sancho Panza riding his broken steed behind the splendorous Quixotes of the reportorial ranks, the photographer is fast acquiring polished armor and manners to make him a don in his own right."[41] Before, they had been the "squires of newspapers' knights, the reporters." Waiting outside while reporters did the interviewing, leaving before formal events began, and generally thought of as "the rogues and boors of the business, uncouth, unkempt, and uncontrollable," photographers often were regarded as unintelligent and uneducated. This perception by other news workers tended, in turn, to foster a gritty self-perception among photographers, one characterized by a willingness to bend or make their own rules. Photographers, perhaps unfairly, were known for their bad manners, such as picking their teeth with toothpicks, propping their feet up on desks, and keeping their hats on indoors. Their reputation sometimes dissuaded the best and brightest from joining their ranks (and attracted eccentric personalities). But that changed by the 1920s with the wider use of photos beyond the tabloids, in "picture magazines" like *Life*, as well as the development of "the telephoned picture," that is, the faxed "wirephoto" and improved lenses and flash systems.[42] Technology made the work of photographers harder, and thus more indispensable, even as their images were more and more part of print journalism and its competition with radio reporting.

A journalistic culture of more impressionistic, story-driven photography also helped, with people being "portrayed as they actually looked." The staged photos of the pre–World War I era were passé. Photographers needed to cultivate a kind of pragmatic artistic sensibility and imagination.[43] But just as publishers could not classify reporters as "professional" due to the subordinate nature of their work, photographers' work was not generally considered "original and creative."[44] The federal 1943 *Manual of Newspaper Job Classifications* defined a "news photographer" and his or her role in the newsroom. The few thought of as "professional" by the standards of the day were found on the staffs of the largest circulation newspapers. This stature came from being "given large general assignments with great latitude as to the method and time of performing his work and . . . [the use] of his own independent discretion and judgment as to the choice of particular subjects." Otherwise, the "routine taking of pictures of news events or persons on a day-to-day assignment basis" classified photographers with working reporters.[45]

As with other newsroom groups, photographers had their own internal norms within the broader newsroom (and journalistic) culture of their time. Even unskilled photographers, "not so good in catching a horse with four feet off the ground . . . will purr when complimented on a picture of the reposeful skyscrapers of lower Manhattan, and will sulk if told that someone else made a better picture." The aesthetic nature of their work mattered.

Because their assignments varied from being sent to get a "pose" (staged) or a "shot" (a more spontaneous image) of a particular person or situation, the typical photographer during the interwar years knew he "must be aggressive, sometimes offensively so; he must know the power of cajolery, and the endless uses of tact." Drawn to action, photographers liked images that told their own stories, and innovative perspectives on news events. They had to engage and outsmart corporate or government figures that did not like bad publicity (for example, railroad companies and airlines did not appreciate the publication of scenes of carnage, and local officials did not appreciate any associations with organized crime), criminals, shy celebrities, and closed-off spaces, such as courtrooms. Photographers competed with one another, resorting to ruses to get an edge on the competition. During the Democratic National Convention in 1932 in Chicago, an AP photographer hired an ambulance to transport an "injured person" out of a stadium, but the "person" was in fact a stack of undeveloped photographic plates.[46]

But these boundary-pushing antics could dance with tastelessness. Photos of mob executions (as well as the state-sanctioned kind) showed readers the uglier side of both underground society and official justice. Controversial photos—such as the infamous image of the 1928 execution of Ruth Snyder at Sing Sing Prison in New York State, covertly taken by Tom Howard, a freelancer working for the *New York Daily News*—could cost photographers needed goodwill with the authorities.[47] Bound by their inflexible ethical code, "which forbids shyster practices, even among this group of hard-boiled buccaneers," photographers also fought for their independence, refusing bribes and destroying their own plates if they decided a picture was unnecessary or harmful.[48] "Snappers" who resorted to dirty tricks to get scoops or beats on their fellow photographers were occasionally looked down upon. Examples of dirty tricks that might earn wayward photographers shaming by peers included posing as public officials, or, more elaborately, getting group shots of celebrities at their weddings and then claiming that there were no more photographers on the way. Sometimes, in fact, there were; this ruse ensured that the latecomers got a cold reception.[49]

Throughout the interwar period journalism experts believed photography was important for the future of print journalism, especially newspapers.[50] Photographers strained to keep up with technological developments. Familiarity was required with the chemical processes needed to develop film, as well as the ability to maintain a complex and sometimes unforgiving camera (complete with shutters, flash and "floodlight" bulbs, and "speed guns," devices that helped to synchronize flashes with the opening of the shutter). More "miniature," or "candid," cameras, early versions of the more dominant 35mm format, made news photography better suited to a larger range of breaking-news stories. A photographer could travel lighter, faster, and with less fatigue to develop his or her film more quickly. By the 1940s a large box strapped to the shoulder no longer announced the presence of a photographer. Smaller cameras meant that sources were more willing to let photographers get close or gain entrance to events, helping to boost the photographer's "social acceptability." Photographers' assignments were also sometimes considered more interesting than regular reporters' stories during this era. Coverage of World War II enhanced this reputation.

Often simply because there were fewer photographers, "their chances of being stuck in the office on darkroom work are not near so great as the reporters' [odds of] having to stay in on a lot of crumby rewrite jobs." While their work could be perilous, and involve climbing out on roofs or dodging fisticuffs in riots to get some "action art," the very danger of their work made it more thrilling, attracting young men and women to photojournalism.[51]

Despite this ability to draw recruits to their ranks, photographers in the 1940s and beyond continued to relish "their legendary status as the clowns of the business," celebrated for their brashness and storytelling acumen. Photographers complained that art, layout, and photo editors tended to mishandle or badly position their photos on the printed page, paralleling the tensions reporters felt with copy editors, and to a lesser extent, rewrite staff. Photographers, for their part, suffered from their own fads, such as overly angled shots (that tended to highlight people's noses seen from below), stylized lighting effects, semiposed shots of people pointing to something newsworthy, and a tendency to look for oddly juxtaposed emotions.[52] Photographers sometimes collaborated with politicians to show the latter in a positive light, too. This was the case with President Roosevelt standing in his leg braces; the press corps agreed to follow a Secret Service directive to not show the president's disability.[53]

### PHOTOGRAPHERS, REPORTERS, AND NEWSROOM CULTURE

From the beginning of the twentieth century, photographers developed their own culture within and outside of newsrooms that paralleled and also shared that of reporters. In some cases, this perhaps came from having their own literal space in newsrooms, in the form of darkrooms. But photographers certainly did not *stay* in these spaces all the time. And as with other groups, rooms adjacent to or generally near the main newsroom seemed to orbit around them, instead of being in a parallel universe. In other words, they *were* connected, both physically and in spirit.

In 1920 a University of Minnesota professor of journalism, Norman J. Radder, urged young reporters to treat a photographer with respect: "Don't treat him as if he were your employee in getting the picture. Of course he is in a way. But you will find that a little co-operation will get you much further."[54] This was not a relationship of true equals, but it was at least a recognition of the other's value as a fellow news worker: "Instead of telling him, 'get a picture of that,' you will get better results by enlisting his interest by asking him, 'do you think we can get a good picture from this angle?' or 'what do you think about getting a picture from here?'" Photographers often knew more about lighting and perspective, but not necessarily more about news values. Ideally, though, reporters and photographers would know a little about each other's work. The reporter had "to see that every detail is included that bears any important relationship to the story. He, as well as the photographer, must see to it that the poses are natural." If a photographer had "good news sense," it helped the reporter get the story. Radder predicted that more papers would require their photographers to obtain experience working as reporters. If the latter could take good photos, then those reporters would "get the most salary," too.[55]

Another journalism instructor later in the 1920s noted that reporters and photographers shared the same stresses and dangers, fostering mutual respect.[56] Both groups received about the same benefits. At the start of the Depression, the *Chicago Daily Illustrated News* organized five-day workweeks for reporters and photographers alike, in an attempt to avoid layoffs.[57] Like reporters, photographers tended to work together, hunting "in packs."[58] But this could be a tenuous equality. Jack Price, a prolific columnist for *Editor & Publisher* and "star" photographer for the *New York World*, observed that it was "within the memory of many photographers when a newspaper photographer was regarded as an inquisitive pest and as such was requested to withdraw. This attitude toward him has been dissipated, and in its place is an attitude of honest toleration." James W. Barrett, former city editor of the *World* and then city editor of the *New York American*, reviewed Price's 1932 textbook, noting that, like the aspiring reporter, "a young man seeking to become a good news photographer learns by hard knocks and severe bawlings-out from editors."[59]

But there were differences, too, between photographers and reporters, ranging from their day-to-day work to their collective ethics, education, and parallel but separate perceptions of the public. These differences both highlighted and caused conflict. Generally, respect from outside the occupation for photographers lagged behind that of reporters. A cartoon from 1936 shows a misunderstanding between an editor and a photographer. Dale Beronius, a cartoonist at the *Kansas City Star*, drew a nonplussed editor interrogating a hapless cameraman, as colleagues look on with amusement:

> "City Editor—Did you get a picture of that bridge being razed?
> "Photographer—No, Boss. They're not razing that bridge, they're tearing it down."[60]

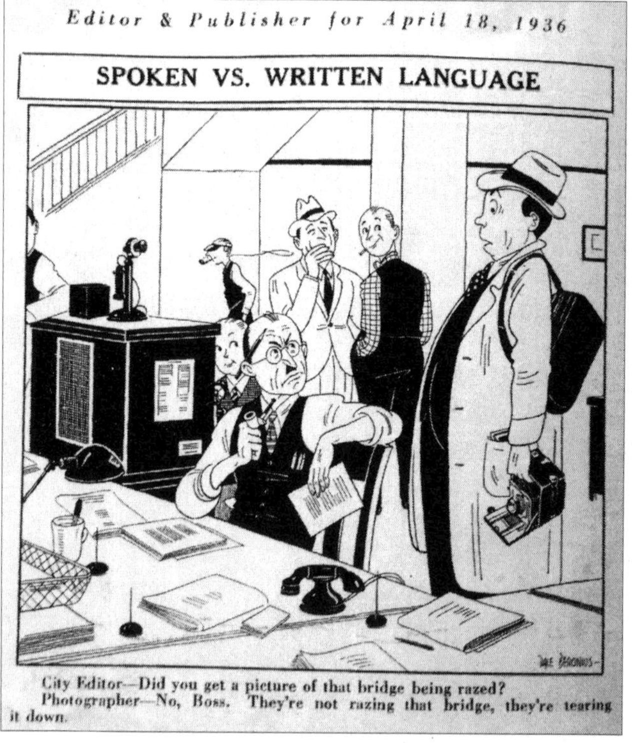


Figure 5. Dale Beronius, "Spoken vs. written language," *Editor & Publisher*, April 18, 1936, 86. In this case, the photographer also represents other news workers of similarly minor influence in the newsroom—but the image of the photographer as a comic figure, sometimes clueless but allowed to swagger more than reporters, was enhanced in these kinds of depictions.

In addition to poetry and cartoons, photographers were often the subjects of newsroom lore. This included elaborate, or often doggerel, verse that lampooned life in the newsroom. It also encompassed anecdotes of dubious origin, passed down from one generation of news workers to the next. One example of storytelling was related by Carroll Byrnes, a photographer on the Utica, New York, *Observer-Dispatch.* Ordered to "make it snappy" and find something newsworthy to photograph, he happily happened on an accident right outside the newspaper building.[61] Photographers, according to another peer's account, needed "pre-natal care" and remained "undeveloped fetuses . . . [who] have obtained employment with the metropolitan press."[62] This teasing, edgy but mostly good-natured, was common between photographers and reporters.

### CONTROVERSIAL CROSS-TRAINING

During the 1930s tensions between the two groups manifested in daily newsgathering routines. They showed up in worries over how well reporters fared when they were tasked with taking their own photos. Many "experienced press photographers . . . resent the blundering and bullyragging which often covers incompetence, and some pictures that newspaper[s] have printed move old-time knights of the camera to bad words and tears."[63] As the use of smaller cameras became more prevalent, reporters, especially younger recruits, needed some basic training. As a result of budget tightening during the Depression, more reporters were encouraged to carry their own cameras to take photos.

Price, the news-photography columnist, was enthusiastic about this trend, predicting that soon "rank and file . . . newspaper reporters" would "also be their own cameramen." These hybrid "reporter-photographer[s]" were "the reporter[s] of the future."[64] While later observers in the early twenty-first century would presume that the reporter-photographer team was a kind of received natural state, for journalism, the reality was that the combination of visual and print work was constructed and rare, in the beginning. Only by trial and error, and over time, would it become a normal state of affairs.

Some editors, such as Stanley Walker, believed that the idea of reporters taking their own photos had some merit under special circumstances, and that some cross-training could succeed if a reporter already had an interest or training in photography.[65] Other newsrooms, such as at the *San Antonio Light*, provided small "Speed Graphic" cameras to their reporters so that they could supplement their news photographer staff as "auxiliary camera-men-reporters."[66] In 1938 the *Birmingham News* equipped its reporters with the Kodak Duo 8, "with Kalert speed gun [shutter-flash device] attachments," in order to "supplement the work of the regular staff of photographers." The idea was to help reporters take photos as needed.[67] Without a "press machine [camera]," photographers coming across news could feel helpless—equipping and training reporters with smaller cameras was a trend that developed in response to the growing and accepted use of photography in daily print newspapers.[68]

And yet this cross-training idea was resisted by older reporters, and even by younger ones too busy tracking down leads and getting quotes to wrestle with the still-bulky cameras of the time. The Guild usually opposed the hiring of part-time photographers, as well as the use of such photographers for work that should, it felt, be done by a reporter.[69] Some managers actively insisted that their reporters learn to use cameras, even as they acknowledged that reporters had trouble taking their own pictures. Someday, reporters who could not take their own photos would "be as helpless as one who can't use a pencil."[70] L. R. Blanchard, an editor at the Rochester, New York, *Democrat and Chronicle*, thought that reporters were not "interested . . . in the picture content of the paper." While some older reporters "felt repugnance at lugging a camera, tiny as the burden was," younger reporters, including women, on the staff seemed more open to the idea, he noted, with the latter proving "especially apt pupils." Even if some reporters could be persuaded, "the backbone of the newspaper's art" remained "the regular camera man with his machine which can be used day or night and under all conditions. The little camera can't replace the big one; it is a mere assistant."[71]

Another trend during the pre–World War II years was the pairing up of photographers with reporters on specific story assignments, a practice made more permanent by the use of the car. In New York in the 1930s, police issued the same credentials to "real working reporters and photographers."[72] But "star reporters" would often get their own photographers for big, breaking stories. These "news crews" would travel together to scenes of unfolding disaster or drama, working as a team.[73] As Price relates, in the late 1930s in any "reporter-cameraman combination" the latter was "theoretically under the direction of the former." Effectively, they were equals, since the disparity in power between the two groups had diminished. Photographers, like reporters, could be assigned to cover news on their own. While given instructions by editors for particular news angles, "the cameras and techniques required for the job are details determined altogether by the photographer."[74]

Early signs of a more equal status with reporters included legal efforts to protect photographers. In the midst of tensions between business owners and striking workers, a 1934 New Jersey law made it a misdemeanor to interfere with news gathering (punishable with up to three years in jail and a thousand dollar fine), specifically if one were to "strike, beat . . . or assault any news photographer or news reporter, while such news photographer or reporter is engaged in the pursuit of his or her occupation."[75] Legal protection in this case was a validation of a closing divide between the two groups.

### TECHNOLOGY AND CONTROL OVER WORKSPACES

Frank Hause, of the *New York Daily News*, reported at a 1935 convention of editors that his paper used about twenty-five hundred photos a month, fifteen hundred of which were taken by thirty-three photographers and seven printers (apparently trained as photographers). He added that generally photo departments were understaffed, with three to four photographers working in a studio and one photographer idle (but expected to be sent out for breaking news).[76] A typical midsized daily, such as the *Des Moines Register*, employed eleven photographers and two darkroom photographers. Many of the former also developed their own photos.[77]

Photographers in the mid-1930s benefited from improvements in transmission technology. Wirephoto, a proprietary facsimile system and photo service launched by the Associated Press between 1935 and 1936, meant that photos of ongoing events, such as baseball games, could be sent to newspapers for updated editions that hit the streets before the games were over, or not long after. AP clients would submit photos alongside stories, contributing to a pool of images that could be used throughout the nation. In time, staged photos would give way to more realistic AP-style action shots. These were more of figures in action versus stationary portraits. Editors could expect more dynamic images, and more images in relatively real time. Even though the change was gradual, this is a case where a technology (a national wire service and its photo network) helped to change the nature of news photography (though of course there were other, human factors involved).

When the service was started, it took forty-five seconds to take a photo, two minutes to get it from the photographers' stand to a motorcycle messenger, seven minutes to get it to the office, and eleven minutes to be developed. A print was then made, dried, captioned, and mounted for transmission back to the newsroom's photo department. It took eight minutes to send, twenty-five minutes to develop and make a print on the other end, and finally thirty-five minutes to make an engraving and prepare it for printing. If accomplished without hiccups, this process could be completed and the paper out on the street by the end of a baseball game. The network handled at its inception about forty "worthwhile news pictures a day," with up to about twelve transmitted regionally. This was a humble beginning, especially compared to the improvements that would come with wartime technological development, but impressive for its time.[78] Postwar experiments with reporting technology relied on the close cooperation of photographers, especially those with radiophone-equipped cars. In one typical example, a *Dallas Morning News* reporter borrowed a radio in a photographer's car.[79] Photographers and their vehicles would, as a rule, become more wired than those of their reporter brethren.

Where they were in charge of their own departments, photo editors controlled their photographers' time and assignments.[80] The physical spaces photographers worked out of underwent some improvements during the 1930s. Newspapers built rooms for their photographers, sometimes designed by photographers themselves. At the *Los Angeles Times*' palatial $4 million new newspaper building completed in 1935, the third floor contained photographers' studios and darkrooms, as well as spaces dedicated to newspaper picture syndicates.[81]

Like other news workers during the Depression, and before the more widespread presence and protection of the Guild, photographers could suffer from sudden dismissal "for any reason beyond the whim of some duffer who doesn't like the cut of my jib or slashes the payroll by checking off every other name on the list."[82] In one particularly egregious case related to *Editor & Publisher*'s Marlen Pew, a desperate photographer in New York City was promised a job in the suburbs and then summarily fired after a few days. The photographer had wired ahead saying he wanted the job, phoning an editor to confirm that he was coming, but had been harangued. Presuming that the editor had just had a bad day, the photographer showed up and completed his assignment anyway, before being dismissed. Pew, for his part, retaliated on behalf of the photographer by refusing any more help-wanted ads from the newspaper in question.[83]

But over time, photographers were rewarded in their quest for greater newsroom respect. With the advent of photographic newsmagazines, and their "new style of pictorial dramatization of the news," photographers were becoming a more respected part of the editorial workforce.[84] Among the leaders in this trend was *Life* magazine, which paid five dollars for each photo accepted, a helpful supplement to a weekly salary that ranged from thirty-five to sixty dollars.[85] In addition to this continued move toward more visual news coverage, there were other developments. As in-house training programs were established, photographers were invited to participate.[86] Other photographers sought improved access to sporting events.[87] Still others called for a separate professional organization just for photographers, at the national and local level, distinct from other news workers.[88] The necessity of photographers for news coverage, even in the midst of tough economic conditions, could be seen in their growing numbers, even on the staffs of smaller newspapers, as noted in a June 1937 report by the Inland Daily Press Association.[89] These "camera knights" had earned their own column in *Editor & Publisher* by this point, written by the prolific Jack Price.[90] It highlighted the exploits of photographers in weekly profiles and also included news about equipment and trends in the field.

Regional groups organizing photographers took the lead during this era to develop codes of conduct and ethics specific to photographers. One such code, drafted by the Southwestern Association of Pictorial Journalists, was adopted at the University of Oklahoma's "short course in news photography." It included such admonitions as:

> Avoid gruesome photos, except where, in its own interest, the public should be informed with them . . . Willingly play no favorites in securing pictures . . . Study to keep up with the rapid advances of our profession . . . Be worthy representatives, both in appearance and conduct, of the best in journalism.[91]

Photography was changing as the 1930s drew to a close. More photographers were coming from "schools of journalism" as fewer were elevated via on-the-job training from the ranks of "messenger boys or motorcycle dispatch riders." Improvements in technology meant that "in the near future newspaper photographers will be rated for their ability to analyze a news story in pictures along with their mastery of the technical problems required to produce the same results."[92] And in another key development, women started trickling into the field. More rarely, however, did they head photo departments or staffs. One exception was on the *Washington Times-Herald*, where Jackie Martin, the "only woman heading a photographic staff on a metropolitan newspaper," helped to pioneer a leadership role for women.[93]

Photographers continued to be the subject of in-house newsroom humor, with cartoons depicting them doing anything to get in position for a good picture, or lazily playing cards in a bar with reporter colleagues.[94] Another cartoon showed a photographer taking a photo of a car crash and instructing the victims to pose.[95] And yet these tropes of photographers and reporters spending time in seedy bars and hiding from newsrooms had a kernel of truth: they *did* push the boundaries of what was professionally acceptable.

### THE 1940S AND 1950S AND THE CULTURE OF NEWS PHOTOGRAPHERS

In the early 1940s, even as the United States geared up to enter World War II, a typical large-circulation newspaper such as the *Dallas Morning News* would utilize five photographers and an editor to cover an average of about four assignments a day. Small-to-medium-sized dailies would employ up

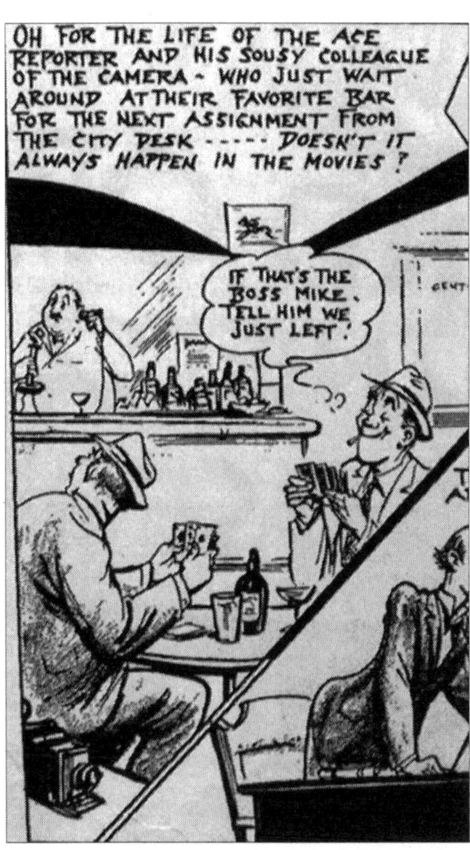


Figure 6. Walt Munson, "Now—you take in reel life," *Editor & Publisher*, April 20, 1940, 54; detail from larger cartoon image. In this cartoon by Walt Munson of the New Haven (Connecticut) *Register*, journalism in film is contrasted to journalism in real life (though the latter is not depicted, the audience would have understood the irony of the more boring world of everyday journalism).

to three photographers (out of a staff of about fifty).[96] On other papers, such as the Oklahoma *City Times* and the *Daily Oklahoman*, an individual photographer might cover up to six assignments a day, working as part of a larger staff.[97] In all these cases, photographers continued developing their own negatives. Photo departments could vary wildly as to organization, too. Some had their own dedicated "executive" in "complete charge of all picture coverage, directing photographic assignments, supervising artists and retouchers, superintending layouts, making subject selections, arranging picture pages and roto pages." This allowed for a filtering of photo assignments from editor to photographers, better management of limited staff resources, "more thorough scrutiny of ill-matured picture assignments suggested by editors; more critical examination of picture copy, [and] speedier remedy of defects in equipment and materials." Photographers generally appreciated being governed by their own. But not every paper had a photo editor, and many still relied on an ad hoc management system whereby other editors would assign photographers to stories.[98]

As the war began, the demand for images increased. Photographers faced gas rations, as did reporters, though due to the nature of their work, some were allowed additional fuel.[99] As with other groups in the newsroom, photographers encountered workforce shortages, too. "Occupational deferment" was sometimes available for key staff, including photographers, but eligibility depended on a local draft board's decision, and as a result there was some confusion as to whom it covered even as late as March 1943.[100] A survey by the National Council on Professional Education for Journalism detailed the extent of staff shortages. Covering 45 states, and 14 percent of all English language dailies, it showed 2,197 vacancies, with an additional 4,169 expected in the 6 months starting in January 1943; 867 of the former were from the editorial side, and 604 were from the mechanical side. Of these, 38 photographers were needed on papers with 100,000 or more circulation (by way of comparison, 102 copy editors were needed).[101]

### WOMEN IN NEWSROOM PHOTOGRAPHY

As a result, some editors reached out to college newspapers, recruiting young men not yet drafted or otherwise ineligible.[102] At the same time, while some photo editors were initially skeptical of hiring women to replace their thinning ranks, others were open to the idea before necessity forced the issue.[103] By the fall of 1942, "women members of the news picture business" were not as rare as before. "Newspapers have been employing lens-gals for years," Jack

Price noted, "but because of this emergency they will become more noticeable." He related how Frank Merta, of Acme News Photos, "asked if he was to place hand [lotion] on the list of supplies." A colleague "replied, 'give the girls anything they need but keep the cussin' to gentlemanly expressions.' 'Amen,' responded Merta." Other parts of the newsroom reacted with similar variations of amusement and, despite the war's workforce reality, resistance. Price himself expressed a changing point of view, believing that "the gals will dish it out also."[104] After the war, some, but not all, female photographers managed to hang on to their wartime appointments.[105] Other women on papers such as the *Los Angeles Daily News* faced an enduring sexism, as photographers continued to be perceived as hypermasculine because of the rough-and-tumble nature of their work.[106] Gender integration came slowly to photo staffs in the postwar years. Sometimes smaller newspapers, such as the *Kansas City Kansan*, proved more welcoming to women.[107]

Thanks to the war, photographers were earning their own bylines. As Price explained, previously, an "unwritten" or "gentlemen's agreement" had kept photographers anonymous. But with the conflict, and with tales of their exploits near battlefronts as riveting for audiences at home as the news stories and photos themselves, photographers were becoming better known to readers. As a result, "cameramen are entitled to the same amount of praise and glory that is given to writers. Surely, they face the same dangers and they often face greater hardships in order to get their pictures. A tardy reporter could easily get all his information from Public Relations Officers and at headquarters but pictures cannot be so obtained."[108]

As the war drew to a close, photographers began asserting themselves in the design of new spaces within renovated and new newsrooms, as well as in regard to the scheduling of assignments. At the *Washington News*, Charles Stevenson, the city editor was "very picture-minded" and believed in "giving the photographers plenty of latitude." Stevenson, perhaps a bit unusually, regularly consulted with his photographers. Despite his photo staff's comparatively small size, they produced twice as much coverage as they might have because of this "close cooperation between the desk and the cameramen."[109]

## EARLY, HALTING, AND FLAWED EFFORTS TOWARD DIVERSITY

Like other groups in the newsroom, photographers in the postwar period faced challenges with integration. The hiring of minority news workers was especially difficult in photo departments. This was revealed in a July 1949 survey of 250 editors conducted by Lewis C. Jones, an African American journalism student at Butler University. About half the survey respondents were white; while more were open to the idea of hiring Black reporters, fewer were open to hiring Black photographers. Specifically, the survey revealed that among the white editors, 35 percent said they would hire a Black journalism school graduate, with 60 percent not answering and five percent saying "no." Of the Black editors, 72 percent said they would, 16 percent said they would prefer a Black reporter but not necessarily a journalism graduate, "preferring instead men with experience." Part of the survey asked which specific jobs at the paper would be open for "equal opportunity" with white journalists; four papers, two in the East and two in the Midwest, said that all positions would be considered open, as such; five papers said that this would be the case with reporters; four papers said that would be the case for their correspondents; three with jobs for artists, two with positions for photographers, and one each for the work done by editorial writers, promotion staff, and mechanical workers.[110]

In 1955, Armistead S. Pride, the dean of the School of Journalism at Lincoln University (near the University of Missouri's famed program), discussed the paucity of African American reporters and other news workers in the white press in the ANG's *Guild Reporter*, identifying just 21 Black news workers out of some 80,000 staffing the more than 1,700 daily newspapers and 9,770 weekly newspapers in the United States, which was "hardly a drop in the bucket, far less than the 10 percent Negro racial proportion prevailing in the total population." Pride went on to point out the formal and informal policies that kept Black workers from being hired in white papers. And as Black dean of a historically Black college, his perspective is invaluable.

"Newspaper executives [in white newsrooms] have a responsibility, beyond editorial proclamations, in helping to bring about more integrated American news staffs," said Price. "Individually, they could start the ball rolling by signing on up-and-coming Negro high school or college graduates as copy boys, thus orienting them to the rigors of office routine and accustoming office personnel to having a dark-skinned worker around," he noted. "Others could get the 'feel' of things as reporter cubs, copy readers, proofreaders, or even advertising apprentices."[111] But it would be another twenty years before this practice became widespread, as will be discussed later.

The reluctance to integrate newsrooms and aggressively court Black reporters was due to racist policies and other, embedded forces, including less blatant, but still nonetheless entrenched, discrimination and segregation.

Editors knew that sources and subjects would often object to being interviewed or photographed by African American staff members, and that their own staff might balk at working with Black reporters and editors. There were early attempts to hire Black reporters during this era, such as Carl Rowan at the *Minneapolis Tribune*, and George D. Forsythe at the *Boston Herald Traveler*.[112] These were critical first steps—and courageous ones, for those few Black journalists who crossed the very bright color line of the typical white newspaper's newsroom of that time. But a coordinated effort to diversify the newsroom would not take place for a generation, under the aegis of the ASNE.[113] Rowan's experiences will be discussed more in a later chapter in this book, on reporters.

### PHOTOGRAPHERS COME INTO THEIR OWN

By the late 1940s photographers had been able to shed most of the remaining vestiges of their second-class status. "Photographers, who more and more work alongside reporters in obtaining the news, need be . . . one-quarter journalist and, in like proportions, artist, technician and dynamo," wrote Howard Kany in 1947. Kany, the AP's Wirephoto editor, believed that "the cameraman should command a status equal to that of any reporter . . . in the matter of privileges and assistance in coverage of the news." Reflecting on his time attending a two-week Columbia School of Journalism seminar on news photography, with representatives from twenty-seven newspapers, he believed that it was important to portray photographers in a positive light. He believed, too, that "occasional staff meetings on a high critical plane are constructive and lead to better pre-assignment cooperation between reporter and photographer."[114] The National Press Photographers Association was at that time seeking press credentials as expansive as those given to print reporters in court coverage. These, Kany argued, should be granted, and bylines given consistently in captions, in order to assist the work of "the genuine news photographer." The latter should be allowed the freedom to deviate from a newsgathering plan. While at the Columbia seminar, Kany observed how the other photo editors present believed that their work got the ax when it came down to a choice between photos and print.[115] Nonphoto editors still had the final say.

The 1950s continued a focus on the value of cooperation between the "lensman and reporter," as radio and TV competed with daily newspapers for local news coverage.[116] Reporters for these new media had fewer barriers to collaboration with colleagues. Television in particular, with its emphasis on visuals, proved a fierce rival for even the most image-friendly newspaper. In response, groups such as the ASNE made editor-photographer interactions the subject of study.[117] Photographers worked more for their own dedicated editors, and less directly for managing or city editors. Joseph Costa, the chief photographer for the King Features Syndicate, noted that photographers' bylines were an increasingly common way "to help build the prestige of personnel," since they helped to give "a man a reputation for good work and it helps open doors to him." For their part, he said, reporters should not refer to photographers with possessive pronouns (as in "my" photographer) and instead present a united front to readers.[118] John S. Radosta, the "picture editor" of the *New York Times*, echoed this perspective: "I think the young cameraman should come to the newspaper with the same background, education and preparation the reporter has. In every way he should be the equal of a reporter in these respects. Intellectually, they should be on a par."[119] While previously photographers would come to work on the staff "out of the darkroom," more and more they should come from other parts of the paper, Radosta argued.

Assignments were sometimes given in advance at the largest newspapers in departments such as sports and society, but otherwise they still tended to be given on an informal, as-needed basis. Other newspapers, such as the *Des Moines Register & Tribune*, tried to formalize their assignment systems. George Yates, "photo chief" at the *Register & Tribune*, attempted to methodically pair up a "lensman" with a reporter.[120]

Photographers continued to be more mobile than reporters, with many of the former having access to their own cars and with gas subsidized by the newspaper.[121] The "team" image of the reporter and photographer, however, remained ingrained in profiles of newsroom life.[122] Some training programs for young reporters, including one at the *Denver Post*, purposely sought to expose them to experienced photographers.[123] Cub reporters, if they were fortunate, would find themselves paired up with a "veteran . . . who knows a reporter's job almost as well as his own."[124]

As will be explored in more detail, photographers used radio-equipped vehicles to compete with one another and with the emerging medium of TV.[125] The use of color, at first on an experimental basis during the interwar years and then in newsmagazines by the 1950s, also promised to make photography more competitive.[126] The acquisition of smaller cameras, a trend begun in the 1930s to capture candid scenes, continued with improved technology in the 1950s.[127] Japanese-made cameras, noted for their quality and compactness, were also coming on the market.[128] Some photographers believed that these less conspicuous cameras got better pictures, as "many people tend to associate the big camera with the more sensational newspapers of the past."[129] A more obtrusive camera "brands the operator as a 'news photographer,'" reported Don Ultang, assistant chief photographer at the *Des Moines Register & Tribune*. Ultang believed that in order to distinguish themselves from better-equipped amateurs, photographers needed to strive for a more artistic and narrative-focused photojournalism to complement routine news coverage.[130] Back in the newsroom, the photo desk underwent upgrades, such as the use of internal intercom systems and more integrated mobile-communication technology.[131] There was a consistent emphasis on making it easier for the various departments in a newsroom to work together, instead of existing as separate fiefdoms.[132] "The press photographer of today stands ready to fulfill his role as a visual reporter and documentarian of the age," declared James Colvin, a former reporter and rewrite staff member for the *Chicago Daily News*.[133] In the face of competition from TV and radio, the "newsphotographer" had "become a reporter to back up the written or spoken word."[134] This competition caused anxiety among some photographers, worried about the ability of newspapers to play technological catch-up.[135] Photo staff tended to be among the more risk-taking when it came to applying technology to their work.

Despite these strides forward, there still existed real tensions between photographers and reporters, especially at press conferences. Walter T. Ridder, a Washington, DC, correspondent for the *St. Paul Pioneer Press* and *Dispatch*, complained that TV and radio reporters were the worst offenders at press conferences with "the mass of lines and wires needed for flashbulbs, klieg lights, tape recorders and live broadcasts, and the bawling of light engineers, cameramen, television production experts, and newsroom representatives." But photographers for newspapers could also be a huge hindrance, he said. An interview subject would be "pushed and hauled and shoved by the photographers as he enters the room until whatever good humor he might have possessed evaporates in a violent eruption of strobolights, flash bulbs and photographers' instructions." Photographers would "yell at the interviewee, at the reporters, at themselves and at anyone else who may be handy, while they take for the fiftieth or sixtieth time 'just one more.' Having ceased at long last their basic task, they lurk on the sidelines, ready to swoop out at unexpected moments to get a candid shot of the interviewee." While Ridder was less annoyed by what he described as "legitimate reporters" (by which he meant fellow print reporters), he suggested a separate conference for radio reporters, photographers, and TV cameramen.[136] Tensions between the newsroom workers still lingered.

Perhaps reflecting the self-confidence and status of news photographers, for both men and women, the term "photojournalist" became more common in the industry by the end of the 1950s.[137] The National Press Photographers Association (NPPA), which was founded in 1946 and by 1952 included some eighteen hundred "working news cameramen," helped to popularize the interests of photographers, who had "a new awareness of their responsibilities in the public interest." They deserved better pay and training in storytelling, as both were "an investment in the future" of the field.[138] At the college level, there were similar calls for more photojournalism courses in journalism programs.[139] At larger newspapers like the *New York Times*, photographers participated in cash-prize contests for stories and photos, with the names of winners posted to an office bulletin board.[140] Calls for better pay and education, along with efforts to recognize their work internally, meant that photographers were no longer regarded as "the stepchildren of the news room." It was now taken for granted that they needed to be good reporters in their own right and to work for "well-qualified picture editors." While a "comparative newcomer," the "photo journalist" was "key man in modern news coverage," as a contemporary put it.[141]

### COPY BOYS AND GIRLS AND PHOTOGRAPHERS IN CONTEXT

Thinking about these workers in the relational space of the newsroom helps to emphasize how their labor was not considered lesser or inferior, per se, by their peers, including the reporters. This was due to its nature as "newsroom work," with its ethos of both collaboration and competition, hierarchy and aspirational meritocracy. News workers believed that with enough good luck, hard work, and pluck they could ascend the latter up into the ranks of the reporters, or, if they were photographers, get steady enough assignments to first get on as full-time staff and then pursue more creative projects, becoming accepted as coequal coworkers to their partners, the reporters. There was an understanding that some of this was "luck," which may have been a coded reference to privilege or other, ineffable qualities that were still soaked in white, male prerogatives and preferences. While physical buildings mattered as part of the containers or contexts for this work, the social nature of the work meant that "the newsroom" was used interchangeably with "journalism" or "the life of the newspaperman," in the parlance of the day. To go to work in a newsroom was to be *at* work, yes, but also *with* others. Correspondents and other more distanced news workers were not considered quite as close to the newsroom community, and thus sometimes regarded with suspicion. But for those who did work with others, closely, certain rewards could be had, even for those, like copy boys and photographers, who would otherwise be on the margins. The social roles of rewrite staff and copy editors will be explored next.

# CHAPTER 3

# Rewrite Staff and Copy Editors

UNLIKE COPY BOYS AND GIRLS, or photographers, rewrite staff and copy editors from the 1920s onward had power over the work of others in the newsroom. As "near peers" of the reporter, they formed a quasi-supervisory group, less empowered than managing and other kinds of senior editors but more in control of the news-production process than reporters. Their role in this process shows how the stratification of work tasks in the newsroom often determined who possessed power, and how that power shifted over time.

Power was represented by control over the story-production process, including how news copy came into the newsroom from the field. Once it was received, edited, and placed on the page, its publication was the end of a long chain of events occurring in a very human context, with many hands touching and shaping it along the way. Technology helped to determine the roles needed to make the newspaper factories of the twentieth century run smoothly, but news workers also exerted their own agency in these roles.

## REWRITE STAFF

Perhaps the "nearest peers" of all to reporters were "rewrite men." But while photographers were close near peers in a junior sense, rewrite men were such in a more senior sense. It should be noted that by the 1940s women were also performing this role, and that the term was commonly used in newsrooms to describe a loose category of newsroom-bound news workers who worked the phones as opposed to reporting from the streets. Rewrite staff in fact often *were* reporters.[1] But because of their technology-driven role in the news-production process, as well as their slightly higher status in terms of authority, hours, and pay in the newsroom, they comprised a distinct class of news worker. Sociologist Warren Breed, for example, thought of them as a separate group from reporters, and from members of the copydesk, in his accounts of newsroom life in the 1950s.[2] The reorganization, or job stratification, that brought this position into its own, however, was the product of many years of gradual change, influenced by various transmission technologies (explored in more depth in the chapter focused specifically on the impact of telephone and car technology on newsroom relationships). Previously, for example, telegraph editors, and before that, "exchange editors," had gathered outside news produced by the wire services into separate sections. That category of work would gradually be encompassed and eclipsed, at least partially, by the work of rewrite staff, and yet the loose title and role of wire-service editor would linger for some time, as the nature of rewrite changed.[3] Finally, to be clear, the "city desk," or main section of the newsroom concerned with local and regional news, would be where most rewrite would occur.

According to the *Manual of Newspaper Job Classifications*, published by the US Department of Labor in April 1943, which strove to define newsroom roles as part of the federal government's implementation of the Fair Labor Standards Act,[4] rewrite men were defined as writers who wrote or rewrote news stories, "working from telephone information and notes prepared by reporters, or received from other sources, or data developed from the newspaper's reference materials."[5] The *Manual* continued, "The day-to-day work of the rewrite man, however, is generally not original and creative in character. . . . it appears that rewrite men almost invariably write or rewrite 'straight' news stories to an extent which would disqualify them from" professional status.[6] Descriptions of rewrite men and their role in the newsroom from the early 1950s emphasized how the job was normally given to older, experienced reporters who had spent several years "grinding out copy under all conditions" before assuming the "heavy burden and . . . exercis[ing] the skill required" of them in that position.[7] As observed by the writers of the *Manual*, rewrite staff also rewrote stories based on clippings from other papers. Rewriting was necessary to avoid directly copying other material (with the exception of quotes) and to cast the rewritten story in the paper's style and format. Often done at the start of a shift, from clippings gathered by an overnight staff on an evening paper, or by the day shift on a morning paper (or by evening paper staff based on what was produced in the morning papers), rewriting in this vein summarized and shortened longer stories, often from wire accounts.[8]

But the primary duty of rewrite men was reshaping phoned-in material. Described as "one of the most important cogs in the news machine," an area known as the "battery" connected leg men to the city editor. A battery was commonly composed of several desks arranged side by side, sometimes arranged near the copydesk in a central position. Rewrite staff knew how many column inches they had to work with and took down a story while seated at a desk, often wearing headphones instead of holding a phone receiver. This freed up their hands to take notes or use a typewriter. The typewriter was usually preferred, due to its speed under any kind of deadline. Unlike writing by longhand, a typewriter gave even a relatively poor typist the ability to write quickly and accurately. The leg man talking to the rewrite desk would know to dictate his or her story in a rough narrative, to minimize rewriting. In an era long before word processors, this was critical. Sometimes, when time was less pressing, and a story could be reworked, a rewrite staff member would overhaul it more completely, but this was rare. "More often than not, the rewrite man is pressed so hard for his copy that sheet after sheet is literally pulled out of his typewriter as he continues his story," wrote one contemporary. This copy was then moved straight to the copydesk, and then to the composing room to be set in "takes," or short paragraphs of type. Seconds mattered in an "unrelenting" job.[9] Rewrite staff existed, and indeed were created, in a newsroom climate of speed. This atmosphere was only reinforced in the 1930s and 1940s as radio emerged as a competitor to both morning and evening newspapers. The myth of the leisurely once-a-day newspaper is not grounded in reality. Newspapers were updated throughout the day and sometimes hourly with multiple and zoned editions.

According to Morton Sontheimer, who wrote a 1941 autobiographical guide to working in journalism, the job was considered "a step above that of reporter" and "coveted."[10] He believed good rewrite men were rare. But beyond broad strokes, the categorization of who filled the job was difficult to pin down. This was especially true before ANG contracts began standardizing the industry's salaries in the 1930s. The rewrite staff could be a fluid group, depending on the newspaper: especially on nonunion newspaper staffs, even by World War II, "rewrite" sometimes still comprised reporters waiting for their next assignment.[11]

But in large newsrooms dominated by the ANG, rewrite staff focused exclusively on drafting phoned-in stories or recreating stories from clippings. In either case, a capable rewrite staffer could write up to about eight hundred to one thousand words an hour. Their norms included the belief that quotes were sacrosanct, and the need to check facts and the words of the reporter when in doubt. Rewrite staff were able to gauge the length of stories. A rewrite staff member would spend four to eight hours actually writing. Between what could be intense sessions, he or she could "relax, get into undignified positions, and read the funny papers."[12]

Many rewrite staffers were occupied by card games, or, more seriously, side projects, ranging from writing feature articles for their or other papers to composing books or novels, though many of the latter remained unfinished.[13] Many reporters thought that too much time at a rewrite desk could turn one into a hack writer, but there was a parallel school of thought that admired the consistent "ingenuity, finesse and literary quality" of some rewriters. Rewrite men and women often took pride in their work. Outside the battery, among the newsroom staffers, rewrite men were known to possess varying levels of ability: "Although there is no placard on their desks to that effect, the best one is always known as 'first-string rewrite,' the next as 'second-string,' and so on." Those among the first-string crew were especially valued staff members.[14]

### REWRITE MEN, REPORTERS, AND NEWSROOM CULTURE

Rewrite men first appeared shortly after telephones entered the newsroom, between about 1900 to 1920. Not until the 1920s, however, did they attain an acknowledged status. The rewrite staff in the newsroom did not have formal authority over their more mobile brethren, including reporters. But in their interactions with reporters, rewrite men did have disproportionate influence and a higher degree of agency in constructing the final news product. An unspoken rule had it that it paid to stay on their good side. Because this rule presumed that rewrite men had power over the news-production process (even as reporters had power over the news collection process), it could produce tension, especially if the reporter's work was seen as heavily edited. But "the reporter-victim of a rewrite man's grudge [could] console himself with the realization that the rewrite man is cutting off his own nose" if the latter failed to work well with a reporter and turn in good copy.[15]

The rewrite staffer's work was only as good as the reporter he or she worked with, ultimately, and vice versa. A reporter out in the field was supposed to dig up facts and the rewrite staff had to assemble these facts into a coherent story. Differing beliefs about the quality of one's work (or the importance of one newsroom norm over another) could lead to clashes:

> While the rewrite man theoretically has the power to order him [the reporter] back to get more, in practice he has no way of enforcing his

> orders except by tattling to the city editor. Even if the rewrite man isn't a squealer, the editor may complain about an inadequate story, and there is nothing for him [the rewrite man] to say but that he couldn't get the facts from the reporter. So it's a good idea to give the rewrite man all the information he wants.[16]

Here, Sontheimer describes a delicate balance. He is addressing younger reporters, but the basic principles also applied to the dynamic between older, more experienced reporters and rewrite men. Trust between the two groups was key. Only then could the "traditional enmity" between rewrite men and reporters (and copy editors) be resolved positively.[17]

Irving Brant, an editorial writer on the *St. Louis Star*, noted in 1920 that a rewrite man, "if he has sufficient prestige, raises a storm if his copy is interfered with."[18] High-salaried rewrite men did not want to take orders from lower-salaried copy editors. Others chafed under rules set by middle management for ever-tighter copy.[19] Rewrite staff, like older reporters, could include "stars" who had carved out more independence than others.[20] The appointment of rewrite staff was ingrained in the larger American journalistic culture. Visitors from the United Kingdom as late as the 1950s were impressed by how much copy was phoned in to rewrite men, and how telephones came equipped with earphones.[21]

In the newsroom, especially in their interactions over the phone with younger reporters, rewrite men could assert their power. Interactions with a rewrite man could be challenging for a young reporter. "You'll be terror-stricken the first time you're called upon to do it," warned Sontheimer.[22] But speaking in short sentences, and pausing when need be, were two helpful techniques. While a cub reporter was anxious about getting the details right, the often-older rewrite man just wanted the details to begin with: "Crowded to the limit about 10 minutes before the edition goes over . . . he hasn't any time to play around. A cub calls up and bothers him with a lot of foolish detail when about 30 words would give the rewrite man time to write a stick or two," claimed an anonymous rewrite man in 1924.[23] Rewrite staff could become impatient and sarcastic with cubs who had trouble organizing their notes or thoughts.[24] There was a steep learning curve involved in talking to rewrite men throughout the interwar years. Many cubs could barely get their "panted words" over "one end of a telephone."[25] At least one reporter suggested that new reporters practice calling into the rewrite desk on less important stories. He also suggested that calling into rewrite should also happen at college newspapers.[26] In these ways, new reporters could get used to telling stories to rewrite staff.

In some parts of the country outside of the major East Coast cities, however, the status of the rewrite staff was less assured. Eric Allen, the dean of the University of Oregon's journalism school, critiqued what he saw as an increasing overreliance on rewrite staff, particularly in New York City: "The cheap reporter, reinforced by a high-priced rewrite man and a skilled copydesk, is a bad combination so far as the possible improvement of American journalism is concerned."[27] Others believed an ideal newspaper should not have dedicated rewrite staff at all. Marlen Pew, editor of *Editor & Publisher*, believed a reporter should be able to "some rapid telephoning" but should also be expected to return to the office to "write most of his stories."[28]

Though they considered themselves set apart, from the perspective of management, rewriters' status in the newsroom (just not their pay) was roughly on par with that of reporters. In the initial years of the Depression, the *Chicago Daily Illustrated News* moved to a five-day workweek in an attempt to mitigate layoffs. Its management kept the rewrite staff on the same schedule as the reporters, since the two groups worked together closely. Accordingly, along with reporters, many rewrite staff members had Saturdays off.[29]

Over time, the rewrite person's role was supplemented by stenographers and dictationists, who "made inroads on the rewrite ranks" by the 1940s. These workers were more specialized in the task of information transfer. But there were sharp differences between reporters and rewrite staff on the one hand and such auxiliary workers on the other: "Some of the biggest newspapers still make their rewrite men take dictation, which is not only a degrading, resented task but an economic waste, when one considers the salary of a rewrite man and that of a stenographer."[30] Dictationists and stenographers had lower status and pay, but the work was an opportunity for more women to enter the newsroom, and, in some cases, make the jump "up" to copy editing or rewrite.

The camaraderie on some rewrite desks could be quite pronounced, as Arthur Gelb related about his experience on the *New York Times* in the early 1950s. Gelb, who started out as a copy boy and moved up in his long career at the *Times* to managing editor, was in a good place to observe the atmosphere among rewrite workers. Having been summarily transferred to the *Times*'s rewrite battery at the insistence of a prickly editor, Gelb was not sure what he would face.[31] Overwhelmed his first night, he was assisted by another rewrite staffer, Billie Barrett, who helped him organize piles of incoming wire-service updates on a winter storm afflicting New England, and who also helped him sort the many phone calls coming in from reporters across the region. As paragraphs of copy were ripped from his Underwood typewriter and taken directly to the city desk for editing, he beat his deadline with just seconds to spare.

"After all my misgivings, I began to feel invincible, euphoric; I was suddenly sure I could handle anything that rewrite required," Gelb recalled. When he thanked Barrett for her help, she replied, "Rewrite's like a commune . . . we all try to help each other, especially on the big stories." Barrett, who Gelb relates was the first rewrite woman on the *Times*, was sometimes mistaken for a telephone operator (a position actually held in high regard by reporters and editors alike) but took pride in earning the "the respect of all the rewrite men . . . [and was] accepted as one of them." The rewrite staff relied heavily on phone operators and the "morgue"—the *Times*'s extensive reference library of news clippings—in their work. Gelb remembered how "the entire battery teamed up to put a story together," particularly when it was a complex one and at risk of not meeting major deadlines, as when the rewrite desk helped to cover Joseph Stalin's fatal stroke on March 4, 1953.

On that occasion, the "rewrite bank" had to work as a unit in order to collect enough information on Stalin's impending death and its ramifications for the relationship between the United States and the Soviet Union. After formative experiences like these, the rewrite desk found it easy to bond as a group. Gelb's rewrite desk even went so far as to create an ersatz dinner group for the night staff, the "Night Rewrite Gourmet Society," which brought ethnic meals to share on Wednesday evenings in the newsroom. On other evenings, the staff would gather at nearby late-night restaurants and bars, sometimes joined by the night copy editors. These events were necessary to unwind after intense shifts, though in time Gelb himself reduced his late nights for the sake of his wife and young son. Gelb and his fellow rewrite men and women continued to pool their resources, occasionally helping one other to obtain "the rare rewriteman's byline—proof of the efficiency of our teamwork."[32]

The rewrite desk also built on its camaraderie outside of breaks for meals or card games. The staff spent time analyzing the early edition for stories worthy of praise or others derided as mediocre. Collectively, they also resisted "periodic cost-saving measures," such as a decree to keep using their soft-lead Ebony pencils (used for taking notes) until they were worn down to a third of their original size. After a clerk locked all the spare pencils in his desk and left early, Gelb and his colleagues reacted against this regulation of an "essential tool of our trade." Grinding nineteen pencils down to stubs, they put them in an envelope and addressed them to their city editor. The pencil edict, Gelb recalled, was rescinded. These acts of defiance helped to deepen the rewrite desk's sense of collective identity and were similar to other news workers' resistance strategies. The actual space the battery occupied, in Gelb's case, helped to build this in-group identity. Other teams in the newsroom were less collegial, and more competitive. When Gelb went to work for the drama department, he moved into a small, glass-enclosed office away from the main newsroom. There, with six other staff members, "we felt like fish colliding in a bowl." This space helped produce a different attitude toward the work, and the "drama enclave functioned on an every-man-for-himself principle."[33]

### THE REWRITE DESK AT MIDCENTURY

World War II changed the culture of the newsroom, modifying its more specialized internal fiefdoms like the rewrite desk. Newsrooms, previously a mostly male domain, began to hire women to fill openings on the desk. But some resisted. Fred M. McLennan, later editor of the *Buffalo Courier-Express*, decried what he saw as the uneven quality of women in newspaper jobs.[34] He complained that they tended to "lose their enthusiasm for the game rapidly. They marry, or drift away when they find that real work and not glamor permeate the atmosphere of the news room." Even as he urged editors to look to smaller newspapers for "good rewrite men," he did not encourage the hiring of women.[35] But as women began to fill the ranks of reporters, including at the elite wire services, the pool of candidates for the rewrite desk began to include them too, especially as the war continued.[36]

One sign of this increasing pool can be found in the "Situations Wanted" ads in *Editor & Publisher* during the war. Among the persons seeking jobs were a self-described "able newspaper woman," another "aggressive young woman," and an "alert woman reporter," all looking for work, and sensing, perhaps, that their moment had arrived.[37] Women were an increasingly frequent sight in the reporter and rewrite ranks, at a ratio of one to five (women to men) by the mid-1950s.[38] But their presence, as elsewhere on many newspapers, was still controversial, especially among older male editors. Some women were welcomed on the rewrite desk. Others were derided in misogynist ways as unintelligent or lazy, and assigned to dictation.[39] But by the end of the 1940s, women were no longer an aberration among rewrite "men." Reflecting this development, the language gradually changed to emphasize "battery," "staff," or "desk" as opposed to the male plural of "rewrite men."

After the war, managers attempted to streamline rewrite desks and put them on par with improved copydesks. Spurred by the growing ability of radio and nascent TV news broadcasts to cover breaking news, these improvements were directed internally, if sporadically. At the *Detroit Free Press* in 1948, inspired by the "continuous production line made famous by auto makers in this Auto Capital," improved coordination was sought between the copy and rewrite desks. With "a specially designed five position Rewrite Desk and eight position Copy Desk, joined by a straight-line working table-desk which places the News Editor, City Editor and their assistants in a compact group in the center," the goal was to move copy more efficiently from rewrite to the city and then to the copydesk "in a fairly continuous process." The ability to hold phone calls from multiple lines was also part of this "modernization" effort.[40] Four years later, at the *Chicago Tribune*, "the entire news flow" was directed by a "center desk," with local, telegraph, and cable desks each having its own team of "rewritemen to handle special stories."[41] Also in 1952, the *Philadelphia Inquirer* renovated its newsroom, providing "button-type mouthpieces, identical with those used by Bell Telephone operators, to its reporters and rewritemen."[42] In Los Angeles at the *Examiner*, a renovation of the "editorial department" placed Agness Underwood, its well-known city editor, as well as the assistant city editor and news and photo editors, next to the "rewrite battery" and the copydesk. Proximity and internal upgrades to phone systems were key.

By the 1950s rewrite staff were increasingly college-trained journalists. Alongside this, there were attempts to prepare new rewrite staff more systematically for the job. Even though many were veteran reporters, as tradition and newsroom norms dictated, some newspapers attempted to craft a training pipeline for them. The *Denver Post*, for example, used its evening edition to train promising young reporters, who could step into more advanced beats, and also the rewrite desk on the day staff, as needed. Exposure to the existing night "rewrite-battery" served as an in-house classroom for young reporters, training them in the interactions necessary between reporters and rewrite.[43] Night reporters in training would spend a month on the dayside staff, starting at rewrite and graduating to general assignment and then more specialized beats, shadowed by a more experienced reporter. This was a step away from the usual use for night desks both as a holding tank for beginners to get enough seasoning to cover daytime assignments and as a "burying place for journalistic misfits."[44] It reflected a more unionized, white-collar newsroom work force, one that could not waste personnel or time. Rewrite staff, as part of this work force, had solidified their position in the newsroom's work culture.

## COPY EDITORS

Copy editors, or "copy readers," held a substantial amount of power in the American newsrooms of the 1920s through the 1950s. More so than rewrite staff, they exercised near-ultimate authority over the news-production process (second only to senior editors), and were the most superior "near peer" to the reporter. Their ranks were populated by both former reporters and those who had entered the newsroom expressly to work for the copydesk, bypassing time on beats or on general assignment. As guardians of print journalism's implicit and explicit rules, they also embodied its cultural norms and existed as a world apart (or a world within worlds) inside many newsrooms. Their conflict with reporters and occasionally other editors was notorious, and both groups often thought ill of the other.

The tensions could reach a distracting point, as reporters complained that copy editors systematically eliminated their best material, and copy editors bemoaned maverick reporters for bending both stated and unstated journalistic standards. Working at the interface between the newsgathering and news-producing sides of a newspaper, such skirmishes were inevitable, and in some cases, healthy. But over time, the two kinds of news workers reached a working détente and learned to share power, as reporters claimed a white-collar status and the authority and autonomy needed to control the newsgathering process. Copy editors, too, were more systematically trained to cooperate, rather than oppose, their necessary collaborators, the reporters. Gradually, younger news workers saw the copydesk as a viable way to start a career.

It should be noted that throughout the 1920s, 1930s, 1940s, and 1950s, copy editors were often identified in textbooks, journalism trade publications, and memoirs as "copy readers." Proofreaders, in contrast, were a different classification of news worker, focused more on the presentation side of the news-production process, examining typeset copy one last time before publication. "True" proofreaders were fading as a subgroup within newsrooms by the 1930s and 1940s, and continued to do so with the advent of cold type and offset printing (which augured less need for hot-type-driven, final page proofs).[45] Contemporaries noted the occasional confusion by outsiders, and observed that the work of proofreaders was much more mechanical than editorial. The work was considered essential but less creative than copy editing and often involved two-person teams of "reader" and "holder," who would read stories twice over for errors.[46] The idea of correcting "copy" versus working on "proofs" captures the distinction, which was clearer to the generation of news workers who operated without word processors. The latter technology essentially eliminated the last vestiges of the proofreading system by the 1970s and 1980s.[47]

According to a 1951 vocational guide to journalism for high school and college students, larger newsrooms could not function without a well-staffed copydesk, sometimes simply described as "the desk." Often a horseshoe-shaped table, it was usually located centrally in the newsroom, with copy editors seated at the edge, or "rim," and a chief copy editor at its head, in the lead spot, or "slot." A "slotman" was slang for the lead copy editor, and "copydesk" short for the whole copydesk staff.[48] A copy editor was considered an "advanced member of the city-room staff," and it was "not conceivable" for a junior reporter to fill a vacancy on a copydesk. Copy editors were among the more experienced people in the newsroom, expected, by newspaper culture and custom, to be "[veterans] of mature judgement . . . and considerable knowledge."[49] Into the 1930s, "the old fellow, from two to five decades of experience back of him . . . [was] called upon to handle the important copy and to write the delicate headline which is to be the paper's main show-window tomorrow morning."[50] A certain nostalgia for a supposedly more freewheeling recent past, as with other groups in the newsroom, characterized perceptions of copy editors during this period. Stanley Walker, the otherwise world-wise city editor of the *New York Herald-Tribune*, characterized them as "hoary and delightful fuddy-duddies . . . holdovers from the days when the copyreader roamed the country like the telegraph operator or the tramp printer." As long as they were not "too far gone in liquor and loss of memory," the "really competent old-time copyreaders" still had job prospects even in the midst of the Depression.[51] As late as the 1920s, before the more widespread acceptance of college and especially college journalism programs as a routine route into the newsroom, copy editors were regarded by their peers as both more educated, and more cynical, than their young reporter peers, and, most importantly, more secure in their positions.

Within their parallel but separate routines, copy editors could be directed by copy chiefs as to how long and how many columns wide a story should be, as well as how wordy—in terms of sentence length and choice—to make a headline, and subheads, as needed. Though they usually worked as a team, editing copy written by beat and GA reporters, as well as that produced by writers working for other sections of the paper, they were under the direct authority of their chief. This chief was "the king of copy," with the "men around the rim . . . his courtiers." A chief was nearly equal in power to the city editor, according to one account. Copy chiefs' power radiated outward, toward their rim editors, almost literally in proportion to their physical distance. Copy, after having been edited by the rim editors, would be returned to the copy chief for a final check before being sent to composing for typesetting. The copy chief, or chiefs, would be recruited from the ranks of the rim editors. The former would be given authority to hire or fire their "rim men" and had "complete authority over the desk and its personnel.[52]

In contrast to most reporters, copy editors were "the most sedentary member[s] of the city room," while also "the best informed."[53] Sontheimer believed that copy editors' duties "approximate a bookkeeper's routine more than any other job on the staff. The grind is steadier, the tenor of the work, despite deadline peaks, more even, the hours more dependable (a copyreader seldom works overtime, sorry to disillusion you, Mrs. Copyreader) and the confinement greater." The job was only for "certain temperaments," but those who liked it could last whole careers enjoying the work.[54] A copy editor was the "unsung hero of the Fourth Estate." His work could be "monotonous . . . he sits on the rim . . . does his stint and then goes home."[55] A routine schedule might be part of a less exciting newsroom role, and one associated with less glamorous news-production work. But it promised stability and "fixed, regular hours," which meant that time off was one's own. The ability to sit down and then leave, with fairly set hours, was "sometimes a sweet boon." This was particularly true before World War II, before the Guild achieved the standardization of the forty-hour workweek.[56]

Since copy editors remained inside the physical newsroom, these characteristics of the job were not surprising. The copy editor was "responsible for the exact form in which a story appears on the printed page." Copy editors were constantly on the lookout for factual errors, libelous content, and errors in spelling, grammar, punctuation, titles, names of streets and local institutions, and so on. Less explicitly, he or she was expected to implement a newspaper's style, to fix or alter (or in many cases, simply remove) awkward phrasings, or as reporters alleged, anything too creative.[57] A copy editor "corrects and manicures" the work of others. The "elimination of verbosity," the primacy of space restrictions, the desire to reshape stories so that the most vital elements came first—all these were guiding norms for copy editors throughout the interwar years and beyond.[58] This came with a fair amount of pressure. Breaking unwritten or written policy directives could lead to a copy editor's firing, and he could "well lose his job for ignorance or carelessness." Headline writing formed another important and less heralded part of a copy editor's job. Challenging to write due to space limitations and rules governing style, headlines and their words had to be composed to order and on tight deadlines. Many of these pithy, active words entered popular culture.[59] This could produce some quirky habits: some editors liked working with pencils instead of typewriters as late as the 1950s. Unlike the typewriter, a pencil allowed you to erase and rewrite, even if just in the margins of a typewritten page.[60]

In response to these pressures, some invented new, shortened words that could fit in tight spaces.[61] Among their peers, copy editors were measured by their accuracy, clarity, speed, and ingenuity with headlines and ability to retain the gist of a story even when cutting details.[62] It was felt they should develop a "nice feeling for the right word, a sense of the clear and the straightforward, a sound knowledge of the people and materials which make news, a retentive memory, a close eye for what is libelous or dangerous, and an incorruptible mental honesty which makes it impossible for him to be unfair." Due to the large influx of copy—one estimate from the mid-1930s was that forty thousand words could pass through a copydesk on a nightly basis—individual copy editors were crucial to workflow for the entire newsroom. Curiously, not all copy editors were gifted spellers.[63] But with their separate "decisions"—that is, their determinations of what had to be changed, or be removed, from a story—there was no appeal except to the copy chief on duty. Reporters were typically not expected to have much, if any, say over their turned-in stories.[64]

### COPY EDITORS, REPORTERS, AND THE LARGER NEWSROOM CULTURE

Sympathetic observers of both copy editors and reporters noted the enduring tensions between the groups. Indeed, reporters and copy editors were prone to conflict due to the contradictory natures of their workflows and processes. Reporters were expected to go out, gather news, come back, and create content, while copy editors remained behind, and even more than rewrite staff, saw to it that this same content was cut down to size and conformed to the newsroom's production norms. Unlike rewrite staff, though, copy editors had even less contact with the outside world. Reporters were given credit through bylines but copy editors remained anonymous. Copy editors worked as a team and reporters were encouraged to work solo. Unless a reporter previously worked on a copydesk, he or she had a hard time thinking of copy editors as "anything except officious dummies, with a gnawing inferiority complex, who delight in ruining the best work of a reporter by cutting out the frills."[65] Folktales of spiteful copy editors were favorites among reporters:

> There is the story of the bitter old copyreader who, reading the copy of a young and brilliant reporter, was unable to restrain his genuine amusement. "Lord, this is funny. I'll fix it." Wherewith his pencil would cut out the very phrases which had moved him to rare bellylaughs.[66]

For others in the newsroom, "the copyreader has traditionally been a worn-out rewrite man or reporter, cynical, skeptical, unappreciative, sour on the world and deriving his only pleasure from murderously disemboweling and emasculating good stories." But that "traditional picture, never wholly correct as to the copyreader's qualities, was losing accuracy in regard to his origin."[67] Stanley Walker half-teasingly referred to the copy editor as the "man with the green eyeshade," noting that a copy editor's "deft touches with the pencil may raise a story out of the ordinary, but it's the handsome, much publicized reporter who gets the credit. Fancy reporters, particularly young ones who have been debauched by gazing too long at iridescent and poetic images, call him a butcher. Rarely do they thank him for improving their efforts."[68] A ditty from a generation before, by the journalist-poet Henry Edward Warner, emphasized the animosity some reporters felt for copy editors, despite their mutual dependence on each other:

> Somewhere there must exist a hell
> For copy-readers who employ
> Their witless minds in killing joy
> And sounding young Ambition's knell![69]

Female reporters were thought to be particularly susceptible to the "the hacksaws of hurry-up copy desks," and supposedly not tough enough for a working environment that included cranky copy editors.[70] But female reporters disagreed. Mildred Philips, author of a column in *Editor & Publisher* in the early 1920s, believed that women could be co-partners in "the land of copy-paper and cusses." Philips also demurred against the perception of some male editors that women would make better desk workers than "go out and go-getters."[71] While their presence would not become common until after World War II, some enterprising women reporters tried anyway. A "situations wanted" ad in a 1934 issue of *Editor & Publisher* featured a female reporter who had "enough backbone to learn copy desk."[72]

The deep disconnect in mentality and mission between reporters and copy editors affected recruitment. As Walker put it, "The copy desk, in spite of efforts of well-meaning journalistic uplifters to interest young and ambitious men in its undoubted charms, remains, in all truth, pretty much a refuge for ageing men who are no longer spry enough to get out and cover assignments." This was not necessarily a bad thing, or always true: "If many old reporters, faced at last with the realization that they were unable to stand the rough and tumble life of collecting and writing news, had taken the time to learn the technique of reading copy, their old age would be much more secure. They could land on the copy desk, instead of whining that they had given the best years of their life to reporting and then had learned too late that there was nothing else they could do."[73] Better to be familiar with how the copydesk worked, because it would "improve your writing, and it may come in handy some day when you want to, or are forced to, become a copyreader."[74] Knowing how to listen to "wise old copyreaders" was a good idea, as "their skulls are full of the accumulated wisdom of decades."[75] Attempts to recruit younger copy editors in the early 1930s met with moderate success.[76]

But despite such admonitions, reporters were reluctant to make a switch—and it *was* a cultural and mental leap—to work for the copydesk. They would far more willingly make the shorter jump to the rewrite battery, or angle for a junior editor's position on the city desk. "Too many of the young men are impatient, and won't stand up under the drudgery. Why should they sit at a desk," Walker mused, "when other young men are writing stories that carry big by-lines, and others are getting around, painting the town red, growing up into special writers, dramatic critics, columnists or feature writers of distinction?" The copydesk had its own rewards, but they were not for everyone. As Walker described it, they were still "members of a strange cult, who suffer from an ailment known in the trade as the itching pencil—that is, they can't leave well enough alone. They think they have to change a few words, or a few sentences, on every page, either to prove that they are working or because of some obscure inner compulsion. Such men deserve all the calumny heaped upon them by heartbroken reporters."[77] In depictions of journalistic communities in 1930s-era popular culture, such as Silas Bent's *Buchanan of the Press*, reporters continued to disregard copy editors. The titular character in Bent's novel, for example, "slowly sinks from the glory of a star reporter to the depths of the copy desk."[78]

### A LATER DÉTENTE WITH REPORTERS AND OTHERS

Some believed that copy editors were grouchy because reporters had made them that way, partially by being worse spellers than copy editors. A spelling contest at the *Sacramento Bee* showed that most of its reporters spelled only 40 to 60 percent of fifty given words correctly. "If copy desk people are as villainous, as empty of humor, as reporters imagine they are, they have gotten that way because of this [tendency to misspell words]," one writer noted.[79] A measure of humor on both sides helped to cushion some of the pointed feelings of dissatisfaction. As a *Los Angeles Times* staff member put it, while copy readers who suffered from "rim-rot" should be euthanized with a "merciful death," beat men could experience "calcification of the brain," and the "immobility of star crime reporters" was caused by "a paralysis due to industrophobia in its most extreme form."[80] Another anecdote poked fun at both sides for their low view of the other: "A photographer guiding a guest through the various work areas of the *Detroit News* remarked as he explained the city room layout: 'On this side are the reporters. They write, but can't spell. On that side are the copyreaders. They spell, but can't writ[e].'"[81] More seriously, senior reporters believed that cubs had a lot to learn from copy editors.[82] Other writers noted that reporters needed copy editors just as much as they needed their fellow reporters or rewrite men: "It is traditional that reporters must damn the copy desk for 'butchering' his masterpieces, but every newspaperman knows that a competent desk is the heart of a good newspaper. The men on a first-class desk are not mechanics. They are professional, in the highest sense of the word. Their technical skill, essential as it is, is only a minor part of the equipment they must bring to their daily tasks."[83]

There was a bigger cultural shift underway in the newsroom by the post–World War II era: reporters were becoming copy editors. More reporters were also going to, and finishing, college. This meant a bigger pool of candidates for the copydesk. And certain practices, like leaving contact information for sources on the top of copy, also helped to increase "interoffice cooperation."[84] William Ogdon, who had made just such a transition, and who was a veteran of the *Toledo Times*, *St. Louis Globe Democrat*, and the *New York Times*, described the "traditional enmity" between reporters and rewrite men and copy readers. He compared it to the disdain reporters had for the "'basement journalists' of the classified advertising and circulation departments who occasionally pass[ed] themselves off to the public as newspapermen."[85] The "logical schism" that divided the reporter from the copydesk could, however, be mitigated by better communication and a chance to review changes made to a reporter's copy by the copydesk before the story went to print. Such practices could lead to a the fostering of a "friendlier relationship" between the two groups, especially on bigger papers where reporters and copy editors did not know each well, if at all.[86] Without active efforts to bridge gaps reinforced by routine, the "pace, the constant vigilance over detail, the exhausting competition, and the strain of the ever-impending emergency are likely to make us inhumane toward one another," Ogdon noted.[87] Other reporters made the move to the copydesk during this era, finding that the reputation of the desk as "a hoary circle of hunch-backed old editors who approached the grave consoling themselves with second-hand glimpses of life from beneath a green eyeshade" was not true.[88] Despite these efforts at reconciliation, there was a lingering fear of getting stuck at the rim, "advancing slowly if at all."[89]

### TECHNOLOGY AND THE COPYDESK

Unlike rewrite men and women, whose newsroom role emerged in the first third of the twentieth century primarily out of technological necessity, copy editors held an older, and more firmly established, position in the newsroom before the 1920s. But technology was still altering their work processes. Some copy editors initially resisted the introduction of typewriters because they were used to estimating the length of articles written in longhand and felt reporters "were getting too much 'space.'"[90] But the typewriter largely replaced the "old-time stylus," and the practice of writing on loose slips of paper faded throughout the newsroom by the 1920s. Copy editors were facing the introduction of the "automatic telegraph printer" and an increasing amount of and reliance on wire-service copy.[91] Often located centrally in the newsroom, the copydesk at larger newsrooms received copy by pneumatic tubes. New buildings from the period emphasized "rapid manufacture." The basic idea, with the copydesk in mind, was to include "the latest devices to make the mechanical work faster and more efficient."[92]

At the Fort Worth *Star-Telegram*'s new building, the copydesk was the center of news production. As "the heart of any news room," its "horse shoe desk" accommodated six copy editors, all working for the "'head' of the desk, who sits in the bend of the shoe." Built from mahogany, it was illuminated by a "trough lighting system, which throws 400 candle power of light direct on the copy but is softened by glazed glass." Copy was carried to the desk via "pneumatic air tubes."[93] And perhaps most importantly, while "formerly every editor and subeditor on newspapers were given separate offices . . . the *Star-Telegram* has found that desks . . . open with partitions eliminated afforded closer team work and co-operation." The open-floor plan encompassed the copydesk.[94] The *Washington Star*'s new newsroom space in 1922 included a horseshoe-shaped copydesk, of "art-metal design, green-enameled steel and brass trimmings, with facilities for handling local, and cable copy. Pneumatic tubes at the chief's elbow communicate with the composing room and other departments."[95] Other newspapers used gravity-based systems to move copy down from the copydesk floor to the composing room.[96]

The *New York World*, taking copydesk reorganization one step further, adopted what was known as a "universal desk plan" in order to handle the increased flow of copy. Designed like a large "H," the copydesk was located in the back of the newsroom, with Hugh Logan, its chief copy editor, sitting in the center. Working with "10 assistant copy editors, [and] a man from the old telegraph desk alternating with a man from the former city copy desk," the new system handled all copy, including material from the formerly separate copydesks devoted to telegraph and local news. With a workday beginning at 5:30 p.m., and with local news dealt with first, before "the telegraph matter begins to flow in," slack "and rush times" were reduced.[97]

The copydesk in the 1920s was also a tempting target for efficiency experts, apostles of Fordism interested in making the newsroom more like a factory.[98] The copydesk's fixed, routinized work patterns naturally lent itself to attempts at making it more efficient. Osmore R. Smith, part of the *Milwaukee Journal*'s planning department, urged a more standardized system for ensuring a better flow of copy to and from the desk. That material "is as much a problem of manufacturing as is the making of an automobile or a pair of shoes," he claimed.[99] Smith, likely an "efficiency expert" himself, urged better cooperation with the mechanical side of the newspaper: "A traditionally minded editorial man may tell you that you cannot control news; that news doesn't 'break' to suit the convenience of linotype operators and must be handled as it comes." That point of view was incorrect, he said.[100]

The copydesk in the mid-1920s faced further calls for efficiency due to an ever-increasing influx of wire news. Some worried that copy editors would be physically and mentally overwhelmed by the vast amounts of prepared copy flowing into their desks. The constant work, or the "treadmill business of desk-plugging," could cause one to fall into a bad "copy-reader mind." This would then affect reporters. "A dull witted, mentally lazy copy-reader can stifle the spark of genius in a budding writer so effectively—by mere dunderhead squelching—that he will be years in regaining his lost enthusiasm even in the most altered environment," a contemporary observed.[101] Increased pay and more regular hours could prevent this, it was suggested. Better internal communication, especially between emergent rewrite desks and the older copydesks, was also thought to be a solution. Keeping related staff members "within speaking distance of each other" could help the copydesk when it got swamped, suggested a staff member at the *Kansas City Star*.[102]

This emphasis on speed meant that the late 1920s witnessed continued improvements to the technology of the news desk. Conveyer belts brought material from the newsroom, often through the copydesk, to the composing room. Soundproofing deadened the dull roar of telegraph keys and "printer machines."[103] Other newsrooms placed their copydesks strategically near centers of editorial power. The *Syracuse Herald* in 1928 positioned its copydesk and editors near the city and state editors, while dampening sound with absorptive ceiling tiles and an internal tube system for moving copy.[104] Similarly, in 1928 the *Cincinnati Enquirer* used nine pneumatic tubes to connect the city editor to the copydesk.[105] Some newsrooms maintained spots on the copydesk for the managing editor and city editor (and his assistant) to sit and work. The desk itself was sometimes improved, in terms of materials and organization, with some made of steel and equipped with "typewriter compartments."[106] In images of newsrooms from this era, copydesks were a prominent part of the environment.[107] These were also sources of nostalgia. The scarred wooden copydesk could make a crude bed, one editor recalled, and "one could sleep on it if he stayed out too late to go home to a suburb and not late enough to start an early trick."[108]

### CHANGES TO THE PHYSICAL SPACE AND ROLE OF THE COPYDESK

Remodels of existing newsrooms and new newsroom spaces continued earlier trends. There was a recurring interest, for example, in moving copy in straight lines across a newsroom, from reporters to department editors to the city editor and managing editor.[109] Copydesks were still being placed for optimum efficiency, sometimes directly above the composing room, as was the case with the *St. Louis Globe-Democrat*.[110] Technical innovations were heralded in profiles of renovations and new construction in contemporary accounts, including the installation of a loudspeaker in the "editorial and composing rooms" of the New Orleans *Times-Picayune*. Located on the copydesk and the foreman's desk, with "an open connection during working hours," in an emergency, "Hold Page One!" could be amplified loud enough to be heard by the entire composing room staff, "reaching the foreman wherever he is."[111] Another newsroom installed an "electronic copy control" device that lit up to indicate "deadline," "too much," or "low" to facilitate communication between the newsroom and the composing room.[112]

As newspapers increasingly focused on economic survival during the worsening Depression, the traditional mobility of copy editors faded. Before, wrote one anonymous copy editor, three years on a desk was considered enough to become a veteran. Now, he said, three years was enough to classify an editor as being among the "newest." No more did they come and go. "Economic uncertainty is an excellent cure for the itching foot of the newspaperman. Whether for good or ill I make no pretense of knowing," wrote one contemporary.[113] The Depression had forced some newsroom staffers into "starvation pay . . . for as long as three years."[114] With uncertainty so high, many stayed put rather than risk losing work. This trend, toward a less nomadic life, had already started in the 1920s.[115]

Marlen Pew, in his "Shop Talk at Thirty" column in *Editor & Publisher*, complained that US copy editors were mere "rim plugger[s]" and were not imaginative compared to their London counterparts.[116] And back home, they still suffered in comparison to reporters. Among other press bromides was this jibe: "What happened on the copy desk? Must be in a trance, for they let . . . an authentic piece of human interest slip into the paper."[117] That the "knights of the green eye-shade" were targets for even sympathetic watchers like Pew speaks to their continued position in the newsroom pecking order. Spoofing the tensions between reporters and copy editors, Pew wrote a short fictional account of a copy editor losing his cool when a reporter misspelled his own name.[118]

The 1930s also witnessed some of the first systematic attempts to standardize the hitherto erratic training of copy editors. Though this would not be fully realized until after World War II, the *Akron Times-Press* was among the pioneers. As part of an in-house refresher program for news workers, Walter J. Coyle, the paper's city editor, made sure to include members of the copydesk alongside photographers and reporters in these kinds of cross-training efforts. Other papers emphasized the responsibility of the copy editor. The *Toledo Blade*'s Raymond A. Werneke, a former veteran rewrite man and copy editor, was designated a "super copyreader" and given the task of checking all proofs.[119]

Despite these early forays into better training and a few reflective efforts at refocusing on the importance of the copydesk under conditions of austerity, copy editors were not considered "professional" under federal labor regulations. Elmer E. Andrews, administrator of the Wage and Hour division of the Department of Labor, sought to clarify the issue in a speech at the sixth annual convention of the ANG in 1939. The fact that "the copyreader is under the constant supervision of the head of the desk, and the sports editor and other departmental heads generally are under the supervision of the managing editor" disqualifies them from any professional status under the Wage and Hour law, he said.

Copy editors, just as much as reporters, were caught up in the larger debate about who could be exempt from overtime pay. Andrews also highlighted the irregular education and training of "the ordinary newspaper worker." Based on then-current understanding of what constituted "professional" status, news workers lacked advanced education and regulated entry into the field, especially as compared to the practitioners of law or medicine.[120] In the newsroom hierarchy, copy editors outranked reporters, but in labor law—and in reality—they fell far below senior editors classified as "professionals" or executives.

## THE COPYDESK IN THE 1940S

The involvement of the United States in the global fight against the Axis affected newsrooms' relational equilibrium as staffs shrank due to wartime mobilization, newsprint became scarce, and both in-house unions and the ANG reached an unofficial understanding that strikes were on hold for the duration of the conflict. As the United States prepared for war, the effect on newsroom work culture was felt in relationships between experienced news workers, a group that included copy editors and their management. While copy boys and girls, photographers, and rewrite staff members were also affected, the culture of copy editors faced some unique challenges.

The draft of young men hit these editors like any other group in the newsroom, with a corresponding influx of women into positions previously not open to them.[121] Since copy editors tended to be older, however, the draft did not reach as deeply into copydesks. But publications and news organizations that had traditionally served as the training ground for copy editors were hard-pressed to fill their ranks with qualified workers, and this, in turn, had ramifications up the ladder. Copy editors were already not plentiful (one study counted them as few as five out of about eighty editorial staff members working for the *Milwaukee Journal* in 1941; the *Journal* could be considered a typical large-city newsroom).[122] One survey by the National Council on Professional Education for Journalism found that on about 14 percent of all newspapers of one hundred thousand circulation or more, copy editors were in particularly short supply.[123] So while relatively few may have been lost to wartime exigencies, their positions were harder to fill. Some papers turned to unusual sources, such as journalism faculty (normally hired in the summers between semesters) to meet their personnel needs.[124]

In Chicago, the City News Bureau was not able to help fill the staffing gaps on Chicago newspapers easily, including the *Chicago Journal of Commerce*. As a result, during the war the *Journal* had an all-female copydesk.[125] Women were hired as copy editors at the *Portland Journal* and *New York Herald Tribune*.[126] The *Tribune* had not hired any since World War I. In both cases, female copy editors were referred to as "copy gals" or "copy girls."[127] Some women objected to being referred to in this way, and to the general tone of coverage of female news workers in trade publications. In a letter to the editor of *Editor & Publisher*, Jessica Bird, a reporter and desk worker from the Riverside, California, *Press and Enterprise*, complained that the prejudices women were facing in the newsroom had been well-ingrained before the war.[128]

Unlike after World War I, though, women remained in the newsroom afterward as a more substantial presence. At the *New York Times* magazine, Virginia J. Fortiner remained at the copydesk.[129] Women also stayed at the copydesks of the *New York Post* and *Mirror*.[130] And while many veterans returned to their newspapers, there were definitely challenges in placing them in positions commensurate with their skills and experiences. This was especially the case in New York City, where the only positions open were entry level, such as for copy boys, according to a 1946 Guild survey of ten thousand news workers employed before the war. Of this number, only about 30 percent had returned to their former positions. And as for the five hundred job applicants the Guild was working with, 90 percent were vets.[131] The copydesk was, however, seen as an ideal place to help retrain them, if positions could be secured.[132]

Despite the war and its aftermath, the basic setup of the newsroom changed only moderately in the 1940s. The Santa Fe *New Mexican*, for example, in its new fourteen-thousand-square-foot office, equipped its editorial staff members with a "clover leaf" desk with soundproofed slots for wire copy.[133] Other incremental innovations included circular copydesks, tried at the *Philadelphia Bulletin* as part of its push to include a more "personal element." Throughout the newsroom, the "flow of copy is expedited by a triangular arrangement with the slowest functions farthest from the copy desk."[134] After the war, other experiments in newsroom design toyed with simple changes to the shape of the desk, including a "modified V" instead of the more traditional "U" shape. The *Wall Street Journal* used this design for its "seven-plus-slotman" staff, in an attempt to provide more room to work. The desk was equipped with two telephones and two to three typewriters, and had more room to spread out, with about thirty-three inches of clearance between editors; each editor had waste bins for paper and "ample leg room."[135]

At the *Detroit Free Press*, a "modernization" program "streamlined" the newsroom's layout in 1948.[136] The major change to the newsroom involved repositioning the rewrite and copy desks. Previously, the copydesk had been across the room from the city desk, "necessitating a constant walking back and forth by news executives as they conferred about the numerous problems coming up for each edition. Now those editors sit side-by-side, or face-to-face, and such problems are settled as fast as they come up." This sped up consultations over copy but also allowed it to move from rewrite to city desk and then to the copydesk with fewer hiccups. This "City Desk-Copy Desk combination" was hardly radical, but it was one example of a newsroom moving away from Depression-era retrenchment to an approach that took advantage of early postwar prosperity to retool the space.[137] Larger newsrooms, including at the *New York Times*, were also attempting to modernize and expand their workspace after the war, focusing on modifications to the copydesk. The *Times*, with a "specially designed city desk," was hoping "to help speed the orderly flow of news copy."[138]

### THE COPYDESK IN THE 1950S AND BEYOND

Efforts to streamline copy processing and publication continued into the early 1950s. At the *Sacramento Bee*, a partial renovation of the newsroom, originally built in 1922, involved the installation of a new, centrally located (and octagonal) "universal copy desk" to speed the "flow of copy."[139] The *Bee* later installed a "double-horseshoe" copydesk.[140] The Philadelphia *Inquirer* provided more spacious desk spaces (instead of the traditional wood, or metal, the new ones were "hard-finished plastic in a shade of soft, gray green").[141] Centralizing efforts continued, moving copydesks closer and ever more in line with the city editor and rewrite battery, as was the case at the *Los Angeles Examiner*.[142] Similar efforts took place at the *Miami News* and the headquarters of Fort Wayne Newspapers, Inc.[143]

Beyond relocations of the desk, there were other attempts during this decade to rethink the role of this group of news workers. The *Chicago Tribune* attempted to systematize its copydesk by encouraging better coordination with the local, telegraph, and cable desks, assigning teams of rewrite and copy staff to each. "Slot men" for each team could decide more proactively how to fill the news hole.[144] The 1950s also brought a renewed focus on systematic training for copy editors. During the war, as well as the more frugal Depression years, training had largely occurred on the job. But the increasing numbers of college graduates with journalism training in the newsroom had begun to change how copy editors were educated. Internal training programs at newspapers flourished, especially for reporters and copy boys and girls. Accreditation efforts by college programs emphasized how the reporter and copy editor, in particular, were benefiting from a more standardized curriculum.[145]

The shift from self-taught and ad hoc training to college and internships as the preferred routes into the newsroom meant that the traditional pathway for copy editors faced changes, too. One program at the *Detroit Free Press* involved up to three and a half years of training on the copydesk. While designed for copy boys, whose Guild contract guaranteed them a trial period on the editorial side of the paper, it was also intended to better integrate new hires into the newsroom workforce.[146] Journalism schools, in a parallel move, pushed more robust courses to prepare students for work on the copydesk.[147] Some editors were also interested in training reporters as backup copy editors. There was some pushback from the Guild against this plan, because reclassification of reporters as copy editors reduced overtime pay.[148]

New technology, including improved teletypesetters, prompted further anxiety about the future of the copydesk. But another reaction was to encourage journalism students to pursue copyediting skills to bolster a backup career path.[149] Especially during the Depression, working on the copydesk had been considered more secure than reporting.[150] Now that reporters who had pursued just such a path were reaching the peak of their careers, their advice percolated down to new staff members.

In the meantime, the tensions "between slot and rim," observed G. Norman Collie, a "slotman" at the *Philadelphia Inquirer*, could be mitigated. Slot men were picked for promotion because they had the copyediting and headline-writing skills needed, as well as "the patience of a Cub Scout den mother, the sympathetic tin ear of a bartender, the flintiness of a drill instructor, the partiality of an octopus, and the jaundiced eye of a deserted wife." Training copy editors was akin to teaching skills in other occupations: "Like other trades—laying bricks, pulling teeth, delivering babies—copy reading can be taught any reasonably literate man of average intelligence. (Women, for some reason I haven't discovered, rarely make the grade)."[151] The latter observation was not uncommon, as women still faced challenges getting hired and remaining on the copydesk.

The social and occupational standing of the copy editor had reached a new, more white-collar status in the newsroom. Carl Kesler, editor of Sigma Delta Chi's *Quill* and a former copy editor himself, said that "nowadays he is listened to with respect even by city editors. He is invited to press parties along with reporters just like a regular newspaperman." Paid better, and sometimes the most powerful among their near peers and with their value more publicly praised, copy readers remained a vital part of the newsroom's relational ecosystem.[152] Part of this status was signaled by a move to call "copyreaders" (an older term) "copy editors." And since "headlines never have bylines," one contemporary believed that these editors deserved to be "made to feel they are part of the team."[153]

### REFLECTIONS ON THE CULTURE OF THE COPYDESK

Some in the newsroom complained about the old, pervasive idea "that the copy desk is a place of apprentices and pensioners." The copydesk had grown up and deserved respect; it had come from being a place "where non-committal heads were written and guide signs put on for the printer" to "the ultimate test of efficiency in handling of copy."[154] Over the decades copy editors were known for their mobility, or restlessness. An anonymous writer at "one of the largest copy desks in the country," commenting on the work culture of the copydesk in 1922, observed that the "genius copy-reader . . . is the original rolling stone, at least until it attains middle age and a thin mossiness or state of vegetation." The desire to travel, soak up "large smatterings of varied knowledge," combined with the tendency of copy editors to get overworked, helped to "enslave a young brain to his green eyeshade."[155] Being "nervous but mercurial" (both qualities, the writer assures us, of a good copy editor), a copy editor had to be managed carefully by a copy chief.

Between shifts, or during lulls during their shifts, copy editors socialized with one another and tended to spend time with each other rather than other news worker groups in the newsroom. Ritualized teasing seemed to be built into copydesk culture, at least on some newspapers.[156] Complaining about reporters' copy was a more outward-focused activity.[157] In addition to reading the paper, writing books, or working on articles for other parts of the paper during these breaks, copy editors would play games.[158] One such game was noted by Joe K. Schmidt, the state editor of the *Cleveland Plain Dealer*, in 1931. It involved a headline-finishing, "ask-me-another" quiz that was popular on his paper's copydesk "during the long morning hours when they are not busy."[159] Others would play practical jokes. The summer weather inspired just such a prank in the newsroom of the *Pittsburgh Sun-Telegraph* on a hot July day in 1946. Charles Wheeler, the paper's makeup editor, yelled from the composing room to "Send up some shorts!" The slot man, Clarence Grundish, "rummaged in a desk and came up triumphantly with a pair of men's shorts, which he stuffed into the copy tube" and launched back to the startled Wheeler.[160] Chicago's extensive "'underground railway'" of the City Press' fifteen miles of pneumatic tubes, linking the AP, *Chicago American*, *Chicago Daily News*, *Chicago Sun-Times*, and *Chicago Tribune*, carried up to 268,291 separate pieces of material each year, including pictures, news releases, and other messages, often to copydesks. Among them, even into the 1950s, were mice, felt hats, and billiard balls that arrived, along with less humorous copy, with a whoosh and a bang.[161]

Even when they had been moved to other, sometimes equally well-regarded parts of the newsroom, some copy editors missed their work. A want ad in *Editor & Publisher* in September 1942 emphasized how a rewrite man, "homesick" for the copydesk, "yearns for a return to pencils, shears, paste pot, cuspidor."[162] Outsiders' perceptions of copy editors could be seen in a 1955 cartoon. A socialite, commenting on a copydesk's inhabitants, remarks that "Not one of these people is wearing a green eye-shade!"[163] Another cartoon showed how packed a copydesk could get.[164]

### CONCLUSION: CHANGING NEWSROOM RELATIONSHIPS

All mutual teasing aside, the copydesk had changed. Less wild and woolly, and separated from the rewrite and local desk, it was staffed by a different, more mellow and stable group of news workers.[165] Copy editing had become more attractive to reporters over time as a career option. In the relational world of the newsroom, it was more acceptable to "stay" on as a copy editor, instead of thinking of it as a route to something better. As noted above, by the 1950s, copy editors were generally younger, trained specifically for the job, and drawn from the ranks of reporters. More openness characterized copy editors' perspectives toward reporters' creative copy. In turn, copy editors felt more respect from reporters, at least on some newspapers. Differences in attitude and skillsets remained, however.[166] The umbrella term of "newsman," "newspaperman," "reporter," or, later, "journalist" was often only conditionally or tentatively extended to copy editors, who nonetheless thought of themselves as such. But as a sign of tribal affiliation, the use of these terms signaled who was in and out of that inner ring of identity.

There were advantages to be had in these indeterminate statuses, however. In some cases, the copydesk was more open to women and younger reporters by the end of the decade. Advancement could come quicker, too.[167] Copy editors were encouraged to become experts in a field.[168] They were recognized for their newsroom achievements more often and participated in in-house refresher training programs.[169] While still senior as a near peer to the reporter, they were also more able to work together as part of a newsroom team. The position would remain closed to people of color for some time, but when newsrooms finally began to integrate, the copydesk could provide a protective place to begin one's career.[170]

Thinking broadly, the period from 1920 to 1960 witnessed the rise of an ever-more industrialized newsroom, as reporting technology and unionization made the space (and the work tasks within and without) more stratified. Groups of news workers tended to operate best within their unique work routines. The sum of these—the relationally driven production of the daily editions at a newspaper—defined the American newsroom's occupational culture. But even as unionization clarified work roles for news workers after the 1930s, there was an increasing emphasis on teamwork. While still distinct, various groups within the newsroom thought of themselves as more on par with one another, especially as related to the centering figure of the reporter. The ranks of rewrite staff and copy editors were more connected to frontline reporters, and vice versa. Copy boys and girls increasingly went to college, were better trained and better paid, and were given a more direct pipeline to the newsroom workforce. Photographers, once considered second-class newsroom citizens, became more important to news coverage, and their ranks became better educated and cross-trained as reporters. When reading accounts of these transformations, it is good to remember the lenses through which news workers *wanted* themselves to be seen, too, especially in trade publications. Taken as a whole, however, these trends were more real than imagined.

The American newsroom of the late 1950s was, if anything, as differentiated as it ever would be. The effects of the ANG on newsroom organization, the rise of college (and journalism education within college, at journalism schools) as a more common route to news work, and a set of reporting technologies that linked news workers to one another—all these impacted "newsroom" identity. Among the near peers of the newsroom, there was a strong sense of solidarity and group identity that cut across differences in routines, tasks, and objectives. This collective sense of self as the midcentury newsroom's culture and workplace developed was different from the more tribalized attitudes of an earlier time, before World War I. After World War II, though, news workers still had their cliques, of course, and as will be explored in the next chapter, among reporters these could strongly influence the course of one's career in the newsroom, as well as one's daily working life. Newsroom relationships were definitional.

## CHAPTER 4

# Reporters and Their Junior Peers

## Routines, Careers, and Status in the Newsroom

AMONG THE VARIOUS groups in the newsroom workforce, the reporters were marked by an intense degree of stratification and diversity of both agency and ability. Ranging from the humble cub, only recently lifted out of the lowly routine of the copy boy or girl, to the exalted and powerful columnist (and his or her more faraway cousin, the correspondent), reporters were "peers" in that they all gathered or created content for the newspaper and enmeshed themselves in a newsroom hierarchy over which, however, they had minimal managerial control. How they cooperated and competed with one another; negotiated differences in age, gender, race, experience, education, and political belief; and formed their own internal working routines helped to define newsroom culture, and thus the American journalism experience, in the twentieth century.

### THE NEWSROOM'S SOCIAL STATUS "MAP"

Historian Robert Darnton reflected on his experiences at the *Newark Star Ledger* and the *New York Times* as a young reporter from 1959 to 1964.[1] He describes an intricate newsroom culture, especially at the latter paper. While no newsroom was (or is) exactly like another, his experiences at the *Times* are illustrative of how reporters created and sustained the newsroom as a space for both work and socialization. Other reporters in other newsrooms had similar experiences.[2] As Darnton recreates it, the newsroom had a distinct power structure. This was determined by spatial proximity to the managing and section editors:

> At the other end, row upon row of reporters' desks face the editors across the fence. They fall into four sections. First, a few rows of star reporters. . . . Next, a spread of middle-aged veterans, men who made their names and can be trusted with any story. And finally, a herd of

> young men on the make in the back of the room, the youngest generally occupying the remotest positions.[3]

Function could determine where certain departments were located, such as sports, shipping news, "culture," and "society." News routines and workflows determined where copy editors and rewrite staff were located in key clusters throughout the space. But how reporters were grouped together was another matter. To a newsroom newcomer, a reporter's status could sometimes stand out "as clearly as a banner headline." Editors claimed they could classify and organize their reporters by ability, but at the same time, even veteran staffers were paradoxically less clear about where they stood, exactly, in their editor's estimation. There were hints, though. Performance on individual story assignments helped to determine how fast a reporter advanced. A reporter who did well could literally "move up to a desk nearer the editor's end of the room, while a man who constantly bungles stories will stagnate in his present position or will be exiled" to coverage of the outer boroughs of the city. The placement and play of stories in the newspaper's daily editions operated like a social "map, which reporters learn to read and to compare with their own mental map of the city room in an attempt to know where they stand and where they are headed."[4]

Since the *Times* gave out bylines fairly regularly by the early 1960s, reporters measured the changes to this status map through compliments from peers and editors. If they came from someone with "prestige," such as the hard-to-please night city editor, the aloof newsroom "star" reporters, or the "most talented reporters in one's territory," they carried extra weight. Supervisors could also hand out public praise, private notes, lunches, or even cash prizes via the publisher. Internally, reporters, including those of the same nominal rank, formed their own social subgroups, which helped to "mitigate competitiveness and insecurity." Organized around age, gender, experience, and socioeconomic status, these groups would eat and drink together, befriend one another's families, and consult and aid one another on challenging stories. A reporter's colleague-friend circle was another layer in a complicated social-work milieu.[5]

Darnton adds that "inter-paper peers"—colleagues from rival news services and newspapers— comprised an outer ring of influences on a young reporter. The influence of these external peers—reflected in efforts to work with them, mimic their career moves, or switch to their publications—was strong. After having made "tenure," or having been "made staff," at a home paper, a reporter could move laterally across peer news organizations if he or she had gained enough status.[6] Moving up was harder and involved a delicate balance of staying within one's peer group and eventually weighing if the leap to the management side was worth the sacrifices along the way. A wrong move might mean a demotion, or, worse, having to leave the journalistic field entirely.

For reporters, working closely with their peers provided the ultimate "occupational socialization." Even editors were constrained by it, as reporters learned the social mores of their newsrooms from each other. Beyond the practicalities of learning beats and boundaries, they gauged how to talk to each other, to sources, and to supervisors, learning the ropes largely by listening, starting as copy boys.[7] This process continued throughout a reporter's career. It did not end when a reporter's cub days were over. Reporters idealized those who had come before them, telling stories to each other of reportorial exploits and victories over deadlines, cranky editors, or obstinate sources. From their first days in the newsroom:

> By listening to shop talk and observing behavior patterns, they assimilate an ethos: unflappability, accuracy, speed, shrewdness, toughness, earthiness, and hustle. Reporters seem somewhat cynical about themselves. They speak of the "shoe-leather man" as if he were the only honest and intelligent person in a world of rogues and fools.[8]

This mythos of the "trench coat" reporter, standing with only a few friends against a crazy world, was powerful and motivating. Because they had "to win their status anew each day as they expose themselves before their peers in print," Darnton recalled, reporters defined their work and their success in relation to peers in this space.[9] In the outside world, these appraisals carried less weight. But in the newsroom, they could make or break careers.

### CUB REPORTERS

Cub reporters only just barely registered on the newsgathering continuum of influence and power. While they could sometimes (in an emergency) do the work of a more seasoned reporter, either by themselves or supervised, the cubs were often given assignments that did not "require the exercise of advanced skill."[10] They instead did background reporting work for other reporters, including copying such prosaic material as marriage and death records, court dockets, and police blotters. They wrote obituaries and ran errands. When they were trusted with more independent work, they were often assigned to a noncritical police station, a lower court, or other local institution of importance to a paper's newsgathering network but not vitally so.[11] A cub's exposure to the city and its "cosmopolitan community" was considered a crucial part of his or her training. Alternatively, and ideally, a cub was paired with a more senior reporter, so the former could observe up close as the latter did their work.[12]

### CAREER PATH: STARTING OUT—FIRST NEWSROOM EXPERIENCES

Even if they were inexperienced, "the line of demarcation between the cub and the senior" was considered "very thin or even nonexistent," and was crossed gradually. Reflecting on his experiences, a former Chicago cub reporter said that "an uncomfortable period of apprenticeship, of adjustment to the, at first, bewildering variety which confronts the newcomer" was just part of the process. Enduring "waiting idleness" that came from sitting in a "city room chair for the duration of my working shift," he was eventually caught "by the coat sleeve" by older reporters on the way out the door. They proceeded "to whirl me to the scene of a news story and keep me there in feverish activity for 24 hours."[13]

Only "day by day" in the midst of such experiences could a cub graduate from apprenticeship, meriting more meaningful, interesting, or otherwise career-enhancing assignments.[14] Small pay increases and increasing trust in his or her ability to pursue leads and develop a story (or react quickly and thoroughly to breaking-news stories) meant that "one day he awaken[s] and find[s] out that he is no longer a cub." Especially before the Guild helped to standardize pay, that transition could be subtle and was not formalized. But even later, it would take the unspoken affirmation of being called by one's first name for the first time, or of being given a special task by "the boss," to clearly signal the unofficial move up from cubdom.[15]

Morton Sontheimer, the former copy boy and reporter on the *Philadelphia Inquirer*, noted in 1941 that new reporters could sometimes go for a full day without lunch when they first showed up for work.[16] Shunted from desk to desk until they found themselves at the edge of the newsroom, they longed for the purposeful gaze of the city editor but were sometimes ignored for hours at a time.[17] This "blisters on the buttocks" period could last for a day or several days, depending on how large a staff was and how much potential a new reporter had for fitting into an editor's system for classifying his or her reporters. Occasionally, a managing editor would dispatch cub reporters on trivial errands, just to get them out of the office, because they were in "eternal dread of the [senior] editor walking in, seeing men sitting around doing nothing, and being struck with a notion to cut down the staff."[18] It was possible to put this "blister time" to good use, learning the city's geography, people, and sources of news. Practicing conversations with strangers in unfamiliar parts of town was "as important to a newspaperman as training to a surgeon."[19]

The "easy informality of the office," which was "unlike any other business place," was full of coatless, smoking, gambling, and spitting men, "gabbing, gadding and griping," some with feet on their desks. Cubs would benefit by embracing it, soaking up newsroom banter over the course of an afternoon.[20] The atmosphere had the effect of warming an "awestruck youngster's heart," even if there were unwritten rules one should not trespass, like no whistling in the newsroom: "try it, and dirty looks will be the least of what's thrown at you."[21] Because these kinds of guidelines were not written down, newsrooms could confound their new inhabitants, but not for long.

Among a cub's first assignments would be overnight rewrite duty. The writing of shorts, "peewees," or briefs, as they were variously called, allowed a reporter to practice writing tightly and simply. Attempts at being clever or "fancy" would expose one as a "callow" cub. Because they did not yet know newsroom norms, cubs' copy was particularly susceptible to the rewrite desk's honing pressure. Sontheimer noted, however, that higher quality papers had aggressive rewrite desks, and that a reporter who bragged about not having his or her material rewritten was either a "temperamental prima donna" or worked for a flawed paper.[22]

Per Sontheimer, cubs should ask the city editor what was wrong with their writing if, after several weeks, their material was being rewritten constantly. An experienced editor would try to help a cub improve, realizing that most needed training in writing. There were rewards in the midst of this indoctrination. The joy of seeing one's first story, no matter how modified, was "one of the unparalleled sensations of the newspaper business. It lifts your feet right off the ground. It gives you an incomparable feeling of importance. It is a hypodermic shot in the ego."[23] A second thrill would come with getting a desk, complete with "spacious drawers in which you neatly place copy paper, carbons, pencils and a pipe and tobacco you brought down from home to help you fill up." After a few months, they would be "crammed with assorted notes, pictures, clippings and gadgets . . . great gobs of stuff will spring out like jack-in-a-boxes every time you open one quickly." But it was not all elation. Discouragement was part of the cub's lot during the "breaking-in period," and the temptation was strong to "lay down on the job." Lasting as little as a few months, or as long as a couple of years, a good "breaking-in" was considered essential.[24]

New cubs were closely watched by older reporters during their first few weeks. These "friendly, but clannish" staffers gradually opened up to and began to like the beginners, usually after the latter had shown that they could handle the work and be trusted.[25] Socialization started immediately, from the moment a cub walked in the door. A "surly old receptionist" might give the cub a "ga[good], morning." Older reporters might pull the cub into a huddle, where in hushed tones (or shouts) they shared their "ceaselessly variable likes and dislikes toward the deskmen, always in proportion to the yield of their assignments." The "tribal spirit" of reporters burned brightly throughout big newsrooms and little ones alike, or in newsroom outposts like a police precinct's press room.[26]

Moving quickly instead of ambling the way a "star reporter lopes out of the office on a big assignment," checking in explicitly with your first few details once on the scene, following the custom of the paper when it came to expense accounts (where to be frugal, or when to "pad"), and voraciously consuming the news—these survival strategies could make life for the cub easier during his or her first few months.[27] A cub would benefit from exploring the paper's various departments outside of the newsroom. In the composing room, among the engravers, riding along with a circulation manager, or chatting with the advertising staff, a cub could ask questions more freely. The former groups would be just as ignorant of the cub's work as he or she would be of theirs, and most would be happy to show off their jobs.[28] But each newsroom's internal culture was different, with some more prone to office gossip and politics than others: "Therefore a young man may feel lost on one paper, and immediately find himself on another."[29]

More college graduates (and the initial graduates of journalism programs) entering the field by the mid-1930s helped to change the nature of the cub experience. Stanley Walker, reflecting on the influence of college from his perspective as the former city editor of the *New York World*, believed that "the fledglings often flabbergast their elders with their erudition—a scholarly but lovely sense of words . . . such a man is likely to outstrip the reporter of the old school in a few years . . . if his legs are good, he can make the older man appear ridiculous." The average older reporter was an "outworn champion pugilist."[30]

The appreciative, inquisitive, absorbing cub would "find, for all the occasional dreary interludes[,] he has been plumped down in the midst of the liveliest and most amusing of worlds."[31] The newsroom was

> like attending some fabulous university where the humanities are [studied] to the accompaniment of ribald laughter, the incessant splutter of an orchestra of typewriters, the occasional clinking of glasses and the gyrations of some of the strangest performers ever set loose by a capricious and allegedly all-wise Creator. The faculty at this fount of knowledge is so grotesque that the young man may be puzzled by the presence of mummified but helpful gnomes, slinking or boisterous yes-men, and thwarted desk-thumpers . . . he is being paid—not much, but something—for attending this place which is part seminary, part abattoir.[32]

Cubs endured drudgery in all this exalted messiness. But it was for a reason, according to newsroom tradition. Through the "searching for details of the most picayune sort," hunting down names, attending mundane meetings in the hopes news was present, he or she had to learn to make mistakes ("at least ten . . . in a ten-line obituary") in order to learn how to report the news and work with sources. The "million boring things that go to make up professional technique" would come only with time.[33]

### CAREER PATH: MAKING IT—BYLINES FOR THE YOUNGEST REPORTERS

Promising cubs could be rewarded with bylines. Internally, their use became much more common during the interwar years. For much of that era, bylines were still thought of as a reward for good stories, or hard work, sometimes in lieu of monetary compensation. Some felt that the more common use of bylines by the 1950s, especially for cubs, had lessened their value, and not all reporters wanted them.[34] But they were still coveted by most. One reporter described the emotional rush of seeing his first byline. Reading the story over and over again, and rushing any corrections back to the desk, he "quickly glances around to see if anyone else has discovered it yet." But it is one's peers (and immediate boss) who help to solidify the experience:

> A while later, when the first-string rewrite man passes by and says, "that's a good yarn you got in on the goatherd," you can see him swell. He [the cub] replies with a quivering attempt at casualness, "ah, it

> didn't turn out the way I wanted it to, but thanks Jim." When the city editor passes a moment later and crackles, "Nice story, McGurk," he almost pops.[35]

This process "will be repeated with each byline, until . . . they become so commonplace you're not even bothered by your name being misspelled." But the bylining experience could also be frustrating. Bylines could be awarded and then taken away, or hinted at but never given.[36]

Awarding bylines had an arbitrary and irregular quality to it throughout the period examined in this book, even if other parts of a cub's work life improved.[37] Reporters generally felt they had to "earn" their bylines, and their use was also governed by norms that varied from paper to paper. Sontheimer said that "all newspapermen belittle bylines, but they all like them." One should never ask for them, however, since it "cheapen[ed] you in the eyes of the city editor" and caused resentment for "putting him on the spot to do it." Writing first-person stories, a relatively rare form, was another way to *not* get a byline, unless specifically ordered by an editor. In order to get one, a reporter had to carefully "inject [his] own personality or opinions enough to make a byline almost necessary." But doing so "has to be very subtle and not too frequent, because the city desk knows all about those tricks and has a special feeling for those who do it all the time."[38] Certain types of stories, including features, were more likely to be bylined.

Anxiety about their use revolved around the idea that too many bylines would dilute their value for readers; among the newsroom staff, bylines were "considered a mark of distinction on a story." They did not always reflect reality, especially for rewrite staffers, who often wrote under the names of the reporters who had initially phoned in stories. Editors also sometimes directed the use of a reporter's name on a story if he or she had become identified with it, even if they did not actually contribute to its latest version or update. This was done with wire-service copy on behalf of a star correspondent or reporter.[39]

Too many bylines by the same reporter could give a newspaper a "rube appearance by making it seem that it has such a limited staff that the members have to do more work than they can adequately cover." Editors did not like giving out bylines in abundance because reporters could also develop an independent identity and ask for more money if a rival paper wanted to draw them away. Reporters, however, continued to believe that bylines were a "reward for good work" and felt that they inspired better writing, signaling to readers that a story was authored by someone with authority, since they thought that "all byline writers [were] expensive." This, many reporters believed, built "up good will for the paper, giving the reader a feeling of acquaintance with the staff." This latter benefit could be enhanced by giving the reporter the same kinds of assignments with a consistent byline, and describing him or her as a "staff writer, political editor or whatever title he may have."[40]

### WORK ROUTINES: NEWSROOM HUMOR AND ADVANCED INDOCTRINATION

New as they were to newsroom culture, where a creative product had to be produced according to a schedule-driven routine, cubs were known for their enthusiasm and willingness to learn. Humor helped make the steep learning curve less intimidating. While a newsroom needed to be "operated as efficiently as the peculiar nature of the materials will permit," it also needed "if it has any life . . . [to be] at times a pasture where salty, jocose spirits lift their hooves and bray."[41]

Hazing was part of this atmosphere and a fact of life for cub reporters and other newsroom newbies. Unless a newsroom was understaffed and faced extraordinary pressure, gags formed a part of the routine, especially after "a very slow day, when everyone's sitting around doing nothing, or at the end of a day of high tension and hard work, when everyone feels let down and a little bit hysterical." As "one of the foremost pastimes of the older members of the staff," teasing, ribbing, and horseplay socialized a beginner. The newer you were, the more you would be exposed to it, and the more gullible one was, the longer it lasted.[42] But reporters felt that an element of surprise was crucial: "the best ribbing is spontaneous and not repetitious," one explained.

Taking advantage of a cub's rawness, an editor or older reporter would send a cub on a "snipe hunt" to find nonexistent newsroom tools. In one such hazing ritual, a cub would be taken to a composing room and told to examine the open space between the type in a page form for "type lice," before the type was shoved together and water, poured into the case beforehand, then sprayed the victim's face.[43] Other, more elaborate pranks included making a cub believe someone was a movie star when they were not, and going so far as to concoct fake stories that forced credulous cubs to hunt down leads and quotes from sources—with some of these in on the joke.[44] These extended gags fostered newsroom comradery and a team ethos.

For their part, senior editors often looked the other way or even approved of the hazing. There were limits, however, especially when newsrooms targeted supervisors. Sontheimer relates one egregious newsroom April Fools' Day prank. A managing editor was led to believe that a newspaper had won a Pulitzer Prize. The editor in chief was told and a story ordered. By the time the hoax was revealed, it was decidedly not funny. The prank had been at the expense of those in power in the newsroom hierarchy. Along these lines, reporters often enjoyed more cerebral jokes versus the practical kind, but there were exceptions. They tended to value physical jokes, and some could be borderline cruel, though most were not meant to be so. Readers, especially those who called late at night to settle arguments, could also fall victim to jokes.[45] Mostly, though, in-house humor was just that—internal.

Cartoons drawn by sympathetic observers used the gullibility of cubs as important plot elements.[46] One common trope was the cub's initial lack of knowledge about the wider world, and especially the newsroom.[47] Cubs could be "as ignorant of craft terminology as is a finishing school graduate of ancient Sanskrit slang." In one common tale, a cub would be sent out to gather facts for an obituary for a prominent local person, only to return to an impatient editor and explain that there was no story because "there was a death in the family." The cub had been so naïve that, when sent to the grieving family's house, he or she was sent away, despite having been sent there to cover that very fact. A variation on this involved a cub being assigned to cover a wedding, only to return with the announcement that there was no news because the bride (or groom) had run away.[48] These tales showed how cubs had to endure ritualized, prolonged, often mean-spirited hazing by their seniors; many recounted these anecdotes years later. Through their exaggerated nature, however, they did show cubs what to value when covering news.[49]

By the 1930s the tradition of having reporters spend their first few months (or first few years) as cubs had been firmly established. Older news workers celebrated the "quenchless, unconquerable" zeal of a young reporter. The "days of his cubdom" would last until "he puts over a story, covered as news should be covered, written as news should be written," and proved himself.[50] A "good cub" was praised by older reporters if he or she endured many small, unimportant jobs, after which growth would come "if he is not fired too often and too seriously."[51]

As they advanced slowly in status, cub reporters faced further hurdles. They could annoy rewrite staff if they were not careful. Interactions over the phone between the members of the rewrite staff and younger reporters could be fraught with misunderstanding. One rewrite man groused that "they [cubs] are under the impression that a college education is a short cut to a byline." These "embryo journalists" needed more seasoning before they could be let loose in the newsroom, and in the larger "hard cruel world of newspaperdom," he insisted.[52] College journalism instructors countered that their programs prepared cubs to get right to work: "The real achievement of the school was that it saved him from pestering the city editor . . . by drilling him [the cub] in alertness, terminology and practices."[53]

Cubs, explaining their experiences to peers, described acculturation to newsroom life as a profoundly transformative experience. A young reporter in Chicago, Phillip D. Jordan, reflecting on his time as a cub in 1923, noted that he was spoken of as "'one of the old boys'" even though he had only been there three years. Painting a picture of his fellow cubs, he described how they would work late, through the noise from the newspaper presses ("the rattling linotypes, the swishing Ludlows, and the proof presses").[54] Busy with tending to the telephones or retrieving tobacco for older peers, Jordan remembered how "the squatty little city ed[itor], who beat newspapering into me . . . kept me on my feet long after deadline and long, long after I should have been in bed."[55] A cub in this environment would change "in that subtle manner that all newspaper men do. Without his knowing it, the deadline horror has brought lines into his face and the constant fear of a scoop has eaten into the complacency of his peace. Our cub is tasting the bitter details of his 'cubship.'"[56]

The use (or misuse) of newsroom terminology during the acculturation process, including references to the "bulldog" (or first) edition of a paper, could trip a cub up. If only because they were unfamiliar, slang terms were easy places for new reporters to slip up, and veterans were attuned to such flubs.[57] To help temper this naiveté, mentorship was crucial throughout the newsroom, but especially for cub reporters, argued a contemporary.[58] It was important to forgive cubs' antics, particularly when a "junior leg man" made mistakes. Giving cubs grace for even egregious mistakes (such as sleeping in and missing a shift) was an unofficial tradition.[59] But cubs did not escape censure for their failures. Verbal correction, sometimes quite vehement—the "bawling out" of memoirs and the recollections found in trade publications—became part of journalistic culture and another method of indoctrinating young reporters.

### NEWSROOM LIFE FOR CUBS DURING THE DEPRESSION

The Depression reduced newsroom mobility within and between newspapers. This meant that cubs fought for positions more than ever: with job opportunities so scarce, work as a new reporter was hard to come by and sustain. The arrival of ANG contracts did bring some job security. The status of cub reporters under the federal government's newspaper industry codes—mandated during the first part of the Roosevelt New Deal reforms—was recognized as unique, even as the length of time a reporter would remain a beginner was debated. Elisha Hanson, attorney for the American Newspaper Publishers Association (ANPA) and a counsel for the Daily Newspaper Code Authority, argued that a cub should be defined as a newsroom "learner" under the code. How long that status lasted "was purely a matter of the man's own ability. If he was good, he shortly would be advanced, and if not, he had better seek employment elsewhere."[60] The Guild argued that starting salaries for cubs and other entry-level reporters were too low.

Even in the midst of the Depression, there were attempts to standardize not just the pay but also the training of cub reporters. The Guild helped lead the way with some of these efforts. The Toledo, Ohio, ANG local arranged a once-a-week workshop with lectures and mentoring for beginner reporters working for the *Blade*, *News-Bee*, and *Times*.[61] College education for cubs became more common. While still scorned by older editors, some were increasingly in favor of it. As one put it in 1930, "The journalistic school cub knows more about the game . . . than the old-time cub could learn in a year."[62]

## NEWSROOM LIFE FOR CUBS DURING THE WAR

The same forces that influenced copy boys (and the arrival of copy girls) also influenced the ranks of cub reporters during the war. Many reporters found themselves doing similar work in the military, though some of their civilian newsroom experiences were not applicable. Waiting for sources, for example, the "time-wasting custom only practiced by cubs," still happened in the military, even if these sources could be superior officers. But unlike in the civilian world, deference toward people in power was expected for reporters in uniform.[63]

Life as a cub lost some of its absurdity as the field mellowed in the face of covering a global war. Many "cub reporters are discriminating young fellows," not young hellions, wrote the managing editor of the *Los Angeles Times*, half-seriously.[64] Cubs tended to be younger, some still in college, and the draft thus dug deeply into the ranks of those eligible for the job. As one consequence, more women than ever before worked as cub reporters during the war. The City News Bureau in Chicago, itself a source of new reporting recruits, ran a training program for newer women reporters. It lasted six weeks and involved two days on the police beat followed by shadowing veteran reporters on the superior and district court beats, the local criminal court beat, and city hall. While an "expensive training process for the bureau, as the girls are on the payroll all the time," it had immediate benefits. Namely, it helped new reporters learn the internal and external routines they needed to know to function on their own, reported Isaac Gershman, City News' general manager.[65] The result proved that they were "neither sob sisters nor club-note specialists, but good, straight news reporters."[66] Gershman, "a firm disbeliever in the 'cold plunge' method of allowing the 'cub' to flounder by himself," believed instead that his cubs, of both genders, did better work when exposed to structured on-the-job training. About twelve of the forty-eight newsroom workers were women, and had, for the most part, been reporters, society editors, or clerical staff at other, smaller news operations.[67]

Some pioneers recognized relatively early on that young women, even in an intensely male-dominated field, should get the chance to work as cub reporters.[68] However, according to Carol Bird, a reporter and feature writer for the *Detroit Free Press*, the youngest male cub reporter would sometimes resent receiving assignments from a woman editor, necessitating "an amount of finesse in dealing with him that no man editor would need."[69] The same kinds of challenges that copy girls faced were faced by women cub reporters. Editors could be unwilling to take a chance on them, resulting in a lack of sustained recruitment of copy girls into cub reporter positions. This, in turn, led to the slow cultural acceptance of women reporters and slowed the integration of younger women. But World War II altered the situation by weakening resistance to women in the newsroom.[70]

While the City News newsroom and other newsrooms pragmatically accepted the presence of women reporters, and female cub reporters, as a wartime necessity, women had "to overcome the deep-seated prejudice against them in the hundreds of courtrooms and the 40 police stations in Chicago." It was "gruff policemen" who initially disliked "the presence of girls in the mens' club atmosphere of squad rooms and district stations." But over time, their colleagues and some of their male sources warmed to their presence (even if there was a definite gendered overtone to this acceptance): "The police desk sergeant, his ears ringing from taking complaints over the phone, enjoys pleasant relief when he lifts the receiver to hear a feminine voice say: 'Sarge . . . anything doing?' . . . It's the City News reporter making her routine checks."[71]

### MARGARET ELLINGTON

A female cub reporter's experiences during the war illustrate how staff shortages changed newsrooms. At the *Baltimore Evening Sun* in 1943, Margaret Ellington was the "first girl reporter hired in many years."[72] When she first entered "the long room filled with assured men typing easily . . . my slight confidence oozed away to nothing," she recalled. As was customary, she sat and waited for hours, until "all at once, a man came over and handed me some sheets of paper. 'Dig some shorts out of these' he said, and walked away." Having majored in journalism at the University of Alabama, she recalled her training and got to work.

At first, she was "completely ignored" by everyone but the city editor. Later, upon reflection, she believed she was "being given a very thorough once-over." To her face she was called "Miss Ellington" and addressed formally, but among the "smoke spirals," she heard wafts of comment about "that blond menace." Over time, however, she found that she gained acceptance, and earned a nickname by an editor, "Duke" (in reference to the band leader who shared her last name). But her challenges continued:

> Being a rank amateur was low enough, but being a girl made the feminine-hating city desk expect much less of me than any male, good or bad. It was up to me to prove to them that being born a girl didn't exclude me entirely from a share of brains.[73]

She found that patience and fortitude paid off. She began by observing news routines and personalities. Ellington noted that the physical office environment was "calm, serene, not too noisy," a place where "everything runs along according to schedule," except "when the copy desk and the city editor are tearing their hair over a story that broke at just the wrong time." Knowing when to speak up and ask for help was vital. "The powers-that-be on a big city daily are too busy and are too concerned with other matters to stop and explain an assignment to a cub," she said. "If it's something that's terrifically important, glance around to find someone who isn't busy and broach the matter to him." The best method was "trial-and-error," honoring the cub's mixture of self-reliance and helplessness. Regardless of gender, cubs were taught to rely on others and themselves. It was important, Ellington wrote, to remember that a reporter would have to be "initiated by pulling some boners."[74]

Ellington gave other, more gendered and specific advice to women cubs. She advised that women "be friendly, but not cute or coy. Let them [male reporters and other editorial staff members] make the first gesture of fellowship and keep just a little behind in the matter of good-natured razzing." There would be "plenty of it," as many men, "from copy boy to editor," went out of their way to stop and talk to her. This would not happen without a chorus of "hoots coming from all corners of the room." In time, however, "they'll begin to accept you as just one of the boys." Dressing modestly was another survival tip, as "men don't like to be too forcibly reminded of your femininity." Ellington felt that it was her mission to help ensure that women stayed in the newsroom long-term, after the war: "We girls are not only going to show the men what we can do in an emergency; we're going to prove that women on the city desk are not an unnecessary evil but a necessary good."[75]

## NEWSROOM LIFE FOR CUBS AFTER THE WAR

Depictions of cubs in postwar newsrooms continued to emphasize their bewildering and disorienting experiences. In one tale, Ralph L. Brooks, a veteran political reporter at the *Indianapolis Star*, welcomed a new reporter he had seen in the office, and explained that "they don't bother to introduce people around here." In reply, the cub responded, "'I've noticed that. I'm new here too.'"[76] Another theme was the lack of control a cub had over his or her assignments. One cartoon spoofed this reality, portraying a cub as having the pick of the best beats, including "sports, drama, politics, [and] finance."[77] That, of course, was very unlikely. Cubs would often get the *worst* beats. Other cartoons played on the age of cubs, or their obvious presence in newsrooms, including one that depicted a literal cub.[78]

According to some commenters, opportunities for advancement during the postwar years could still be hard to come by at larger dailies. Extolling the virtues of starting at smaller papers, including more chances to write and work independently, one author said that cubs might get stuck for "months and months writing nothing but deaths."[79] As with copy boys and girls, positions at big papers could become dead ends if the cub was neglected. Even if he or she was not ignored, work often entailed being "occasionally sent out to cover relatively unimportant events or to obtain minor interviews which will appear (if there's space) somewhere between the classified section and the comic page."[80] Others doubted that the newsroom was a good place for a young reporter to learn. Cubs were especially prone to getting lost in the crowd.[81] But this perspective was that of the minority. While still uncertain to some degree, a position as a cub was thought to offer a strong point of entry into future newsroom work. In the meantime, many editors remained ambivalent about college preparation for cub reporting, according to a 1949 survey.[82]

But as more college-trained journalists entered the newsroom, postwar attempts to improve training included cubs. At the *Denver Post*, the managing editor declared that "good reporters don't just happen. They are the result of proper, well-rounded training, support [and a] background of adequate education." That education involved a "school for cubs" that met every day at 4 p.m. at the rewrite desk and was led by the night city editor, who insisted on "literary perfection for each piece of copy produced. He stresses writing or reading 12 hours hence." This informal training program helped the paper's management know whom to retain, and whom to release early. While the program was initially opposed by the ANG local, enough members gradually became sympathetic to the paper's position and backed the process.[83] The *Post* had been using its night-side shift as a training ground since the early 1950s for copy editors, rewrite staff, and older, general-assignment reporters.[84] Training alternated between the day staff and intensive coaching that was then carried on at night by the evening staff, when newsgathering routines were less busy, barring emergencies. At the later hours of the day, and into the night, there was just more time for mentorship and feedback.[85] In these kinds of settings, a gradual, mutually reinforcing pattern emerged between college education and unionization. Where previously the Guild and many other, non-Guild staffers who had little or no formal education may have opposed training, as college degrees and then specialized journalism degrees became more common, it become helpful to inculcate in new graduates—and thus new cubs—the need to be part of a white-collar union from the beginning of one's career.

Making time for mentoring cub reporters in the near-constant work of the newsroom remained a challenge. An editor at the *Washington Star* observed that "one of the commonest complaints of young reporters . . . [is] that nobody on the city desk has time to talk to them."[86] His paper ran a training program lasting three months, with each new reporter given their own desk and typewriter and told to start with an autobiography of two thousand words. The idea was to see "whether the man is the kind who punches out about ten words, lights a cigarette, stares out the window and goes on. If he is, the supervisor begins right then and there to try to force him to write his first draft, at least, fast . . . he starts inculcating in the man's mind the habit of turning out copy to be ready for deadlines."

Another editor, from the *San Diego Union*, recommended assigning an experienced staff member to provide direct feedback to cubs, as well as rotating cubs to different beats, from obituary to police, to courts, to city council, shadowing and being mentored by a more experienced reporter.[87] An example of a more formalized training system could be found in Gannett's twenty-one-week-long, in-house orientation program for new reporters, with three weeks working in the circulation department, two weeks in the mechanical department, and "twelve weeks in the department for which the trainee is being prepared." Any remaining time would be used to help get the trainee up to speed on a weak or undeveloped area. As with more informal programs, rotation and mentorship were a part of the process. The idea was ambitious; it was to be an "internship affording all the personal dignity to be found in the internships of older professions."[88] Variations were advertised in regional trade publications to garner a wider pool of recruits.[89]

Cubs remained low in the newspaper hierarchy of power, deferring to almost everyone else except for copy boys and girls, and perhaps the librarian and other support staff. They were under the authority of many, starting with the city, managing, copy, and other senior editors.[90] Editors had immense influence over the future of cubs in their or other newspapers' newsrooms.[91] The traditional power dynamics of these spaces were slow to change for workers with less agency, reinforced as they were by well-developed customs and culture. Even so, cubs remained a celebrated part of newsroom life.

## LEG MEN AND GA REPORTERS

After one had passed through the fires of the cub experience, the next step in the newsroom's hierarchy was work as a "leg man" and then GA reporter.[92] These positions were occupied by a majority of the newsroom's reporters, and some would spend an entire career in one of these roles. In the internal hierarchy of the newsroom, the "leg man," or field reporter, was regarded as an extension of the rewrite staff. As an "outgrowth of modern journalism . . . he did not exist in the days when there were no telephones and when competition and mechanical development did not necessitate publishing portions of a story that had not yet been fully developed."[93] The telegraph editor had been a precursor (since that position also juggled incoming long-distance news reports), but the telephone was a more disruptive technology, creating new linkages to and from the newsroom. Leg men had a unique relationship with rewrite staff. They inhabited a niche position in the newsroom's reporting system, with one contemporary noting that "leg men with only mediocre ability are frequently not at all unaccustomed to public speaking when it comes to beating a deadline with a twirl of a telephone dial and a few well-chosen words."[94] Of course, "public speaking" in this context referred to skill using the phone. A leg man had to be good at more than dictation. He (or she) had to tell stories rapidly, often in fragments and through dubious connections. Despite these abilities, leg men complained that their contributions were not recognized. The unsung workhorse of newsgathering, the leg man's "name is rarely seen on a by-line story since he seldom if ever does any [actual] writing," wrote an observer in 1935.[95]

Phoning in updates wherever he or she pursued a story, and checking in throughout the day, a "leg man" was named such because he or she was mobile and not tied to a specific beat, though they could be assigned an area of the city and a broad beat, including crime. As a "master of the shortcut," leg men and women knew their sections of the city and the people therein "as well as it is possible for any newspaperman to know a beat."[96] While writing was not their strong suit, some leg men and women devoted part of their day to it and could become adept at translating their newspaper's style into various news items. For example, a leg man assigned to cover courts would phone in stories for an evening paper in the morning, and then in the afternoon work on longer updates to be used the next day. Instead of returning to the newsroom to do so, though—and this is a crucial difference between these more mobile reporters and GA writers—he or she would often stay in designated press rooms out in the field. Expertise at news *gathering* was what they were known for, among other reporters and their editors. As such, too much time away from the newsroom as a leg man or women, as "fascinating and exciting" as it could be, and staying "out of personal touch with the newspaper office" could lead to being forgotten by editors. It was felt that leg men or women should not spend more than five years at this job if they wanted to advance to GA or beat reporting.[97]

## WORK ROUTINES AND NEWSROOM STATUS

Not all police or crime reporters were leg men, nor were all leg men crime or police reporters, but because of the nature of the reporting involved—calling in updates on spot news across a city—leg men over time became associated with crime coverage. "Police reporters," as some leg men and women who focused on local crime beats were called, were "somewhat removed from the reporters of the city room," according to Arthur Gelb, reflecting on his experiences as a cub on the *New York Times* in the early 1950s.[98] There were class differences, too, between leg men and women and beat and GA reporters. The latter two had better sources (including politicians and large business owners), tended to be better educated, and, at least in New York City (and in other large cities), came from more middle-income backgrounds. In this way they resembled their middle- or even upper-class sources. Leg men or women tended to be more working-class and self-educated.

Gelb observed that his new companions in a Lower East Side police station's reporters' "shack" had been hired for "their street smarts and ability to ferret out facts swiftly." Many were the sons of Italian, Irish, and Jewish immigrants, had not finished high school, and were "dese, dem, and dose kind of guys." They often shared the same backgrounds as the police and criminals they covered. Communicating with the newsroom could be challenging, as some of the field reporters had thick accents. Once, a leg man's report that a woman had died at the hands of a "poisson" (person) or "poissons" unknown had translated into the headline "Funeral Follows Inquest with Verdict of Death by Poison." Gelb, having gone to college, was initially regarded with suspicion in this environment.[99] He had to show that he could report *despite* his education. Work in the field, and hunting down facts for the crime beat, was considered such a part of the job that "legging" became shorthand for this kind of reporting.[100]

Others distinguished leg men from "the routine men," "the specialists," "investigators," and "dynamiters"—while the latter group could "blast out the stories that are hard to get," members of the first group "do the running around" needed to find details about breaking-news stories. Despite the humble status of the leg man, he or she was expected to travel constantly from one news source to the next, "and is always expected to be miraculously on the scene of every newsworthy incident practically immediately on its happening." Sometimes also called a "district" or "beat" reporter (though not to be confused with an older and more educated beat reporter), he or she would occasionally work alongside a dedicated police-beat reporter. Familiarity with sources, including the constant making of rounds, was crucial foundational work for a good leg man. Knowing ordinary police officers, neighborhood-level politicians, local shop owners, and the various individuals who hung out at quasi-legal watering holes could lead to solid sourcing when the time came. Relying on carefully cultivated friendships with police officers, but also knowing when and how to bluster, bully, or appeal to their bosses, fell within the general sphere of the leg man or woman.[101]

But engagement with cops could have definite downsides. David Halberstam, later famed for his coverage of the civil rights movement and Vietnam, reflected on his experiences covering crime in Nashville, at the *Tennessean*. As a young reporter in 1956, he was proud to be working in the newsroom of a moderate paper committed to—especially for its time—avoiding stereotypes of Black people in its stories and committed, too, to listening to their concerns. Coleman "Coley" Harwell, the paper's editor, drove his reporters, especially his younger ones, to aggressively cover issues of race. Halberstam remembers that this made interactions with the white police force difficult: "The police beat was the great test for young reporters, particularly those who were like me, young and Eastern and Ivy-bred and in some way or another in this profession that was without rules, trying to develop their own definition of personal integrity. It was where the paper tried to find out how much inner strength its young reporters had. It was the least genteel of places."[102]

Halberstam writes about how, for example, the police officers he would encounter would try to bait him into using and saying the n-word, on the job, as a kind of a test of willpower: "It was very much in their vocabulary, used as easily and readily in those days as any minor bit of profanity. They knew very well that the new young reporters on the *Tennessean* did not use the word, that it was in some way abhorrent to us, and they were testing whether we could be bent." By using it, you could easily become "one of the boys," and maybe get assistance with your work, but if you did not, the best you could hope for, eventually, was a kind of reluctant respect. And in the meantime, a reporter would face much more resistance.[103] Such ethical tradeoffs, or temptations to compromise one's beliefs, happened continually on this beat and when interacting with law enforcement. But such choices were not always as stark (or starkly racist). Sometimes a less morally clear concession was required.

This could be a delicate balance. Too much cooperation with the police could result in missed stories or abusive departments. Too little and leg men and women would not have access to the personalities that drove stories. Handling an editor back in the newsroom also presented challenges for a leg man or woman. Sometimes unaware of conditions out in the field, editors could issue unreasonable orders. Sontheimer advised junior reporters to "use your own method," since getting "your assignment done . . . [is] all they care about." Doing everything one was told would "probably get you killed or go nuts, or even miss a lot of stories." At the same time, it was important to not let the city editor know one had diverged from the latter's directions. In that vein, senior editors could be skeptical audiences, having heard many failed pitches before, but Sontheimer counseled that a young police reporter should write extra features anyway, if only for the practice.[104]

The more junior a reporter was, in fact, the less leverage he or she had over sources if not backed up by the paper. This could be mitigated by being adopted by more experienced reporters, or sympathetic sources, or both.[105] Young "district" reporters also faced temptation in the form of bribes from people eager to have their names kept out of the paper, from lawyers courting business, or from those hoping to see their names *in* the paper. Getting entangled with sources was unwise in the midst of this pressure, since it might lead to lost independence.[106]

### GA REPORTERS: THEIR ROLE IN THE NEWSROOM

The line between experienced reporters and leg men could be indecipherable, but generally the former could be defined as those "not tied down to a district, a desk, a beat, or a specialized department." Other key markers for a "senior" were the kinds of assignments given, skill, and pay—sometimes experienced reporters preferred the independence and variety of stories pursued while on "general assignment."[107] GA reporters also differed from leg men in that they did, in fact, return to the newsroom to finish their stories and interact with editors. This was a crucial difference. Working on everything from several assignments a day to one every few days, weeks, or even months, "seniors" could also act as specialists or de facto correspondents. GA reporters would cover news within a city or its immediate environs. "A senior of the first rank" would, by the early 1950s, have been someone who had usually held a variety of newsroom positions including, occasionally, positions as copy editor or section editor. Returning to reporting work without a demotion in pay, a senior reporter often had at least five years' worth of experience on the job.[108] Four to six years became the typical yardstick against which Guild (and even non-Guild) contracts measured seniority. Reporters could then advance from GA work into a number of other, more elite positions in the newsroom.[109]

GA reporters were often positioned as a kind of reserve force. This "ready availability" gave managers confidence that they could cover any kind of breaking-news story. It also ensured that editors could keep track of their best reporters when they were not out in the field.[110] At the *New York Times* in the late 1940s, city editor David Joseph liked to use his "star" GA reporters on the rewrite bank, where they would play cards or read the paper while taking turns handling calls from leg men and women.[111] As late as 1949, editors debated the merits of having their reporters remain generalists or "whether they [should] be allowed to specialize."[112] Into the 1950s, however, leading editors believed that a cub should be trained so that he or she could eventually become a well-rounded GA reporter.[113] As part of this GA ideal, the 1950s brought with it a new pride in the nomenclature reporters used to identify themselves. "Newspaperman" was still customarily reserved as a proud and lingering epithet that should be used exclusively by members of "the editorial department." Other news workers claimed the title as part of "a continuous, though ineffectual, attempt to arrogate the proud word . . . Ever hear a newsman pass himself off as a circulator or adman?"[114] This tribal pride, and sense of belonging to a special group within the larger newspaper organization, resonated throughout the period from 1920 to 1960, and, if anything, grew in its special intensity. This happened both within and outside of print journalism in the United States, as newspaper memoirs attracted general-interest readers and popular culture's depictions of reporters in radio, films, and television gradually became more positive.[115] It became important, too, as rival broadcast newsrooms emerged to compete with print newsrooms.

### CONCLUSION: WORK ROUTINES AND NEWSROOM STATUS

Some veteran reporters, even those with varied experiences, confessed to enjoying GA work the most. As one former GA reporter put it: "It is the one spot on a newspaper where you come to work in the morning not knowing where you'll wind up or what you'll be doing at the end of the day, where you get the greatest diversity of assignments and experiences, where you're more likely to meet the unusual and have a greater opportunity to write about it."[116] The work and the prestige could vary widely depending on the paper and the individual reporter, from the most prosaic spot news coverage of fires, meetings, and celebrity visits to the most important stories a paper published. The latter, often calling for multiple editions or saturation coverage, were the special charge of an elite group called "star reporters."

While not always officially called such, these were GA reporters with enough skill and experience (and clout) that they could easily work complicated beats but who were instead used and trusted by editors for emergencies and one-off projects.[117] Other reporters at the paper knew and looked up to these reporters. Assigned with teams of photographers to report on disasters that affected whole regions, states, or countries, star reporters could roam far afield of the newsroom.[118] They could be leaders within their newsrooms, *and* outside them, as when Evelyn Shuler, a former "star reporter" for the *Philadelphia Ledger*, helped set up an "employment office" in her apartment for former fellow unemployed *Ledger* workers after that paper folded in 1942.[119] Star reporters were sometimes the first to try out new technologies or reporting strategies.[120] They could also become pioneering reporters in early newsroom inclusion efforts, as with Carl Rowan at the *Minneapolis Tribune* in the early 1950s, as will be explored in the next chapter.[121] Their chief attribute was their independence, the measure of freedom they had earned from close oversight by editors. While some beats had to fight the influence of their sources, as with the interactions between younger reporters and cops discussed earlier, high-powered GA reporters could transcend them.[122]

Within a newsroom, star GA reporters could serve another purpose: inspiring cubs and other younger reporters. A. R. Holcombe, the managing editor of the *New York Herald-Tribune*, believed that having "a star reporter of as great versatility as possible, for the other men to shoot at" would help the cubs become "fired with an ambition to be as good a man as he is." Their example could help these younger reporters "dream at night . . . of being someday as able a reporter as the star."[123] As a rule, these reporters comprised a very small percentage of newsroom staff, so there was plenty of room for inspiration.[124]

To maneuver through a career in journalism was to know the nature and kind of community one found oneself in. Savvy news workers—depending on their individual goals—had a great deal of relational work to do, as pathways and promotion were not always clear. While not quite a tribal society, it was, nonetheless, a relational one—you defined your success and status by your next-desk neighbor and the placement of that desk in relation to your editor. You knew if you did well or badly based on how your colleague fared in a pitch meeting, and if you got a decent assignment, and so on. That relational posturing process is examined more in the next chapter, focusing on the experiences of the rank-and-file reporter.

## CHAPTER 5

# Reporters and Their Senior Peers

## The Myths and Realities of Upward Mobility

THE REPORTING STAFF of a typical newsroom from 1920 to 1960 contained two broad kinds of reporters: those more junior, including cubs, leg men, and GA reporters, and those more senior, such as specialists, feature writers, columnists, and editorial writers. The degree of independence marked the dividing line between the two groups, though GA reporters straddled it. For specialized senior reporters, this translated into a greater degree of control over their work. They were more empowered and more "professionalized" than their colleagues, and self-aware of this superior status both in and out of the newsroom. While both broad types of reporters were focused on news *gathering* (and were thus distinguished from those who helped to *produce* the news, including support staff such as copy editors, rewrite staff, and desk-bound senior editors), the power differential between junior and senior reporters justifies a separate, if related, examination. When thinking about the relational ecology of the newsroom in the era of industrial journalism, it is important to consider those who held relative privilege and power. These more powerful players helped to define the value of news work and set the limits of the agency and autonomy of their fellow news workers.

The distance on the continuum of newsroom power and success between leg men or women, GA reporters, and beat reporters could be short. But dedicated beat reporters, unlike the other types of reporters mentioned thus far, focused their routines exclusively on following, checking in on, and developing the same set of sources, traditionally including officials in educational institutions, hospitals, courts, and local, state, and federal governments. Like leg men or women, they remained focused on a particular place or set of places and often left the newsroom in pursuit of stories. But unlike leg men, and more like GA reporters, they were expected to write their own stories, and not call them in. They were also expected to become experts on their beat. This practice could vary by newsroom, however. If a beat man stayed out of the office too long, he or she could be overlooked, similar to the leg man or woman.[1] But on the plus side, beat reporters earned a certain amount of autonomy from their editors. Keeping confidences (and knowing when to break them) gained in importance, as the nature of covering a "building"—city hall, city, state, and federal courts, federal offices, or the state legislature (if a newspaper was in a capital)—meant spending time with more sophisticated, in-the-know sources.[2] Being close to sources with power reflected these reporters' own increased autonomy. At least one observer recognized that "many of the most important beats are those which have a topical rather than a geographical basis."[3]

### CAREER PATH, COMBINATIONS, AND GROUP WORK

While other kinds of reporters faced them, too, it was beat reporters who were most enmeshed in "combination" reporting.[4] Others referred to this practice as pool reporting, or "reporter's combines."[5] This collaborative approach to newsgathering involved reporters from competing papers pooling their resources. While the practice was prone to abuse, some observers defended it as a necessity. The informal system was especially common on the more routine beats, including police and government.

In the pre–World War II Washington, DC, political press corps, sociologist Leo Rosten found that correspondents would routinely help each other outside of the Associated Press or other wire-service networks.[6] This assistance included consulting one another for expert advice about regional or technical issues, such as interpreting press releases from the US Department of the Interior, or seeking help in writing about the auto industry. Sometimes reporters who attended the same press conferences would help each other find new or different angles for their stories.[7] Most directly, however, reporters would share carbon copies of their news dispatches with each other. These "blacksheets" provided critical information and sources and were the manifestation of the wealth of tips and gossip political reporters passed among their friends and colleagues. These practices were prevalent among reporters from different markets or regions, but correspondents from the same city also cooperated. This was not just limited to data—practices like the sharing of blacksheets helped to shape news priorities and opinions among reporters.[8] If a reporter knew what was important to his or her colleagues, they knew what was important for them, too. And it was no accident that correspondents shared their work so freely: they had learned to do so at home.

During the late 1930s, the choice to join or resist a combination was a critical one for a new beat reporter. If the reporter chose the latter, he or she had to be determined enough to "work like hell and maintain a never-ending, nerve-racking vigilance to keep from being scooped."[9] Sometimes one dissident beat reporter was enough to break a combination, at least for a while. In retribution, a combination might "gang up on the renegade" to generate enough scoops to get the dissident in trouble with an editor. Breaking away from a combination required good communication, and "an understanding," with one's editor. While many editors tolerated the formation of these combinations, for reporters caught up in them, it was important to sell the boss on the virtues of either staying in them or trying to leave. Both decisions had consequences for the quality of coverage.[10] But it was sometimes wiser to wait. A new beat reporter needed help to learn the lay of the land. This was not always possible outside of a combination.

Sometimes a combination of beat reporters would be excessively "clannish" to the point of exclusion. Happily, other combinations could be more welcoming, and would help the newcomer.[11] The ideal combination would focus its efforts on certain topics, with other topics designated as free-for-all. This was not always easy to keep up, as the temptation to scoop one's rivals was real.[12] If a "non-co-operative or over enterprising reporter" attempted to cultivate a series of scoops over time away from a combination, the latter would sometimes work especially hard to counterscoop the renegade "until the city desk howls, and the nonconformist gives way."[13] Even if a reporter decided to stay with the combination, it could possess bad or inaccurate information, and an individual reporter, otherwise known for his or her accurate reporting, would suffer from an overreliance on colleagues. This could damage reporters' relationships with their home newsrooms. But any fraying of ties to home newsrooms could be avoided by careful collaboration, including verification of tips, or, better yet, volunteering to be part of the smaller subset of the combination which did the actual reporting, to make sure it was done correctly.[14] Looking at a generation before, Smythe found similar collaboration at work.[15]

### BEAT REPORTERS AND OTHER FORMS OF COLLABORATION

Away from their individual newsroom spaces, competitive tensions could be eased by the camaraderie of the "press room," or "reporters' room," the assigned workspace for reporters in or near sources of news, including city hall, the courts, and police stations.[16] A great deal of work, at all hours, would take

Figure 7. "The Fourth Estate," *Editor & Publisher*, March 27, 1948, 36. As this cartoon shows, reporters' combinations could quickly become focused on gaming and socializing.

place in these shared journalistic workspaces. Telephone connections back to home newsrooms and typewriters were shared. These rooms were also places to swap stories, smoke, drink and, infamously, play endless card games. Some reporters even pooled resources to make meals for one another.[17]

Reporters would also help each other in less systematic ways. If a reporter was late to a press conference, "it doesn't matter in the least whether he is an old friend or a complete stranger; it is a matter of course to give him what we call a 'fill in' on what he has missed," wrote Frank Adams, a veteran *New York Times* reporter, in 1945. Reporters did so when their peers missed something through no fault of their own, expecting to be helped, in turn, later. This was part of a larger sense of collegiality. With its "goldfish-bowl lack of privacy" and a daily product open to inspection by the "City Editor, fellow reporters, and friends," work was consumed and compared to others' constantly: "This is more effective in keeping reporters on their toes . . . than any system of rewards and punishments that could possibly be devised." This need for the ready measurement of comrades was acutely felt in its absence. Adams noted that some of his friends, covering distant parts of the Pacific and European theaters during World War II as correspondents, wrote to him about the sensation, when far from the civilian newsroom, of living and working "in a void."[18] They looked forward to being back in an all-encompassing work environment.

**ARTHUR GELB**

Arthur Gelb's second police beat in the late 1940s for the *New York Times* involved covering crime in the evenings on Manhattan's East Side. Sharing one room on the first floor of an old brownstone, just two doors west of the precinct station, it was a quiet assignment, with two public telephone booths shared by a handful of reporters.[19] But his first assignment as a police-beat reporter had taken him to the much larger Police Headquarters building, with a correspondingly more complex "shack" for reporters. This space had three floors of offices, rented as separate spaces by the city's newspapers and news services. It was housed in an old tenement building purchased as an investment by a former reporter. On the outside of the building, fire-alarm bells—via three rings—signaled that a conflagration worth reporting was happening somewhere in the city. Colored lightbulbs, also on the outside of the building for each paper, summoned a reporter in from the street. The *Times'* workspace contained two phones, desks, and typewriters, to be used by leg men and women and beat reporters before returning to the office.[20] Press rooms were open constantly, and the presence of friends and rivals helped to develop a kind of newsroom in miniature, Gelb recalled:

> When a report came over the police radio, I did indeed follow the pack as they ran from the shack with homemade notepads of folded copy paper stuffed into their back pockets and thick, soft-lead pencils enabling them to scribble fast. By foot, cab, bus or subway, we converged on a scene in a haphazard frenzy. Though we rushed to meet edition deadlines, we didn't compete against one another. Before anyone called the office, we came together and shared every scrap of information we each had gathered.[21]

This provided the reporters with a "sense of security," protecting them from reprimands by bosses. Not sharing facts could result in shunning. But even this group work resulted in some individual stories, since the rewrite staff back at their home newsrooms would inject their own "sensibility . . . wit . . . [and] skill" interwoven in the newspaper's style.[22] At Gelb's and other large newspapers, leg men and women, beat reporters, and rewrite staff interacted in a constant and self-contained milieu of peers and near peers. He relates how he knew the "pack" had accepted him after some of the more hardened police reporters showed them their revolvers and let him in on their sources and routines.

Reporters in the pack were loyal to each other to an intense degree, helping one reporter who could barely write because the police "loved him for his natural Irish wit" and gave him exclusive tips. Later assigned to the Mid-Manhattan Magistrates Court, Gelb left the comparatively tight company of the police beat and had to learn to work with a veteran AP reporter, Dick Feehan. A gradual and more one-to-one relationship of the junior-to-senior kind ensued, with Gelb sharing information with Feehan before calling in his own stories. Eventually, Feehan accepted and mentored him in this more challenging beat.[23]

### CARL ROWAN

Carl Rowan's pathbreaking career at the *Minneapolis Tribune* began in 1948 when he was hired to work as a copy editor, on the express orders of John Cowles Sr., the paper's progressive publisher. He had been freelancing for the Baltimore *Afro-American* at the time and had just finished a master's degree in journalism at the University of Minnesota. Writing years later in his memoir, Rowan relates that Gideon Seymour, an editor, had told the personnel department to alert him if "one of them showed up." Rowan later learned that Cowles had said that "he did not believe in all of America that they could not find a single Black man or woman capable of being a reporter on his newspapers."[24] Rowan would face the immense challenge of stepping into an all-white newsroom.

The Twin Cities were notoriously anti-Semitic and struggled with a deep-seated racism, which, while not as aggressively explicit as in the South, was still nonetheless present, Rowan recalled. After two years on the copydesk, he became a GA reporter but resolved to not become a token. To that end, he made a deal with his executive editor, Bill Steven. "You will not assign me to any story simply because I'm a Negro; you will never deny me an assignment simply because I'm a Negro," Rowan said. Steven agreed. In time, though, Rowan felt that he had to speak up and speak out about racism in his community, through truthful, challenging journalism. He noted that he had only heard of *five* other Black GA reporters working in white newsrooms across the country by 1950.[25] Rowan details his struggle to fit in in the face of racist resistance, but also the advocacy of a select group of editors, including Steven. Their hospitality—despite racist pressure from neighbors—to invite him and his wife, Vivien, over for dinner, helped Rowan feel less isolated.[26]

Rowan not only succeeded as a staff reporter—he also persuaded his editors to fund an ambitious, award-winning reporting trip through the Deep South. His resulting series, "How Far from Slavery?," won numerous awards and led to a book, *South of Freedom*, published with Knopf in 1952. Rowan went on to become a beat reporter covering civil rights, a syndicated columnist (among the very first African Americans to have that role in white newspapers), a foreign correspondent, and then a distinguished civil servant.[27] His career in journalism was exemplary, on his own merits, but it is telling that it would remain unique for another twenty years. In time, however, Black journalists like Rowan would become a more common presence in white newsrooms, mirroring similar struggles for gender equality: slow, painful, with setbacks, but then some (eventual) progress. By the late 1960s, "the black press lost its near exclusive access to black journalists, and the white press began to reluctantly reconsider how it wrote about African Americans and other minorities."[28]

### WORK ROUTINES: NEWSROOM LIFE FOR BEAT REPORTERS DURING THE DEPRESSION

While long an undefined category, since "beats" could extend from the relatively easy-to-start-in police beat and range all the way to powerful political beats, by the 1920s many beat reporters (especially for any beat beyond cops and crime) were regarded as newsroom veterans.[29] But veterans or not, by the early 1920s the collaborative nature of some of the more routine beats was firmly in place, reinforced by a lingering pay-by-space system in which reporters, even those nominally on staff, would be compensated only for what appeared in the paper. This led to an ingrained sense that work should be shared, since there was too much of it anyway. Others criticized this phenomenon, which continued into the era when salaries became more common. Too often, "beat men from the various papers sit around waiting for something to turn up," and when something did, they would often "delegate one of the men to go and get the story and bring it back to share with the rest."[30] Even after the influence of the Guild was felt in many newsrooms, reporters could agree to "syndicate" while on a beat. The practice was too ingrained to give up. One editor feared that this camaraderie among beat reporters would erode good coverage: "When reporters are 'palsey-walsies' on a beat there is no use of keeping more than one of them on the job as their comradeship has eliminated rivalry."[31] Reporters, however, seemed fine with the arrangement.

### WOMEN AS BEAT REPORTERS DURING THE INTERWAR YEARS

Prestige beat reporting, due to its perceived "masculine" challenges—with the police beat, especially—remained a tough field for female reporters to break into before World War II. There were pioneers, however. In Seattle, Mari Brattain, a University of Washington journalism student, guest reported and edited for the *Seattle Star*, and Lucille Cohen, another UW journalism major, covered the police beat. Both took a hard-edged approach to covering Depression-related local news.[32]

But these sorts of isolated experiments were just that—not part of a trend. Long-term cultural change in the newsroom would have to take place for women to work regularly as beat reporters. Some veteran editors, such as Stanley Walker, thought so too. Among tabloid newspapers (which had fewer qualms about hiring women for positions considered more appropriate for men), Walker pointed to the examples of Grace Robinson, Edna Ferguson, and Inez Callaway (also known as Nancy Randolph), employed by the *New York News* in the mid-1930s on challenging assignments, including everything from sensational murder trials to off-limits-to-the-public society events. On more conventional daily papers, he noted, other women were pioneering beats traditionally covered by men, including Lorena Hickok, who reported for the AP in New York, and Genevieve Forbes Herrick, who worked for the *Chicago Tribune* in the 1920s and early 1930s. The latter advocated for a wider scope for women, beyond "the woman's angle in journalism," since "typewriters are sexless." Better assignments from editors who treated them as reporters, not as *women* reporters, were also crucial, she said in a 1933 address to the Chicago Woman's Club.[33] Many women reporters did not like the traditional advancement options they were offered, in which all career paths led to "society" editorships, and instead preferred to "think of themselves as regular reporters."[34]

Staff shortages during the war meant that more women worked as reporters on the police and other beats. This was the case, for example, at the *New York Daily News*. Some women, such as India McIntosh at the *New York Herald Tribune*, believed that the war "hastened" the arrival of a more "benevolent" openness to the presence of women in the newsroom. "The woman reporter got the biggest chance she ever had to prove that she could cover, at home and abroad, anything that came under the heading of news," she reflected. McIntosh believed women had already established a strong "beachhead" in the newsroom and were no longer "considered a damn nuisance." Women reporters were a more accepted and expected part of many newsrooms, and not just in supporting roles but as part of the reporting team: "She is seldom reminded of her sex or her supposed limitations by the men with whom she covers fires and homicides, meets ships, shares taxis, and sits in on that diabolic institution known as the press conference [;] . . . most of the men in her office seem to like her."[35] The larger question for McIntosh and others was, "How are women treated by the city desk, that upper-case POWER which can annihilate with a word, a knitted brow, or a pantywaist assignment every major triumph that the girl reporter has gathered unto herself?" Whether working as a GA or beat reporter, woman reporters endured the same challenges and then some as men, were "joshed, instructed, bawled out, or complimented in the same manner as a man," and so deserved the same kinds of "running stories—the big stories, with many facets, which splash page one for days or even weeks, surging to a climax or boiling over into half a dozen stories or fading to a one-line head as imperceptibly as the Cheshire cat faded to a grin."

But women were too often assigned "tidy little episodes that can be packaged in three-quarters of a column and then forgotten." Compounding this, the male-dominated city desk, "with all its democratic leanings, is wary of the woman reporter's emotional equipment" and hesitated to give higher-stakes stories to women. McIntosh nonetheless remained optimistic about the future of women in the newsroom. Women could use existing prejudices to their advantage, including the still-pervasive belief that they could write better than men about other women or children. They could also take advantage of "Worthy Cause" stories, ordered either directly or indirectly by the paper's ownership, to showcase their work. They could use cultural biases toward women, including an inclination by male sources to give women reporters an extra tip, to their advantage. While many women were not driven to use this advantage and "indulge in feminine sorcery," many felt that "being pleasingly feminine, in the better sense of the phrase," could not hurt.[36]

But the stereotype of the "jittery, tough-talking, picture-snatching girl reporter of the mystery thriller" had less and less basis in reality. Most women were as down-to-earth and practical as their male counterparts. They could be distinguished from their "glamorous magazine . . . trade journal . . . [and] radio" counterparts at press conferences, despite the latter's nominal possession of press cards, by the way the print reporters behaved. Some of their male colleagues insisted that female reporters be identified first by their workplace identities ("reporters"), and less by their gender, especially in the presence of newsroom outsiders.[37] After the war, women were able to break into some of the more "he-man" beats, as one contemporary put it, including covering the timber industry in Oregon.[38]

Some women tried the more dangerous sides of police reporting, such as immersing themselves in daily inner-city life.[39] Other women had the opportunity to cover the courts.[40] And still others advocated for themselves, and for chances to prove their worth as beat reporters.[41] Pay disparities remained and were sometimes stark: a survey conducted by the Ohio Newspaper Women's Association in 1958 found that while rank-and-file reporters made an average of $106 or more a week, society editors made just under $74, and suburban editors—a position often held by women—made $70.[42]

### NEWSROOM LIFE FOR BEAT REPORTERS AFTER WORLD WAR II

After the war, specialized beats remained one of the places on a newspaper where openings were more plentiful, due to the influx of returning former reporter-veterans in more GA-oriented jobs.[43] Beat reporters resumed or kept up their old habit of group collaboration, even on more specialized beats, such as coverage of federal courthouses.[44]

Some beat reporters stayed in their beats "for years and years," becoming experts in their fields and transitioning more toward niche writers and columnists.[45] Unionization brought more standardized pay scales, which affected most experienced reporters and encouraged them to stay at a paper longer. The location of beats was changing as well. Beats in the suburbs of the postwar years could encompass thousands of square miles in the West and Southwest. In Houston, the reporter on the country beat had to sell news to the city desk, "where much of the mental emphasis of desk men is on the . . . 'city.'"[46]

Back in the newsroom, reporters from similar beats were sometimes positioned near one another.[47] In Rochester, New York, during the 1940s and 1950s, the two rival daily newspapers, the *Times-Union* and *Democrat & Chronicle*, possessed highly refined, and similar, beats, including science, health, education, labor, the arts, police, and politics. Three or four reporters were regularly assigned to the latter two beats at both papers.[48] This concentration of beats reflected the city's technology orientation as the home of Xerox and Kodak.

As the 1950s drew to a close, some vocal editors felt that fewer reporters should be assigned to routine beats, but also, somewhat ironically, that newspaper staffs with increasingly specialized beats were already too complicated, "great factory operations" that had "become gigantic tails on the editorial dog of Pekinese dimensions."[49] Still, most considered beat reporting essential to thorough news coverage, especially in the face of new TV (and radio) newsrooms that could beat newspapers at breaking news. Business reporting, for example, continued to be regarded as a consequential—and influential—beat.[50] In the late 1950s, the *Wall Street Journal* experimented with "team reporting," in which a veteran reporter would work as a "team leader" of a group of beat reporters "and with as many reinforcements as the story demands, coordinating and directing the overall effort on the spot." This brought faster and more thorough coverage of "top stories" and promised independence and scalability as reporters led themselves, apart from direct supervision by editors.[51] These elite beat reporters would sometimes form the basis for investigative teams on larger metropolitan newspapers, setting the stage for the investigative reporting movement of the 1970s and 1980s.

### STATUS IN THE NEWSROOM: A HIERARCHY OF BEATS

Newsrooms had a hierarchy of beats, and reporters could either intuit from their stories' prominence in the paper or from the ways their peers talked about their work, or the kinds of stories they were allowed to pursue, which beats were more prestigious than others. Some, including religion, were thought of as comprising sleepy church news and were "not usually handed to the stars of the street and rewrite staffs."[52] Later, some reporters sought such work, claiming that innovation and advancement were possible.[53] Other beats were driven by technological or scientific developments. Aviation in particular surged in popularity after World War I, later supplemented by aerospace and science beats.[54] The latter could produce a "city room prima donna complex," warned one such writer in the mid-1950s. Such a complex could result in a reporter becoming "petulant if his copy is changed or trimmed, or left out." The identity as an expert sometimes conflicted with the idea that he was "a newspaperman first."[55] Reporters practiced various rhetorical strategies to distance themselves from this apparent contradiction. Specialized reporters engaged in this boundary-work in order to reinforce their own status in the newsroom.[56] Science reporters, for example, sometimes insisted that they had "come up" via the newsroom and had fallen into their beat by accident, acquiring a taste for science along the way. They were often called "doc" by their non–science reporter colleagues, who tolerated, and sometimes appreciated, their eccentricities.[57] Generally, beats dealing with local, state, or federal government, especially the latter, were thought of as steps toward work as a specialist, columnist, or correspondent.

## NEWSROOM OUTLIERS: SPECIALISTS, FEATURE WRITERS, COLUMNISTS AND EDITORIAL WRITERS

Reporters who were not tied as closely to the daily (or even hourly) cycle of news and who could devote their time to specialized beats were sometimes called "specialists." These "nonconformists of the newspaper profession" had arrived at the pinnacle of nonfiction writing and remained "away from the grind of the city room."[58] While still working out of it when they wanted, the true specialist was "more than a newspaperman, because in addition to being a skilled writer he is an authority in a chosen field." Freed from most daily newsroom chores, a specialist was the envy or his or her peers, who aspired to the position.[59] These were essentially beat reporters who had advanced in autonomy and authority.[60]

Under this broad grouping could be considered popular sports writers and the writers for sections on fashion, beauty, business and finance, science, agriculture, food, drama (including music and film), politics, religion, art, books and radio and television, travel, labor, childcare, photography, real estate, or education.[61] Feature writers were a related, if also rare, breed. Employed by bigger papers for their Sunday sections or the occasional longer piece in the daily newspaper, feature writers were known for their interviewing and investigative skills. Often bylined in an era when that was still uncommon, they could make up to three hundred dollars a week by the early 1950s.[62] Some feature writers were able to travel the world and write books about their experiences.[63]

While specialists could write for a variety of sections, labor, politics, and finance were particularly prized. Labor coverage could affect a reporter directly, especially if it involved the Guild. It was also a growing field, as other industries unionized or as existing unions expanded, especially during the Depression and right after the war. But it was politics that offered "just about the best steppingstone in the office to bigger things." The local and state political beat, and the nominal editorship of both, could lead to postings far *from* the newsroom, as Washington correspondents, or *in* the newsroom but very much aloof from its daily work life, as an editorial writer. Access to publishers, who often harbored political aspirations, did not hurt in this regard. Political writers had "more of a sense of power than any other on the paper," due to their external influence on readers and office holders and internal influence on the paper's informal and formal positions on issues.[64] Young politicians were known to seek the advice of experienced political reporters. At the state level, these kinds of journalists would eventually come to know those in power, an invaluable set of connections if they had ambition.[65]

But as a corollary to perceptions of access to power in and out of the newsroom, contemporary observers noted that just because a reporter had a title with "the imposing word 'editor'" did not mean they had actual power over either coverage or peers. Rank-and-file reporters turned special writers knew that they were sometimes paid less than a reporter's salary. An extra title was "often dished out to unlucky rewrite men as part-time responsibilities." The best way to get out of the rut that a superfluous, nonauthoritative "editorship" offered was to work hard and hope that your supervisors "realize you're fit for better things, or to do it so poorly (without getting fired) that they'll have to take you off it."[66] Navigating "dinky editorship titles" could just be another part of surviving at a larger, more compartmentalized newspaper. Despite this reality, some positions, which on the surface seemed like dull dead ends for reporters—including section editing of financial, ship news, society, and art beats—could provide interesting breaks from traditional beats or GA reporting and could become careers unto themselves.[67]

During the Depression, working as a specialist was thought to bring you extra job security.[68] In the midst of this difficult economic time, Helen Rowland, a syndicated advice columnist (of "The Marry-Go-Round"), advised aspiring reporters to "find a specialty," since "your reputation is a cumulative thing."[69] Reporters sought bylines, in some cases, in order to build enough of a reputation to someday become columnists. Leveraging detours was a hallmark of the savvy reporter. At the end of World War II, Hanson Baldwin, himself a military analyst and specialist for the *New York Times*, reflected on how experts were "now a fundamental part of the modern newspaper," with a definite trend "toward departmentalization of the news." Reporters and specialists were similar, he said, and "indeed, I claim that a specialist has to be a good reporter." While some GA reporters at the *Times* were part-time specialists, some specialized departments could staff dozens of dedicated writers (though only at the biggest papers). A specialist was in the unique position to fuse "facts, background and opinion—with *particular* accent upon *background* and *interpretation*" (italics in the original).[70]

Baldwin was quick to add that while specialists had tacit and explicit permission to engage in what was then called news "interpretation," or analysis of current events, they were not, strictly speaking, columnists.[71] They could be roving, as was the case with Ernie Pyle, who died while covering combat operations on Okinawa in the final days of the war. A more comfortable parallel for Baldwin, himself an in-demand specialist, was reporting, and he argued for the role of specialist reporters, an important, if category-collapsing clarification in a newsroom united by the act of creating a daily and weekly product but also subdivided into groups of peers and near peers. A specialist could occasionally diverge from the paper's editorial policy, and have a wider latitude than the ordinary reporter in doing so. In Baldwin's case, perhaps because of the unique situation of the war, and his own expertise, this was not uncommon.[72]

Within newsrooms, creating specialist reporting jobs was a trend that outlasted the war. By the 1950s an observer noted that the "age of specialization in the news room" had arrived.[73] A generation earlier, "any reporter worth his salt was confident that he was competent to cope with whatever assignment came his way, whether it was a general alarm fire, a juicy murder, or interviewing the latest literary lion." But the traditional expectation of reportorial flexibility had changed, he said, with an increasing emphasis on, and encouragement of, specialists at even smaller newspapers.[74]

### COLUMNISTS: CAREER PROGRESSION, WORK ROUTINES AND STATUS

Columnists were a breed apart in the newsroom's editorial universe. While specialists were considered experts among newspaper people and the public alike, they still focused on news and developments in their particular field. Columnists, likewise, were specialists on particular topics, but far more focused on developing a first-person persona. This distinct voice was critical. Successful columnists approached topics from a unique angle that readers enjoyed.

The only requirement was consistency, up to about five hundred to one thousand words per day for the more gossipy columnists, a.k.a. "the keyhole boys," who needed to be "lively and not too libelous."[75] They could of course, also write and break news. Circulation boosters, columnists could range widely in content, from advice, politics, drama, and history to sports and humor. They could "make more money than editors and have more fame and fun."[76] The freedom to consistently write under their bylines daily or weekly was about all many columnists had in common, however, as their salaries and backgrounds could vary, from humble, small-town daily newspaper columnists to the high-powered, well-remunerated, and nationally known columnists such as Dorothy Thompson, Walter Winchell, Walter Lippmann, Ernie Pyle, Heywood Broun, or Westbrook Pegler.[77] On the lower end, full-time columnists could make as much as a GA reporter, but on the higher end, he or she could take home as much as ten thousand dollars a year or more (far more, in the case of Thompson, Winchell, Lippmann, Broun, and Pegler). In some rare cases, with extra income generated by lectures, books, endorsements, and appearances on TV and on the radio, columnists could make up to two hundred fifty thousand a year, an extraordinary sum for the time.[78]

Columnists found time for these extra activities if they could confine their drafting work to a few hours a day, which the wealthier were able to do.[79] These highly successful columnists tended to be in the widest syndication, their material filling up editorial and feature pages in hundreds of newspapers around the world. With "this volcano of the newspaper field," column writing and columnists were a big business, and they had an outsized influence on the opinions of powerful and ordinary Americans alike during this period.[80] The extreme disparity in pay between reporters and columnists concerned some editors, however. "We are workers," one managing editor in Chicago noted in 1931, "and to my mind, there never could be any sense in paying a columnist $25,000 a year, and maybe syndicate percentages, and then having a fellow who is writing for the first page all the time, paid $100 a week."[81] The majority of columnists, however, made a more modest income. A survey in 1960 of 153 managing editors found that veteran reporters and columnists made an average of $8,344 a year on newspapers of 150,000 circulation or more; extra compensation brought that closer to $8,705.[82]

Cultivating material could be challenging. A columnist, even a creative one, could run his or her "subject so far into the ground it should come [out] in China, or in Chinese." It was important to develop new sources.[83] Starting out involved getting as many bylines as possible and writing guest columns, as well as working steadily on "some dinky local column on fishing, radio, ship news, sports or such," so that over time, and "with enough individuality, good writing and pungent observations . . . somebody will 'discover' you for a real columning job."[84] Cementing their reputation as newsroom elites, columnists often got their own offices, putting them on par with senior editors, cartoonists, and editorial writers.[85] Barring that, they might get their own corner spot in the newsroom.[86] Either move signaled status and removed columnists from the work and social spheres of regular reporters.

Women as well as men could be successful columnists. Many of the former were advice columnists, focusing on relationships and romance.[87] Others, however, covered broader social issues and politics.[88] Columnists of both genders were advertised in trade publications, with some newspapers hoping their local talent could be syndicated nationally.[89] Later, columnists added TV to their repertoire of topics.[90] Some papers looked to replace syndicated features with local, "signed" columnists.[91] This was an attractive option if an editor could save money while also increasing circulation with a locally known writer. Colorful and capable, columnists were a prized asset for a newspaper. Some editors advocated for treating local news columnists as direct extensions of the newsroom's reporter pool, and part of the team instead of somehow orbiting outside of it. Columnists could include the "pundit," the "reporter-commentator," gossip-driven "loss-and-tell boys like Winchell," and "the funny boys like Bob Hope and Gracie Allen."[92] Giving reporters latitude and paying them a little more to use them as commentators was a better use of resources, versus paying "out millions," one editor insisted, "for canned columns."[93] Some local columnists, contrary to their aloof reputation, enjoyed interacting with newsroom life and with rank-and-file news workers.[94]

### EDITORIAL WRITERS: ROLE IN THE NEWSROOM, CAREER PATH, AND WORK ROUTINES

The most anonymous and routine copy was produced by the editorial writers at daily newspapers. On smaller newspapers, the more powerful editors, such as the managing editor and editor-in-chief, wrote the editorials, which became the official point of view of the paper.[95] Editorial writers were "of high rank," after having commonly worked their way up. While the job was known for attracting older news workers, due to its "sedentary nature" and its more reflective routine, by the early 1950s it was attracting younger writers. In either case, former and current specialists in certain beats made good editorial writers, depending on the topic of the day.[96] Not as limited by space and free to opine (at least in accordance with the official and unofficial policies of the paper), editorial writers worked on teams as large as the copydesk at larger newspapers. This was done in conjunction with an editorial board, often including the publisher, the managing editor, available editorial writers, and any other interested section editors. Assignments for individual and group-written editorials would flow from this meeting.

Thus operating in a world apart from the newsroom, editorial writers were the most loosely affiliated "peers" of more ordinary news workers. They felt "less the excitement, glamour, and press urgency of most newspapermen" but were still considered part of the broader newsroom team, definitely more closely aligned with the writing side of the paper, for example, than any staff

Figure 8. Louis A. Paige, "The other fellow's job," *Editor & Publisher*, April 18, 1936, 70. News workers sometimes envied their peers' work routines.

member on the business side.[97] Along with other newsroom groups, they had their stereotypes, too. As Hugh S. Balllie, executive vice president of the UP, reminisced in 1935, "The editorial writer usually sat on a pile of back numbers and had his office so stuffed with old papers and musty paste pots that it constituted a fire hazard."[98]

It was considered comparatively easy, steady work, with hours much more akin to a non-newspaper job and a compensation higher than other newsroom jobs. "The work is seldom heavy and is accomplished in an atmosphere of quiet and leisure compared with news writing," noted one reporter. An editorial writer, however, often labored in "complete anonymity," so much so that it was "not unusual for even most of the staff to be unacquainted with the man in the little private office who pounds out the editorials."[99] Removed as it was "from the rushing, tearing, glamour centers of newspaper production," it was sometimes not much sought after and thus had more openings than other jobs at the paper. Pitching opinion pieces steadily, ideally to a city editor, but barring that, to an existing editorial writer, increased a reporter's chances of becoming one of the latter. Learning by trial and error to not criticize the publisher's "pets" and instead align oneself with his or her perspective, helped. Only over time and after editorial writers had established themselves could they gainsay the opinions of the paper's ownership. A well-rounded education on everything from "transit to totalitarianism" was also necessary.[100]

### EDITORIAL WRITERS BEFORE THE WAR

Editorial writers remained physically separated from the rest of the newsroom, enhancing their status as quasi-outsiders and aligning their perspectives more with ownership and management than with their rank-and-file colleagues. This was partially pragmatic. In an era when newsrooms were as lively and loud as a "firecracker," with telephones, typewriters, pneumatic tubes, and shouting editors and reporters creating a rich aural landscape, it was helpful for editorial writers to have their own space apart to think, debate, and compose.[101] There was also the traditional, and increasingly stark, separation of "opinion" from "fact" on many newspapers, as objectivity became an entrenched norm and more overt political patronage receded further into the past.[102] The editorial page and its writers were the paper's best avenues when it wanted to express its official response to business and government activities and decisions. It was imagined as a powerful, activist counterforce to state and federal governments.[103] Internally, next to the business office, it was as sealed off as possible from the workaday concerns of the regular newsroom.

In contrast, some editorial writers, even those who worked as newsroom supervisors, felt that editorial writing kept them close to the pulse of the newsroom. H. V. Kaltenborn, associate editor of the *Brooklyn Eagle* and later a well-known radio commentator, enjoyed writing editorials. As a profile on Kaltenborn put it, doing so "keeps [him] in the class of working newspapermen and keeps him also in active touch with the news department."[104] But the arrival of the Depression—and the ANG—caused some anxiety as to the role and status of the editorial writer. The generally pro-publisher *Editor & Publisher*, for example, worried that unionizing the newsroom would lead to a less creative, less independent worker, especially if that worker was coming from a position that required more creativity and independence to begin with, including editorial writers.[105] And while there were some exceptions, editorial writers remained a minority on most papers. A survey by the ASNE estimated that small- to medium-sized daily newspapers employed two editorial writers out of about fifty dedicated newsroom staff. A typical range was about one to four on staffs that totaled between twenty-five and sixty-eight.[106] One study of the *Milwaukee Journal*, a relatively large daily with a circulation of two hundred sixty thousand found only a single dedicated editorial writer out of the fifty-five men and women surveyed in the news and "other editorial departments" (and with a total staff of eighty-four).[107]

### EDITORIAL WRITERS DURING THE WAR AND BEYOND: AN ELITE STATUS CONFIRMED

Newspaper buildings and newsroom in the 1940s and 1950s continued to apportion separate spaces for editorial writers, putting them on the same level as artists, critics, senior editors, and feature writers.[108] Editorial writers' proximity to power was obvious. The *Los Angeles Examiner* in 1956 located its editorial writers close to the office of H. H. Krauch, the managing editor, with his corner office in the renovated newsroom.[109] Even when not as ostentatiously placed near supervisors, they were commonly removed from other writing news workers, occasionally located on their own floor.[110]

Editorial writers remained a breed apart from other newsroom workers, and especially from beat and other kinds of reporters. But they all shared the mission of writing "material which will interest the public and keep the paper sold to the public."[111] Like other more fixed creative news workers, editorial writers continued to battle perceptions that they were less relevant than the news reporter and hardened editor.[112] They were thought to live in their own "Ivory Tower" as part of the "egghead department" and were seemingly aloof (and privileged to be removed from) the concerns of the newsroom, the newspaper, and readers in general. Other reporters thought they "enjoyed an undeserved sinecure." Editorial writers "sat with their feet on their desks and gazed thoughtfully into space. The end result of a day's work was less than any competent rewrite man could turn out in less than an hour," noted a newsroom observer in 1958.[113]

Reporters and other lower-level newsroom staff usually "did not achieve the dignity of an editorial writer's chair until the years began to weigh on him." And so younger reporters, including cubs, came to believe that the "sole qualifications for the assignment were a lack of bounce . . . [in the step] . . . and a mentality not quite quick enough for the copy desk." But some argued that these narratives were either not true, or the basis for them was changing. There were still unique stresses to the job, and editorial writers did, in fact, help to influence their community for the good. With its "own compensations," or benefits, an editorial writer need not live an "austere existence behind the sterile walls of his Ivory Tower." Editorial writers were writing "much closer to the news" and were more willing, especially as they began to include younger newsroom staff and former reporters, to "stick their editorial necks out with far more abandon."[114]

While editorial workers remained quiet members of the newsroom, there were also attempts to capture more information about them. A survey by the University of Oregon's School of Journalism found that fifteen of the twenty-three editorial writers working in the state from 1950 to 1951 had other journalistic duties; two covered regular beats and three wrote for the AP and *Oregonian*. The average age was fifty-six, and average weekly time spent on the job was sixty hours; all but four belonged to some kind of civic club, echoing a more general involvement in life outside the news organization.[115] The American Press Institute, started in the wake of the World War II and holding meetings hosted by Columbia's School of Journalism, held a special session just for editorial writers, putting them on par with managing and news editors, "picture editors," and specialized reporters, including those covering city hall and labor.[116]

In continuing public debates with the Guild, representatives of the ANPA contended that reporters and editorial writers, due to the independent nature of their work, qualified as "professional" workers. Because they produced creative work outside of the direct control of their supervisors, "all of them must be inspired and motivated in their production efforts by considerations that are intellectual and creative and must, of necessity, therefore, have qualities of studiousness, scholarliness and trained thinking."[117] The ANG disagreed, claiming that reporters and editorial writers alike faced severe restrictions on their work.[118] In other ways, editorial writers continued to operate with a more traditional set of newsroom customs. They remained even less diverse in terms of gender and race than the rest of the newsroom. Whereas women and minorities were slowly, though haltingly, hired to fill other news-worker roles, many newspapers' editorial writers remained primarily older white men.[119]

## CONCLUSION: DIFFERENTIATION AND EXTENSION OF LABOR IN THE MIDCENTURY AMERICAN NEWSROOM

Reporters' roles, power dynamics, and levels of autonomy in the newsroom were varied. But within this variegated milieu, they formed a unique *occupational community*, with its own norms, standards, ethos, and mythos. As the newsroom ethnographers of the late 1960s and 1970s (and 1980s) discovered, this community shaped the meaning and form of news. It also shaped and formed the newsmakers. The work-saving and sharing practices detected by Leo Rosten in the mid-1930s and the subtle policy-shaping pressures from editors picked up by Warren Breed in the mid-1950s foreshadowed this.[120] Other contemporaries, including a number of memoirists and writers for trade publications, reflected on how cub reporters, leg men, GA reporters, beat reporters, and other newsroom-based writers operated within their own larger circle (within the broad category of news gatherer), distinct from other newsroom support staff (who were more focused on news production).[121] Of course, as with any other autographical writing, the challenge is filtering reality through recollection, or lack thereof. While there were prominent women and Black specialist and syndicated writers who broke through into the white press, especially by the 1960s, including James Baldwin, Louis Lomax, William Worthy, and Philippa Duke Schuyler, most where older white men.[122] With race, the barriers to entry were high already for the rank-and-file. This continued to be the case the higher up one got within journalism's elite. With some very notable exceptions, then, many established white reporters did not usually mention race or newsroom integration and its challenges, at least not for another generation. Columnists, correspondents, and editorial writers and other elite journalists were definitely beneficiaries of privilege. But in examining the totality of these accounts, certain trends emerge.

Reporters of various kinds became *gatherers*. Copy editors, rewrite staff, and middle- and senior-level editors became *producers*. Within the inner circle of gatherers, both junior and senior reporters created their own subgroups, with idealized pathways to independence. Junior reporters had less power and autonomy. Senior reporters had more of both. But through their own discourse about themselves, their work and their workplaces, reporters, as the centering figures in the newsroom, also created their own interpretative community.[123] As Barbie Zelizer describes it, through this discourse reporters navigated changing circumstances, technologies, and the status and role of their work in American society.[124] Gatherers and producers needed each other, and their interrelationships formed the unique newsroom work culture.

These micro–workplace communities could create intense tensions and rivalries. They could also create necessary relational space, an important buffer against the ups and downs of work in print journalism. Whether working together out in the field or in the physical newsroom space, recent recruits formed friendships, packs, and symbiotic connections. Their presence near one another was crucial. It was no accident that newsroom proximity had profound social and occupational meanings for these workers. The very physicality of the newsroom space helped to foster this sense of occupational and interpretive community. "The newsroom" was again shorthand for the relationships that formed and were fostered there.

Within this space, a "secondary socialization" was part of the division of labor and the hazy hierarchy of relationships; it was led, determined, and bounded by peers. With this socialization, news workers engaged in a social construction of their workplace reality and roles.[125] Due to the special similarity and immediacy of their work practices and products, reporters tended to identify strongly as part of groups, even as an ideology of individualism was also present. These contradictions were reinforced in reporters' reactions to the demands of their near peers and peers. Reporters who had more power—including "star reporters," specialists, columnists, and editorial writers—were held up as different and important among their colleagues and inspired junior reporters' aspirations to autonomy. Finally, reporters were shaped by the authority of editors, and how that authority pushed against their own aspirations for agency and control over their work routines. The relational capital of editors—and thus their authority—will be the subject of the next chapter.

## CHAPTER 6

# Reporters and Their Bosses

## Power Sharing in the Newsroom

THE TRADITIONAL TENSION between reporters and editors has been the stuff of newsroom legend, and for good reason. For the purposes of this chapter, "reporter" will refer to "leg men," GA reporters, beat reporters, or specialists (with the latter two categories often overlapping). As centering figures in the newsroom, reporters exemplified the supervisor–news worker interaction that is examined in this chapter. Other types of news workers, including support personnel such as copy editors and rewrite staff, could, of course, experience versions of this relationship. But for the sake of my argument and the overall occupational-social history of the American newsroom, reporters and their editor(s) will remain our focus here.[1] They were a broad and sometimes fuzzy group of newsroom actors and so part of the challenge for media historians is parsing out what their actual power and influence within a newsroom would have been. Even as great a contemporary scholar of newsrooms and the news industry as A. M. Lee, writing in 1937, conceded that newsroom authority structures were complex and in flux, as reporters flexed their newfound power. While the role of higher-order bosses was clearer, the exact interrelationship of various under-editors—for example, the telegraph and Sunday editor, the assistant editors—was highly variable, depending on the newsroom in question. One newsroom saying though, helped clarify the situation: "The longer the title, the shorter the pay check," Lee observed.[2]

Regardless, for generations, reporters of all kinds thought of editors as "friendly enemies."[3] Focused on getting and writing the news, reporters constantly pushed for more autonomy. Editors pushed back. They believed they had to be a "fountain of knowledge; a glutton for work and able to put over a bluff," in order to both engage with their paper's enigmatic ownership and the erratic tastes of their readership.[4] Sometimes reporters and editors could agree. Often they could not. The latter was nominally in charge, but the paper could not function without the former.

Some of this tension is steeped in nostalgia, or romanticized heavily, and is thus perhaps overemphasized in the trade publications that detail it. The authors of the *Quill* and *Editor & Publisher*, after all, were often either established reporters or editors themselves. Countervailing perspectives from the *Guild Reporter* and news workers' memoirs, however, do show that editors were reviled *and* loved, despised *but* needed—and that a great deal depended on where and when you were working, a topic that will be discussed in more detail below.

But in the forty-year period from 1920 to 1960, editors changed from being top-down "bosses" to managers. As with other American business organizations, newsrooms were in the midst of a white-collar shift, with college becoming a more acceptable way to enter the field. As Richard Edwards has argued, a "system of control" pervaded this process, with direction, evaluation, and discipline enacted within a shared workplace.[5] Newsrooms, though, as I have argued earlier, were unique constructs, with their own rich traditions. The paternal, if at times autocratic, attitude some owners and senior editors held toward their reporters would give way to a more strictly managerial, or corporatized employer-employee dynamic. This did not happen overnight, or easily.

The arrival of the ANG made arbitrary decision making more costly for editors, who found that their supreme power to hire, direct, and fire news workers was fading. They also found that their prerogatives had to be shared with human resources departments, which functioned as a new institutional structure that regulated authority. Reporters, for their part, went from surviving and tolerating abusive bosses to interacting with them if not quite as equals, then on less terrified and increasingly respectful terms. This chapter tells the story of how the newsroom's hierarchal dynamic changed.

### A BRIEF NOTE ON THE HIERARCHY OF NEWSROOM POWER

At the outset, it is important to clarify, briefly, the hierarchy of power in a "typical" large daily midcentury newsroom. First, the editor in chief would preside over the total operation of the news factory, but that person—and it was almost universally a white male—would also often be concerned with the business side of the paper, or keeping the publisher happy (or in some cases, *was* the publisher). Below him, the managing editor was the boss of bosses in the newsroom, in charge of editorial policy, hiring and firing, and the daily news production of the paper. But just below this figure was the city editor, often called a news editor. This person had the most contact with rank-and-file reporters and also the greatest day-to-day authority. He (and again, it was almost always a he) was tasked with managing not just reporters but also photographers (though usually sharing that responsibility with a photo editor), copy editors (alongside the copy chief, or head copy editor), and other, specialized figures, such as columnists or subsection editors. More discussion about the organizational structure of a typical big-city daily follow below, including the conflation of the managing editor's role with that of the city editor at some newspapers, based on contemporary sources from that era; but in sum, the newsroom had a definite collection of bosses, with some looming larger over reporters than others.

The often-conflictual relationship between the newsroom's leaders and its nominal followers was messy. Both groups thought of the other as a distinct "them" and sought to minimize and share the other's power. Reflecting on his experiences in the early 1960s, one reporter remembered how editors thought of themselves as "idea men." Reporters, for their part, thought of editors as "manipulators of both reality and men," operating within their "own, separate hierarchy" designed to enforce conformity.[6] As Warren Breed described it, the newsroom's "social control," centered on these editor-reporter interactions, was subtle. It had much more to do with editing marks, quiet nods, and unvoiced acts of shunning than it did with verbal correction, shouting matches, or thrown objects. Editors were enforcers of newsroom power. But this control (and resistance to it) did not exist in a vacuum. Breed's examination of newsrooms in the 1950s, for example, took place during a relatively white-collar era.[7] He noted an overarching collegiality to most newsroom staffer interactions, even between those of different ranks, and postulated that news workers controlled themselves more than they were controlled by others. Far from being a top-down workplace, power was *shared* among newsroom inhabitants (granted, with newsroom bosses still retaining its preponderance). From their entry into the newsroom, reporters learned on the job and from each other, as well as from interactions with their bosses, during a "wiring-in" period.[8]

At the same time, through the middle of the century, however, newsroom life retained elements of a more blue-collar existence. The work of reporters, involving long hours, unreliable transportation, and time outdoors or standing for long periods, could tax even the most energetic of people. Stress was ever-present, and not just from these and other external factors. Working closely together, reporters and their editors had ample opportunity to display their frustrations. Reporters and their bosses engaged in conflict, fighting for control over their shared work processes. Editors sought to tightly direct their reporters' workflows and products. Reporters, in turn, resisted efforts to be controlled and sought to direct their own fates as much as possible.

Editors and reporters tended to be wired differently, a fact that had to be taken into account by the former when managing the latter. While both groups were more normal than might be expected by outsiders (not the "screwballs, alcoholics, dope addicts and so on" depicted in films, novels, and later television), it was also felt that "editors tend to be much more serious than the successful reporter." Reporters were more socially aggressive and were "more like salesmen." Unlike editors, they did "not mind getting out there and knocking on doors to get a story."[9] Editors had power and used it. But reporters and their bosses were also similar. They engaged in collaborative activities, sharing aspects of their work and its processes. This involved establishing and respecting routines and boundaries with time and workflow management. As in the conflict and collaboration between copy editors and reporters, an uneasy détente could be reached. Ideally, editors and reporters recognized that they worked best when they respected each other's agency. In addition, both roles and routines were set by the production needs of the newspaper.

Writing in the mid-1930s, a city editor noted that his job was "a little less piratical and adventurous than in the old days." With larger, better organized staffs, editors no longer had to rule as much by fear and could manage more through collaboration: "He may compare himself with the manager of a baseball team, impresario of a road show, the driver of a mule team, a school teacher hammering knowledge into the backwoods crackers, an overworked and underpaid hangman, the boss of a chain gang, a priest with a parish in Hell's Kitchen."[10] Editors could be crafty and cruel, insightful and distant. They could come in "hard, soft, and medium" flavors, and tended to be "hard-boiled." There were reasons for this almost chameleonlike set of characterizations. As "the boss of the city room," the editor needed to maintain a powerful persona, complete with a certain fierceness of temper. He (and it was nearly always a "he" during this era) was also human, suffering from "migraine and buck fever," and subject to "moments of fumbling and fright."[11] At this time, there was a noted decline in the presence of the angrier, louder type of editor who had inspired old stereotypes. But contemporaries observed that "sometimes, it may be, there is too much politeness and consideration. The moderns may be at times too soft for the good for the business. The 'good fellows' can overdo it."[12]

## NEWSROOM ROUTINES

While journalism textbooks from the 1920s through the 1950s outlined a tidy set of procedures for how reporters should interact with their bosses, newsroom routines were often deeply affected by personalities within both groups. Routines, while helpful, could be circumvented, replaced, or modified. Pew made this clear in his portrayal of a typical newsroom scene:

> Flushed reporter enters, throws off coat, yells to the city editor, "The mayor has thrown us down," [and] starts to pound the keys of his typewriter. City editor tears out a sheet and puts a flashing eye on the purple line of words. Managing editor approaches from his office. City editor tells him the news. Managing editor disappears behind the door of the editor's office. Talk registers indignation. An editorial writer puts a fresh sheet in his typewriter, and punches out the line, "triple-lead and lead all."[13]

In this environment, workers fulfilled preset roles: the reporter gathered the news and wrote up stories, the city editor and managing editor edited content and argued over policy, and the editorial writers interpreted it.[14] This was a process of control, subject to change, dependent on the memories of those involved, and rarely entirely smooth. Because assignments and newsroom routines were often unevenly written down, especially before World War II, the presence of older news workers, and in some cases, retired editors, helped to maintain consistency. These could include old reporters-turned-semiretired editors, sometimes working less-taxing jobs that still allowed them to be present in the newsroom and thus available for quick questions or longer conversations.[15]

Routine making and maintenance by editors and reporters was a stressful process. "Almost everything in the news field demands that workers strain their capacities to the utmost and errors creep in when tension is high," wrote an editor in 1929. This "high-pressure work" could drive workers "to achieve the seemingly impossible," but the very routines that drove fast production schedules could produce tensions.[16] Outside the newsroom, editors had less control, but their presence could still be felt. Even overseas correspondents, arguably the news workers with the most independence, could find it helpful to think like their bosses back home and be their "own city editor," in the absence of clear direction from the far away newsroom.[17]

The transition to the role of editor could occur gradually and was itself a kind of collaborative process. A "top-ranking reporter" could find himself helping to plan coverage and develop stories and could become "an authority while covering some major assignment himself." While having "managerial ability" did not often result in a formal title, it could result in higher status in a newsroom. This could occur even if the reporter in question explicitly rejected the trappings of a management position.[18] The idea of a meritocratic newsroom hierarchy remained part of newsroom culture. If a reporter "really wants to succeed, he must always be preparing himself for the next job ahead." The best, brightest, and most driven reporters, so this mythos went, eventually became editors, and from there eventually aspired "to the city desk, the city editor to the managing editor's chair, the managing editor to the position of publisher, and so on." This brought a "singleness of purpose" to the newsroom and drove a culture of internal advancement that honored loyalty while also somewhat paradoxically rewarding mobility.[19] Conversely, an editor could fall from power and still work in a newsroom, just with diminished power. Newsroom lore included tales of defrocked editors who reverted to the role of reporter.[20] Nomadic copy readers were rumored to be "fallen managing editor[s]."[21] Editors' fortunes shifted in both directions. If an editor worked for a chain, he or she would be shifted around. Sometimes one city, such as Cleveland, would serve as a training center for a chain (in this case, Scripps) from which multiple editors would be sent.[22] If a newspaper was locally owned, editors tended to be promoted from within. Editors in chief and managing editors could be nomadic, too. Expanding chains exacerbated the trend. When it came to middle management, however, junior editors could just as easily emerge from within an organization as without.

### NEWSROOM ROUTINES: THE EMERGING ROLE OF THE DAILY "CONFERENCE"

For a newspaper to be a "masterpiece of cooperative brains," with words speeding "over telephone and telegraph and cable and wireless," it had to be edited by editors and reporters who "deliberated, toiled and gave of their best" efforts.[23] An editor, sometimes differentiated from a copy editor by the title "news executive," had the exclusive discretion to review finished stories before they went to the copydesk. They could also "kill" or cut a story before it went anywhere else, or send it back to a reporter to be rewritten by either the latter or a rewrite staffer if it had "taken the wrong perspective or is otherwise defective."[24]

Managing editors helped set but were also bound by newsroom routines. When to intervene and when to let events play out could be a tough call. Many erred on the side of action. A managing editor at the *Chicago Tribune* in 1941 believed that he should "butt in all I can" and "operated on the general theory that a 'kick in the pants and a pat on the back' is the best method of getting good results." At the same time, he felt that an engaged "M.E." should deliver "more pats on the back and fewer kick[s] in the pants." As much delegation as possible was desirable and seen as a sign of confidence, and not weakness.[25] Within the assignment system, editors were ultimately responsible for the kinds of stories uncovered and how well their staff performed. If reporters performed badly, it could be because their editors had given them bad assignments or unclear directions.[26] Reporters expected "competent supervision by editors who know their business," even if they rebelled against it on occasion.[27]

Several specific practices were designed to enhance the efficiency of newsroom routines: streamlining workflow by redesigning or moving desks, organizing meetings, and maintaining written records of current and future reporting activities. The postwar renovation of the Detroit *Free Press*'s newsroom included centralizing copydesk operations, and brought the telegraph editor, the copy chief, the photo editor, and news editor physically closer together. It was important to place the various section editors within "easy reaching and conversing distance of the News Editor." This kind of workplace conversation was thought to reduce tensions and mistakes and improve morale.[28] An increasing emphasis on the need for weekly or daily conferences followed, even if it took some time for these to catch on. Internally, this innovation paralleled the instillation of a dedicated photo editor, especially as photo staffs became more mobile and worked in conjunction with, rather than just for, reporters.[29] Staff meetings ranged from an occasional informal gathering of star reporters with a city editor to a regularly scheduled encounter between the managing editor and the entire staff down to the lowliest copy boy or girl. Meetings were used to lay out any aspects of new routines, update old routines, assign stories, and troubleshoot staff issues.[30]

How meetings worked out varied in practice. But on afternoon newspapers ranging from the smallest to the largest dailies, newsroom routines often included a midday huddle with the senior editorial staff, including the managing editor, city editor, news editor, and makeup editor.[31] Meetings of the "bull pen" could prevent future problems, address current issues, and debrief past ones.[32] Work rhythms on afternoon papers also often dictated earlier starts, at around 9 a.m., for city editors, with reporters and lower-ranking editors arriving throughout the morning.[33] Keeping a "future book" helped some city editors track their reporters and their assignments. Often written as a story-planning calendar or "an enormous ledger," it included clippings from recent stories and notes, as well as summaries of information from rival papers. Tips from reporters and readers and event calendars from civic groups suggested coverage ideas.[34] As a way of bringing a level of certainty to an uncertain day, the future book also helped manage reporters and their varying abilities, from green cubs to jaded veterans.

When Agness Underwood became the pioneering first female city editor of a major metropolitan newspaper, the *Los Angeles Evening Herald & Express*, in 1946, she relied on just such a future book to navigate and "to disprove expectations that a woman would be too scatterbrained to cope with a fast city desk."[35] Underwood's daily routine involved considerable bookkeeping that could not be delegated, including working with the rewrite desk and managing the "slugsheet," which contained details on story assignments for that day. Underwood found that maintaining a written record of her routine helped to settle disputes between reporters and the copydesk. It helped keep other senior-level executives and publishers happy.[36] Editors like Underwood cultivated relationships among friendly or supportive groups in the newsroom, including, in her case, news photographers, whom she made a career-long point of treating well. As a former reporter, Underwood found it difficult to direct newsroom routines as an editor rather than being driven by them. In her recollection, a "city editor is paid to direct and co-ordinate the activities of the city-side staff," not to "spank a typewriter" or spend time "hotshotting around."[37] Letting reporters police themselves helped maintain good newsroom morale, she found. Still, she would not "take any back talk, insulting loafing, or smart-aleck insubordination" from her mostly male reporters.[38]

### NEWSROOM ROUTINES: THE SHARED RITUAL OF SCHEDULING

To process the never-ending flow of information-turned-news, editors, especially assistant day city editors, came in early in the newsroom's day. For morning papers, this could be around 9 a.m., and for afternoon papers, around 6 a.m. Some newspapers would vary this schedule, but generally morning papers had a later start because their staffs would work into the evenings, producing issues that would come out early the next day, while the staff at afternoon papers had to start as soon as feasible, to get their evening editions out in time for the late afternoon. Reviewing stories from rival papers, the latest from local and national news services, and material left over from the previous shift, the first junior editor-in-charge would make initial assignments and prepare the way for his boss, the city editor. The latter would arrive by about 10 a.m. on a morning paper and by about 7:30 a.m. for an afternoon daily. The assistant city editor would brief the boss on news tips and potential story ideas, set up a tentative coverage schedule, and decide which GA reporters would go where—that is, once they reported in at around 1 p.m. or 7 a.m., at morning or afternoon papers, respectively, with photographers to follow throughout the day. City editors would have to keep an active account—a kind of mental map of the city—of which of their reporters had been sent out and which reporters had remained behind to gather more information, just in case the stories they had been assigned developed in certain directions, or not at all. Many editors on morning papers were so concerned about being scooped or shorthanded that a reporter, photographer, and rewrite staffer acted as a newsroom reserve.

A mid- or late-day conference of the various editors, including the city and managing editors, copy chief, and makeup editor, would resolve differences or discuss how to make up shortages of copy, but these decisions and their consequences had to be passed on to the managing editor, who would often arrive later in the afternoon. On morning papers, the late afternoon and evening hours could get particularly hectic, with "incoming and outgoing telegraph wires clattering; messengers coming and going; pneumatic tubes clicking; news being written, edited and set in type; proofs arriving at the managing editor's desk;" and late-breaking stories, changes in layout, and other last-minute modifications demanding precious time. This was when a good editor would take the "helm of [the] city room," until the various editions went out and the "late watch" arrived, with the "dog watch man," or "sunrise editor" (often a senior copy editor), remaining in charge until morning came again. This "night managing editor," as the position was sometimes called, "was the nearest person to a czar," a "despot whose word is law when the question of news space is disputed by the city, telegraph and other desks."[39] Even as editors mellowed and became more managerial in style and less stridently boss-like, they could still summon their old habit of claiming absolute authority in emergencies. Depending on the circumstances, this was justified even by the more independent reporters, who recognized the need for top-down control in the midst of crises. Morning editors felt doubly pressed because they had to set the news agenda for the day without the benefit of as much material from rival papers. Normally the late editions from these other papers could be checked throughout the day for major scoops or stories to follow up on. But once they went to press, morning papers had to be a bit bolder, sometimes without knowing as much about their cross-town competitors.[40] Afternoon papers, in contrast, might face more pressure to work faster and update stories with wire copy.[41]

These afternoon papers had as their busiest part of the day the late morning through the early afternoon. Because of their schedule, afternoon papers often updated morning newspapers' stories and pursued different angles to stories that had already been written. Reporters would be assigned stories by about 7:30 a.m. and their progress tracked. As with their morning paper counterparts, it was important for editors to stay aware of what was being covered, how much space was left in the various upcoming editions, and what to do with late-breaking news. Afternoon papers had a staggered shift system in which reporters and support staff (copy editors, rewrite staffers) would leave throughout the afternoon. A skeleton crew would be in place by about 6 p.m., including a makeup editor designated as the "editor-in-charge" of all but the sports section and its editor, who remained independent. Some afternoon papers had more rewrite staff than "writing reporters" present since the latter tended to stay out of the newsroom on assignment. Editors would reassign them by phone as needed throughout the day, sometimes to the point where they would not return to the office. On both morning and afternoon dailies, a high level of coordination and control was necessary to manage limited resources, namely, the number of personnel available at any one point.[42] While technology enhanced an editor's ability to track and instruct reporters, both in and outside the newsroom, most editors had to make do with educated guesses.

Cost-saving pressures could also inspire city editors and other newsroom leaders to carefully watch who was being sent where and why (and who needed to remain in the newsroom). Tracking absences, avoiding duplication of coverage by news services, having reporters not otherwise employed write evergreen copy, and training reporters to take photos in a pinch were considered good practices. The shift to thinking of reporters more as resources to be spent or saved, instead of as personalities, was uneven, however. Most editors struggled to implement these kinds of efficiency-driven routines.[43]

Regardless of their publication schedule, on those newspapers with circulations of more than one hundred thousand, a typical newsroom might have around thirty-five dedicated staff members, with about four to five editors.[44] But in a 1930 study of 211 newsrooms, organizational structures varied wildly. Only a handful maintained an organizational chart prior to the study.[45] Many utilized a loose system in which a comparatively small group of powerful editors determined the day-to-day operations of the newsroom. They negotiated enough functional independence for their staffs from publishers and business managers to be able to cover news with as little interference as possible (except when "policy" was infringed, or "something unusual" arose that necessitated a meeting of senior editors with ownership).[46] Newspaper chain organizations differed from those held in family ownership when it came to pathways for promotion: the former would promote and send editors to other papers, while the latter would promote and keep them local. In both cases, within the "operating organization," a senior editor, often identified as the managing editor, would collaborate closely with the editor in chief, who was associated more directly with the publisher or owner of the paper. Newsroom routine dictated that at most of the papers analyzed in the 1930 study, midlevel and junior editors reported, in turn, to the managing editor. Sometimes this power was shared with a city editor, or news editor.

The news editor position eventually evolved into a senior-level position between managing and city editor roles, since the managing editor often focused on personnel issues and interdepartmental cooperation, and the city editor concentrated on local news operations. This middle role, of course, could vary, if it existed at all.[47] Managing editors still set overall newsroom practices and could hire and fire section editors.[48] More detailed newsroom routines were the purview of city editors, who could hire within budget limits and fire reporting staff within union constraints. But "personal factors" drove most power-sharing arrangements over time.[49] Temporal power management, and journalistic values such as speed, were enhanced by the newsroom routine, including its relentless focus on timelines.[50]

### CHANGING NEWSROOM DYNAMICS: THE EARLY INTERWAR YEARS

Reflecting on newsroom life in 1925, a writer noted that the "newspaper office often seems a hard, cold semi-military institution in matters of discipline, a machine that takes little thought for the individual, yet there is passion for service, [and an] ideal of duty, often tucked away there."[51] The authority of editors could be the envy of foremen on the mechanical side and was similar to that of a classified-advertising manager, with the latter's direct control over a "telephone staff."[52] The power of editors was such that they could "ruin" reporters through "unsympathetic treatment."[53] Reporters could be and were summoned by shouts, intercoms, loudspeakers, and buzzers.[54] If a reporter failed to come back to the newsroom or phone in copy, or, worse yet, was scooped by a rival paper, he or she would often endure a familiar ritual, a "session with the old man."[55]

A textbook author noted that a city editor acted as the "commander in chief" during breaking news, directing the "activities of his troops—the general assignment, beat and special reporters, the leg and rewrite men." Operating "like an advancing army," the newsroom demanded of its members "organization, discipline, partition and specification of duties and co-ordination." Editors prized, perhaps ironically, both obedience and independent initiative.[56] The military metaphors continued: "Like a company of soldiers, the entire staff may be shifted or realigned by the editors as the day's events dictate."[57]

Other commentators noted that over time the distance between rank-and-file reporters and their bosses had begun to ease. A generation before, editors were "hell-roaring," and would pride themselves on their ability "to curse out a reporter and . . . [a] willingness to 'fire' him on very slight provocation." Some editors were so well-known for their rages that they earned a kind of celebrity for "their tendency to go into perfect paroxysms of rage, to climb on their desks, tear their hair and then rush through every department of the paper like a cyclone, leaving terror and confusion and vacant jobs in their wake." Editors and reporters only talked to each other when they needed to, and the former's "aims and purposes were a mystery" to most of the latter.[58] This mythos was a mix of fact and newsroom gossip, with the typical editor known to arrive at 6:30 a.m. and leave after 5 p.m., "frantically shouting, storming, criticizing and laboring throughout the day."[59] Managers "ruled" their newsrooms and were known for their "sharp" words that instilled a self-driven desire in reporters to avoid the "humiliation of being beat on a story."[60]

Despite a discernible mellowing of this tradition of angry editors (who used their anger to maintain control in often-rowdy newsrooms), a strong psychological barrier remained for generations between the two groups. Top-down, or unilateral, was the most common management style. Reporters rarely met with editors to decide assignments. Daily conferences occurred on some newspaper staffs but did not catch on more widely until the 1940s and later.[61] Instead, editors would typically tell reporters their assignments without preamble, or pass them out at the beginning of a shift based on their estimation of a reporter's ability. Depending on how much they liked a reporter's "originality and style, the city editor naturally singled him out for the fattest assignments thereafter." Before World War I, this personality-driven assignment process awarded those whose talents meshed with an individual editor's tastes, and punished those whose did not. Being paid on the basis of space, this tendency could create real economic hardships for reporters, who risked being relegated to "sit around the city-room for a week and never earn a cent."[62] Gradually, the assignment process was systematized as salaries became common. But assignments and other directives still retained an impersonal air in many newsrooms, large and medium-sized alike. An editor in Springfield, Massachusetts, demonstrated this when he posted signs around the newsroom admonishing his reporters to "CONCENTRATE YOUR MIND," "WRITE LEGIBLY," "TAKE TIME," and not to "SPEAK TO YOUR NEIGHBORS AT WORK."[63]

Newsrooms were often laid out so that editors could keep a close watch on their reporters. For example, the managing editor at the *Wichita Daily Eagle*, John Reed, would watch his reporters at work in the city room: "If I hear one reporter calling to another: 'is there one t or two in City Manager Elliott's name,' I watch that fellow." If this kind of questioning continued, Reed would provide a "regular sermon on the beauties of accuracy."[64] Editors were by tradition trained to be observant. They developed an "eagle eye" for trouble or perceived loafing.[65] Reporters, for their part, noticed when their bosses were monitoring them and changed their behavior accordingly.[66] Into the postwar years, designed (or redesigned) spaces helped editors to see who was and who was not working, even when the former were otherwise busy or on the telephone.[67] Editors placed their desks in prominent places, such as at the front of the room, or had them raised in the middle of the newsroom, so that they could be seen and heard in a chaotic workplace.[68] As late as 1951 this practice of "visual control," in the words of an editor from the *Yakima Morning Herald* and *Daily Republic* in Washington state, could be practiced from a corner office with walls partially made of glass.[69] With shades of Foucault-like *surveiller et punir*, the watchful eyes of editors were legendary. As Robert Darnton, himself a former reporter, put it, "The most expert eye in the city room belongs to the city editor. From his point of maximal visibility, he can survey his entire staff and put each man in his place, for he alone knows the exact standing of everyone."[70]

Other editors tried to appeal to a reporter's "pride of workmanship," believing that correcting errors every time they occurred was "the very best medicine in such cases." Posting errors on bulletin boards, listing common errors in in-house newsletters, and, less indirectly, calling reporters into an office and questioning them about their mistakes were all ways editors exerted control over work processes and workers.[71] Editors were expected to be active, inspirational, and advocate for their staffs in the face of pressure from circulation and advertising department heads. They were also supposed to drive their staffs to perfection. Some editors practiced "chivvying," which included harassing, volatile behavior like yelling or screaming.[72]

Editors had different styles of verbal rebuke. Some, like the managing editor of the *Cincinnati Times-Star*, preferred a direct approach. The wielder of a "sort of beneficent czarism," he was a self-described "boss," and "a cross between a dynamo and a mule's kick," according to a contemporary. Instead of privately reprimanding a reporter, "he prances into the workroom, fixes the offender with a stabbing sort of stare, and then proceeds to burn him up. He is an expert in this sort of newspaper arson." Nonetheless, when he liked a reporter's or copy editor's work, he would just as publicly praise him, which his profiler claimed made him popular among the staff, who would "walk down Vine Street in Cincinnati town, clad in a one-piece bathing suit," for him.[73] This mix of anger and staff loyalty was a theme in accounts of newsroom life. Editors who had a "terrible temper" could also be accessible and fair to the "lowest paid reporter."[74]

## EDITORS IN THE LATER INTERWAR YEARS

Even while the openly frank editors of the later interwar years were heralded for their gruffness, some of the more belligerent tendencies of editors were discouraged by peers. Some bosses were known for their "uncomplimentary never-ending directness" toward those they believed unworthy, including women.[75] But editors who focused on "picking little flaws and brutally insulting those who make them, are particularly obnoxious and incompetent executives," noted Marlen Pew from his perspective at *Editor & Publisher*. It was important to recognize how the combination of human fallibility and high-pressure work could lead to mistakes, he believed, and how highlighting the latter too much could undermine a newsroom's morale.

Editors could be imbued with a "high-speed spirit" and still be fair to their workers, he argued.[76] Pew represented a more progressive approach to newsroom management that foreshadowed things to come. A good editor set the tone for the rest of the staff.[77] It made sense, then, for that editor to be consistent as a source of inspiration and motivation. Younger reporters, especially, needed good mentorship, but older reporters could also sense "the spirit of the office" and would work harder if a paper's leadership was competent.[78] "The problem is to get a good City Editor, and turn him loose," claimed a managing editor in 1930.[79] Another believed that "if you have a fellow at the city desk who is good-natured, nervy, well-balanced, and knows enough, you are through with your problems." Granted, this emphasis on leadership from above came from those already there. But good editors seemed to recognize that there were limits to their power. Morale could be built and reinforced "through encouragement," not by "crabbing" or grouchy "post-mortems."[80]

And yet there was a general sense, too, that reporters had become the focus of newsroom work, and that the age of larger-than-life editors had passed by the early 1930s. Editors, while still powerful, found themselves in a more supportive position (in terms of workflow). Reporters got the glamour and attention in popular depictions of newsrooms, despite the poor pre-Guild working conditions. "The editor's thoughts may find exposition in the editorial columns, but it is the Reporter's life blood that goes into the news story," noted an industry observer in 1922.[81] Reporters were to be the new "power generators," even as they needed the strong leadership of editors.[82] And their clashes with editors were not limited to disputes over assignments or angles on stories. They could also disagree over more mundane issues. When the staff of the *Chicago Daily News* moved to a new building in 1929, a reporter dragged a battered hat rack to the new newsroom, much to the consternation of "an executive who had a good deal of respect for efficiency." Ordered to remove it, the reporter responded, "Well, then I quit." Another executive intervened and a compromise was reached, wherein the rack was placed in an unused area of the new space.[83]

These kinds of low-level conflicts could prove to be a sore spot and involve the arbitration of the publisher or editor in chief. Below the managing editor on many larger newspapers sat the city editor, who was often "permitted full authority over the local news and personnel," and who helped interpret and direct policy as set by the managing editor for the various section editors. He or she could also operate as the point of contact for the "eternal struggle between the composing room and the editorial department."[84] But city editors who acted counter to a managing editor's wishes, including firing entry-level reporters without consulting their immediate boss, could find themselves in trouble.[85] In smaller daily newsrooms, the managing editor shared power with other editors more equally. The larger the newspaper, the more power was disbursed or negotiated. In any event, editorial power dynamics might best be seen in a more concrete example.

### ROBERT DARNTON AT THE *NEW YORK TIMES*

Robert Darnton, reflecting on his experiences as a young *New York Times* reporter in the early 1960s, noted that reporters and editors engaged in a delicate dance of shared agency. Editors knew how to manipulate a subtle reward system "from the other end of the room," though how this worked was not always clear to reporters. Upon getting a run-of-the-mill story, Darnton explains, a reporter could "[console] himself with the hope that he might get a better assignment . . . but . . . [know] that the story did not make his stock rise with the assignment editor."[86]

For a more important story, a city editor or other assigning editor might purposefully make his way over to a reporter's desk and "discuss the story with him in a kind of conspiratorial huddle before a sea of eyes." If the editor did not like the copy that the reporter wrote, he would summon the reporter back to his desk via the public-address system. The reporter would meet the editor in "enemy territory" and then walk back through a room full of appraising peers. After writing a version of the story that he felt was closer to his editor's perspective, but still reflected some of his own thoughts, he might worry about his position with the editor. In either case, "he does not enjoy walking the tightrope between his desk and the city editor before the crowd of reporters waiting for his status to drop."

Younger reporters felt this power differential more than older ones. Many learned "to escape to the bathroom or to crouch behind drinking fountains when the hungry eye of the editor surveys the field." Editors used this discomfiture, and the competitiveness among their reporters, to their advantage. Reporters tended to wish for their rivals to get so-so assignments or to fail on important ones. Editors knew this and would "sometimes try to get the best effort out of their men by . . . advocating values like competitiveness and 'hustling.'"[87] In one example:

> "Did you see how Smith handled that garbage story?" the city editor will say to Jones. "That's the kind of work we need from the man who is going to fill the next opening in the Chicago bureau. You should hustle more." Two days later, Jones may have outdone Smith. The immediacy

> and the irregularity of reinforcement in the assignment-publication process mean that no one, except a few stars, can be sure of his status in the newsroom.[88]

The situation at the *Times* was exacerbated by that newsroom's status in American journalistic culture. Not every newsroom was as intensely competitive.

But editors at other large metropolitan dailies were aware of similar tendencies among their reporters and, to different degrees, were capable of manipulating them. Too much of this could lead to "peer-group solidarity [developing] as a counter-force to the competitiveness." This development could, in turn, lead to a rift between even newsroom veterans and editors, with the former thinking that the latter were guilty of "selling out to management and for losing contact with the down-to-earth reality that can only be appreciated by honest 'shoe-leather men.' This anti-management ideology [created] a barrier to the open courting of editors and [made] some reporters think that they write only to please themselves and their peers.[89]

### EDITORS' SHIFTING POWER

Many sources of conflict animated newsroom life, but most revolved around issues of hiring, firing, retention, and pay. In the days before HR departments, newsrooms would handle hiring through word-of-mouth and on an as-needed basis. This was done on the spot with little in the way of formal interviews. Sometimes a reporter would be asked to go through a brief trial, or be told to track down a lead, as a kind of final test. References would sometimes be called. But otherwise news workers were hired by editors haphazardly. Applicants took care to be deferential to their potential employer.[90] Personality fit and experience mattered more than college education or formal vetting.

A senior editor was the "Man Who Hires and Fires," in the words of a self-deprecating newspaper librarian.[91] A key aspect of the boss-worker dynamic in many American newsrooms during the early to mid-twentieth century was the stark power difference between editors and reporters. As has been explored elsewhere, the arrival of unions in the early 1930s tempered the power of the editors. The economic reality was that firing an experienced, unionized reporter could be an expensive proposition, due to the required severance pay a union contract demanded and the time expenditure involved in training a replacement.

Some editors worried about the erratic standards that guided their decision making. "Too often the editor does not know just what he wants, or why," noted James Pope, managing editor of the *Louisville Courier-Journal*, in 1947. "He cannot explain to the confused youngster what was wrong, what was right." Facing competition from radio, editors had to do better, he urged.[92] It was believed that the city editor (an often vaguely defined position only just below that of the managing editor's) was best suited for the actual rituals of hiring. A reporter was considered more loyal (at least by some city editors) if he or she possessed a "consciousness that the man who gives him his orders is the man who gave him his job and who, within a somewhat more limited range than heretofore, can take his job away from him." Even if the city editor was not able to hire at will, it was considered good internal policy to have the managing editor check with various department heads before hiring a new staff member.[93]

Likewise, editors in different departments at some larger newspapers would "very carefully channelize authority to maintain administrative order," avoid wasted effort, and reduce personality-driven conflict.[94] Editors would continue to complain of newfound union prerogatives to influence, object to, or at least limit their power.[95] Even sympathetic editors who agreed that the Guild and other unions had a role in newsrooms believed that they themselves still needed to retain some kind of control over wages and hours, and that they could do a better job than a union representative at determining staffing levels.[96] The union intervened and restructured the dynamic between reporters and editors, altering the critical "individual relationship between the writer and editor," these editors believed.[97]

By the early 1920s some editors were frustrated by what they felt were wasteful tendencies in hiring reporters. The "employing factotum" would ask if a casual applicant was a "desk man or a street man," the new hire was "broken in," but then would quit a few weeks later or was fired because "he cannot make good." A second new hire would replace the first, meaning two salaries would be paid for the same job over the course of a week.[98] "In cities off the main run," such as El Paso, Texas, the turnover for a telegraph editor could be as frequent as every week and a half. In one instance, a managing editor returned from an absence of three months to find just two familiar faces. While rarely this extreme, a lack of familiarly between middle-level leadership and lower-level editors and reporters involved "disruption of the entire force."

Moving staff members around, the active management of reporters, the use of meetings, good pay, encouragement, life insurance, and other quality-of-life factors like maintaining a clean, well-lit, and well-ventilated office, were thought to help with retention. No longer could you let the "editorial department just run itself." An "efficiency system" had to be put in place.[99] "Efficiency" systems were, of course, a long-running fad in the industry beginning around the turn of the century and continuing through the 1950s.[100] Some of this concern was driven not by worries about how workers were being treated but by anxiety about maintaining healthy profit margins in a competitive industry.

Editors were aware that they sometimes had limited actual day-to-day control over the movements of their reporters once they left the newsroom. Many otherwise "hard-boiled" editors also knew their own capacity for misjudgments with personnel.[101] Mistakes could cost stories, readership, advertising dollars, and ultimately revenue. But abundant self-confidence was more common. To achieve their positions, editors had to survive office purges, multiple moves across a region or the country, and sometimes treacherous newsroom politics. While "superior to the average reporter because he can answer all his questions," a middle-grade editor was less important to the newsroom hierarchy than a managing or other senior editor. But ultimately a good midlevel editor "recognizes his readers' appetites and dishes it up a la mode."[102]

Editors valued their independence and resisted efforts to become "reduced to the ignoble status of a floor-walker and glad-hander for the Advertising Department." Succumbing to business pressure would lower "his respect for his own paper and his own work may be destroyed."[103] An ideal newspaper, at least from the perspective of many editors, would operate with only minimal influence from the business staff. This world, "in which the men from the advertising department are not permitted to enter the editorial rooms, and where the business manager merely agrees with everything the managing editor does," was the aspiration.[104] The reality could be more complex than some editors would have liked, however. During the Depression, newsroom managers felt compelled by necessity to collaborate more with the business side of the newspaper. No longer could they function "in watertight compartments."[105]

### EDITOR POWER: PAY AND REWARDS

Issues of pay were flashpoints of newsroom tension between reporters and editors. The former were often either confused or frustrated by the latter's apparent stinginess, and the latter either felt pressure from ownership to keep payroll costs down or genuinely felt some workers did not deserve pay raises. This was especially the case if managers had requested raises from management but had been turned down themselves. Conflict was sometimes tied to bylines, which for the first few decades of the century implied a definite status in the newsroom. Considered a "rarity" on many papers, they were "only given as a reward for a scoop or a story written with a special flair." But because "they were bestowed with no prior notice by the city editor," this became a "tormenting tradition that all local reporters believed had been designed to make their lives a misery and drive them to drink."[106] As discussed earlier, editors often held the final power over this act of peer (and public) recognition, to the chagrin of reporters. It was not until the awarding of bylines had become more routine, by the late 1950s and early to mid-1960s, that their connection to pay and status (due to the continued effect of Guild and other union contracts) became less associated with editor-reporter confrontations.[107] Some editors also simply avoided conversations about pay, a passive approach satirized by cartoonists.[108]

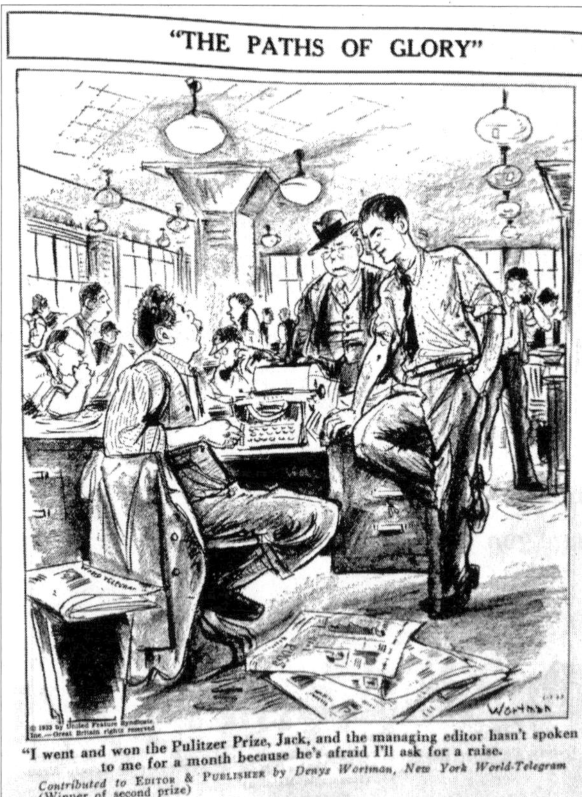


Figure 9. "The paths of glory," *Editor & Publisher,* April 21, 1934, 17. In this cartoon by Denys Wortman, of the *New York World-Telegram,* an ambitious reporter is kvetching to a peer about their editor.

Figure 10. "I need a two-dollar raise," *Editor & Publisher*, September 8, 1956, 34. Editors as well as reporters felt the need for raises at midcentury, as unionization in some papers (but not all, especially in the South) meant that salaries could vary wildly.

While many editors avoided or stubbornly refused to budge on raise requests, others took a more proactive approach. An editor at the *Buffalo Courier-Express* urged his peers to reward reporters with bylines more often, instead of only discussing stories at length when "you want to 'bawl them out.'" Giving five-dollar or other small raises with an admonition to "keep up the good work" could be more effective for retaining quality reporters than ignoring or lambasting them. This also had to come with a willingness to cut staffers who were "dead timber . . . drawing large salaries and not worth a tinker's damn but kept on for sentimental reasons."[109]

Low pay could discourage reporters, since many less-educated workers, including auto mechanics, or any number of workers on the mechanical side of a newspaper, could make more per hour, especially before the Guild asserted itself. As one managing editor noted in 1927, "We already have too many editors and not enough good stuff to edit."[110] The largest newspapers, such as the *Los Angeles Times*, could regularly raise pay across the staff, even in the midst of economic downturns as severe and prolonged as the Depression.

These kinds of standardized pay raises rewarded "particularly brilliant work, long service or [were used] to encourage promising young reporters on the staff."[111] They also demonstrated how variegated the industry was in terms of pay—in one city, reporters and editors could have wildly different salaries.

### EDITOR POWER: CONSTRAINED BY A CHANGING WORK CULTURE

During the interwar period and into the early Cold War, the US Department of Labor helped to differentiate the rank-and-file from their bosses. As has been noted elsewhere in this study, most American publishers, represented by the ANPA, argued for a "professional" status for news workers, while the Guild countered that the vast majority of workers were not "professional" because they lacked final control over their own work routines and products. As late as 1948 the ANPA's general counsel proposed that "executive" status be restricted for the purposes of contract negotiations to someone "who can hire or fire and directs the work of others and makes at least $30 a week," and that an additional status, that of "administrator," be defined as someone who worked for an executive and was "engaged in transporting goods or performs responsible outside work of a specialized or technical nature and makes at least $200 a month."

This widening of a "professional" status would exempt more workers from nonexecutive standing (and thus union membership). Publishers chafed under industry codes and later more permanent federal rules that limited their ability to define this status.[112] While this definitional tussle related to boss-worker tensions during early newsroom unionization, clashes over what constituted the best path toward professionalization (and whether news workers could and should aspire toward a "profession") would continue through the century.[113]

More to the immediate point, however, many publishers continued to view reporters as working independently, "beyond immediate control," due to the "creative nature" of newsroom work. They argued that reporters could, in fact, act as "their own bosses, regulating their own time" and were "inspired and motivated in their production efforts by considerations that are intellectual and creative." Their work was *not* measured by quantity alone, the Associated Press Managing Editors (APME) claimed, as was the work of "non-professional workers." The Guild disagreed strongly, citing a 1927 essay by H. L. Mencken:

> [The journalist] remains, for all his dreams, a hired man—the owner downstairs, or even the business manager, though he doesn't do it very

> often now, is still free to demand his head—and the hired man is not a professional man. . . . even the most competent journalists face at all times a severe competition, easily expanded at need, and cannot afford to be too saucy.[114]

Of course, newsroom life had changed considerably in the years since 1927. But the Guild's case was bolstered by previous federal appeals court rulings, as well as by federal policy that defined reporters as not being professional workers due to a failure to meet then-traditional benchmarks of professional status (examination for entry to the occupation, a license to practice, a mandatory college education, and so on).[115]

For all that, news workers successfully pushed back against claims that they were not "professional" people. This influenced newsroom hiring practices and led, in time, to a flattening of hierarchies of power. A more systematized process for hiring reporters was in place by the end of the 1940s, in which editors worked with reporters who were "better trained, more carefully chosen, [and were] prayed and watched over for the first sign of flair for any specialty of the business." Editors still tended to "lean heavily on the instinctive newspaperman who recognizes the exceptional story, handles it competently and plays it hard before the competition realizes what has happened." In other words, they relied on the "veteran," a critical resource in many newsrooms, where the difference between lower-echelon editors and experienced reporters could be a narrow one, at least in terms of experiences.[116] Editors believed that they had a quick and even innate ability to "discern a promising young newspaperman."[117] Knowing how to reward that reporter—and knowing when to do so—was an additional talent.[118]

### EDITOR POWER: CURTAILED BY "HUMAN RESOURCES"

By the 1950s, and even earlier, "scientific hiring" with help from HR departments, sometimes called "personnel administration," was increasingly advocated by editors. Screening an applicant would help "avoid hiring the glib youngster who may make a good showing in his early years and then turn into the office drunk because basically he didn't have the stamina, the drive, the integrity and character for the work." While not all editors appreciated or liked the power of an HR department, others felt it provided a more convenient and efficient means to organize and staff larger newspapers than previously existing practices.[119]

Despite this trend, an editor at a 1955 panel on personnel and recruiting observed the slow pace of adoption of more modern personnel departments, claiming that with more than 275,000 workers in the industry, "an appalling amount of mediocrity finds its way into our organizations because of hit and miss methods of screening, hiring, training and handling of staff."[120] Retaining good staff members involved creating opportunities for the development of new skills "over and beyond the routine . . . when he [a new reporter] first got the job," argued a journalism professor on the same panel. Enhancing "mobility in the newsroom" for new staff members, and the chance to be "a useful cog in the news machine," was crucial to the overall functioning of the newspaper.[121] As concerns about recruitment manifested themselves in the 1950s, editors fretted continually about competition with radio and TV newsrooms. New newsmagazines also sought recruits from print journalism, as did corporations such as General Electric, General Motors, and Westinghouse, which had large and expanding advertising and public-relations departments that could outcompete any salary and incentives the newspaper industry could muster.[122] In more traditional fields, such as law and medicine, a young hire was made to feel like he could "he can stand on his own feet, if he will, and gain a sense of personal status and, thus, of personal satisfaction." In journalism, it was harder to establish the same "human relations with the organization."[123] Editors were trying to compete with these industries in terms of pay and prestige, and scrambled to adjust their own attitudes and behaviors toward the labor market. Other editors during this era worried that "the level in our seed bin is going down" in the competition with other white-collar jobs. With "uncomfortably empty application files," even the military had begun to seem preferable to life in the newsroom. A woman reporter had left to join the Air Force, decried one editor: "We didn't blame her. It seems that our newsroom couldn't compete with the marriage opportunities of an army camp." For too long publishers had tried to pay their reporters in "romance instead of cash," with "wampum, glass beads and cigar coupons," while paying their composing-room staffs competitively.[124] In this more white-collar environment, though, editors had to treat reporters better, and not just in terms of pay, if they hoped to keep them.

## MANAGEMENT CULTURE: OFFICES, AND OTHER FORMS OF DISCIPLINE AND CONTROL

Long before the 1950s some editors had actively resisted their tyrannical image and asked for the walls to literally come down between themselves and their staff. Management culture was changing. Merritt Bond, a managing editor at the *New York Evening Post*, insisted on moving from his "goldfish bowl" of an office to a desk "out [in] the center of activities." Sitting within "arm's length" of his telegraph and city editors, this editor wanted to avoid a "cyclonic" style and instead insisted on using praise and cooperation. It was his duty, he thought, "to strive for [a more] co-operative effort than to boss."[125] By contrast, editors who worked out of private offices, unless they were titular editors in chief, risked being labeled "pseudo-hermit[s]."[126] In this vein, O. O. McIntyre observed that after World War I, "the boss who thunders orders at an underling is likely to receive in reply a quaint travel suggestion not included in Cook's itinerary." Lower-level managers, including city editors, had found that getting reporters to work *with* them instead of just *for* them made for a happier newsroom dynamic.[127]

The representation of the fearsome editor gradually gave way to depictions of him as the "captain of a team, a captain who plays as hard a game as his teammates."[128] Being in the "thick of things," as when the editor of the *St. Louis Times* ordered that his desk be moved to an airfield during an air race, was another way of describing the better kind of editor.[129] The city editor, or other senior editor, had the "dual responsibility of getting news and handling a large body of men." This meant that he had to be a "cross between a steel trap and encyclopedia," who needed to know as many movers and shakers as possible, along with a fair collection of people from less wealthy walks of life. His telephone should "always be jingling."[130]

The "perfectly poised director," such as Edward S. Beck, the mellow managing editor of the *Chicago Tribune*, was the new model. Beck acted "like the general who directs the battle, and affairs move so swiftly that one is scarcely conscious of the power [of] leadership which he exhibits." Directing activity from the middle of things, and not from the corner office, meant that regular staffers could have "the greatest confidence in his fairness," as well as access to the boss. This was in an era when most reporters rightly believed that a typical "managing editor hardly knew they were on the payroll" and had a habit of doing "spasmodic things."[131]

The managing editor of the *Chicago Evening American* after World War I found this to be the case, at least according to a profile in *Editor & Publisher*. His "boys" gave him their "100 percent esteem" and insisted they "work with, not for him." He kept his staff's "confidence in a quiet, unassuming way, and without the slightest apparent consciousness of the importance of his own position in the local room," partially due to his insistence on "working right with his men out at the battered news desk." Reports like these are almost *too* glowing—after all, *Editor & Publisher* was a pro-management publication.

Figure 11. Johnny Anderson, "Circus day," Editor & Publisher, April 20, 1940, 36. Editors felt pressure to perform social roles not in their official job descriptions, including recruiter, morale officer, life coach, friend, and, of course, "boss."

But there was some truth to the idea of working with the troops as a way of gaining their trust and affection. Eschewing the private office was a way to gain the respect of lower-level editors and reporters.[132] Separate offices were a sign of achievement and status. They provided privacy in an open work environment. Throughout the era, they belonged exclusively to senior-level editors, some star columnists, cartoonists, and ownership.[133] To purposively give these up meant something. British visitors to American newsrooms noticed this, too. Representatives of the Newspaper Society of Britain marveled at American innovations like a heavier reliance on rewrite staff, horseshoe desks for copy editors, and the universality of cigarette butts, ice-water dispensers, and air conditioning, so much so in the latter case that "architects are not concerned with windows." But among their most intriguing observations was of the open floor plan and the role editors played in it. "Editors have no private room," they noted. They thought that the idea was to motivate reporters, and in their words: "'See that guy there! We have him right on the floor, so's the other fellas see they can be managing editor too!'"[134]

Younger editors were more inclined to lead from the front. As a twenty-two-year-old managing editor argued in 1925, his place was "in the news room from 7:30 in the morning until the final edition has gone." The same editor found that he "can't keep in fighting trim and on his toes unless he knows every major story going over the desks," and believed that "only constant leadership in the news room brings about the proper fighting organization." The "old routine methods" needed invigoration, and part of that came from direct leadership.[135] To a generation of reporters and editors who had experienced World War I, this perspective made sense. After World War II, it would continue to resonate.

Some publishers noted a decline in the older and more paternalistic management approach, in which the publisher (or, in some cases, a senior editor) acted as "the Old Man" and "father confessor, fixer, and financier." They blamed the Guild and unionization, but also an increasing emphasis on chain ownership. The "thinning of that tie between the employe[e] and the boss" meant that there were fewer publishers and senior editors who would "keep a man on the payroll long after his useful days are past and find him work that will not lower the man's respect for himself." Instead, a distant and corporate approach was taking over, in which profit margins and "'strictly business' methods" were encouraging a removed, though recognizably modern, office dynamic. Some publishers went further and blamed this new environment for rising conflict between ownership and the Guild.[136] A flashpoint for this concern was the 1937–1938 Guild strike of the *Brooklyn Eagle.*

*Editor & Publisher*'s Arthur Robb believed that such strikes were endemic in this new, more hostile environment. The "old paternalism" was being replaced by interactions conducted on a "complete[ly] impersonal basis."[137] It should be noted that this move to corporatized leadership was slowed briefly during World War II. Because editors were sometimes considered "essential men" and were often older than their reporters, copy editors, photographers, or copy boys, they did not face the draft in as many numbers as these latter. Of course, younger editors could be drafted. But for those who remained, including managing editors and other senior newsroom supervisors, double duty was expected, with some acting as copy editors to help make workforce ends meet. Throughout this time, editors continued to work more than the Guild-mandated five days a week.

### MANAGEMENT CULTURE: BEST PRACTICES FOR "GOOD" NEWSROOMS

Ideal editors, "the plain unvarnished short-sleeved editors," were regarded as earthy but engaged with their staffs and readers alike.[138] These idealized editors worked long hours, did not force their ideas for stories on reporters (unless they judged it necessary), refined content but did not overedit it, and inspired their people to greatness, which could include awards but mostly consisted of the creation of a healthy work environment where personalities collaborated instead of conflicted. The better editors in mid-twentieth-century American newsrooms recognized the importance of turning their reporters' abilities toward stories, and not against each other or in opposition to their bosses.

The age and backgrounds of editors, like those of all newsroom denizens, could vary wildly. Generally, however, editors were older, often former reporters, and, as time went on, college graduates. There were always exceptions, of course. Some managing editors were exceptionally young. But while "the boy wonder" was perhaps not as wondrous a phenomenon as it once was by the early 1930s, especially on smaller papers, it was still a comparative rarity. In a field known for its physically and mentally demanding nature, gray hair often meant that a reporter had transitioned to the role of an editor.[139] They had undergone years of newsroom rituals, including working overnight or early-morning shifts. The "dog watch," or "lobster-trick" overnight position was sometimes used as a way to test out an up-and-coming reporter-turned editor.[140] As one editor explained, looking back on his career, which included years as a reporter, "traditions were baked into a reporter's marrow, and by the time he was offered a promotion to editor he was in no doubt about what his paper stood for, and how and why its standards had to be fiercely protected."[141]

### MANAGEMENT CULTURE: "GOOD NIGHT" RITUALS

In "an extremely healthy situation" a reporter rose to management not by taking shortcuts but by "pulling an oar along with the other galley slaves."[142] The norms that governed day-to-day routines in newsrooms could center on the most mundane things. As Arthur Gelb reflected back on his life in the 1940s at the *New York Times*, he observed that even "quirky habits" were accepted "if they did not impede the sacred task of getting the paper out on time." Insubordination, however, was "dealt with severely." At the *Times*, as on many other papers, an unofficial rule called for reporters to check in with their editors before leaving, and not to go home "until you received a 'good night' from the editor." Leaving without it "was tantamount to a felony." The ritual was not unreasonable, since it gave the editor an opportunity to raise questions about a reporter's copy before he departed for the night. Because reporters were otherwise hard to reach, this ritual was not just about control—it was necessitated by the paper's relentless production schedule.

One evening, a reporter failed to tell Bruce Rae, the city editor, "good night." This reporter was known as "the gumshoe," since he "served as in-house informer," digging up unsavory details on those in the ranks who had caused trouble for management. For this reason, of course, he was uniformly despised by both reporters and editors. Rae dispatched a clerk to retrieve the errant reporter:

> "What's it about?" Gordon [the reporter] asked, assuming there was some hot story or other breaking [news]. "I don't know," said the clerk, "but you'd better get back, quick!" Gordon dashed for the subway and started the long commute from his home to Times Square, raced to the city room and presented himself at Rae's desk, breathless. "What's up?" he asked of what seemed to be a strangely calm city editor perusing some paperwork. Without looking up, Rae paused a moment and said, simply, "Good night."[143]

Editors sensed that demanding obedience in small matters like this would pay off later. They knew, too, that conceding too much too soon could result in an unmotivated newsroom. Unlike other occupations, daily print journalism was not as merciful to those who rose through the ranks by marrying into the owner's family or through office politics. While those kinds of maneuverings still helped, many editors prided themselves on at least the aspirational idea that their work ethic and ability to lead newsroom staffs had led to their promotions. Many city editors and other senior leaders believed they had survived being "scorched by the same flames" they ordered their "assistants to plunge" into every day. Fakes could be easily spotted:

> For all his suavity and dignity, or for all his brusqueness, and bark, the word circulates that "he's never done what we're doing; he hasn't been up against the things we're running into." Newspaper folk are independent enough, irreverent enough, to enjoy letting "the boss" know what they think of him. If he is executive in fact as well as name, he must be genuine.[144]

City editors knew their communities, friends of the paper and reliable sources, as well as those outside actors who could be manipulative, including political figures. Editors also knew the paper's policies, readership, and people. Editors needed the fresh talent and perspective that new reporters could bring to a staff. Considering this, it made sense for new reporters to stay on staff in order to get properly acculturated to their newsrooms. This allowed them to get used to, and then work more effectively with, their peers and bosses.[145] A belief in potential could motivate both groups.

Contemporaries believed that newsroom bosses should "blend the work of always disparate groups, talented, creative and sometimes temperamental," including the composing-room staff and the editorial staff, who tended to have contact "most often during moments of tension." Getting the paper published through the day's multiple editions involved the work of a personality "conductor," who could "create harmony of persons and their products."[146] This metaphor of music making was apt in an era of big bands with equally big personalities.

When it came to controlling their staffs, some editors were subtle and avoided direct confrontation, appealing instead to powerful peer pressure to conform. The managing editor of the *Chicago Daily News*, when faced with the prospect of losing reporters to another paper due to higher salaries, counseled that an editor appeal to newsroom friendships, and to tell the reporter in question, "You are not going. You belong with this gang and you are going to stay here." The idea was "to convince that fellow that he was just adventuring when he moved away."[147] Under deadline pressure, savvy editors had another tactic for controlling their workers: simply standing close to them. "A newspaper reporter in civilian life is inclined to believe that he is working 'under fire' when the city editor, standing behind him as he writes 'hot' copy near deadline, tears short takes from his typewriter almost as fast as the reporter puts a period to a sentence," wrote a US Marine Corps correspondent.[148]

### MANAGEMENT CULTURE: THE UNLIKELY POWER OF BULLETIN BOARDS

Bulletin boards were a communal space, often regulated by editors and management, but showing workers' spunk too. Particularly active reporters were recognized through notes tacked to them.[149] Prizes or praises could be posted. Important changes in newsroom policies, including the introduction of the five-day workweek, were noted on these boards.[150] Less kind, or conflict averse, editors preferred edicts on boards to in-person announcements, but some used both. And while satirical signs could be posted in other parts of the newsroom, it was the bulletin board that garnered the most attention.[151] News workers knew that these boards were read by everyone, and were thus the best place to post jokes or wordplay. Reporters pushed back against their bosses with their own unauthorized protests via written or typed messages. As sites of newsroom discourse, the boards belonged to both parties.

Editors as much as reporters engaged in "relentlessly" chiding each other, but especially beginners, for errors in newsroom routine or clueless early attempts at imitating a newspaper's unique style.[152] Editors were also easy targets of this kind of teasing. Managing editors, wrote a *Quill* columnist in 1942, were "housebroken . . . and know the kidneys can't stand anything stronger than milk." Self-possessed city editors tended to be "ambitious young men who can handle eight telephones at a time but only one blond." And managing editors, again, could not really wrangle their cubs, even if they were "fortified by the publisher and a writ of habeas corpus."[153] Awarding nicknames, too, was the informal specialty of editors and senior reporters, who shared in the ability to christen new reporters.[154] Junior staff were singled out and incorporated into a newsroom's community through this process.

Figure 12. "Yesterday's news today," *Editor & Publisher*, April 21, 1934, 92. The editor-as-lion metaphor was common in newsroom memoirs, cartoons, and even poetry—powerful and pernicious, but also somehow human and fragile.

### MANAGEMENT CULTURE: A SHIFT TO LIMITED COLLABORATION

Concerns about newsroom staff recruiting and retention in the late 1950s again focused attention in journalism's trade journals on the dynamic between supervisor and reporter. As an editor for the *Washington Star* put it, "the biggest factor in any man's morale is his relationship with his immediate boss." This relationship depended on recognizing the reporter "as a human being, with his peculiarities and idiosyncrasies, not as just another piece of office machinery." Encouragement, opportunities to improve, and increasing responsibility helped to maintain a healthy rapport between boss and reporter.[155] At meetings on how to stem the flow of talented young people out of newspaper journalism, editors were told that more individual care and attention, conducting exit interviews, "finding out what makes" workers "tick," and developing relationships could help. "Get to them," one panelist urged, "Get to know them. Everybody will understand much better. You'll be amazed at how they'll decide you're not such a bad guy after all, and really interested in them."[156] With the avowed goal of avoiding grinding a "reporter into revulsion," interest could be expressed via the sharing of reporters' stories around the newsroom, and recognizing that good work involved more than a byline. Bonus pay could help, but so could backing up reporters in "controversial situations" with upper-level management. As a rule, too, "the older an employee, the more he has to be led, rather than pushed."[157]

Despite the occasionally autocratic nature of newsroom relationships between management and workers, there was often an underlying ethic of democratic input, at least among near peers. As early as the 1920s, some newspapers took great pride in labeling their newsrooms "democratic."[158] This was often an idealized ethic, but was claimed nonetheless in the rhetoric of editors like Norman Shaw, associate editor of the *Cleveland Press*. A "firm believer in what we call democracy in the news room," Shaw believed this meant that "everybody can offer ideas and criticism to anybody; that the editor himself should not be locked up or even put away in a corner in his office, and that you should be able to see him without having to make an appointment with his secretary." This principle of accessibility—not authority—extended to sharing ideas. "A good newspaper is built on ideas and the more people who are offering ideas, the better it is," declared Shaw. A copy boy or girl should be able to "catch the managing editor or the city editor at the drinking fountain or on his wanderings around the room" for a quick conversation. Some of the architecture of the day sought to inspire this democratic mingling, as Nikil Saval explores in his study of early to midcentury American workplaces.[159] Newsroom management guides also emphasized the democratic nature of the newsroom. "Industry has become more social minded," and therefore there was more interest in training, claimed one such text: "Everyone in a democracy must have equal opportunity to improve himself and his family according to his ability."[160]

Reporters were integral to a newspaper's daily operation, and an editor could not "function were it not for the reporter."[161] Due to their more stationary (or as some of their reporters might argue, sedentary) nature, editors could lose touch with the world outside their newsroom, becoming "mahogany-bound hermits." Aware of this old concern, editors were told to cultivate their reporters' gossipy tendencies, in order to avoid ending up like chairbound department store executives. Reporters should be encouraged, a crime reporter noted in 1937, to "bring him [the editor] all the gossip, all the street-talk, even all the dirty stories that they may hear."[162] A good editor would listen in on conversations, contribute to them, and be seen casually engaging with reporters throughout the newsroom.

To outsiders, editors and reporters tended to emphasize their better collaborative selves. In *Without Fear or Favor*, a 1940 book that profiled the journalism industry for the public, newsroom staff members were portrayed as "fast-functioning machines, one of the most competent of this age of efficiency. The reporter and his city editor are quiet, capable, and educated gentlemen."[163] While they might deviate from this refined characterization, most newsroom mangers and reporters were keen to be perceived as advocating for their readers.[164] Internally, they would highlight conflict, but even then mutual reliance was held up as the better path.

A kind of craft pride in mentorship also connected some reporters more closely to their editors. This pride often came from the top down, as when a "long-suffering" city editor from a newspaper in Sheboygan, Wisconsin, proud that he had "broken in quite an array of new men," urged young reporters to "try to pick a good boss, keep your feet on the ground the first couple of years and be fair to your city editor, because he will be fair to you." Loyalty to editors could manifest itself in refusals to accept better offers on other papers.[165]

Loyalty that led to mentorship benefited reporters because they could gain newswriting skills more quickly and thoroughly. Reporters chosen for unofficial mentorships could advance quickly in their careers, getting plumb assignments or good beats. While this could come with some accompanying resentment from their peers, reporters weighed this against the potential pluses. From the editors' perspective, they could develop reliable and loyal workers. Positive interactions between workers and their bosses were ideally also interesting, for both parties, and not just a kind of duty. As *Editor & Publisher*'s Marlen Pew explained, it was a "deadly thing to work for a dull person in the newspaper business, mainly because ideas are our stock and trade and to lack them is to lack all."

As a young cub reporter, Pew had an editor who took a personal interest in marking his reporters' stories. They were "used by the chief as the basis of pungent, humanistic notes addressed to members of the staff, roasting the tar out of them when they blundered, praising them for strokes of genius, suggesting this and that, and in generally keeping red hot the contact between the editor and the men who worked for him." This kind of commentary built newsroom morale and was "proof that the good chief was not asleep at the switch."[166] As collaboration could be informal most of the time, overt displays of camaraderie could be rare. It might take a citywide disaster, such as a flood, in which all hands were needed and appreciated, to help reporters feel better connected to their editors. The closing of a newspaper could also move emotionally reticent workers and bosses to express appreciation for each other.[167] If an editor suddenly died in an accident or of natural causes—and editors passed away not too uncommonly from heart disease or strokes on the job, that is, "in harness"—reporters would grieve the loss of their "chief."[168] Stress was thought to be a leading contributing factor to editors' mortality rate.[169] Because editors, especially senior editors, were expected to be present or on call, taking vacations could be challenging. This was especially the case on smaller newspapers.[170] In one instance in the summer of 1956 in Chicago, two city editors on the same newspaper died in rapid succession.[171] More happily, national recognition via journalism awards, or coverage of a story of national import, could foster newsroom bonds. Such acts of newsroom affection included profiles of staffers, impromptu parties, group visits to local bars, bonuses from management to editors and reporters alike, or just quick huddles of casual conversation in the midst of the newsroom workspace.[172]

### A NEW NEWSROOM: THE ADVENT OF "PERSONNEL RELATIONS"

As management strategies shifted with the postwar world, human resource managers and departments claimed that refined "scientific" methods would help newspapers retain quality staff and quell labor strife. Toward that end, the Newspaper Personnel Relations Association was formed in 1949 and held its first convention that year. Donald Wood, an early proponent of the use of then-new HR methods in newsrooms, wrote *Newspaper Personnel Relations*, a textbook for newsroom HR managers, a few years later.[173] It foreshadows later management texts, and, as noted elsewhere in this chapter, the resulting concern that corporate interests and attitudes were permeating newsroom culture.[174] But it was also part of an existing, if niche, subgenre within then-existing journalism literature. Published by the Newspaper Research Bureau, Wood's book was intended for supervisors, reporters, and journalism students. But because it outlines how to administer an internal personnel-management and training program, it is really designed for junior bosses, specifically the versatile "department heads," whose actual job was to hire and fire. Wood acknowledges that most newspapers did not and would not have the resources to run a dedicated HR department, but his solution was to encourage the creation of more concrete management and training programs.

With the exception of a handful of pioneering efforts, such as at the *Milwaukee Journal* in the late 1940s, the majority of newspapers, even larger dailies, leaned heavily on their younger management for the day-to-day indoctrination and supervision of reporters. In Wood's study, less than a third of ninety-four newspapers surveyed had an HR department, and instead deferred the job of management and training to these junior or middle-grade supervisors.[175] Newspapers had, of course, long been slow to adopt more formal business-management methods, or what Wood called "scientific personnel programming," from other industries.[176]

But that was changing. Before the 1950s, "more attention was given to [the processes of] editing, manufacturing and selling newspapers, than to the human beings who were the newspapermen responsible for the publisher's success," Wood claimed. Those former times, "when more attention was given to machines than to human beings," were gone, and, by the early 1950s, the newspaper industry was starting to adopt best practices from other fields. These recognized "that the greatest wealth of any and all business is . . . the human beings in the organization."[177] Among these was the field of public relations, whose firms were believed to be good models for management practices despite tensions with journalism.

In his text, Wood discusses the need "to break in a new man," emphasizing how important it was to introduce a news worker to the publisher, if possible, but also to the editor, the advertising director, and all available department heads. Workers should be made to feel "at home" and "part of the family."[178] In an era of increasingly depersonalized relationships, his choice of metaphors is telling. While management and labor forces were keen to move on from an older, more paternalistic model, the desire to preserve a familial level of interaction lingered. Wood believed that a new hire's career began with these kinds of cozy introductions. These would give the new hire "a feeling of importance and loyalty at a time when it is necessary." That worker would "never forget the courtesy extended to him" and would be more effective as a result.[179]

The underlying goal of more systematized training was "maximum efficiency at minimum costs." This efficiency could come, Wood claimed, through better training. The middle of the century brought a "new era of management-employee relationship," one that had "resulted possibly through a more educated class of workers, a growing awareness by management of their responsibilities toward employees, unionization, and government intervention."[180] Wood believed that "most employees are driven by the basic desire to better themselves" and were eager to improve their pay, secure their current jobs, and gain more responsibility. It was important to involve both management and the rank-and-file in training sessions, and for the former to be responsive to feedback, because "the employees will not be sold" on the idea otherwise.[181]

Getting the "old-timers" involved, and going further and building a program around them, would help draw in younger, or newer, workers. A "wise manager" would recognize and work with this reality: the nature of newspaper work, with much of the hard-won, how-to knowledge passed on verbally, required the participation of peers. It was important for any training to take place on company time, because "most employees, no matter how conscientious and ambitious, are jealous of their leisure hours."[182] Alongside more informal meetings designed to train the trainers, other formats recommended by Wood included conferences and lectures. The former could help with the collection of material needed for handbooks, manuals, or new programs, and were the most effective at helping older workers pass on their knowledge. Lectures were less ideal, unless carefully planned, on topic, and short.[183] Other helpful elements of a training program, from management's point of view, included the use of in-house publications, which ranged from highly produced magazines to mimeographed sheets. Even an unassuming "house organ" could reduce labor strife. The use of "academic schooling" for one-off correspondence courses in newspaper management, advertising, "industrial relations," and "office procedure . . . benefits . . . the company as well."[184]

"Department heads should not expect miracles overnight" from their training, Wood advised. But "the pulse of the staff" could be quickened and morale generally improved, even if gradually, through it. Satisfied and better-trained workers ultimately needed less supervision. For supervisors doing the training, the goal was again to increase efficiency and reduce personnel costs by determining who was worth investing in for the long haul. Before, a lower-ranked editor or supervisor, the "sub-department head," was "the forgotten man of industry." Now newspapers needed to adopt a "scientific business management operation." Wood quotes the business manager of the *South Bend Tribune*, in Indiana, who called for faster selection and training of managers. Due to an aging management class, "personnel departments will be looking for young men who will be future department heads," he predicted.[185]

The team-based nature of newsroom work created opportunities for the delegation of authority, but not for ceding responsibility. Younger or newer editors were taught to use strategic praise of their workers, since it was the "greatest human relations tool available to any executive." As always, Wood tied this to the theme of efficiency: "decadence and inefficiency" were hallmarks of a poorly led and trained staff. Staffs could forget that "criticism, flattery, and public reprimand are taboo, and will kill the morale of any group." Power sharing, coupled with encouragement, brought "a feeling of belonging."[186]

While reeking a bit of pop psychology, even for its time, Wood's guide borrowed from then-current literature on personnel management (including material from the American Management Association) to emphasize the importance of open communication between workers and their supervisors, as well as workers' growing insistence on job security.[187] Various "security programs," including life and hospitalization insurance, severance pay, sick leave and pensions, helped keep workers happy with their bosses. A "progressive personnel program" provided information to newspaper workers about these kinds of benefits, which were new compared to other aspirational white-collar occupations.[188] Wood reiterated that a good personnel director also assisted with core functions such as staff selection, job introduction, training, and evaluations. Initial hiring was overwhelmingly done by department heads at most newspapers (only about 1 percent of the newspapers Wood surveyed deferred to nascent HR departments). But more general screening was done at newspapers, using batteries of aptitude tests, in combination with editors using their discretion. Perhaps the best early example of this could be found at the *Minneapolis Star and Tribune*, where Phillip J. Kruidenier worked as the paper's personnel director, pioneering more quantitative methods for staff selection. More often, if a newspaper possessed personnel staff, or editors with personnel as their collateral duty, their job was to track and train new hires brought in by department heads. Wood conceded that a more active role for any new HR departments or personnel-management programs would have to wait "for the future."[189]

## CONCLUSION: FROM DICTATORS TO MANAGERS

From the end of World War I through the start of the 1960s, the social and managerial roles of editors in the newsroom changed dramatically. While editors remained the "boss," they recognized that they functioned increasingly as a firm's managers and not as its dictators. Many still resisted, if not resented, the label of "manager" and continued to lead their staffs in idiosyncratic ways. But even these more traditional editors were less powerful than their predecessors. While they retained the ability to hire, fire, and direct the daily routines of reporters, photographers, lower-level copy editors, rewrite staff, and other support personnel, their power had been reduced and shared. Whereas before reporters lacked agency, they had developed much more their own power and had become far more assertive.[190] While not a workers' nirvana, the newsrooms of the 1950s and 1960s were places where reporters could do their work more independently, and where they had more hope of advancement and security. This affected management in several ways.

Newsroom bosses and management styles changed because the industry had changed, as had the wider business world around it. But more than that, the workers and the organizational structure of newspapers had changed. Newspapers were more complex, influenced by a broader corporatization and consolidation of business culture. The presence of HR departments and personnel directors were responses to these changes. And while middle management had existed for some time in American firms, newsrooms gradually adopted an intermediate class of bosses that meant most news workers did not directly encounter senior editors or ownership. At smaller newspapers, interactions with the latter groups continued to be the norm. But the larger dailies became ever more variegated and complex. A reporter would engage with some kind of "boss" only a few years older and more interested in his or her problems than with the editors of half a century before. This is not to overstate the professionalization process—reporters still had limited autonomy, and this had to be negotiated. Autonomy also varied greatly across newsrooms, especially smaller to midsized dailies.

While strikes and external conflict continued, some of the more explicit internal conflicts had diminished. Collaboration had become more common, and editors took more pains to get their staff to work *with*, rather than just *for*, them. Power-sharing rituals, such as the daily or weekly news conference, a more organized assignment system, and new technology tools such as the car and portable phone—covered in the next chapter—helped to inscribe these changing values into newsroom routines. As more reporters ascended the ranks to their own editorships, they brought these practices with them and normalized them. Editors no longer felt they had to, or even could, scream and shout to motivate their workers. They could let them work in peace and expect them to finish the work of reporting. If yelling was felt to be necessary, it could be done behind closed doors, and this was considered a better practice than a dressing down in front of the whole newsroom. As the occupation continued to aspire to a more "professionalized" standard, and as bylines became more common, newsroom bosses could control their workers in subtler ways, using the existing hierarchies of power already present in the newsroom. Control was still there. It had just grown more sophisticated, in ways that Warren Breed picked up on in his 1950s-era newsroom studies.

Editors had given up some of their power in the face of the newsroom's unionization. This dovetailed with editors' own white-collar aspirations. They, too, wanted a more balanced and well-compensated working life. Reflecting the rest of the country's middle management, and white-collar occupations in general, newsroom managers were still deeply embedded in the top of the hierarchy of power. But a general flattening of this power meant that reporters, previously portrayed as heroic underdogs, became more powerful. As Kevin Lerner has shown, the 1970s would witness the publication of dozens of new alternative journalism trade publications, reflecting a shift toward the reporter as the most important force in the newsroom.[191]

But severe problems remained. Many editors, and not just in the American South, resisted racial and gender integration and hired Black reporters and women only under duress, if at all. Despite pressure from publishers or senior editors, middle-ranking editors could be the worst offenders as creators and defenders of race- and gender-based barriers to entry, applying higher, unfair standards to African American applicants or women than to white men.[192] Others, however, could become staunch, in-the-trenches advocates for the hiring and retention of people of color and female news workers. In time, these latter groups would be represented in newsroom leadership (though long after the time period in question).

When imagining the future of the newsroom later in the century, editors believed their role would be as important if not more important than it was at the time studied here. Even as technology promised more mobile reporting, the coordination and control of stories was still expected to be under the purview of a team of editors.[193] As will be examined in the upcoming chapters on technology adoption in the newsroom and the impact of unionization on working life, editors remained vital to a newsroom's healthy cultural and working life. But their tyranny, if they ever exerted it completely, was over. They, and the newsroom, had mellowed.

Caught as they were in the shaping forces of newsroom social life, editors were not immune to the collective white-collar shift within journalism. While it would be a simplification to say that corporate middle management culture came to the newsroom's relational world of work and was both shaped by it and helped to shape those relationships, in some ways this did, in fact, occur. Granted, this process happened alongside many other influences, as noted above, but it is again critical to think of no one subgroup of the newsroom as totally isolated from any other—instead, their fates were deeply intertwined. A competent editor knew she or he had to motivate a desperate collection of individuals, and would do so by appealing to each group of workers in ways that were effective, whether that meant giving more flexibility in work hours to reporters, better onramps to newsroom careers for junior staff, or specialized roles for more senior members of that community.

Newsroom bosses were savvy force multipliers and massagers, authoritarians and egalitarians, sounding boards and distant, by turns. But they had learned these so-called soft skills, or relational awareness, from their own careers in the newsroom's communal universe. The remainder of this book will turn to the other forces impacting the social life of the newsroom during this era, namely, technology tools and unionization.

CHAPTER 7

# Technology and the Newsroom

## Phones, Cars, and Radio

AS A FIXTURE in the workday world of journalism, telephones connected those who gathered news with the newsroom staff that processed and produced it. They also connected those *inside* the newsroom with the larger networks of sources and rivals *outside* of it. Reporters telephoning the newsroom, or calling out of it, became a common motif in popular-culture representations of news work ("give me rewrite!"). Journalists' own accounts of their work lives sometimes matched Hollywood portrayals of the role telephones played, as suggested by this 1941 vignette:[1]

> *Elbowing a group of professional bondsmen away from the police blotter, the station reporter gets the framework for this story. Then he climbs up to his ivory tower [his press room] in the police station. He picks up his phone (a straight line to the newspaper's PBX board).*
>
> *"Hello, Sweetheart. Wake up and buzz the desk for me," he says familiarly.*
>
> *"Say, Mac, I've got a few paragraphs on drunk drivers and a new angle on that Tenth Avenue hold-up." (The C.E. signals a rewrite man, who puts on the earphones as the call is switched.)*
>
> *And back in his ivory tower the police reporter says "OK," bug-eyed and beetle-brained, "ready to take some arkmalarky on what our guardians of law and order are doing?"*
>
> *The man under the earphones replies, "Shoot the copy to me, Sloppy!" And the "crime author" glances at his scrawly notes and begins: "A man listed as . . ."*[2]

The telephone and other newsgathering technologies had been used in the newsroom since the late 1800s. But increasing access to them by the mid-1930s meant more agency and autonomy for news workers, now freed from having to either share phones with colleagues in the newsroom or fight for access to phones outside of it (at least not as much). Granted, not every newsroom was awash in phones. Increasingly, however, after 1920 reporters' phones became as common a vocational tool as typewriters. The car closely followed, and soon the two technologies were united, via radio, on an experimental basis in the "radio car." This latter technology allowed the reporter to increase his or her reach (and independence) beyond the newsroom. As "tethering" tools, these devices allowed for a more expansive, distributive journalism culture that set the scene for further disruptions brought by the computerization of the newsroom. This chapter briefly explores the adoption of disruptive technologies on newsroom relationships and news workers during the twentieth century.

## SITUATING TECHNOLOGY IN THE NEWSROOM

The adoption of the phone and car as reporting tools accelerated a trend in US journalism in the early part of the century: the increasing divergence between the process of gathering news and the related but separate process of writing, editing, and publishing it. The telephone encouraged this bifurcation, particularly in urban areas, especially as its use in businesses and other institutions increased. The telegraph and its descendants had paved the way.[3] This could be seen in how technology emphasized differences between a newspaper's "leg men"—reporters out in the field—and an ever-more complex newsroom staff structure to support them. While this has been discussed earlier in this book, further nuance is necessary for understanding how certain tools impacted news routines in the past. When it came to both newsgathering and news-production processes, newsrooms had long functioned as simultaneously reluctant and innovative testing grounds for communication technologies.

The telephone is a complex technology, neither coming from a single path of development nor following one route to commercial adoption. Instead, it comes from numerous streams of innovation.[4] Its physical network was a network of networks from the outset. Numerous entrepreneurs, companies, city and state governments, and other parties all vied to commercialize and sell a device that had, at first limited utility. Newsroom adoption of the telephone reflected the larger struggle to usher in a national telephone network. As the author of a history of the device has written, the telephone ultimately overshadowed its sibling "technologies of reach." These had emerged (or come into their own) in the mid-nineteenth century onward, and included the telegraph and the railroad.[5] As larger and more complex firms emerged by the end of the century (including the sprawling and powerful railroad companies), their need for organization and communication became more acute.[6]

In time, the confluence of a gradually centralizing telephone network, the standardization of telephone switchboard technology, decreasing costs for local and regional (though not quite yet) national calls, and an increasing familiarity with the telephone as a commercial tool led to its widespread use by newspapers. These happened neither overnight nor smoothly, which led to the use of the phone in some parts of the country by reporters while it lagged behind elsewhere. Newspapers needed the large profits of the post–First World I years to roll money back into physical newsroom renovations. These often included wiring for telephone connections and rooms for operators, as well as increased access to electricity. A newsroom wired for electric lights was also often one wired for sound via wires to the outside world. A caveat, though: telephone connections were locally oriented for much of the twentieth century. It was expensive to call long distance, and so most news gathered by phone was within a state or region.

And so by the 1920s, within and without these newsroom spaces, news workers' relationships with technology, and the effect of technology on their own relationships, had been formed by intricate, contingent choices. The twin technologies of the telephone and the car exemplified how these choices amplified news workers' agency, giving them increasing autonomy to do their jobs, as well as the ability to coordinate and compete better with colleagues. This is not to say that newspapers and their reporters, columnists, and correspondents were not focusing on analysis and in-depth, "interpretative" reporting in their long competition with radio, and (later) TV. They were. They were *also* reacting continually to the incremental and sometimes unclear developments and directions of their world, much in the same way we are today. As scholars such as Nikki Usher, Kevin Barnhurst, and Richard Kielbowicz have shown, it is wise to avoid simplistic presumptions about the spatial and temporal realities of news production and news work.[7] The common narrative of the interwar years in particular focuses on the struggle between new and old journalistic forms and ways of telling stories, when in fact they coexisted, as journalism's various forms also do today.

But both the desk phone in the newsroom and public and private phones outside of it limited this agency. By creating a *tethering* effect that bound news workers to their supervisors (i.e., editors), it reinforced what economist Richard Edwards has defined as control within a production process: the ability of "managers to obtain desired work behavior from workers."[8] The ability to both leave the newsroom space to do work and to be more autonomous in that work was thus limited by editors, who, from afar, attempted to curtail it. And yet the phone and the car remained particularly disruptive newsroom tools, even as they built on older routines and power dynamics. As they helped to inspire new routines, they created new centers of power.[9] As Bruno Latour has described in his "sociology of the social," technology can alter "power relationships between the different *actors involved in the development of an innovation* in a newsroom."[10] Telephones may have been purchased by publishers, and their use may have been regulated by editors, but it was reporters and their peers who made full use of them, utilizing them to streamline and enhance their work and express their independence in the newsroom space. The telephone helped to spur a "titanic transformation . . . in newspaper operations."[11]

The use of technology has reflected power differentials in newsrooms through the twentieth century. Susan Keith has shown this with her examination of ubiquitous newsroom-work objects, including the horseshoe-shaped copydesk, the stylebook, the pica measuring stick, the photo-proportion wheel, and the paper page dummy.[12] By looking at how "frontline newsworkers" have used tools, or the "objects of editing," Keith examined how copy editors, reporters, and later, designers, changed their power status in the newsroom.[13] As Keith points out, comfort level, speed of adoption, and innovation with that adoption impacts who has more control over their work in a media organization's dynamic workplace. Generally, the faster and more creative one was at adopting a technology, the more autonomy one enjoyed or carved out. This is important, as technology adoption tends to shift control among groups of peers and near peers in the newsroom. Control over work processes, as empowered by technology, is one of the hallmarks of a professional identity.[14]

Comfort with technology, and the ability to use it in one's routines as a news worker, has a direct connection to the reskilling, multiskilling, and deskilling processes that simultaneously occur in journalism work, according to Henrik Örnebring.[15] He defines the act of news gathering as the locus of "journalistic labor," or the process of finding, selecting, and presenting the news. News workers regularly acquired new skills and modified old ones.[16] Technology use in multi- or reskilling processes grows out of "existing value systems, and these value systems have cultural, social and economic roots."[17] In our case, these systems encompassed work routines in journalism that had been driven by discourses of speed, economy, and efficiency.

These arose during the era of factory, or industrial journalism, during the first two decades of the twentieth century. These routines have continually been modified by technology, not suddenly and recently. The telephone and the car are lingering examples of that long modification. News workers were made both less and *more* mobile through the use of the telephone. On the whole, though, as tool, it helped reporters "be" in more places at once than ever before. Even if these devices were stationary, and not always physically portable, they nonetheless created a culture of mobility and extended newsroom routines outside of their physical spaces. More broadly, newsgathering technologies like the phone tended to entrench established work routines, while also creating new ones. New or emerging work patterns, such as the use of the telephone for interviews, or the use of the radio car to wirelessly update a newsroom from a distance, take time and experimentation to develop. But news workers during this era were committed to such innovation, at least when given the time and training to master the new tools.

As labor historian Marianne Salcetti has noted, the technology driving the creation and revision of work routines also created unique divisions of labor in the newsroom, not always to the benefit of workers.[18] But the advantages were undeniable. With the arrival of the ANG and other unions, even replaceable reporters were harder to fire.[19] New technology, and the arrival of rival media, such as the radio, meant that new skills were required. Rival newsrooms that relied on broadcasting could more readily beat newspapers in breaking news. But newspapers, adopting and refining both the phone and car as reporting tools, were able to maintain an edge in a competitive media ecosystem. This also enhanced their ability to focus on analysis and longform journalism. At the same time, the broad division of many larger newsrooms' workforces into those who gathered the news and those who edited and published it increased the need for the kinds of skills needed to operate newsgathering technologies.

As has already been discussed, the more skilled, stable workforce produced by this process helped reinforce the importance of reporters by the 1920s and 1930s. Management benefited less from culling annually from a pool of skilled, hard-to-fire workers—who possessed familiarity with the phone, and later, the radio car—and instead gained more from maintaining, training, and equipping them. In other words, management in fact gained by not firing news workers, as well as by acquiescing in some situations to union demands. This confluence led to a better quality of life for news workers, as their agency was strengthened, even as it was contested and in flux.[20]

### TELEPHONES: ADOPTION BEFORE THE 1920S

Telephones gave agency to news workers, who for the most part gladly—though only eventually—adopted them in their work. Their incorporation into the newsroom and newsgathering routines, however, was neither inevitable nor swift. And some news workers were unsure of, or not comfortable with a relatively new technology. Telephones had been in the newsroom since the late 1800s. By 1901 the *Fourth Estate* could depict the reportorial accomplishments of the *New York Evening Post* in describing a boat race via telephone reports from its correspondents in Poughkeepsie, some eighty-seven miles north of New York City.[21] Other newspapers in Ohio and Missouri were also experimenting with the use of phones for newsgathering. In the latter case, the editor of the *Sturgeon* [Missouri] *Leader* called a network of farmers and others to collect the news, holding his desk receiver with one hand and taking notes with the other.[22] Another small paper in Missouri was in the process of establishing a similar rural phone network for its correspondents and trained its staff, including printers, to operate the telephone switchboard. Telephone operators, conversely, were trained to set type.[23] This was not unusual. Many mechanical workers earlier in the century were cross-trained. Only later, with increasing specialization, did such training become rarer. Still, the appearance of the phone in newsrooms around the turn of the century could startle or amuse a newsroom's reporters and mechanical workers alike. When H. L. Mencken was a young reporter on the *Baltimore Herald* in 1899, he noted that there were only two telephones, "paleozoic instruments attached to the wall," and that "no one ever used them if it could be avoided." He also noted that there was no phone on the city editor's desk until he himself took the position in 1903.[24] In contrast, one early adopter was the *Memphis Commercial Appeal*, installing its first phone in the mid-1880s, when there were fewer than fifteen hundred in the city. By the first years of the new century, the paper had "enough telephones to make the device convenient to reporters and to advertising salesmen."[25]

The second decade of the new century saw further experimentation with phones. *Telegraph and Telephone Age* noted how much faster stories could be sent by telephone. Seventy-five words per minute on average could be sent over the phone by an unskilled operator, it was claimed, versus the forty to fifty words a minute by a skilled telegraph operator writing in Phillips code (with a receiver decoding it).[26] The advantage to sending stories, or parts of stories, in whole words versus in code increased the number of potential correspondents as well as the flexibility of newsgathering. Being able to update stories over the phone allowed a paper to receive last-minute news up to the moment of going to press and helped eliminate "the waste of special [copy] delivered too late for the press that day," noted a contemporary.[27] The adoption of the phone by news workers was both a deskilling process, because less technical savvy was needed to phone in a story versus transmitting it via telegraph and decoding it, and an upskilling or reskilling process. Not only did a reporter have to be able to operate a phone, they now had incentive to focus on *telling* their stories, versus writing by longhand or typing up them on a typewriter in a newsroom in the presence of peers.

Anecdotes from memoirs by reporters who worked in this era make frequent reference to how the best of their number could start writing stories in their heads before finding a phone or reaching the newsroom. As a news-gathering tool, the telephone did not cause a loss of skill among reporters but did emphasize certain skills over others, contemporaries realized. This happened as a culture of timeliness increasingly pervaded newspapers and journalism in the early era of radio.[28] Newspapers, which had always exhibited considerable interest in scooping one another to get the latest news, became more and more focused on breaking news, covering it with hourly updates. By enhancing these latter, they could make continual news more commonplace—not quite "live," but close.

Some speculated that the telephone could help speed copy directly to the typesetter. An early experiment to that effect in South Carolina, in which a short news article was telephoned directly to a linotype operator in Columbia from a transmitter in Charleston, hinted at the possibilities. Still, the rewrite man would soon serve as an intermediary between the wire and the process of setting type, before the technical challenges could be worked out further. The rise of new newsroom technology could, of course, result in the loss of jobs, especially on the production side of the newspaper. A case in point: when automatic telegraph machines were adopted in the 1910s and 1920s, thousands of telegraph operators lost their jobs. Western Union employed thirty-five thousand such operators in 1913 but only ten thousand in 1928; the AP cut its force down to six hundred from twelve hundred during that same time period.[29] "Before I get lost in the story of the derelict telegrapher, permit me to point the moral," warned one author: "Do not learn one trade, and only one trade, on which you are wholly dependent. . . . A machine may come along almost any day which can and will do your job better than ever you could. And then where are you?"[30] One news account from 1928 reported that a forty-nine-year-old AP operator (who had worked for the AP and the UP for thirty years) on the Jamestown (New York) *Journal*, apparently committed suicide "within 72 hours after losing his position . . . as the result of installation of a 'printer' [automatic telegraph machine]."[31]

The implication was that because his job was replaced by a machine, he lost his will to live. Less grimly, the position of telegraph operator, with a team of assistants, was solidified even with the arrival of automated equipment.[32] There were also attempts, partially successful, to retrain older telegraph operators.[33] But concerns about job displacement were generally overshadowed in journalistic trade publications by a pervading optimism. In the future, it was predicted, typesetters would have "head telephones" and chest-mounted transmitters to speed their work (these gadgets would in time, become part of the gear of the rewrite desk).[34] The AP, for its part, adapted the telephone to deliver thousand to five thousand–word news reports to about thirty papers at "regular intervals at day or night."[35] News was typed as it was heard over the phone, after speakers and listeners perfected their rates of speaking and copying to adjust to the new process.[36]

In many newsrooms in the early 1920s, there were few phone lines, and reporters and editors alike had to share access. This was especially the case on smaller dailies. An illustration for a "space-saving table" in 1919 shows a desk meant to accommodate four reporters, with drop shelves for four typewriters and a telephone on a "top shelf for use by all four workers."

This was in the office of the Wausau (Wisconsin) *Daily-Record Herald*.[37] Similarly, a 1921 profile of the Chattanooga (Tennessee) *News* describes how "in one corner of the editorial room a telephone booth has been arranged."[38] This booth would have been, presumably, used by all the paper's reporters. The Washington *Star*, exalted for the efficiency of its newsroom, had desks made of "the inevitable restful green metal, flat topped, with disappearing typewriters." Two desks were served by "telephones on flexible brackets."[39] Indeed, in the 1920s it was more common for business department staff members to have telephones than for reporters.[40] Advertising teams used the telephone to contact clients, and so it is possible that the success of these uses influenced the decision by editors and owners to invest in the technology.

Even though they were not yet on every reporter's or even every editor's desk during this decade, telephones had already altered work routines. Journalism textbooks, initially distrustful of their use, for fear that a reporter could be duped by someone claiming to be someone else, gradually advised on their best use. Face-to-face interviewing and observation still held

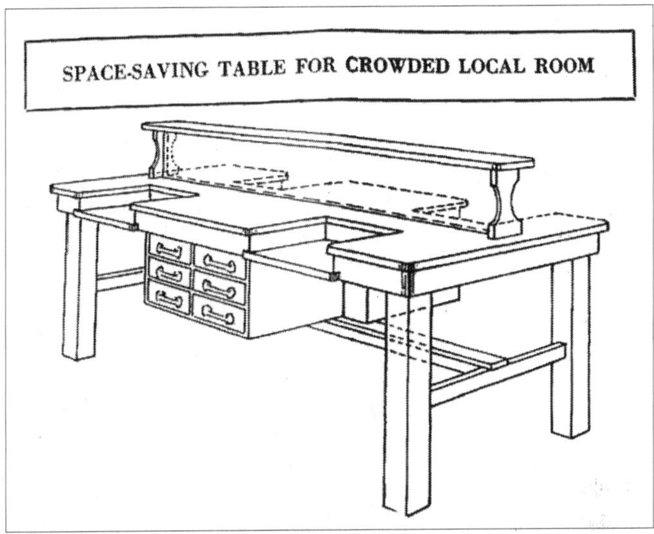


Figure 13. "Space-saving table for crowded local room," *Editor & Publisher,* August 7, 1919, 19. This table combined a relatively new technology, the telephone, with another new idea: "efficiency" and turning an office space into a factory. This sketch shows how a reporter's shared desk would have appeared at the Wausau, Wisconsin, *Daily Record-Herald.* It was meant to be shared by four news workers. Made from birchwood, it contained "drop shelves" for typewriters and other reporting gear, with one phone for all four reporters.

primacy of place in journalistic practice, but the telephone had become a useful auxiliary. Beat reporters started to use telephones to call back to the newsroom. Roving reporters on general assignment checked back in with the newsroom and their editors repeatedly throughout the day. The device was both a tethering and a liberating force, reinforcing the hierarchy of power in the newsroom between the reporter, the city editor, and the managing editor, but also allowing the reporter to cover more ground and be more independent, within and without the newsroom and its constraints. Editors could both control and better coordinate coverage of unplanned events.[41] It might be hard for us to envision what having more access to one's own phone would mean for a reporter, either at a desk or out in the field, but overall it meant more agency. The phone was a sign of freedom.

As the phone was slowly adopted in the newsroom, it changed news routines, though slowly at first. Instead of it taking hours to gather the facts, return to the newsroom, and write up a story, breaking news could be related from the scene of a story by a reporter via a rewrite man, who "whips the happenings into a story as rapidly as he can write it," according to a 1923 account by a *New York Times* reporter. This same reporter claimed that "all the greatest stories of the last decade have been telephone stories." Indeed, after about 10 p.m., any breaking news would be covered over the phone, by calling *out* and not just calling *in*. Some of the issues concerning this phenomenon of "calling out" are addressed in chapter 4, in the discussion of leg men and GA reporters.[42]

By 1923 the New York Press Association was using the telephone to great effect, with reporters letting their editors know where they could be reached. And long before any "sensational fire, murder, or robbery" occurred, private phone lines could be secured in certain neighborhoods. This would save the reporter time from having to hunt down a "coin booth box" and allow other reporters to be sent to the vicinity to aid in newsgathering.[43] Long-distance phone calling also helped the larger newspapers in New York, which would have staff members check in daily with correspondents, sometimes several times a day, in other big cities, such as San Francisco, Washington, DC, Chicago, St. Louis, and Detroit. By the early 1920s reporters were finding that some of their subjects preferred to be interviewed over the phone. A busy source could seek to control an interview, keeping it, for example, to a specified length. Although some reporters still preferred to see their sources in person (or, more commonly, were harangued by their editors into doing so), even if they needed descriptive details, many were content to have limited contact with their sources via a phone call versus none at all.

On the *Boston Globe* in the years after World War I, telephone calls were used to check on press releases or stories rewritten by the night-shift staff for the morning edition. They helped the smaller, less-talented overnight crew cover any news that happened to break at night.[44] Another *New York Times* reporter from this era said that a "telephone interview makes it easier to confine a man to the subject you want him to talk on. We have found that a big man is better pleased to talk to reporters over the telephone than face to face in his office."[45] A phone call, it turned out, improved access to some sources. It could save face, even a generation later, when a rival paper had a major scoop or story not reported in your paper. In New Orleans, the competing *Item* and *States* relied on last-minute phone calls to include bulletins in later editions if one had a story the other did not.[46]

Guy F. Lee, a reporter manning "the dog watch," or overnight shift, for the *Chicago Tribune* in the winter of 1921, used the phone to monitor news across the sprawling city. For long stretches of the night, he would be "left alone with the rodents and the office boy," composing poetry on a "battered old typewriter." But a phone call would invariably break this reverie, as a "sleepy police reporter" called with news of a bomb explosion, for instance. Lee would rush into action, typing up a story based on the call and supervising the night shift composing-room crew. But the same cause of his interruption enabled him to perform his solo work. Once the story was set for the morning paper, he would resume his poetry and keep "hammering at his typewriter while the rats rustled across the paper-littered floor of the local room and the phone clamored intermittently at his elbow."[47] While romanticized, perhaps, the account shows that the telephone was a force multiplier, and an extender of the newsroom's—and the news worker's—capability.

Even in this early era of the phone, reporters needed to learn how to convey details to the rewrite desk. Young reporters, who had perhaps not used the phone for more than the occasional social call during their college years, would not know what to do. An anonymous rewrite man complained in 1924 that "the first time a new reporter gets hold of a telephone, he looks at the transmitter and forgets his name." The story would tumble "out backwards and upside down" since "his voice is not tuned to the receiver, and his story, to the rewrite man, sounds like a lot of mixed signals." The author urged journalism schools to spend six months practicing "talking over the telephone." The room for error, even when using a relatively new medium, was slight for "embryo journalists."[48]

The use of the phone was not only difficult for beginners. Some reporters and editors complained that this newsgathering technology was changing journalistic standards, and not always for the better. In 1925 Karl M. Anderson, managing news editor of the *San Francisco Chronicle*, said that "fifteen or twenty years ago, before the day of the telephone and the early edition, when a story broke, a man went out and got it, cleaned it up, came back to the office and wrote it. If it wasn't written right, he got hell for it." Now the "wretched telephone . . . the biggest detriment and the greatest help the newspaper world has ever known" had changed stories into "fragmentary bulletins and scrap-ends."[49] News workers, tending toward nostalgia, had found a reason to rue the day that this new newsgathering machine had appeared.

This sense of greater haste, of a faster newsroom pace, spurred by the widespread adoption of the telephone in society at large as well as in the newsroom, found its way into news workers' attempts at poetry. Stewart

Emery's "Big News," from a 1920 issue of *Editor & Publisher*, describes what happened when news broke in the newsroom, aided by the phone:

> There's a room of racked reporters pounding type keys to and fro. And a harried desk a-slaving with their reeking pipes aglow; Crazy telephones are jangling and the "boss" is yelling speed, Never mind the fancy English, simple facts are what we need. It's "emergency," a welter of wild orders, rush and noise, And the staid dramatic critic's chasing copy with the boys.[50]

In addition to the mechanical clanking of the typewriters, the constant ringing of the phone, even if reduced by removing the receiver (a trick a reporter or editor would resort to if a caller were particularly insistent) became part of the barrage of aural stimuli. It was a constant accompaniment in the newsroom. Throughout the interwar era, the soundscape was characterized by the ubiquitous presence of phones on reporters' desks. One editor who worked in the women's department of the Pittsburgh *Sun-Telegraph* noted that "you'd have to seal yourself in the wall or climb into an empty file drawer to escape the noise around this place." With fifty reporters who "think out loud, and countless voices who scream out for copyboys, janitors, candy salesmen

Figure 14. "Modern appointments of newest metropolitan newspaper building," *Editor & Publisher*, July 13, 1929, 13. Note how news workers' desks in the *Chicago Daily News* newsroom have their own individual phones.

and telephone repairmen," thirty typewriters "with the hiccups," and eight telephones in her department alone, the rings were indistinguishable from one another: "If a call happens to come into the society department announcing the engagement of the Wild Man of Borneo to the daughter of the Neanderthal Man, all the phones ring with the same dialect."[51]

The pace of reporting had changed. More disturbingly, for some older news workers, especially editors, the phone affected the underlying relationships that in their opinion had steadied and inspired the newsroom. The era of "daring individual journalism" had arrived, and its power was "now vested in the reporter instead of the editor," according to an anonymous editorialist in 1922. The failures of this power shift from his perspective lay with the "men who give assignments. It is they who have not kept pace with mechanical advancements, except in a mechanical way." The writer quotes Victor Murdock, the vice chairman of the Federal Trade Commission and former editor of the *Wichita Eagle*, who called the reporter the new "high priest of the craft." This worker was weakened at the same time by a new spirit of "haste, the telephone, a practice called 'rewrite,' multiplied editions, and other innovations." Reporting was more than "accurate narration" and needed the "expression of opinion, vigorous or otherwise."[52]

J. Charles Poe, the executive editor of the *Chattanooga News*, complained, in this vein, in 1931 that the quality of applicants to his newspaper had declined. Too many, now that they were on salary and married, spent less time at the paper or out on the town pursuing leads. Some would make "one feeble effort to get the story over the telephone, and failing, report to the desk that the man wasn't in."[53] Other editors also complained about their reporters' use of the phone. They would hang around the newsroom instead of heading out of the building. Or if they had gone out, they would stay out. Arthur J. Sinnott, managing editor of the *Newark News*, chaired a "Shop talk" panel on "building a city staff" at the 1931 convention of the American Society of Newspaper Editors. Reporting was now so fast-paced, he said, that "very few men that are out in the field come in or have time to come in." Now that the "telephone intervenes," most reporters either chose to, or had to, telegraph or phone in their stories, which led to "the most curious and idiotic mistakes—getting names wrong, the fellow blurs it or something on the telephone." The convenience of transmitting information had consequences, he said, such that "the telephone is our great friend and enemy."[54] Another writer related that "before telephones, reporters would write their own stories. Now they do so only where the time element is not so important."[55] As late as 1957, editors were meeting to find ways to "discourage reporters from depending on the telephone."[56] Or, if they did use the phone, they were encouraged to call *and* then go out physically.

But while some editors and older reporters feared the telephone would encourage lazy reporting, younger reporters were using it to manage their own independence both in and out of the newsroom. This conditional independence was reinforced by the phone, which both connected and distanced a reporter from the immediate control of his supervisors, with the balance of power shifting slightly in favor of the reporter as a result. Mitchell Charnley, a reporter-turned-journalism professor, related how he, having been assigned to cover a divorce early in his career, encountered the divorcee's mother. She begged him and another reporter from a rival paper to not publish her daughter's story. As Charnley relates it: "I was new at the job, and, although I was most willing to accede, I felt that the presence of my seasoned, hardboiled rival (he was a rat-faced little chap and it was easy to believe all that had been said of him) would force me to print it. He must have sized up my attitude, for he didn't even consult me." Charnley was surprised at what happened next, however.

"'Okay,' he said. 'We'll kill it.'" The older reporter then called his city editor, and spoke into the receiver. "'Nothing to the story,' he reported, 'bum steer.'" Charnley left the house, and the other reporter turned to him. "'You got to do that now and then,' he explained. 'That old girl got to me. No sense in putting her on the spot just to satisfy a lot of moron readers.'"[57] This was a relatively rare case, but editors did delegate to their older reporters a certain level of judgment as to the newsworthiness of stories, once on the scene. Reporters made use of telephone technology to carve out their own freedom of action.

Some reporters could push this phone-empowered independence to its limit. Orien W. Fifer, an editorial writer for the *Indianapolis News*, recounted the story of a reporter who had taken advantage of a quiet afternoon to see a movie. He thought he was playing it safe when he called from the theater to check in with the newsroom one last time. As it turns out, however, he only narrowly avoided missing the breaking story of the governor's resignation. He was saved by a friend from a rival paper, who knew he liked to frequent movies on slow days and found him in time.[58]

Even at larger newspapers into the 1930s, telephones appeared only gradually on individual reporters' desks, their acquisition dependent on the whims and priorities of publishers. But reporters came into increasing contact with phones and their use in their work. When the *Los Angeles Times* opened its

Figure 15. Eugene S. Pulliam Jr., "Just Seat 20 Next to Each Other: How to Streamline a Big City Newsroom," *Quill*, February 1950, 8–10. As managing editor, Pulliam was interested in designing, or at least reworking, the existing newsroom space at his family's paper, the *Indianapolis News*. By midcentury, older routines that once made sense were less relevant in the face of TV and radio competition, such as having such tightly drawn newsroom roles (rewrite vs. copy vs. news desks).

new $4 million building in 1935, its lavish, air-conditioned spaces included a 4,576-foot "city room" on the third floor that contained two rows of steel desks for reporters. On an opposite wall was a row of telephone booths to be shared.[59] Other newspapers ranged telephone booths along a wall for their reporters, separate from their rewrite space.[60] Designated rewrite "batteries" with multiple desks became a common sight in newsrooms.[61]

In August 1937, when the Toledo (Ohio) *News-Bee* renovated its building, every reporter's desk had a phone installed.[62] A reporter reflecting on his early experiences in journalism during this era recalled how his local daily paper used phones, and how every reporter's desk was "equipped with headphones" for dictation.[63] A 1928 photo of the new newsroom of the Canton (Ohio) *Repository* shows that most of the editors and reporters had access to a phone.[64] Other images show a similar trend. Some twenty years later the *Dallas Morning News* had renovated its newsroom to equip each reporter's desk with a phone.[65] The *Oregon Journal*'s newsroom had "ample space for each reporter to have his own desk, telephone and typewriter" in 1948.[66] Similarly, photos of newsrooms by the early 1950s show plentiful telephones on nearly every news worker's desk.

Cartoon depictions of newsroom life from this time also showed the prevalence of individual phones on reporters' desks.[67] Phones had long been considered a critical part of the daily workflow.[68] One young cub reporter working summers at the *Wenatchee World* while an undergraduate at the University of Washington in the mid-1950s described them as ubiquitous.[69]

### TRAINING AND ACCULTURATION

By World War II, "telephone reporting" was ingrained in journalistic culture. The phone's presence in US journalism during the 1930s and 1940s had expanded beyond the simple addition of a new tool in the newsroom. In 1942 new reporters at the *Washington Post* were told to call or "personally report to the desk" when they went on and off duty for the day. If they were away from the newsroom during the afternoon or evening on city or suburban assignments, they were expected to call at least once to check in (or face the reality of editors calling *them*). If traveling out of town, the city desk had to be informed of where they could be reached. Even leaving the newsroom during the workday, when not on assignment, required some kind of notification, especially if a reporter was expecting an incoming call. Before answering machines, a memo "saying what the telephone call is about and where you probably can be reached" was needed.[70] A reporter was expected to call in to the newsroom and to his or her editor more often, particularly during and after covering a story, and especially if he or she had been assigned a photographer.[71] Photographers were limited newsroom resources. Phone-call status updates ensured they could be deployed effectively. These norms had already been established. But technology reinforced some aspects of them, while creating others.

At bigger papers, cub reporters and copy boys were expected to staff the phones, not for rewrite, necessarily, but fielding incoming calls from readers and sources, or calling them to confirm details. There was an expectation that learning the phones was one of your first experiences in the newsroom.[72] Women were also working more as dictationists, regarded as a lower-level stepping-stone to reporting work, by the early 1940s.[73] There were more opportunities for women in these newer areas of the newsroom's workforce, perhaps because they had not yet been claimed as thoroughly by men. This was a trend that would be replicated later in the century, with newsroom computerization.[74] Skilled rewrite men and women, who worked primarily over their earphones and typewriters, were valuable: they were "almost as important to this type of coverage of local news as are those who write with their voices instead of their hands." In a fast-paced environment, both ends of the information-collection system were in fact vital, since it was "not easy to go back and edit over the telephone."[75]

Telephones in the workplace influenced how new reporters were indoctrinated into newsroom culture. Sam Justice, a special-assignment reporter for the *Charlotte Observer*, noted how the "news room force" enjoyed playing pranks on each other so much that it seemed that "it is April Fool's Day every day." One common trick was leaving fake messages for the less-savvy members of the staff. While veterans would check numbers in a directory before calling back, others, "hopeful that it might be that big story, will grab the telephone first and do their reporting later." Teased and chastened by their colleagues, these reporters would go back to work. In time, however, they, too, would break in new reporters using similar tricks. Looming deadlines and demanding editors, alongside continually ringing phones, meant that one's "patience punches the time clock and goes home when an old sister from Route 3 calls to find out 'what that peculiar light is in the north sky.'"[76]

There was basic decorum that covered the use of the phone in the office. While this was often unspoken and reinforced by casual reminders, such as pranking each other, some newsrooms operated under more explicit rules. The "office conduct" code for the Glendale (California) *News* admonished reporters to answer the phones promptly, and not "leave it for the 'other fellow' to do." Tact was expected, along with instructions not to argue or "hang up" or otherwise express personal views while on the job with a caller. If management felt the need to be so exacting, these behaviors must have been prevalent.[77] And it is unclear how effective explicit rules actually were. Other rules tied the telephone to authority. *Washington Post* reporters were told in 1942 to give their names immediately, with their title.[78] A reporter was better off saying his or her paper's name, and not their own, first, since "it carries greater prestige than the individual and usually the business at hand can be transacted more quickly, in the name of the paper."[79] Outside the newsroom, telephones were sometimes positioned near recurring sources of news, as part of newsroom outposts. In that vein, Bill Cunningham, a feature writer covering sports for the *Boston Post*, appealed to stadium and racetrack owners for sturdier press boxes. He noted that his peers,

> The gentlemen of the press . . . are chained to their seats, even as the Germans were chained to their machine guns. They must take notes,

> keep charts, operate typewriters, feed wires, use telephones. They can't raise umbrellas and they can't leave their stations. Furthermore, their hands must be free to work their various instruments that perforce must be spread wide open.[80]

As newsrooms and their auxiliary spaces became more wired, news services led the way with innovation. In 1924 one such service, the Standard News, installed a customized phone system in its offices in New York City that bypassed a switchboard and took calls from reporters straight to the rewrite desk, where a system of lights and bells would show which calls had not yet been answered. Especially during peak news cycles, this had the effect of "economizing on every hand the minutes that count."[81] Six years later, the *Buffalo* (New York) *Courier-Express*'s new building used an internal phone system that did not rely on switchboard operators.[82] These developments would bear fruit later in the century.

### MORTON SONTHEIMER

In 1941 Morton Sontheimer, writing semiautobiographically for young men and women interested in breaking into journalism, outlined how one would go about reporting a story via the phone. Echoing older tales of competition, Sontheimer encouraged the "tricky little art of tying up phones." These "lines of communication are as important to you as a reporter as they are to an army." Among your first actions when arriving at the scene of a developing story, whether in the city or out the country, he advised, was to find a phone and secure it until you needed it: "You don't know what sweat is until, with a hot story burning your fingers, you run from one phone to another, only to find an opposition reporter phoning in oceans of detail on each one and none left for you to use."[83]

Though he did not explicitly endorse this, Sontheimer observed how some reporters faked talking on a phone to "tie up the wire," and how it would be a "handy thing for a newspaperman to know how to disconnect a phone neatly at the bell box by simply loosening the connection, and then later restore service again."[84] He was hardly alone in these practices. In Detroit in the late 1920s, competition over beats or scoops on stories drove similar stratagems and strategies. Even photographers were advised to "carry plenty of nickels," because "many news cameramen who did yeoman service on coverage found themselves short of the necessary small change when they rushed the pay phones to report to the desk."[85]

Ray Girardin, a veteran crime reporter on the Hearst-owned evening *Detroit Times*, faced rival reporters from the Detroit *News* and from the morning paper, the *Free Press*. He recalled how one day he "raced from a courtroom to a nearby telephone booth but found an 'out of order' sign on the door." Immensely frustrated, and facing a deadline with minutes to spare, he dropped a coin into the phone out of desperation. It worked, and Girardin made his call, suspecting a rival's purposeful obstruction.[86] AP reporter Dick Feehan, covering a suicide victim's jump from a 160-foot-tall ledge in Manhattan in 1938, tossed another reporter out of a nearby phone booth. Dialing the AP's rewrite desk, he asked "his rewrite man to keep the line open."[87] Having a clear view of the scene, he reported what he saw directly to the AP desk. He then unscrewed the phone's mouthpiece, "put it in his pocket, and walked away," leaving other reporters to scramble for working phones and earning himself a five-minute beat (a five-minute head start on the competition). This was especially upsetting for Feehan's rivals in an era when papers updated their stories to the minute and the hour.[88]

All hints of vandalism aside, Sontheimer observed that the telephone could either reinforce lazy reporting or aid more thorough work. Calling someone had an advantage over visiting them, because asking rapid-fire questions in an authoritative voice could get results if the person on the other end of the line thought you were a police officer or other authority figure. Phone companies would assist a reporter looking for someone in another town, since most were eager to generate a toll. Generally, however, editors were frugal when it came to long-distance calls. "Even the big American papers, with large sums to spend on coverage, do not squander near the tolls that British newspapers used to pay on long distance phone calls all over the world," Sontheimer noted, describing American editors as "thrifty" by comparison, and more willing to rely on wire services for updates on national and international stories.[89]

The telephone was not an ideal medium for interviews, or stories needing details, he believed, unless a reporter was on the scene and could describe what was going on. "Vicinity phoning," or the practice of calling known addresses near a fire, murder, or other news event, was one way around this. Sontheimer recalled how an editor working the "lobster trick," or dog watch (overnight) shift would readily rouse citizens to find out what was going on in a particular neighborhood, before dispatching a reporter. The equivalent in our own time would be crowdsourcing or checking social-media reports first.

Aggressive use of the phone could lead to scoops. While working for the *San Francisco News*, Sontheimer called an address mentioned in a police bulletin and found himself "talking to the surviving victim of a double shooting before police or ambulance had arrived." He got an account of what happened after assuring the victim that a doctor was coming, a "true enough statement."[90] He also urged young reporters to stay on the "'dearie' list" of the newspaper telephone operator, that "hard-boiled prima donna of the plugs and cords," equally capable of "trading wisecracks with reporters and talking back to impatient editors."[91] A generation later, such operators, even as their positions evolved, were still important.

Margaret Whitesides, a city desk coordinator, sat across from the city editor at the *Chicago Daily News* in 1959. She worked as an important part of the social glue that kept the newsroom's various factions on schedule and connected to one another.[92] A receptionist played a similar role at the *Indianapolis News*, taking messages and answering incoming calls to the city desk, the city editor, and reporters.[93] Telephone operators, sometimes called "phone girls," were a vital part of the reportorial support staff at the *New York Times*, especially for the rewrite desk. Perhaps the most proficient of any newsroom staffers in the use of phones, telephone operators could find unlisted phone numbers to track down elusive sources, cross-reference phone numbers to addresses, and had sources of their own among friends who worked as city switchboard operators, if they needed help contacting more distant locales.[94] Like Sontheimer's newsroom, these later newsrooms were webs of relationships between staff members.

## EARLY RADIO CARS AND PORTABLE CAR PHONES: REACTIONS TO RADIO

In the wake of World War II, newspapers reacted to radio as a rival for breaking-news coverage, and even for some longform storytelling. The telephone by then was a proven technology, soon wedded to another proven technology, the car. This, in turn, would be tied to a third, but even newer, technology: the mobile, short-range radio. The result was the "radio car," quickly followed by handheld radios.

Contacting the newsroom wirelessly became feasible even before the United States entered the war. Newsrooms were by this point acquainted with using phones to remotely contact reporters, or vice versa. Existing norms for telephone use served as the foundation for newer norms for more wireless devices. Moving beyond a dedicated phone line on some newspapers was an innovation that came in two parts. First, portable photo labs developed as a way to speed image transmission to newsrooms.[95] These large vans or trucks, which could cost up to about $1,000 (in 1946, or about $12,700 in 2020), not counting the chassis or car body, allowed the development of photos from near the scenes of stories.[96] The developed images would then be either raced back to the newsroom by courier or other car, or in some pioneering cases, sent by early photo-transmission equipment, as a wireless facsimile.[97]

Dedicated car phones, or portable radios fitted into cars (i.e., "radio cars") were a second, distinct development that would "permit city editors to keep in constant touch with roving reporters," it was believed.[98] Unlike photo cars, radio cars served as mobile reporting stations for leg men getting their stories back to rewrite desks. An early example of this could be found in 1939, when a newspaper reporter used a telephone installed in his car to cover the sinking of the USS *Squalus*, a US Navy submarine, off the coast of Portsmouth, New Hampshire.[99] Not until after the war, however, did newspapers begin to invest in making radio cars a reality as the technology was more commercially available and as resources were freed from wartime contingencies.

A variety of newspapers throughout the country began experimenting with these devices, installing them in cars and instructing their reporters to use them to increase both their breaking news and beat coverage. Between 1946 and 1948, these papers included the San Francisco *Examiner*, *Chronicle*,

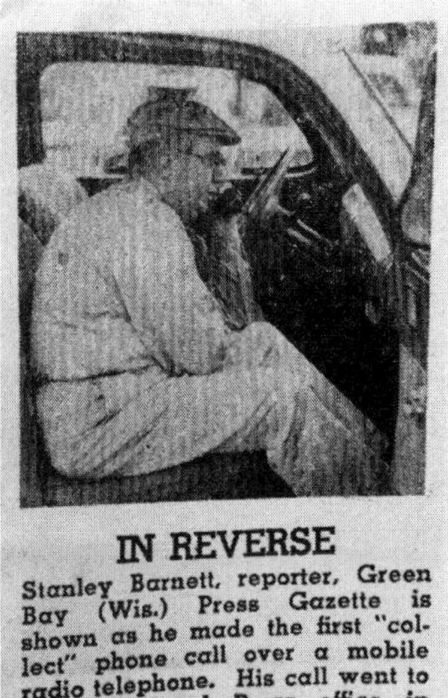

IN REVERSE

Stanley Barnett, reporter, Green Bay (Wis.) Press Gazette is shown as he made the first "collect" phone call over a mobile radio telephone. His call went to the Associated Press office in Milwaukee.

Figure 16. "In reverse," *Editor & Publisher*, September 14, 1946, 81. The AP was interested early on in investing in innovative ways for its correspondents to file stories, both domestically, as seen here, but also outside the United States.

*Call-Bulletin* and *News*, the *Boston Traveler*, *New Orleans States*, *Dallas News*, *St. Louis Star-Times*, and the *Denver Post*. The trend also reached smaller papers such as the *Green Bay* (Wisconsin) *Press Gazette*. In the latter case, reporters could call the regional AP office directly in Milwaukee.[100]

Radio phones increased the range of leg men, allowing for "two-way radio-phone communication for covering a news story" via the rewrite desk.[101] The early installation and use of these devices was not without its challenges, however. The radios, and the batteries that powered them, despite advances in miniaturization brought by the war (and the fact that many such batteries could be charged by the car), were still bulky, taking up trunk space.[102] Looking at the deployment of a radio-car system in one West Coast city may help to illustrate these obstacles.

### SAN FRANCISCO

For the system shared by the four daily metro papers in the Bay Area, sixteen cars (four at each paper) received 25-watt transmitters from the Pacific Telephone and Telegraph Company for a one-time fee of $25 and a $22 monthly rental. The phone company had to treat all four newspapers the same, in terms of service and equipment. Messages cost thirty cents each, with most of the papers running well over the minimum monthly charge of seven dollars. Most of the newspapers made ten calls or more a day on a six-day-a-week schedule, with the whole venture racking up about $1,153 each month. A reporter-photographer team was assigned to each car, and its respective newspaper would contact one of their radiophone cars by dialing a special number on a regular phone; an answering operator switched the call to a central 150-watt transmitter, relayed via six receiving stations positioned throughout the city.[103]

"A light flashes on . . . the dashboard, a bell rings, and the hapless reporter is again in the clutches of his boss," related the reporter who profiled the system. But all the other bosses could hear these commands, too. Since in this early experiment the four papers shared the same fifty-party radiophone channel, they could listen in on each other, and in response reporters and their editors developed a kind of secret shorthand to communicate discreetly about breaking news.[104]

The presence of the newspapers on an in-the-clear radio network had another side effect. Some reporters found themselves "smarting under [a] phone company order to pretty up their language, for newspapers aren't the only radiophone users." City editors, for their part, liked the extended coverage the system brought, enjoying the confidence that breaking news could be covered more thoroughly. This early system had a thirty-mile radius, not much beyond the "public nickel phone area." Still, photographers and their assignment editors liked the ability to coordinate photo coverage. Reporters had more mixed reactions: "The disadvantage of being continually under the desk's thumb is outweighed by the saving in leg power. The reporters are getting more stories, more fully covered, in less time."[105]

The older method of calling in from stationary phones (or calling out to them) had provided more freedom than having to call in routinely via a radio. And the open nature of the network was again a distinct disadvantage. Private lines, which would come not long after, would encourage rapid adoption and use by individual papers. Less time would be spent hunting for open phones, and more time providing extra details for the next edition. Indeed, in the then-near future, the role of rewrite staff was expected to become more important. Using radio-equipped cars, as well as "walkie talkies," would make the reporter "little more than a mechanism for placing gifted rewritemen in contact with the actors on the scene of a story."[106] At the same time, breaking news would become more thorough and vivid. With television in its infancy, newspapers were keen to compete with its live broadcasts.

And yet, the radio car was thought of as enhancing, not supplanting, other kinds of coverage, especially the visual: "Photographers will get to the big fires while they're still big, to the murders and wrecks while they're still gory, and to rescues still in progress."[107] But no longer would editors worry that a big newsbreak would catch an empty newsroom off guard. They could position their writers and photographers near news faster than ever before.

### INCREASING ADOPTION OF RADIO CARS

The reality, of course, was messier, and contingent on local circumstances, including economic expediency, how competitive a local news market was, and how much a newspaper could invest in purchasing equipment and training its staff. Small advancements in radio-car technology enabled the installation of photo-transmission gear, such as when an AP WirePhone machine was modified to fit in a truck by the Southern Bell Telephone Company for use by the *New Orleans States*.[108] The "wirephoto-radio telephone reporter" car and its portable photo lab were cutting edge for the time.[109]

The *Denver Post* also operated a dual-purpose vehicle built on a Chevrolet Suburban chassis. In addition to a photo transmitter, its operator could tap

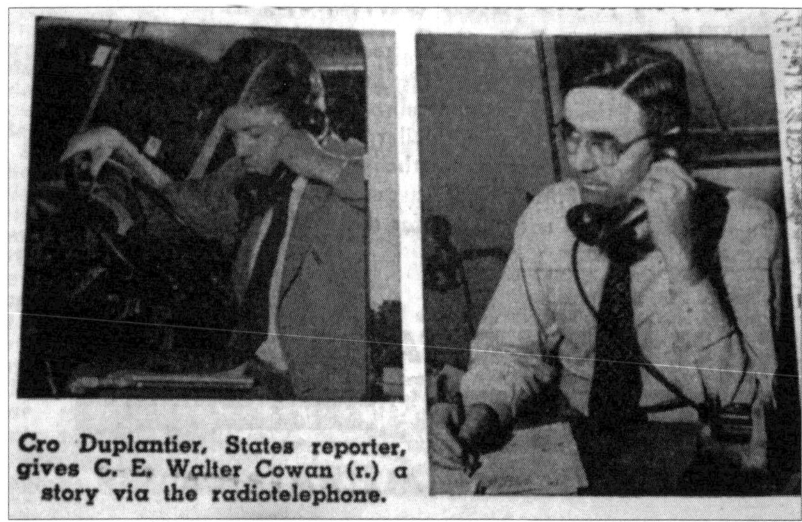


Figure 17. "Pictures and stories 'phoned' on-the-spot," *Editor & Publisher*, January 4, 1947, 28. While probably staged, this image shows how early "mobile" tech also tethered reporters to their newsrooms via their editors.

Figure 18. "Pictures and stories 'phoned' on-the-spot," *Editor & Publisher*, January 4, 1947, 28. Example is from the *New Orleans States*. In this diagram of a "novel car being used by the New Orleans, Louisiana, States newspaper for transmission of photos and voice from the scenes of stories," the "1" refers to "negative developing tanks," the "2" refers to the "enlarger and printer," the "3" refers to "print developing trays," the "4" refers to "print dryer," the "5" refers to "wirephoto transmitter," the "6" refers to "photo chemical storage," the "7" refers to the "radio telephone transmitter," and the "8" refers to the "radio telephone antenna."

into telephone lines, with permission from phone companies, using a portable kit. The radio-truck and photo lab was used to cover remote stories in Utah, Colorado, and Wyoming, and in the course of a year had transmitted more than one hundred photos.[110] Other modified vehicles from the time relied on a mix of off-the-shelf and custom-built components.

By the start of the 1950s, photographer-reporter teams assigned to radio cars were becoming less of a novelty. The ANPA lobbied the FCC to keep open their access to part of the commercial wavelength spectrum, opposing any efforts to reduce this access. The publishers argued that "the present experimental relay press wave-lengths over which news reports and pictures are transmitted from reporters' cars [should] be placed on a permanent basis."[111] As newspapers such as the *Des Moines Register & Tribune* and *Los Angeles Times* adopted radio cars, a more standardized method for their use was worked out. At the latter paper, using an intercom in the newsroom, assignments were usually relayed from the photo manager through to the city desk. These were informal arrangements, however, and supplemented by individual reporters' cars fitted with police-band radio scanners to provide the paper with "spot news coverage otherwise not obtainable.[112] The use of radio cars was a work in progress, as seen in a spoof of one such car in action.[113] Another cartoon, by the same artist, also pokes fun at radio cars, pointing out the ironically interconnected nature of radio cars and newsrooms.[114]

Despite the technological challenges, the *Chicago Tribune* invested in a fleet of thirty-six cars: twenty-nine dedicated to supporting photographers and seven assigned to reporters. All were equipped with Motorola-manufactured radiophone sets, with a 250-watt base station in the *Tribune*'s building that was "remotely controlled from the City Room by Chief Photographer Lyman Atwell and Assistant City Editor [George] Schrieber." All *Tribune* photographers, except for those on society, sports, Sunday features, neighborhood, and other regular (i.e., non-breaking news) beat coverage, had radios in their cars. The seven reporters driving the radio-equipped cars covered "hot assignments." The paper had an old system, costing $1,200 to $1,800 a month, that involved dialing out of the city room to a telephone exchange, which then called the car, and then back again when the car called the city room. Its new "radio relay system," which cut out the intermediate step, had been installed in April 1952, and was expected to cost $600 to $900 to operate. Generating about ten calls a day, the radio gear was installed in the vehicle's trunk, with cables running to the transmitting and control unit in the dashboard.[115] A General Electric-designed system at the

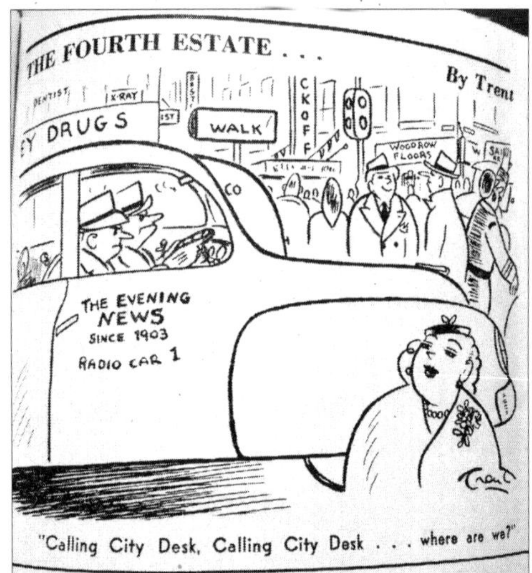


Figure 19. "The Fourth Estate," *Editor & Publisher*, February 18, 1956, 47. New technology often found itself reliant on older technology, as least in spoofs of the former.

*Indianapolis Star* included a base station and "13 mobile units in the cars of staff photographers and reporters." With a 35-mile range, the system's antenna was mounted 170 feet above the paper's building in the middle of the city. It had been planned by Joe Jarvis, "news picture editor," who had worked with GE engineers.[116]

Some reporters were already reflecting on the change in their news routines that more plentiful telephones, both in and out of the office, brought. Joe Finn, a reporter for the *Ottawa Citizen*, was impressed by the mobile telephone unit that had been installed in the paper's photo-car. "No mad dash for a telephone anymore when you are out in the country on a story. Just [get] back to the car, pick up the phone and ask for the city desk. Not like the old days," he observed.[117] Though this is a Canadian example, it does show how a more mobile reporting culture was emerging in response to TV and radio.

### THE *NEW YORK MIRROR*

John J. Reidy, Hearst Newspapers' "mobile radio coordinator," doubled as the *New York Mirror*'s chief photographer. He outlined at a 1953 conference how his newspaper used mobile-communication technology to coordinate coverage.[118] The *Mirror* used the "two-way mobile radio to quickly assign staff photographers to spot news stories or to feed additional information such as changes in location while the photographer is underway." Using a radio-equipped car with Motorola transmitters, along with a customized

International News Photo Soundphoto machine, allowed him to send a 3.25-by-4.24-inch photo that could be enlarged to 6.5 by 8.5 inches, a sequel to a system that used a darkroom-equipped car to send 8-by-10-inch photos.

These transmissions, and assignments of the photo or radio cars, were controlled from consoles in the newsroom. One console was located in a soundproofed "radio room in the photo department" that had "a sliding window looking out on the City Room between the City and Picture Editors." The other was located in the photo desk out in the city room. Headsets connected both desks, and a switch was installed that allowed "radio control from three rewrite desk positions to which points reporters may radio in their stories direct from the news scene."[119] Headsets, headphones, and earphones had already been in use as a way to minimize disruptions in the newsroom. With the sounds generated by the use of other reporters' telephones in particular, headphones were helpful for the rewrite desk.[120] To further avoid disturbing reporters and editors nearby, the speakers for the radio-intercom console in the newsroom were turned off except during the early morning "lobster" shift. A reporter was assigned to take calls in the soundproofed space and to handle tips.

But when a photographer called the desk, the radio conversation could be relayed back via the intercom and the headsets to editors. Reidy noted that the *Mirror*'s rivals, including the *New York Journal-American*, used photographer-reporter pairings "cruising the city," together with the radio as a news-reporting dispatch for their photographers out in the field. The versatility of Reidy's radio cars was increased through the use of nine- to eighteen-pound "Handie-Talkies" ("small low-powered transmitters"), connected via the radios in the cars to the newsroom:

> When a photographer or reporter goes on an assignment he will be transported into the immediate area of the story by the vehicle which is carrying the automatic relay equipment. It is only necessary to keep the engine running, set the control switch on relay and lock the car. He will then be able to operate with his lower-power two-way portable all over the area as well as from within buildings. The Handie-Talkie signal has only to get to the receiver in his car. The main station because of its power will be able to reach the portable directly and without the relay. This is now under development and when put into regular use should be a forward step in wider acceptance of two-way radio by newspapers and press associations.[121]

By using the car's more powerful transmitter, and by allowing the reporter and photographer teams to split up and get closer to the scene of the action, the paper had a distinct edge over its competitors. Reidy predicted other papers would follow suit, noting that the *Mirror* was working on developing an even smaller hand-carried radio, the "Micro-Handie-Talkie."[122] This increasing portability and mobility enhanced the agency and ability of news workers to exercise independent news judgment, even as new means to coordinate, and control, their behavior were introduced.

### WALKIE-TALKIES AND TAPE RECORDERS: MORE MOBILE REPORTERS

After the technological developments of World War II, batteries and radios grew smaller, more reliable, and longer lasting, complementing the increasingly compact radios that were integrated into a newsroom's routine. Technical innovations introduced on the business side migrated slowly but steadily to the editorial side of most newspapers, foreshadowing how computerization would enter the newsroom in the 1960s and 1970s.[123] In the same way that phones had been more common in newspaper advertising offices, tape recorders and answering machines would become more common in the newsroom itself. Other changes meant that reporters were easier to contact, from the outside, and could call out more easily.

Newspapers moved away from using switchboard systems to providing their reporters the ability to take outside calls directly. As early as the 1940s,

**STANDARD EQUIPMENT** for newsmen nowadays on fast-moving stories like the Inauguration of President Eisenhower is the powerful lightweight walkie-talkie developed by RCA Victor for the U. S. Army Signal Corps. Here you see Rewriteman Paul Gocke taking the story via walkie-talkie from Art Edson, who rode the atomic cannon in the Washington parade.

Figure 20. "Standard equipment," *Editor & Publisher*, February 14, 1953, 41. Newspapers and magazines showcased their capacity to equip their reporters with the latest in mobile technology.

newspapers had their own directory listings, for their own internal switchboards.[124] But in ways that transcended the experimental use of radio cars, reporters added new tools to their technological arsenal, or at least dreamed of acquiring them. In 1945 Robert U. Brown, editor of *Editor & Publisher*, speculated about the effect of the war on reporting technology. He imagined reporters in the near future having the ability to cover a big fire, or other large-scale disaster, "filing an eye-witness story direct to the desk as the event is unfolding before him." Even the coverage of routine news, including that of ship and police beats, could be improved. He visualized "a network of 'walkie-talkies' linking the star reporters of a newspaper all over town who [then] can work in unison on a single story without waiting to contact the other by telephone. Think even of the time saved by a reporter not having to locate a phone."[125]

While he says he was "dreaming a little," he also pushes back against "the experts' claims that [the] 'walkie-talkie' will not be of value to newspapers because anyone can tune in on the conversation." Treating the newspaper use of radios and walkie-talkies as a de facto "party line" would probably lead to fierce new competition in the field, he said. But "scrambling devices" could negate that disadvantage, down the road, despite their then-considerable bulk.[126] However, the fact that he combined the concern about eavesdropping with reflections on the time gained from not having to search for a free phone highlights how Brown and others were thinking of these devices in terms of older technologies.

Within a few short years, Brown's predictions were becoming a reality. During a visit by recently reelected British prime minister Winston Churchill to New York City in January 1952, two reporters from the *New York Journal American* used two-way, walkie-talkie radio sets to cover the British politician's cross-town appearances. The portable radios "enabled them to give on-the-scene details of the running story instantly to the city desk and to rewrite men."[127]

Other ventures into mobile reporting included a then-rare 1947 air-to-ground telephone interview by a reporter from the *Grand Rapids Herald* with the two sitting Michigan senators, and the installation of a two-way radiophone service, based on FM radio, to "speed news coverage through the Lehigh Valley" at a newspaper in Allentown, Pennsylvania.[128] The *Dallas News* used a "radio mobilphone" in a news photographer's car to report a plane crash in 1947.[129] A cartoon from 1953 shows a reporter equipped with a backpack radio interviewing a public official; the caption reads (spoken by an onlooker), "Hi Betty, this is Al; give me the Desk." The other people in the frame seem to know Al's routine—and are perhaps annoyed by it.[130] The spread of this technology to areas far beyond the West and East Coasts (and out of Chicago) shows its adoption away from elite news organizations. To be clear, though, most newspapers could not afford the large-scale deployment of advanced technology tools such as mobile radios, opting instead for more targeted use.

The mass-market introduction of the transistor and its adoption by manufacturers increased the portability of reporting gear by the end of the 1950s. William R. Hearst trumpeted the edge "transistorized two-way radiophones" would give his reporters at "political conventions, keeping Hearst reporters and photographers in constant touch with central headquarters."[131]

Portable wire and tape recorders also made their first appearance during this era. Raymond Moley, a political columnist for *Newsweek*, used "the Dictet," a "portable voice recorder" manufactured by the Dictaphone Corporation, weighing in at two pounds, eleven ounces, for research and interviews. It had enough tape for an hour-long recording.[132] A compact recorder produced by the Mohawk Business Machines Corporation sold for $229.50 in 1954. Roughly the size of a book, it came with its own shoulder holster. Before, the "enthusiastic scribble of a quote which may make or break a story" could be recanted by a source in the presence of a notepad. The recorder's size and relative portability, combined with "several microphone attachments which may be hidden from the interviewee's eyes . . . behind the wrist watch, on the tie clasp, or behind the lapel" could lead to a candid interview. The recorder could also be attached to a telephone receiver. In the latter case, bringing two kinds of technology together helped reporters hone their ability to tell complex stories.

The ethical issues raised by such devices were not often discussed in the enthusiasm over their labor-saving potential.[133] Even student newspapers were experimenting with these technologies. In 1948 the staff of the Syracuse University paper, the *Daily Orange*, used an off-the-shelf wire recorder owned by a student to help cover a campus political debate. Retailing for about $150 at music stores, its spools cost $2, $3, and $5 for fifteen-minute, thirty-minute, and one-hour versions, respectively. Because one fifteen-minute spool and then a second one (on a second recorder) was needed to capture speeches, there were downsides. A reporter had to carefully coordinate swapping spools, for example. But the overall idea was to avoid accusations of being misquoted. The spools themselves could be reused.[134]

AP reporter Herman R. Allen used an early tape recorder to help cover the 1955 convention of the National Association of Secondary-School Principals. Allen noted that he "wrote stories from playbacks of his tapes," recorded during the convention, a novel technique at a time when reporters still took notes by hand, wrote them based on memory, or dictated them over the phone. National Editorial Association publicists were so proud of this innovation that they distributed mimeographed copies of Allen's stories to attendees.[135] A pair of Oregonian reporters, William Lambert and Wallace Turner, used tape recorders (in their case, recording audio via a wire worn by an informant) in 1956 to write a series of stories on corruption in Portland.[136] The high-profile nature of their exposé warranted the use of a then still-relatively rare piece of reporting technology. Reporters pooled resources to share this kind of equipment, which was otherwise the purview of celebrity reporters and writers into the 1960s. Tape recorders were prohibitively expensive, costing more than one hundred dollars a device. According to the Bureau of Labor Statistics, that would be the equivalent of $1,600 in 2020 US dollars.[137]

The infrastructure used to support this more mobile reporter was improving by the end of the 1950s, a development that affected more traditional landline desk phones. The *Detroit Free Press*'s newsroom underwent modernization in 1948, with a new, "streamlined" layout designed to increase efficiency, inspired by the "continuous production line made famous by auto makers in this Auto Capital." Instead of an older "push-button multiple setup in which reporters fumbled around piccolo-style with the buttons to get the caller," the paper had a box system, which allowed for the "taking or holding of calls at eight positions," as colored lights showed which lines were "clear, in use, or in 'HOLD' position."[138] Classified ad departments, as well as business departments in general, were responsible for pioneering more advanced phone systems that eventually spilled over to editorial departments, as has been noted.

Innovations with phone systems were happening throughout the country. An advanced setup could be found in the ultramodern UPI Newspictures bureau in San Francisco, based in the *San Francisco News* building. Individual calls could be fielded from external phone lines and transmitted to internal intercoms installed in the newsroom.

## CONCLUSION: THE LEGACY OF NEWSGATHERING TECHNOLOGY

Writing in 1952, *Editor & Publisher*'s Robert Brown speculated, jokingly, that "it won't be long before we will have a completely automatic newspaper—one

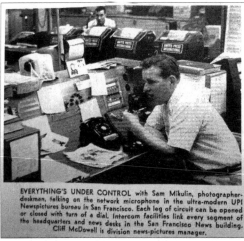

EVERYTHING'S UNDER CONTROL with Sam Mikulin, photographer-deskman, talking on the network microphone in the ultra-modern UPI Newspictures bureau in San Francisco. Each leg of circuit can be opened or closed with turn of a dial. Intercom facilities link every segment of the headquarters and news desks in the San Francisco News building. Cliff McDowell is division news-pictures manager.

Figure 21. "Everything's under control," *Editor & Publisher*, February 6, 1960, 36. The coordination and control of radio cars and other mobile technology affected improvements in more old-fashioned desk phones, as direct lines and other innovations came to the fore.

that puts itself out without manpower of any kind." Eventually "automatic devices" would combine to squeeze the humanity from newsrooms and newspapers, he claimed. Even the cub reporter and copy boy might find themselves replaced by "pneumatic types and automatic coffee and soft drink dispensers." These fears were farcical, but they contained a grain of truthful anxiety and spoke to worries about how newsroom relationships were being altered by technology.[139]

The telephone and the radio car, along with some of their ancillary newsgathering technologies, including battery-powered tape and wire recorders and hand-held radios, both disrupted and created work routines in and out of the newsroom. They gave agency to news workers, requiring a new set of practiced skills for their mastery, whether it was giving dictation over the phone or using a radio-equipped car to beat the competition. Conversely, the power of editors to coordinate and control their reporters was enhanced. As disruptive objects of newsgathering technology, the telephone and radio car were two-way, negotiated tools, freeing and tethering, empowering and disempowering reporters vis-à-vis their supervisors. The affordances brought by these technologies changed newsroom routines, culture, and the power dynamics between reporters, other types of news workers, and their editors.[140] Reporters and other news workers, including photographers, continued to answer to editors and other supervisors. Simultaneously, the new or updated technology allowed reporters to carve out more freedom in their work routines. It was neither a panacea nor a harbinger of doom. Workers deskilled, but also reskilled and upskilled with its introduction. On balance, though, the typical American newsroom, as *Editor & Publisher* columnist Jack Price described it in 1937, had become a "hair-sensitive organization equipped with every known device for receiving and translating news into reading matter with incredible speed."[141]

Media technology is renewable.[142] Its history in and out of the newsroom reflects this lived reality. That is, while its uses may evolve and change, it is hard for any one piece of technology to truly "die;" its development, retooling, abandonment, and repurposing do not follow a linear, easily predicted pattern. Telephones integrated themselves into the daily work lives of news workers so thoroughly that it remains hard for the latter, even today, to understand a world without them. This is true despite the fact that smartphones (itself a transitory name for what may prove to be a lasting piece of technology) are primarily computers. So it was that by the middle of the century most histories of newspapers did not actually mention the adoption of telephones into the newsroom, even if they mentioned other elements of their physical newsroom spaces. The telephone was too embedded, too essential, to be described explicitly and separately *apart from its use as a reporting tool.* This fact leads to a few key observations about newsroom technology during this era.

First, the cousin cultures of timeliness and mobility were already ingrained in the heart of much of twentieth-century journalism practice and encouraged a spirited, if uneven, adoption of technology. The impulse to seek out news at its source, to send it back to the newsroom, to publish it rapidly (and to update it whenever possible), was enhanced, and not lessened, by telephones and radio cars. These devices would never have been taken up as journalistic tools with as much enthusiasm and innovation if they had not tapped into the existing practices and motivations driving news workers and their bosses. If anything, they drove them faster, whether in the realm of enduring practices (calling sources) or more experimental ones (driving to the scenes of breaking news and then calling the newsroom). As Keith suggests, journalistic tools, like the editing software that appeared in the 1970s onward, reflected larger newsroom trends but also drove them.[143]

The second observation is that while the adoption and use of technology was part of a long-established pattern of news workers using tools to increase their storytelling prowess, this was not done in necessarily intentional ways. This was not a profound process. Rather, reporters and editors were pragmatic, and thought of themselves as such. They were reacting to new realities as much as adopting on purpose. For example, new tools required new ways of acculturating young reporters to their effective use (say, using the telephone), and established new routines built out of and on top of (or sometimes within) older ones. This meant that in-house training programs, when instituted, helped to maintain morale and eased concerns about the impact of these tools on employment (being good at calling in stories would not get you demoted, but maybe actually lead to promotion), and so on. Thus, while the accounts in trade journals tended toward a reflexive enthusiasm, a careful reading shows the nuance that comes from a human-driven construction of technology.

Third, the use of new communication tools shows how developments on one side of the newsroom—toward mobile technology—reinforced older technologies, such as desk phones. As newsrooms adopted computers for sorting data and word processing in the 1960s and 1970s, they continued these trends.[144] Business departments continued to drive innovation. With a vested interest in efficiency—part of a legacy from the era of industrialized newsrooms—ownership invested in modernization. Reporters and editors sometimes resisted, and at other times co-opted, these changes. By "efficiency," though, again, it is important to remember that rank-and-file news workers did not usually approach the use of new tools in any kind of holistic way. Rather, like us, they reacted to the introduction of new devices and adopted as best they could, with day-to-day exigencies driving their acceptance or rejection of tools. Coming into a space already structured by both vertical and horizontal hierarchies of power, the potential of radio, the car, and then the radio car was mitigated and molded by an existing, immersive culture of work practices. This culture accelerated and then cemented the separation of news gathering from news production, and set the stage for the computerization of the newsroom.

Fourth and finally, it remains vital to place newsroom technologies in their historically relational contexts. Without considering the *community* of workers that composed the newsroom's social life, tool adoption and its impact makes little sense. The phenomenon wherein, for instance, a reporter would feel both liberated from his or her newsroom with a radio car, or annoyed and tethered to their editor if called in that same car, is only understandable when considering that the sensation of continuous connection and freedom was *from someone else*, specifically, one's editor. It was not from a depersonalized newsroom building, but from the *people* within it. Socialization and reception by peers greatly affected how a news worker felt about, and used, a new technology tool, whether it be a radio car, a tape recorder, or other device. Affordances were and are only as good as the relationships that enable and sustain them.

## CHAPTER 8

# Unionization in the Newsroom

## Organizing and News Workers' Quality of Life

For a generation, reporters and other newsroom workers looked for relief from their daily newsroom toil through socialization: "Loyal, unorganized and proud, [they] sought satisfaction in their labor or quenched their burning humiliation or relaxed their exhausted bodies and minds at the nearest bar."[1] They adapted new technologies to their work. They organized hierarchies of power and the control to delegate, gather, and produce the news. But they also organized themselves, fighting for a better quality of life through the American Newspaper Guild, in-house unions, or aspirational-professional organizations like the Society of Professional Journalists. It was the unions, however, and the unionization of the newsroom, that brought about the most dramatic changes in working conditions in newsroom culture for the rest of the century. Shorter hours, better and more consistent pay (and annual raises), paid vacations, binding promises of job security, some control over the hiring and firing of peers, agreed-upon job descriptions, health insurance and healthcare, pensions, and even incentives to get married and have children were either the direct or indirect fruits of unionization. Gradually gaining force in the early to mid-1930s, by the late 1950s unionization was becoming the norm and not the exception in newsrooms. This paralleled a broader development, one in which unions of all kinds reached an apex of popularity and influence during this decade.[2]

While previous chapters have explored intranewsroom dynamics involving peers and near peers, peers and bosses, the impact of unionization on those relationships changed news workers' lived experiences. The history of the ANG and the legal maneuverings of publishers regarding white-collar regulation have been explored before by other scholars.[3] But as Bonnie Brennen has pointed out, the actual day-to-day lives of news workers during and after unionization has remained underexamined in traditional media histories.[4] Other studies of newsroom unionization have focused on the early years of the ANG, on specific newsrooms or sections of the country, or the

ANG's relationship to larger organizations. But only a handful have tried to put newsroom unionization in the larger context of industrial journalism, especially outside of the northeastern United States.

Granted, not every reporter was a member of the Guild, or even supported it as it transformed from a loose confederation of reformist newsroom workers in the 1930s to a more traditional labor and then an "industrial" union by the 1950s. Some worked hard to stay affiliated with the American Federation of Labor (AFL) after the Guild moved toward affiliation with the more radical Congress of Industrial Organizations (CIO). Others formed alternatives. Some unions fought over the right to represent news workers, sometimes requiring the intervention of the National Labor Relations Board (NLRB) under the Wagner Act.[5] Alfred McClung Lee, in his classic history of American journalism, noted in 1937 that seven news worker chapters of the AFL lasted through 1936, but that five of these eventually joined the ANG.[6] Since the CIO generally encouraged the unionization of all trades working at a newspaper, some reporters and editors wanted to distance themselves from these industrial unionization efforts.

The unionization of the newsroom went through several stages. The successful organizing movement that began in 1933 was at first widely diffused, with its main centers of power in New York City and Cleveland. Others sprang up in parallel, including in the Twin Cities and Philadelphia. The unionization movement reacted to the efforts of publishers attempting to evade federal regulation, with a proactive "guild" response, focused on improving wages and hours. After the failure of more overt attempts to regulate industries like newspapers after 1935, unionization took a more militant, or industrial, turn, interrupted by World War II, but resuming in earnest afterward. From about 1945 through the early 1960s, unionization took root and became part of the newsroom workers' aspiration to white-collar status.[7] This was part of their larger professionalization project and coincided with postwar generational, societal, and cultural changes reflected in the newsroom.

Unionization was more than a legal movement. It disrupted newsroom dynamics, reinforced old patterns, and created new ones. It lessened the power of bosses, empowered more established reporters and editors, and created a more standardized workplace in terms of pay and advancement. When women and minorities had the opportunity to enter largely white, male newsrooms, the union also advocated for them. It helped to enable their agency as workers and treated them less like pioneers and more as colleagues. But it was not a cure-all: publishers and senior editors still retained power, new personnel still endured newsroom indoctrination, and some reporters were marginalized when they declined to embrace total unionization, whether through the ANG or its alternatives. The unionization of the newsroom is worth its own examination, then, because workers struggled against existing constraints while creating new patterns of power.[8]

### BEFORE THE GUILD: FIRST ATTEMPTS

Early efforts to form a union for news workers on the editorial side began in earnest after World War I. Workers at newsrooms across the country attempted short-lived affiliations with International Typographical Union (ITU) chapters. Most of these did not survive into the 1920s. But for brief moments, in the early 1890s and from 1919 to 1920, unionization of newsrooms seemed possible.[9] Media labor historian Daniel Leab characterizes the ITU as an umbrella union for mechanical workers in the newspaper industry, which attempted to organize reporters and editors as part of a bid to strengthen its own bargaining position with publishers before the turn of the last century. The ITU did so at a time when many editorial workers could still set type and perform other mechanical tasks on the production side of the newspaper. In this capacity, some helped to break strikes by full-time mechanical workers. But efforts to organize faltered. Of the fifty-nine local ITU chapters chartered with the express purpose of organizing editorial workers in more than forty US and Canadian cities between 1891 and 1923, only a handful—six—survived for more than five years, with most lasting no more than a year or a year and a half.[10] News workers either could not afford or simply chose not to pay the relatively expensive ITU dues that were used to fund pension and insurance plans. They also tended, due to their opportunity-seeking nature, to move from city to city, and idealized their occupation as being above or not in need of unionization. Reporters were supposed to be different: working with their heads and not only with their hands. Of course, production jobs still called for intelligence and hard work, but a sharp cultural divide emerged in the interwar years.

After World War I, as the cost of living spiked some 15 percent, newspapers closed, and millions of young men returned to the job market, there was renewed if fleeting interest in the ITU. Fifteen ITU locals were authorized in 1919 alone.[11] As news workers joined a national movement that was already prone to labor agitation, the summer and fall of that year held potential for further unionization. Walter Williams, dean of the University of Missouri's

School of Journalism, predicted that as long as publishers invested in their machinery more than in "the salaries or wages of the men and women whose brain cells feed the presses and machines," nonmechanical news workers would be tempted to join forces with the ITU.[12] Even the conservative *Editor & Publisher* commented that with the dollar having lost half its buying power, salaries for the men "upstairs" (i.e., in the newsroom, versus the mechanical jobs at the paper) were inadequate. As *Editor & Publisher* put it, "it would, indeed, be hard to find a publisher who does not admit that a capable reporter should receive at least as high a wage as a capable printer."[13]

But that moment faded as most publishers struck back hard, blackballing reporters who organized ITU locals and refusing to cover their efforts in the news pages. When they did merit coverage, news workers' rancor and collapse tended to be highlighted, especially after the initial wave of interest had passed.[14] As one publisher, W. B. Bryant of the Patterson (New Jersey) *Press Guardian*, explained, he had been open to negotiating with editorial workers' groups if they did not unite with mechanical workers. But once they did, he and others refused to negotiate. Newsrooms, already workplaces where news workers held comparatively little power, stayed that way. The reality remained that if the ITU did not support reporters and editors, newsroom unionization would have little teeth. Opposition was framed as a freedom-of-the-press issue, as it would be during the 1930s and 1940s. Characteristically, Bryant wrote, "Which, I would ask, would be in the majority. The mechanical or the brain workers? Could there be an independent press under those conditions?"[15] In New York City during the summer of 1919, despite support from the Typographical Union No. 6 (the "Big Six"), arguably the most important ITU chapter in the country, the ANPA's chief union negotiator expressed skepticism that a "skilled newspaper man" would want to be "fettered by an arbitrary wage scale," since so many treated reporting as a stepping stone to "some other kind of work that pays them much better."[16] This skepticism was not unfounded. Editorial workers themselves continued to resist organization, falling prey again to their own self-perceptions as entrepreneurs first, and a class of workers second.[17] The larger suspicion of collective worker actions during the era of red scares did not help, either.

Only a handful of ITU locals continued into the new decade, including the Scranton Newswriters Union, founded in 1907. A 1932 *Quill* profile identified the "benign" nature of the local ownership as responsible for its survival.[18] More often, these nascent chapters folded; if they survived, they became a more pliable in-house union, as happened in Rochester, New York, where the Newswriters' Union No. 16 of the ITU became the Rochester Newspaper Writers' Association.[19] For most news workers, even in cities with more than one competing newspaper and multiple owners, such as Chicago, New York, St. Louis, Seattle, and Boston, organizing was a hot or cold proposition.[20] Unless they tapped into a preexisting source of unity, such as language or ethnicity, there were simply too many competing interests, and little experience with organizing.[21] In St. Louis, where the ANG would later have some of its most ardent early supporters, reporters and editors managed to organize themselves enough to successfully demand, and receive, a cost-of-living bonus. This approximately five-dollar-a-week increase in salaries at the St. Louis *Times*, *Post-Dispatch*, and *Republic* empowered the reporters and editors of that city, who reveled in the rare 20 percent overall boost in pay.[22] This success was self-defeating, however: ultimately the concessions undercut any resolve to organize newsrooms there further.

But their "St. Louis Plan" helped to inspire the short-lived formation of the American Journalists Association (AJA), complete with its own column in *Editor & Publisher*.[23] This organization lost momentum by 1925, co-opted by publishers and subject to the same malaise that seemed to afflict all news workers.[24] In 1923 the ITU disbanded its attempts to organize nonmechanical news workers. The AFL moved into this vacuum, chartering six locals over the next decade, but three soon collapsed and the survivors had only limited memberships, such as in Chicago, where members worked primarily for that city's Jewish-language newspapers.[25] It did not help that by the mid-1920s the American economy had improved and workers felt less urgently drawn to protounion efforts. Foreshadowing later developments, Heywood Broun, the well-known *New York World* columnist and animating spirit of the ANG during the 1930s, petitioned the AFL for a charter for his small "Organization of News Writers" (identified elsewhere as the "New York News Writers Union"). Some seventy-five members strong, it kept most of its members' identities secret for fear of retaliation by publishers.[26]

## NEWSROOM RELATIONSHIPS BEFORE UNIONIZATION

Historian of late nineteenth and early twentieth-century reporter culture Ted Curtis Smythe has examined the brutal newsroom work conditions of the last turn of the century, and other historians have touched on them too.[27] They are worth revisiting here, briefly, as they pertain to the early interwar period. News workers, in their memoirs or in union-friendly publications such as the *Guild Reporter* (or mostly union-neutral publications such as the *Quill*), recalled an uncertain time, even in larger cities on bigger publications.

Reporters were hired and fired haphazardly, publishers and owners generally intervened readily and directly in the smallest details of work life, and news workers were often mobile between and within cities. This was the generation preceding the working détente arranged between publishers and editorial staffs, as described by Daniel Hallin, in which the former gave the latter freedom to oversee their internal affairs in exchange for a product that produced a steady profit.[28] How one recalled pre-Guild conditions depended distinctly on whether one exercised supervisory power in the newsroom. Most middle- and senior-level editors disputed the idea that unionization was necessary. Many reporters, however, even those who later soured somewhat on aspects of "industrial unionism," appreciated the Guild's influence.

Figure 22. "Afoul of those rules," *Guild Reporter*, November 22, 1937, 3. In the conflicts between the ANG and the ANPA, among other groups, the ANG often pointed out the arbitrary rules imposed by powerful, anti-union publishers.

Moe Raiser, a member of the San Francisco-Oakland Guild and a reporter for the *Call-Bulletin*, recalled how "you never refused an assignment, no matter how many extra hours it took, if you wanted to hang onto your job." To do otherwise led to being "fired on the spot." Wage cuts appeared arbitrarily. First they might appear on a bulletin board with an apology, then via a note without an apology, and then reflected in paychecks. Some more humane bosses would give time off in lieu of pay, or try to give some kind of notice of pay and hour reductions, but others would either fail to track time off or track it haphazardly, or announce cuts without preamble.[29] According to a former treasurer of the ANG and former staff member on the New York *Evening News*, the average weekly wage in 1934 for reporters was $30, with no set hours, which were "stretched to fill all the time in which any news developed."[30]

But from the perspective of management, the culture of work was beginning to transform even before the Guild and unionization helped to change newsroom life. Writing two years before the formation of the ANG, the executive editor of the *Chattanooga News* noted that reporters used to work "for the joy of chasing news and cared little for the comforts of life so long as they could . . . borrow a cigarette."[31] Now, however reporters had changed, and went home as soon as possible "in their own car" and had the free time to "to help [the] wife plant roses or take the baby for an airing." Better educated, they enjoyed "poring over a book of poems or writing a book review for the literary editor." Salaries meant investment in real estate, stocks and bonds, radios, or automobiles. And even their conversation was less salty, involving "philosophy or the latest play or their golf scores rather than about some brewing political scandal." Having forgotten the "art of intelligent loafing," this meant, from the editors' perspective, that their reporters were less keen to take on tough stories, government pressure, or business influence.[32] This was an unfair conclusion, as editors typically felt more pressure from advertisers and local politicians than a typical reporter. Some editors, in contrast, acknowledged the negative sides of the arbitrary work conditions of the pre-Guild era. An editor at the *Cleveland Press* remembered how his peers used to be able to "sweep out a lot of people on a Saturday afternoon and on Monday morning hire a lot of others to replace them." But the Guild meant more security, other editors admitted, which meant there were "fewer men leaving jobs and fewer good men being fired and the time is past, it seems to me, when any newspaper can expect to find good men wandering around looking for jobs." It also meant that "good men are staying on their jobs. They are not being fired and they are not quitting and, when a vacancy comes, if there is not somebody already in the organization ready to fill it, then the chances of getting competent help in that job are not very good."[33]

Even later management skeptics of the Guild, like Marlen Pew, at least initially believed it could provide a needed safety net. He predicted in September 1933 that "brutal uncertainty, lack [of] appreciation, surly official snarling, cynical disrespect of sensitive and striving people in some offices are bitterer pills than low wages and long hours." If and when unionization occurred under the federal government's New Deal industry regulations,[34] "it will not be half so much because they are impoverished in pocket as that they have been kept miserable in their souls." Hiring practices that only recruited "hard-boiled, ruthless and essentially ignorant people" and that looked out first for the interests of a publisher, with low pay and morale pervading newsrooms, could be an "explosive" combination.[35] Less than a month later, Pew's magazine, responding to dueling ANG and ANPA estimates of average newsroom salaries, conceded "that editorial pay is scandalously out of line, in view of the creative character of the work and the obligations the editorial department places on employees." Still, this begrudging acceptance by industry observers such as Pew had its limits. The ANG, *Editor & Publisher* also commented, was developing too quickly "into a radical labor union, with A.F. of L. affiliations, called 'co-operation,' and publishers in general are rejecting it."[36]

"Shop Talk at Thirty" columnist Arthur Robb, commenting in *Editor & Publisher*, for which he also served as the editor in chief after the passing of Pew in 1936,[37] found the expansion of the Guild into the *New York Times* hard to understand in 1941. A victory for the ANG, it helped to legitimize the spread of unions to other elite East Coast newspapers.[38] Particularly confusing to Robb was the all-encompassing approach the now-CIO-affiliated Guild had taken, and why the writing and editing members of a newspaper would want to be associated with office support staff.[39] Reporters and editors had been "sold" and "swindled" on "the idea that they were mechanical craftsmen." He believed this meant they were now the "tail of the guild kite, outnumbered and outvoted by people of far less importance in the newspaper picture," and that this was "another evidence of the insane years through which we have been passing." But he did concede the ANG's raison d'être. Reflecting on its first ten years and rocky expansion, he admitted that "the championship of such men as Heywood

Broun, Kenneth Crawford, Harry Martin, and other sincere writing people who looked to it for no personal gain but as a necessary protection for their fellows" gave it legitimacy.[40]

Writing later in the *Quill* in 1956, the managing editor of the Louisville *Times* acknowledged that the "Guild came into being because of the blindness and the economic stupidity of newspaper owners." While "it was the inevitable development of a fantastic imbalance—of a period when the pay to printers was double that of skilled reporters," the Guild had become a "trade organization dedicated to a leveling process." That process pushed against publishers, who were still "fundamentally dedicated to the proposition that profits have to be maintained even at the expense of responsible performance.[41] Also in 1956, Carl Kesler, then editor of the *Quill*, admitted that he still had mixed feelings about the Guild. While he was not entirely sure of the soundness of management's argument that the "union accent on minimum salary scales, particularly in the starting brackets and the semi-editorial classifications, takes the money that might go into merit raises," he believed a different kind of work culture had taken root in the newsroom. Without the Guild and its "flat unionization," the "old pro," or older reporter, "would have been cherished[,] . . . kept around on most newspapers without . . . contracts saying just how well he would be treated."[42] Other critics believed that the Guild had moved from its "original craft union purpose into a vertical industrial union," in that it had merged "the editorial forces and many other kinds of employees on newspapers and periodicals."[43] Opposition had generally increased from publishers when the Guild moved toward its affiliation with the CIO in June 1937 and away from its initial affiliation with the AFL. The latter had taken place less than a year before, in July 1936.[44] Publishers accused the federal government of favoring labor over their interests and encouraged criticism or published their own.[45] Franklin Roosevelt's perceived prolabor bias supposedly fueled "coddling laws and practices."[46]

The Guild, though, speaking through Milton Murray, its president in 1947, was proud of this merger and of its identity as more "industrial" than "craft." In a rare speech to publishers at their annual convention, and representing a slight thaw in the tensions between the ANG and the American Society of Newspaper Editors, Murray defended the legacy of the former. Murray focused on the issue of wages, claiming that "the Guild is raising the standards of journalism by raising the rate of pay." Raising pay had helped to keep young workers in journalism who would otherwise have "drifted off into other fields." Publishers and the Guild shared the same basic goal of hiring "competent and capable staffs." Ultimately, Murray defended the Guild's "industrial union" status as "a community of interest among newspaper employees" and encouraged a continued working peace.[47]

### NEWSROOM RELATIONSHIPS DURING THE ANG'S FORMATION

In 1933, as editorial workers around the country endured a deepening Depression, they found themselves again at the mercy of their publishers and the industry's habit of weathering economic storms by cutting both salaries and jobs. Mergers and closings hastened further job loss. Attempts by the federal government to intervene were often rebuffed by newspaper owners. News workers reacted to publisher resistance to the efforts of the National Recovery Administration (NRA). But unlike in former times, they were better organized, motivated, and led. Inspired by the "prime mover," Heywood Broun, now a columnist for the *World-Telegram*, some of the first and largest efforts to organize came in New York City. In an early August 1933 column in the *World-Telegram*, Broun called for a "union of reporters."[48] Two months later "a massive meeting of New York newspaper writers" helped to create "the Guild of New York Newspaper Men and Women." In announcements posted to newspaper bulletin boards throughout the city, the group called for a forty-hour, five-day work week, thirty-five-dollar minimums for those with a year or more of experience, paid vacations, discharge notice, minimum wages, and elimination of clause 14 of the revised publisher's code (which discouraged unionization for collective bargaining).[49] The nascent New York chapter of the Guild starting meeting in August and September during the lead-up to the NRA's industry code hearings in September. It formed officially on December 15, 1933, and quickly began to organize locals throughout the country.

Other newspaper workers in other cities, notably Cleveland, had also been organizing haphazardly before Broun's column. Reporters repurposed newsroom mimeograph machines, and their personal networks of friends and colleagues, to rally support for the cause, even if it was vague beyond opposing the publishers' proposed code.[50] As before, reporters had a hard time staying united. Meetings were fractious, erratically attended, and unfocused, as many had little or no experience creating such a collective enterprise as a union. The labor reporters among them were often elected to leadership positions because they, at least, had some exposure to how union meetings were run.

But the hearings themselves, taking place September 22 and 23, 1933, formed a further rallying cry for the first wave of unionizing editorial workers. With the organizing efforts of the New York City group, eleven spokespersons, representing fifteen proto-ANG chapters, were present at the NRA's meetings at the Department of Commerce in Washington, DC. They testified after the publishers' delegates, calling for a five-day, forty-hour week, with a minimum wage scale of twenty dollars a week for news workers with less than a year's experience and thirty for those with one to two years' experience. They also asked for a discharge notice except in egregious cases and appealed provisions in the temporary code banning unions from representing workers. Three months later the NRA would ignore these appeals and ultimately adopt most of the publishers' demands, including hour-and-wage exceptions for those deemed "professional" by their bosses, based on a forthcoming Bureau of Labor Statistics (BLS) survey of "news department worker" salaries. The temporary code, with its thirty-five-dollars-a-week standard for that "professional" status, was not replaced by a baseline dollar figure, pending the results of the BLS survey. This caused confusion within the ranks of news workers, who insisted that they were not "professional" workers if that meant they could be paid less. Despite their protests, the final code went into effect in February 1934.[51]

News workers won one minor concession: the removal of a clause ensuring an "open shop" status that would have practically blocked organizing. Otherwise, the nascent groups that would form the ANG in December were dissatisfied—fueling the birth of the national organization. Leab believes that if the code had made even a few more concessions, the ANG would never have developed enough momentum to develop as it did. More importantly, for the first time, news workers had spoken on a (more or less) united front on a national stage, "as workers consciously concerned with common economic problems" and speaking on behalf of their fellows.[52] The publishers, for their part, remained unconvinced their industry needed to adhere to the code in either the spirit or the letter of the law. Of the 540 codes (essentially, binding legal rules) adopted, it was among the most difficult to write and administer, as well as being continually opposed by owners, who believed, sincerely or not, that their editorial freedom was in danger.[53]

Two schools of thought guided how and why to organize in the Guild's early, formative days: the first emphasized an *economic* orientation—its goal was to raise salaries and advocate for better hours. In this regard, it was a *traditional* union. The second kind of organization effort wanted a more "professional" approach that highlighted career development and vocational advocacy in the vein of the British Institute of Journalists (versus the more pragmatic and working-class National Union of Journalists).[54] As Benjamin Scott has argued, the ANG was pursuing autonomy from publishers as part of a more professionalized identity.[55] Ultimately, the economic orientation prevailed, but an element of the professionalizing faction remained.

The later success of the ANG in unionizing the newsroom remained constrained by several factors. ANG contracts never covered an overwhelming majority of working reporters and editors. While pro-union or at least neutral sources like the *Guild Reporter* and *Quill* tended to emphasize the growth and power of the Guild and in-house unions, publications and organizations antagonistic to the Guild (such as *Editor & Publisher* and the various monthly and annual publications of publisher and management groups) downplayed the newsroom unionization movement. They also highlighted in-house union activity, especially when it was friendly to publishers.[56]

Undaunted, the Guild claimed an exaggerated membership of more than ten thousand by May 1937, with eighty-eight active chapters.[57] Some of these estimates were skewed toward the higher end as non-newsroom office workers began to affiliate with local ANG chapters. In 1938, for example, out of a claimed membership of 16,797, some 3,292 were "commercial" workers. And more than half of the Guild's growth over the previous year was due to the latter kind of member.[58] Data from the Department of Commerce and Labor identified a field with 51,844 men and women working as reporters and editors in 1930, 58,253 in 1940, and 90,325 in 1950.[59] This shows that even as the Guild grew to more than seventeen thousand reported members in 1941, and then twenty-six thousand in 1951, its membership never encompassed the majority of American news workers.[60] At most, it was an influential minority. A labor historian of the era notes that "the Guild was essentially a big city organization, based upon several strong points, and extending into smaller communities mainly where these were already strong union territory." Guild influence was not felt in rural areas and smaller cities (or even in larger cities in the South, where the Southern Newspaper Publishers Association remained opposed to Guild contracts) to anywhere near the degree it was in the larger cities. The limited impact of the Guild was a subject of some derision in the pro-publisher trade press, at least initially.[61] Still, as the union's numbers and chapters grew, so did a working détente with publishers. After World War II, publishers became more pragmatic and accepting in their interactions with the Guild, even as they still complained about its power.[62]

Figure 23. "Pardon us for pointing—" *Guild Reporter*, October 1, 1942, 12. In this cartoon, the ANG is portrayed as a positive force for quality-of-life benefits, even in the midst of World War II.

## NEWSROOM RELATIONSHIPS AFTER THE ANG'S FORMATION

A result of this détente could be seen in the development of a new, union-influenced, newsroom relationship dynamic during the 1930s and into the 1950s. Editors and managers were dealing with a new kind of reporter. News workers had become more college-educated, assertive, and independent. Publishers and senior editors could no longer act as unilaterally in the newsroom as they could previously. This became clear during strikes organized by chapters of the ANG. Publishers believed strikes over wages and hours were "clear evidence that management has lost the control it ought to hold." To reassert control involved remaining calm during negotiations with union leadership over contracts: "It takes genuine manliness, as compared with the spurious variety that resorts to the punch in the jaw, to convince a negotiating committee that their demands are impossible and that the proposition is the honest best that can be offered." A publisher could be concerned about the wellbeing of his or her workers but could not "carry it into the conference room with labor unions." It is perhaps telling that for publishers, union assertiveness meant "the idea that a man has an interest in his job—a new and unproven concept of the relations of employer and employ[ees]."

For many employers, the presence of unionized workers represented at first a threat, then a sustained interruption, to their power.[63] Some reacted with subtle threats. Speaking through their managers, publishers told reporters and junior-level editors that Guild activity could cost promotions or would result in a more unpleasant work environment. Even if they were not fired, reporters or sometimes editors could be reassigned to different beats, or even to the newspaper's library (i.e., its "morgue") in retaliation.[64] Sometimes reporters or other newsroom staffers would be told directly that they had to quit organizing or leave the Guild if they wanted to keep their jobs, especially before World War II. After a prominent rewrite staffer at the San Francisco *Call-Bulletin* was intimidated into resigning for his union activity, a copy editor at the same paper was lectured by a managing editor, who said that the Guild was "an 'anti-Hearst organization . . . run by a bunch of crack pots.'" The copy editor was also told that he was "making a mistake by putting your neck in a noose."[65]

While more formalized, negotiations themselves were a sign that publishers had lost the ability to ignore or effectively punish attempts to organize. As the ANG formed, publishers sometimes refused to sign their names to union contracts, agreeing to demands informally through representatives or via posted signs, in what a contemporary called "the bulletin-board agreement era." That ended when the NLRB recognized the Guild increasingly in the 1940s and 1950s as the majority bargaining agent on newspapers that had voted to elect the union as its representative with ownership.[66] While the transition of the ANG to a more powerful force within the industry was heralded by many rank-and-file workers as a good thing, many publishers already opposed to the Guild believed that it had encouraged a "gleeful haste from a quasi-professional status into the security of unionism."[67] By the 1950s staff relationships had moved to the "impersonal," and the emphasis for many newspapers was on financial imperatives, especially in the wake of the Depression. For a generation, there had been consequences to applying "'strictly business' methods to the artistic and professional side of putting out a newspaper," claimed one industry observer. Among them was the creation of an overzealous union, in which "radical labor union tactics" had tended to play "to the gallery and, intentionally or not, forced drastic action when the mutual interests of both parties indicated moderation."[68] While this impersonal management style was portrayed by publishers as more antagonistic toward workers, it reflected a broader change for many US firms: fewer papers were owned by local business people and more were owned by chains and corporations.[69] This new reality represented, in the words of the general manager of the *New York News*, a "division of interests."[70]

Early and brief forays into proactive collaboration between management and unions were not unknown, though. At the Los Angeles *Daily News* in 1942, a management-employee advisory council was formed to manage the multiple unions, not just newsroom workers, but mechanical, business, and circulation, to name a few, that could exist on the same newspaper. Representatives from management and the AFL-affiliated, CIO-affiliated, newsboy, and typographical unions would meet regularly to engage with specific departmental problems from "all angles of the question involved." This sort of power sharing was ahead of its time, spurred by the effect of World War II on union relations (in the newspaper industry, this meant setting aside severe disagreements for a time). While there were strikes by mechanical workers, the ANG generally avoided aggressive confrontations with publishers, holding to a truce during the war years.[71]

After the war, the role of mediator (or arbiter) was taken up in some cases by newly formed human resources departments. As discussed in chapter 6, these HR units negotiated to reduce tensions at larger newspapers such as the *Philadelphia Inquirer*. There, Stewart Hooker, the personnel director and a committee member of the Newspaper Personnel Relations Association, affiliated with the ANPA, emphasized screening and placement of news workers on the editorial side. Working within a more unionized environment, HR directors like Hooker could not only recommend but directly hire reporters or other workers. With fifteen union locals represented at the paper—five alone in the rotogravure (or photo-printing) divisions—and thirty-four hundred workers, Hooker had a busy job.[72] Some publishers had to engage with up to twenty-five separate unions.[73] HR managers thus took on an important role as part of a growing middle-management class within newsrooms.

By the middle of the 1950s, newspaper unions could negotiate from a stronger position. This was helped by an intervention-inclined NLRB and rules like the so-called "Kiss-and-Tell Doctrine," which required management to share their payroll data with unions, including "jobs, names, [and] amounts received in salary and merit for the purposes of collective bargaining." Publishers worried that this rule and others like it would further disempower them from offering raises based on merit.[74] Several years later, the NLRB would limit the expansiveness of this transparency measure, deciding that unions would have to be content with consolidated tax returns and

Figure 24. "Grin and bear it," September 26, 1952, 7. In this cartoon, published in the ANG's *Guild Reporter*, a labor negotiator is unceremoniously tossed out of a door window. Cartoonist George Lichty drew the image for the Chicago Sun-Times Syndicate.

financial statements during wage bargaining with management.[75] But the ANG was not going away, and indeed had already influenced the industry, bringing it more in line with other white-collar occupations.

Debates about reporters' "professional" standing did not fade away in the midst of this, however. The ANG continued to advocate for the older standard of a $500-a-month salary as the definition of a "professional" person. This higher salary level meant that the upper echelon of newsroom management could be restricted from labor-union membership. Unions, for their part, wanted to expand their membership, while keeping ownership-influenced senior editors out of their ranks. Ultimately, according to a contemporary, the debate over "professional" status "centered on the type of work performed, with the editorial and reportorial workers being the focus of difference."[76]

The ANPA had argued unsuccessfully since the second stage of New Deal–era reforms for the widest possible application of a "professional" standing for news workers.[77] Somewhat ironically, the gradually growing acceptance of college as a route into journalism was tied by publishers to these professional claims (as understood at the time). As part of the federal government's test for professionalism in an industry, the ANPA believed that "an individual who has studied at a school of journalism may be regarded as professional; newspapermen, who have not attended such institutions, non-professional."[78] Some publishers also felt that the consistent use of bylines could help distinguish "professional" reporters from those not considered as such.[79] Keen to minimize the power of unions to grow and organize, these definitions were based less on altruistic desires to elevate news workers than on financial concerns about the increasing personnel costs brought by an assertive Guild presence.

From the federal government's perspective, the capacity to hire and fire remained the crucial distinction between an employee and a supervisor during the 1930s and 1940s for all news workers. Elmer E. Andrews, administrator of the Wage and Hour division of the Department of Labor, addressed the 1939 ANG convention regarding this point. For example, a copy editor was "under the constant supervision of the head of the desk, and the sports editor and other departmental heads generally are under the supervision of the managing editor," and so was not independent enough to be considered an "executive" and not "professional" enough to be exempt from negotiations. Andrews and his office (and his successors) disregarded the liberal sprinkling of "editor" in titles. As a result, Andrews urged, the ANG and other unions were right to contend for a much more restricted definition of "executive."[80] The unions were concerned with actual control over work processes and workers. In a way, they foreshadowed more holistic definitions of "professional" status as defined by sociologists later in the century.[81]

### SALARIES AND BENEFITS: TRENDS UNDER UNIONIZATION[82]

Unionization generally helped raise and stabilize, as well as standardize, news workers' wages, even in non-ANG newsrooms. In time, the union's presence also helped to raise salaries to levels on par with other white-collar jobs. While this took a generation, news workers in 1960 were far better off than they had been in 1920: they worked shorter hours, made more money more consistently per week, were better protected from dismissals, layoffs, or misfortune, were better educated, and had more opportunities to venture outside of journalism into lucrative fields like public relations (and within journalism, try upwardly mobile careers in other media such as radio and television). A general rise in weekly salaries lay at the root of this improved socioeconomic status.

The Guild was particularly successful at boosting salaries for those in the lower pay brackets, including entry-level reporters, younger editors, copy boys and girls, and photographers. Editorial staff who had been fairly well paid, comparatively, before the advent of unionization (copy editors, rewrite staff, senior editors, correspondents, columnists, et al.) continued to be well paid.[83] While management and some reporters and editors worried union contracts would keep less-talented workers employed and thus have a flattening effect on achievement, that did not generally prove to be the case. Instead, news workers enjoyed a rare parity with colleagues in business, banking, marketing, government, and to a lesser degree, engineering. Medicine and law continued to far outpace journalism's pay scales, but as part of the field's acceptance of college graduates, weekly salaries had never been better for newsroom staff by the end of the 1950s, even factoring inflation to a degree (see chart opposite).

While variable, pay for reporters and editors had been slowly improving in the years before the Depression. In a general move away from the "space" system (in which reporters had been paid only for what was published, not too unlike members of the "gig economy" of the 2010s), the industry had reduced uncertainty by moving to weekly salaries. But the lack of any sort of collective bargaining meant that these salaries, and any raises, were entirely at the whim of the employer. Job security was also extremely tenuous. While many publishers thought of their role as paternalistic, others did not hesitate to cut payroll (either by reducing pay or firing people for "economic" reasons). Prior to the emergence of the Guild, the payroll of newsroom workers was one area that owners could reliably trim to lower publication costs.

In contrast to the ITU's members, reporters and editors had no one to appeal to if they were laid off. This led to a national 12 to 16 percent decline in wages for reporters, photographers, and "desk men" (a broad category that included copy editors, but also special-section editors, assistant city editors, and news editors) between the spring of 1930 and the fall of 1934. In contrast to executives (i.e., senior editors), who faced a 10 percent decline, rank-and-file newsroom workers could not hope for quick restorations of these cuts. Neither could they leave for other jobs in the same city, as newspapers

Weekly salaries for US reporters and editors compared to selected white-collar occupations, 1920–1960

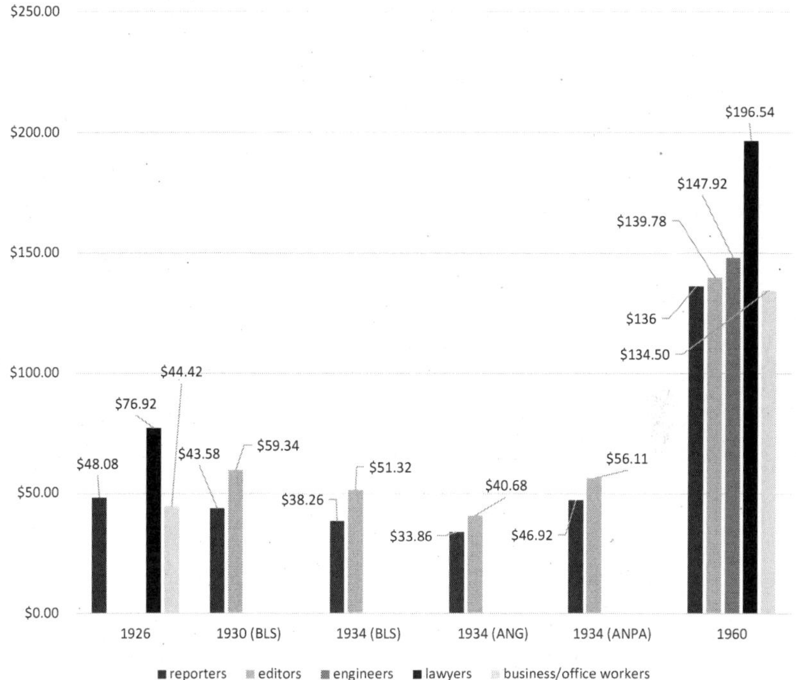


Figure 25. In this chart, self-reported salaries show how much reporters and editors made compared to some of their professional peers in other occupations. Created by the author.[84]

closed and consolidated in many places.[85] As Philip Glende and Leab have pointed out, the ANG's arrival coincided with a grim forecast in the economic outlook for lower-ranking news workers. But unlike other moments when these workers tried but failed to sustain organizing, white-collar news workers were successful, ultimately, in raising their base pay across the country. The Guild did not accomplish this on its own—the national mood tolerated unionization generally across industries—but its plucky efforts and motivated members brought publishers to the bargaining table.

Publishers were more confident and comfortable negotiating with the ITU. In the words of S. E. Thomason, publisher of the *Chicago Times*, in 1941, "the guild had not attained that degree of responsibility shown by printing trades unions which enjoy closed shop conditions."[86] The concept of the "closed shop," in which newsroom workers could not be hired unless they joined the ANG chapter or an in-house or other union, was firmly opposed by most publishers, who feared further erosion to their ability to hire and fire staff. But critics not associated with either the ANG or the ANPA believed that some publishers overreacted to the ANG's demands. The editors of the Topeka *State Journal* and St. Louis *Star-Times*, while decrying what they called a "mob union," pointed out that calling a "Guild shop" a "closed shop" was unfair, and that there was a place for some kind of worker representation, especially since reporters' wages were particularly vulnerable to cuts.[87] Another divisive issue was "maintenance of membership" contracts. These required editorial workers under union contract to maintain membership in their local chapters of the ANG.[88] Members could be dismissed for failing to renew their membership, which in some cases could be renewed automatically. ANG chapters and locals believed this would help stabilize or even increase their numbers, while publishers and some dissatisfied staff believed this limited their freedom to hire and fire.[89]

After the war, the Guild became more assertive and sweeping in its demands, at least symbolically. In 1946 the ANG set as its national goal a salary of $100 per week for "experienced employees," including reporters, with a $50 minimum. In 1951, claiming to adjust for inflation, the Guild raised that standard to $138.40 and in 1954 adjusted it up to $150. The first $100 minimum contracts appeared in 1948, with eight such contracts issued. By 1952, twenty-six contracts had some kind of $100 minimum. This fit the ANG goal of "full union security" for its members.[90] And though this was much more of a reality in the big East Coast cities, especially New York, other large metro areas, including Chicago and the Bay Area, were also known for high salaries. In San Francisco in 1952, the Guild was able to ask for a $140 minimum for workers with more than six years' experience, compared to the original pay scale of $113.50. Management opposed the increases, claiming that profits, and not the cost of living or differentials in pay, should drive the ability of owners to raise salaries. Eventually, with help from an outside arbiter, the Guild local was able to win $2 to $6 increases, with "top reporter minimums" for those with more than six years' experience topping out at $119.50, meaning the area's reporters were among the highest paid outside of New York City.[91]

But even as reporters' and editors' salaries improved, there were lingering worries from unionized news workers about the sustainability of the "living wage." Many issues of the *Guild Reporter* through the 1950s contained anxious analyses of cost-of-living increases in a generally improving US economy. Their authors pointed out that even as baseline minimums hit and then exceeded one hundred dollars a week for many reporters (not just experienced workers), this development still only brought the typical worker to within approximate parity with non-newsroom office workers. Anxieties also persisted that unionization was not doing enough to stem the perceived tide of college graduates into other fields. As college was normalized as a route into newsrooms and up the ladder of power within, minimum salaries of $77.50 a week were considered too low by some observers in 1956. Advertising and public relations remained especially lucrative alternatives for print journalism graduates, as well as for established news workers, who could work more regular hours and earn more with less stress in those fields.[92]

Such was the attempt to portray print journalism as a college-graduate-friendly career that the ANPA put ads in the *Quill* in 1954 claiming that reporters could make fifty to seventy-five dollars a week to start, and five thousand to seven thousand a year after five years, with newspaper executives making ten thousand a year; pension plans and hospitalization insurance were offered too, it claimed. Part of this white-collar appeal was the idea that "the newspaper office . . . presents an atmosphere so relaxed as to compare favorably with the annual picnic and clambake of more prosaic places of business." Reporters could stash their coats and keep on their hats, and the grooves on the desks were probably inflicted as much by heels as elbows, contemporaries claimed. In an era characterized by formality in office settings, newsrooms stood out for their sense of "comradery" and social bonhomie.[93]

In an admonition to newsroom managers in 1955, the authors of a journalism business textbook summarized postwar Guild expectations for salaries. The authors claimed that the newspaper industry had reached or exceeded pay equality with other industries in the United States, citing the BLS Wage-Hour Report to prove it: in May 1953 the average weekly salary of *all* nonsupervisor news workers was $92.48 for a 26.7-hour week, as compared to "all manufacturing" workers, at $71.63 a week for 40.7 hours of work. Newspaper workweeks could vary depending on how shifts were arranged—the lower average hours per week for news workers reflects the fact that mechanical workers (often grouped together with editorial workers by federal salary surveys) generally worked fewer hours but also made more money and earned better benefits. To put it another way, the way that data was gathered about news workers sometimes conflated the higher wages of mechanical workers with those of editorial workers.[94] Mechanical workers made an average of $2.17 an hour at an average of 37.2 hours per week in 1948, the ANPA's official history claimed. That would translate into $80.72 a week.[95] Contemporary data from the US Bureau of the Census indicates that in 1945, the average weekly pay rate for newspaper printers was even higher industry-wide, at $116.70.[96]

Publishers would routinely claim this as proof that the industry paid its workers well, refuting accusations that they underpaid their workers compared to, say, those who worked in public relations, but such claims nearly always focused on the high-paying ITU-protected jobs, and not on the lower-paying newsroom positions. Weekly wage data from the BLS for mechanical workers from 1955 (assuming a 40-hour work week for those in the "printing and publishing industry") shows a $90.40 national average (translating into about $4,680 a year). In 1960 that rate would increase to $107.20 a week.[97] Note that this is a simple average, and a typical reporter, or other editorial worker, on the average daily newspaper would be making closer to sixty or seventy dollars to start in the early 1950s.

For all that, the reality on the ground was improving. A 1953 survey of Ohio State University's School of Journalism graduates anecdotally confirmed that better pay was becoming a reality, even for younger reporters. The average annual salary for that year for those with newsroom jobs was $3,492, or $67.15 a week. The end of the decade would see an increase of 85 percent (the average salary, according to one study, of editorial workers in 1959 was $6,378, or $122.65).[98] In other areas, too, editorial-worker pay was improving markedly.

### HOURS: FROM TIME OFF TO OVERTIME

Before unionization, many newsrooms operated with an informal system that gave reporters, photographers, and editors unpaid time off when they worked late, on weekends, or during holidays. This was necessary because breaking news, or developing stories, meant that reporters would sometimes work for days on end. Both bosses and peers expected an on-call mentality when it came to news coverage. This vocational expectation became embedded in work routines. Morning newspaper staff members, who worked late into the evening hours, were sometimes paid a "night rate" higher than those who worked for afternoon newspapers, who worked during the day. Even on their days off, reporters were sometimes expected to call and check in with the newsroom. Early Guild contracts, however, often specified that time worked above and beyond a set number of hours each week had to be compensated. This could be either at the same rate or higher than regular pay. Editors routinely complained that their reporters worked overtime on purpose, or were lackadaisical when it came to finishing their stories or returning to the newsroom, in order to accumulate overtime pay.

A recurring battle cry during early ANG contract negotiations, especially as federal industry codes were enforced during the FDR administration, involved calls for five-day work weeks for nonexecutive staff. By the late 1940s these became routine parts of many contracts. But even before the advent of the ANG, some employers had begun to switch to shorter workweeks during the Depression. In an attempt to keep workers on the payroll, they moved to a five-day work week from the more typical pre-Guild six.[99] The 1934 BLS survey of newsroom wages also found a general decline in hours worked between 1930 and 1934; in April 1930 average hours ranged from 45.1 to 50 for just over half of all news workers, to more than 50 hours for 10 percent, with the remainder working less than 45 hours a week.[100] Still, longer hours for noncontract workers could go significantly beyond forty- or fifty-hour-a-week norms.

As newsroom unionization became more widespread, union members pressed for more than better hours and pay. Concerns about "speeding up," or increasing the rate of production for a news worker (which could take the form of asking reporters to cover more beats, for example, or just write more throughout the day), or combining or changing jobs, would sometimes draw union protests, formally or informally. In 1940 the *Philadelphia Record* tried to hire part-time photographers and use these workers as leg men. The union objected, concerned that this would take away work from full-time reporters.[101] Most of these conflicts faded by the 1950s, especially as union contracts grew more specific about job classifications. One result of unionization, then, was stabilization of newsroom roles. This benefited photographers and lower-ranked reporters and editors.

The ability of unions to intervene in the hiring and firing process generally increased during this era. In 1941 the Third Circuit Court of Appeals ruled that the NLRB could not "police," in its words, "relations between employer and employee after a collective bargaining agreement is in operation," in a case regarding the reinstatement of a Newark (New Jersey) *Ledger* rewrite reporter, Agnes Fahy. The local Guild unit protested, claiming that Fahy was fired for her Guild activities and was, in fact, competent enough for the job.

This was a rare loss for the ANG. Most of the time the NLRB sided with, or gave the benefit of the doubt, to union claims as long as the unit in question was the majority bargaining unit.[102] The Guild also intervened when workers under contract were fired without back pay, usually challenging the grounds on which an employer would try to disqualify a worker from receiving that pay.[103] At first these interventions were relatively ineffectual. With growing unionization, though, they became increasingly effective. Editors began to change their behavior as a result. Newsroom life lost more of its uncertainty.

### HEALTHCARE/INSURANCE AND UNIONIZATION'S EFFECT ON FAMILY LIFE

As American print journalism and newsroom life experienced the kind of workforce trends affecting other aspiring white-collar occupations by mid-century, on-site health care and health insurance became more common. Some newspapers incentivized loyalty in the unionization era by providing health insurance for family members. On larger newspapers in the biggest cities, providing employee insurance, either life or health, was not unheard of before the Guild. On the *Chicago Tribune* in 1924, the Medill Building and Loan Association was run by employees with the blessing of management. It offered home loans, insurance, and a pension plan.[104] It was typical in the sense that it was employee organized and led. Owners would sometimes match funds or provide seed money but would leave further development to workers. This burnished the owners' image while allowing their employees to make what they would of the plan, at low actual risk (and expense) for publishers. In some ways, these early collectivist behaviors presaged the onset of the Guild.

Workers who bought houses and believed their company would take care of them if they were injured on the job or when they retired tended to work harder and longer. "Security" in this broader sense for quasi-white-collar workers was not widespread and could attract reporters and editors from rival newspapers. It could also reduce turnover, keeping the natural churn of new staff to a minimum.[105] Other types of job security included funds to help pay for funeral expenses.[106] In time, some Guild locals offered health insurance for workers and their families.[107] While these benefits tended to be found only on larger newspapers, smaller papers could and did offer them too.[108]

Their inclusion in Guild contracts tended to increase as time went on, as workers began to expect and ask for them.[109] The Guild, not to be outdone by publishers, sometimes offered life insurance through its local chapters.[110] While the details are difficult to glean from contemporary accounts, a typical example for smaller papers was that of the New Bedford (Massachusetts) *Standard-Times* and the Cape Cod *Standard-Times*, whose owners insured workers up to $1,000, with $1,000 accidental death and dismemberment insurance, $10-a-week accident and sickness benefits, $5-a-day hospitalization benefits, and $150 surgical benefits. Employer-led efforts like this tended to get positive press, but like pension plans, they were not always guaranteed.[111] The ANG and publishers by the 1950s were trying to win hearts and minds by making these plans available to workers, or by calling for them. The more generous plans covered dependents, including children up to eighteen.[112]

For reporters and editors, the important point was that life and health insurance was now within reach. Before, newsrooms were places for single people, or at least people who prioritized career above family obligations, for the most part. But the introduction of corporate- or family-owned social safety nets allowed news workers to cultivate their own family lives. Occupational humor in the form of poetry and cartoons acknowledged this new reality, as workers were increasingly able to afford the cost of children and subsidize the presence of a spouse at home, either part- or full-time. Juggling work and home life was a new and welcome challenge for many news workers, who, like other aspirational white-collar workers in the postwar period, enjoyed the idea of owning their own home, a car, TV set, and other amenities.

## FAMILY LIFE AND GENDER RELATIONS

Family life outside of newsrooms reflected changes within them. A telling development was the increasing number of news workers who married each other. Women became common in the newsroom in the 1940s and 1950s, in support jobs such as circulation, transcription, and other administrative positions as well as in editing and reporting roles. While any definitive statement on marriage rates (or on the longevity of these unions compared to other occupations) among these workers would be tentative, a representative reading of the trade publications and memoirs in this era hints at the normalization of working spouses in the newsroom. Unlike other occupations where workplace marriage would be frowned upon, or even thought of as dangerous, a healthy tradition of news-worker spousal partnerships had formed in American newsroom culture by the 1950s, enough that it could be spoofed for a generation in such popular depictions of newsroom life as *Deadline—U.S.A.*[113] While women would sometimes marry and then retire early to focus on homemaking (a social norm that affected newsrooms as well as other workplaces throughout the midcentury) to the ire of editors, who unfairly complained of wasted mentorship and training, others remained or returned to the newsroom once their children were older. Some women, in fact, felt a higher degree of respect from male colleagues after marriage that allowed them to operate with more independence in a chauvinist workplace. They used this identity to leverage their own agency and cover beats reserved for men. Dorothy Ducas, a staff writer for the International News Service, noted some of the limits of this phenomenon in 1932:

> There is nothing very romantic in the association of newspaper reporters. How could there be? Have they not seen each other early in the morning and late night, looking tired, bedraggled and worried? Have they not split the bills in speakeasies, fought for the use of telephones, carried on joint interviews for weeks, months, years? They borrow money from each other, tell each other how terrible they look and feel, share inside tips on stories, and confide the secrets of their hearts during those long waits for verdicts in trials or the deaths of famous men.[114]

The result was often "solid and lasting friendship" for many news workers, since "most newspaper people think each as glamorous as a ham sandwich." Reporters respected each other for their work if it was good, and this helped to transcend some of the barriers between the genders. According to Ducas: "If he [the reporter] does a swell job, he is apt to be thought a pretty swell person." If a woman reporter was "very attractive, she is called over-conscientious, a bore—'just another newspaper woman!' Just as, if she is good-looking *and capable*, she will be spoken of everywhere she goes as 'the best little reporter in—[the] City!'" Generally, though, a woman "who does her work thoroughly" was accepted by her "poorly dressed, unshaven, unkempt, [and] sometimes ungrammatical" male colleagues, who did not have to be as "presentable" as their woman colleagues.[115]

One reason for Ducas's success was that she was "happily and permanently married" and thus shared in the family-oriented disposition of many of her peers: "The photographs of wives and children I have seen are legion. I am convinced reporters are as much domesticated animals as salesmen or telegraph operators." Marriage helped keep everyone's focus in the newsroom on the work.[116] On the mechanical side, too, women were also married and working. A 1951 survey by Florida State University's School of Journalism showed that of the 123 recent women graduates working in mechanical press rooms in Florida newspapers, 85 were married, and 71 had children.[117] Sometimes employers encouraged these unions, even before unionization. Perhaps reflecting how many news workers married each other, in 1924 the *Chicago Tribune* offered newly married employees a chest of flat silver, or two weeks' vacation with pay.[118] This paper maintained a strong tradition of married workers. Six couples worked together in the newsroom in 1960.[119] A survey of University of Oregon journalism graduates showed that between 1916 and 1928, 257 had worked in journalism, 224 were still involved in the industry, and 26 were married to fellow news workers.[120]

The *Guild Reporter*, usually focused on the advances (and, more rarely, the reversals) of the ANG in court battles and the development of local chapters, noted examples of reporters or other newsroom staffers marrying each other. Many happened, of course, to be members of local Guild chapters.[121] Some stories also noted that rates of marriage went up during strikes.[122] Reporters got married more often and had families when the Guild provided "some promise of security" with increases in contracted base pay.[123] How much this was actually a result of Guild influence is hard to measure, of course, but like other aspiring white-collar workers, it is reasonable to speculate that reporters and editors found assurances of continued employment and promotions equally encouraging for their own formation (or expansion) of family. Reporters' memoirs note that bigger homes and apartments (and often families) followed promotions or pay raises. The editor of the *Toledo Blade*, Grove Patterson, described a "humanitarian aspect" in the hiring of reporters with families. The *Blade*'s "automatic rule" was to hire a reporter at no less than $45 a week if he or she had a family. This was in 1931, and for the time, especially during the Depression and outside of the large East and West Coast cities, generous. As Patterson put it, "We felt that it was required for a decent living standard."[124]

By the 1950s news workers generally felt more secure in their occupation, at their individual newspapers, and thus more settled in the pursuit of family life. Especially after industry codes mandated five-day weeks, and wages allowed for a comfortable margin of spending and saving, supporting a family became reasonable for even junior reporters and editors. News workers' ads seeking employment noted marital status as a sign of stability and loyalty (or, conversely, singleness as a sign of flexibility and independence).[125] Some employers, however, would not hire married women as copy girls.[126] The mostly male editor-panelists at industry conventions confirmed this tendency to avoid hiring women, or at least remained skeptical because women were supposedly more likely to leave newsrooms due to marriage.[127] Male colleagues would sometimes mock their female coworkers for their tendency to leave.[128] The Guild, for its part, advocated for women against what it called an "unwritten law" in the newsroom, arguing for their reinstatement if fired for getting married.[129]

In this the Guild had support from the NLRB, and its wartime equivalent, the National War Labor Board (NWLB). The latter ruled in a case between the owners of the Allentown (Pennsylvania) *Morning Call* and the Lehigh Valley chapter of the ANG in June 1944 that women could not be paid less based on gender alone. The *Morning Call*'s ownership had attempted to classify women reporters as "society reporters" and pay them $30 after five years. Regular male reporters made $41.54 with the same experience. The NWLB proposed that the former's pay be brought up to $34.50 because "women . . . doing the work of reporters . . . should be classified and compensated as such." It is notable that the pay raises did *not* mean parity with male coworkers. But it was a sign that the ANG could get support from the federal government even during wartime for the former's contention that women reporters should be paid at the same rates as men. While the NWLB hesitated to wade into definitional disputes between the Guild and ownership, in this case it backed the Guild assertion that "the existence of a separate Society Reporter classification is an indication of sex discrimination."[130]

Unlike in other work environments, newsroom relationships between male and female peers depended less on power differentials. In non-newsroom office settings throughout the period, male employees often held a position of power over women. In hospitals, laboratories, factories—the same dynamic was at work. But in newsrooms, a male reporter and a female reporter were at least nominal equals (the same with male copy editors and female rewrite staff). Of course, male workers had a place of innate privilege. Newsrooms were not immune to larger social forces. As Linda Steiner has shown, women struggled to normalize their presence in newsrooms.[131] But the parallel unionization of the newsroom, as well as the role of college as an equalizing route into it, meant that news workers were among the first vocational peers in a white-collar work environment to marry while holding similar jobs.[132]

### GUILD OUTREACH TO BLACK JOURNALISTS

In its attempt to recruit as many new members as possible, the ANG also made some efforts—tentative as they may have been—to reach out to the Black press. As early as 1944 the Guild signed a contract with news workers at the *Chicago Defender*, the first such formal agreement with a Black newspaper.[133] In the waning days of the war, the Guild also courted the newsrooms of the *Pittsburgh Courier* and the *Baltimore Afro-American*, while also making inroads at the *New Amsterdam News* and *Los Angeles Sentinel*.[134] This outreach to prominent and well-respected Black papers was intentional and continued into the 1950s. Fletcher Martin, the first African American to receive the prestigious Nieman Fellowship at Harvard, and a former World War II correspondent, wrote about his experience with the Chicago chapter of the Guild in the *Guild Reporter*. Fletcher, writing with Milburn Akers, the executive editor of the *Chicago Sun-Times*, affirmed the Guild as being a force for newsroom integration (Fletcher worked briefly at the *Sun-Times*, and was an important figure in reporting on civil rights).[135] The *Guild Reporter*'s coverage of these efforts is an important contrast to that of *Editor & Publisher*, which sometimes took a patronizing or othering tone toward the work of the Black press. At the same time, however, there are glimmers of genuine interest and cooperation between the primarily white mainstream press of the era and its Black counterpart. In August 1945, for example, the editors of *Editor & Publisher* invited a group of eight African American publishers and editors to discuss racial conflict and the role of newspapers in helping to mediate it. Some of this coverage was, frankly, optimistic at best (one section of the story is labeled, "reporters work together," describing how Black and white reporters could collaborate).[136] And yet it is the start of the long road toward integrated newsrooms that is discussed by Gwyneth Mellinger, Fred Carroll, and Calvin Hall.

## CONCLUSION: UNIONIZATION SOLIDIFIES A WHITE-COLLAR NEWSROOM

The Guild had negotiated 216 contracts through 1959, with 151 contracts covering 185 newspapers, nine wire services, four weeklies, twelve magazines, two radio stations, nine foreign-language papers, thirteen labor publications, three racing papers, and thirteen miscellaneous publications. While impressive, this was a minority of the total number of newspapers in the country at the time, with more than seventeen hundred dailies in operation in 1960.[137]

And yet it was still an influential number, because of the kind of publications that were unionizing. The wire services and big-city papers in Los Angeles, Chicago, and New York were particularly critical, as they largely set the tone for much of the rest of the nation's journalism. In addition to improved hours and wages with these contracts, the Guild also worked to protect "reporters against the use of their bylines over their objections" and to provide opportunities for outside work, leaves of absence for fellowships and scholarships, and a share of the proceeds from the syndication and reuse of work, if a photographer. But as a longtime ANG member put it, "of the many things [the Guild] has contributed to the newspaper industry, however, perhaps none has been of more lasting impact than the increased self-respect it has brought to those individuals who work in it."[138] Reporters and lower-ranking editors had a new class consciousness, and the desire to act on it.

Publishers and individual union locals still clashed, of course, but the principle had long been conceded: unionization was a newsroom reality. The ANG had made joining a union, and the union's advocacy on behalf of news workers, normal. "Its negotiations with publishers are not as bitter and irreconcilable as in its early days," the author of a career guide noted in 1951. As "the first union in the news-writing field," the ANG had increased its influence at the organizational and national levels within the occupation, normalizing worker power and limiting the ability of bosses to control every aspect of newsroom life.[139]

This built on former newsroom norms of independence and assertiveness. News workers had always found a way to push back. But unionization strengthened and provided legal force to these norms of autonomy and helped to build new norms of collective identity, action, and the expectation of white-collar benefits and quality of life. This was a trend across industries and individual businesses throughout the United States during this era, though it had a unique effect on creative workers. It allowed them to operate with independence within a larger organizational culture in ways previously unavailable. By pushing back against a "professional" identity—the identity that publishers wanted for their workers—journalists won major concessions from ownership.

In the more oppressive era during and before World War I, news workers had little in the way of recourse when they were fired, laid off, or docked pay. They were subjected to the complexities of an advertising-fueled free market, one in which publishers looked to cut costs by slashing the payroll as needed. Even when they did push back, news workers were either quickly punished by being blacklisted or, due to their own vocational culture, lost interest in sustained organizing efforts. Their time just had not arrived. That changed with the Depression and the subsequent intervention of the federal government with the white-collar regulation of the newspaper industry. The survival of the Wagner Act and other federal legislation that allowed for collective bargaining—over the objections of publishers—was another critical factor in the success of the Guild. Federal protection of labor unions' right to organize and bargain with owners was a necessary condition for their spread, even if the latter was limited.

The formation of the ANG came about due to a confluence of factors, including dissatisfaction by rank-and-file workers with how publishers tried to mitigate or avoid federal industry codes that regulated wages and hours. Affiliation first with the AFL and then with the CIO moved the ANG toward a more traditional labor union.[140] Reporters and editors alike were conflicted about what to do next. Generally, however, most reporters and lower-ranking editors appreciated the ANG's and other unionization efforts to improve working conditions. "Salaries went up and hours went down, and needless firings began to drop off when each one meant several hundred dollars in dismissal pay," noted Morton Sontheimer, reflecting on changes already occurring in employer-employee dynamics in 1941.[141] Instead of trying to negotiate with individual news workers, publishers had to deal with union locals. While some workers left the ANG, others stayed or remained sympathetic to it, and the union survived the war years to become a potent force in newsrooms across the country. Publishers, even those unfriendly toward unionization, accepted a détente with the ANG and with unionization more broadly, partially due to the fact that other attempts at regulation of their industry had failed, and, of course, the helpful additional fact that their papers were generally very profitable.

New reporters, fresh from college journalism programs, a still relatively new source of workers, were expected to join Guild locals upon their arrival in a new newsroom—provided, of course, that a Guild local was present.[142] That was not always the case. But it nonetheless marked a cultural shift in newsrooms, as the expectation of a unionized newsroom would have been alien to earlier generations. That it was a reality at all had not been a foregone conclusion. After all, other college-educated workers, and white-collar workers in general, had resisted efforts to organize, and news workers themselves had failed to organize coherently during at least two distinct moments in their history. A few conciliatory moves by publishers earlier on, or a less severe Depression, or even the absence of key unifying figures like Broun, could have led to yet another failed attempt at newsroom unionization.

But it was the ultimate, even though not universal, success at organizing that solidified a general trend toward a more secure white-collar status, one in which workers could reasonably presume to afford the expenses associated with families, cars, and their own homes or apartments. While their salaries reached only a rough parity with comparable white-collar occupations by the end of the 1950s, for many reporters, the independence and security achieved by union representation, or its influence, were enough to look back on the era as a kind of "golden age."[143] Some in the industry, in fact, believed that this new white-collar standing was making it, ironically, increasingly difficult to attract young workers. This was a good problem for those who thought that reporters and editors needed the security of a job more akin to the members of a public-relations firm: well-paid, well-heated in the winter (well-cooled in the summer), managed by human resources departments, and staffed by specialized college graduates. This worried self-educated, older reporters and editors, who felt that unionization had taken something of the romance and excitement out of newsroom life.

And yet most workers preferred to have union representatives negotiate with publishers rather than find their salaries summarily posted on bulletin boards. Worrying less about their next paycheck helped them to focus more on their beats, aspirations to join the copy desk, or their goal of becoming a correspondent, and to expect, with a reasonable amount of certainty, that they would have a job tomorrow, next week, and next year. The unionization of the newsroom allowed its workers to realize both the aspirations and enjoy the benefits of middle-class status. Reporters and other news workers felt more settled in their jobs as a result of unionization. They were "men [and later women] of family, registered voters, members of the Parent-Teacher Association." Less nomadic, they could have "savings accounts and worry about mortgages," reported a contemporary. They were thus "no longer harum-scarum, feckless and addicted to bad habits" and would "plod home at day's end with the utmost docility, mow lawns, shovel walks, help with the dishes and play Canasta with their wives instead of helling around town and worrying their families."[144] While it would be a little simplistic to give the credit for this cultural change to unionization alone, it would be a mistake to ignore the day-to-day impact of the ANG and other unions—they helped to bring news workers and newsrooms into the ranks of the American middle class. While ineffable, to some degree, that feeling should not be downplayed.

Class and socioeconomic status mattered to the people living and working alongside one another in these spaces. When reflecting on the relational nature of the newsroom and its community of workers, thinking about its place in an early information economy and its relationship to adjacent occupations that enticed its workers away—public relations and government jobs, among others—can help one get a better sense of the external forces shaping internal newsroom dynamics. Having a middle-class background and a college education enabled reporters and other news workers to have more options for leaving the field, or provided a margin for those undergoing rough patches in their careers. In contrast, not having a social safety net, or other career prospects, might relegate them to less glamorous newsroom work. Unionization was an attempt to both retain people who had other options and to protect those who did not. Its impact was uneven, but it did tend to shape the social life of the newsroom in positive ways.

CHAPTER 9

# Conclusion

## The Newsroom in American Journalism, 1920–1960

THE SOCIAL HISTORY of the American newsroom is the story of its workers and of their larger occupational community. It is also a story of their physical workplace.[1] News workers were well aware of what desk placement meant, who had a telephone, and the importance of reliable access to each other and editors. This occupational space was not a cause, but a context, within which American journalism formed. The relational- and organizational-level workplace communities known as newsrooms created a unique, shared identity. This identity was aspirational.

The reality of relationships and the communities of work within the newsroom were much more complex than this, however. Power differentials meant that some news workers could determine the day-to-day work routines of others. From copy boys and girls, photographers, copy editors and rewrite staff, and reporters (from cubs to veterans), to supervisors drawn from the ranks of former peers (i.e., editors), workers were arranged along a continuum of control. Until World War II (but not for a long while after) this was further divided along gender lines, with rare exceptions. And until the 1960s, where this account of newsroom life ends, it was divided along racial lines, as well, with only glimmers of a future effort toward integration. The newsroom was not a democratic place, or a real meritocracy, but a place and idea—an institution of institutions—deeply embedded in the prejudices and prerogatives of its own time.

The "newspaper" and "newsroom" served as the flawed vehicles for the modern, professionalizing, journalistic identity of the twentieth century, with all its aspirations and contradictions.[2] These terms encompassed whole systems and networks and are of course simplified shorthand for journalism writ large. But flawed and unequal as it was, the newsroom was also a web of relationships—the centering place for those relationships, a place where a confusing mass of reality was condensed into processed, produced news and distributed to reading publics. This reality—and the many individual acts of news labor needed to produce a daily newspaper, often several times a day—was, also, ultimately, "the newsroom." Conceptualizing "space as constructed out of interrelations" means that "the social is inexorably also spatial," as Doreen Massey has argued.[3]

It embodied, via news workers and their many varied backgrounds, the beliefs and values of industrial journalism. These norms existed only in the context of the newsroom. Many other fine scholars, such as David Mindich and Henrik Örnebring, have studied the origins of objectivity and autonomy, respectively, as *the* ideal values within and without the newsroom.[4] But without the encompassing relational world that was represented by the newsroom, objectivity would not make sense, and neither would autonomy, just like the technology tools described in a previous chapter. As a social construct *and* a community of labor, then, the newsroom represented far more than a physical building, as romanticized as these spaces rightly have become.

## NEWS WORKERS, POWER, AND PROFESSIONALIZATION: NEWSROOM CULTURE EVOLVES

It was in the newsroom that the power relations between peers made sense and were organized. The *relationships* of these workers were shaped at multiple levels, but especially by those within individual media organizations and their routine practices.[5] Some of these practices were unique to the historical development of individual newsrooms. But broadly, by midcentury, workers pushed back against the various forms of control deployed by those in positions of authority over them. They collaborated on and coordinated work routines and devised time- and energy-saving strategies. They resisted overt forms of supervision, working mostly outside the newsroom; upon returning to it, however, they acquiesced to supervision as needed.

By the 1950s, in a "good" newsroom, there was mental room for flexibility—editors exerted their authority but yielded to the judgments of their experienced reporters and copy editors. Humor was encouraged. Editors could laugh at themselves. Editors could stand up for women and people from minority backgrounds and give these individuals rare opportunities to enter a previously homogenous, white, male world—or at least accede to the need for eventual integration, and not resist it. In a good newsroom, there was space for creativity, job security (sometimes enforced by a union) and space for a life outside of it. In short, there was a healthy level of autonomy and a respect for, if not objectivity and professional behavior norms, then something like fairness or a basic moral code.

In "bad" newsrooms, editors ruled with arbitrary cruelty, in a top down, not bottom up, manner, and excluded women and minorities, beyond, perhaps, token positions on women's pages or on the race beat. Editors in these rough workplaces denied their staff any kind of autonomy, forcing them to put aside any professional impulses and follow the publisher or owner's editorial line, and were generally cruel. It is telling that in such newsrooms occupational humor, including poetry and cartoons aimed at bosses, was forbidden—the editors did not want anyone to laugh *at* them, because they could not laugh *with* anyone, least of all their staff. Choices were driven not by any kind of ethical compass, but by fear.

News workers took note of these kinds of bad newsrooms, and left them when they could. This sometimes involved a move to bigger cities, following the traditional path from a small weekly to a small daily, to a big daily, or perhaps a magazine or the radio or TV. But sometimes it meant lateral moves, or even transfers to less prestigious publications. The trade publications of the 1950s and early 1960s, in particular, identified this trend. It was thought that it was better to leave for the same pay, or even a bit less, and have a better quality of life, than to stay and work for tyrants. As journalism became a white-collar occupation, white-collar considerations made more sense. News workers were getting more exposure to parallel careers that offered lucrative offramps to journalism, especially public relations, and higher salaries were also an incentive to *leave* the field (for more on that phenomenon, see below, and the appendix on newsroom salaries).

### NEWSROOMS EXPAND WITHOUT, AND GROW IN COMPLEXITY WITHIN

Another phenomenon was the expanding outside networks reporters and editors were operating in by the middle of the century. News workers had more sustained outside engagement with fields adjacent to their own. This meant that they occasionally brought the newsroom's norms with them, and, more often, left others behind, when they went to work for the government or into public relations. Rival reporters combined efforts when working out of police stations and city halls, gathering news together and writing it separately to suit the tastes of their individual publications. When back in the newsroom, they argued with copy editors and rewrite staff. Copy editors and rewrite staff complained about reporters when the latter were gone, and often while they were there. Newsroom relationships reflected these themes of resistance and change. Newcomers to the newsroom endured rituals of initiation. These "cubs" earned their way into the ranks of regulars and then veterans. Editors would sometimes assist in this process, or at least tacitly endorse it, themselves a product of newsroom hazing.

Once in the pool of rank-and-file reporters, news workers would further subdivide into groups based on relational, socioeconomic, education, gender, race, and political status. More commonly they split based on career goals. Those fast-tracked for success sat apart, both literally and figuratively.[6] Junior editors faced frustration and were placed farther back in the newsroom, away from the locus of power and control that was the copy editor's and rewrite staff's desks. But all reporter subgroups aspired to independence, expressed through roles as rewrite staffers, copy editors, columnists, correspondents, or other specialized writing jobs.

Reporters were able to think of these upwardly mobile paths because the newsroom had changed. The physical and social spaces it comprised were far more fluid, and more secure, for the generation working in newsrooms in 1960 than they had been in 1920. The community of journalists working at midcentury remained fiercely loyal to the idea of working in and for the newsroom, and their occupational mobility within individual news organizations speaks to the strength of the newsroom as a centralizing place.

Reflecting on nearly a century of studies by fellow sociologists, Andrew Abbott examined aspiring professions such as journalism as "exclusive occupational groups" that apply "somewhat abstract knowledge to particular cases." Abbott was chiefly concerned with "the actual work that is done and the expertise used to do it": professional structures and cultures are built out of abstracted work practices.[7] Abbott focused on contested jurisdictional claims in an intricate ecosystem of occupations. Different occupations contend for the authority to exercise the right of inference, or control, over the most "professional" part of a work process, that is, the most inferential.[8] Occupations making professional claims (and counterclaims) over these processes involve a complex and dynamic topology of tasks. Abbott emphasizes the role of history in understanding the rise and fall (and rise again) of individual occupations as they successfully, or unsuccessfully, make these claims. This matters for our consideration of newsrooms because these spaces were where claims of authority were often made or disputed.

In a critical move for journalism-studies and media-history scholars, Patricia Dooley takes Abbott's professional-work stages and applies them to journalistic work, examining reporting, evaluation of news/sources, and the presentation or content. Journalistic identity markers, including editorial independence as forged in newsrooms, helped to preserve news workers' occupational space and their political role in US society.[9] Abbott is not very interested in journalism's "inability to monopolize" its work routines (and whether or not that precludes it from being a profession). We should not be either. If one were to focus unduly on a supposedly failed "professionalization" process, journalists would be a rather dull group—what matters more is how their contested societal roles drove ideas of professionalism from both within and without journalism, and within and without newsrooms.

## NEWSROOMS AS SITES OF TECHNOLOGY ADOPTION AND WHITE-COLLAR UNIONIZATION

Technology and unionization disrupted and reshaped newsroom dynamics. The adoption of the office phone, internal switchboard systems, and, later, the mobile phone, either as a radio phone via cars or accessed via static points in the field, further bifurcated the gathering and producing processes within and without newsrooms.[10] These tools created whole new classes of news workers (i.e., rewrite staff), enhanced the status of others (copy editors), and restructured the internal workings of even otherwise cohesive groups in the newsroom (separating "leg men" from reporters, the latter able to write up their own content back in the newsroom or substitute as rewrite staff, as discussed earlier).

As journalism textbook author Robert Neal noted in 1942, "each department is the direct outgrowth of inventions. The machinery of the newspaper is elaborate, expensive and premeditated. It didn't develop by chance."[11] They were chosen tools, created by humans, imperfectly utilized. Technology upended established routines and created new ones. It shaped and was shaped by its users, with news workers acting as pioneering members of a future information economy. Dealing in data, they shaped that data into coherent, constantly updated stories. News workers during the precomputerized era, that is, before the 1960s and 1970s, wrote for the press-service wires, multiple editions throughout the day, and, in some cases, allied radio or TV stations, gathering and producing news with an immediacy that rivals their digital descendants. Far from being reticent to embrace technology, news workers—if they received training and were motivated by their peers—were sometimes enthusiastic and early adopters of technology . . . *if* it helped them solve day-to-day issues and did *not* threaten their jobs.

Social construction theorists and technological determinists both describe the American newsroom's (and its workers') relationship with technology as complex, and one that defies both simplistic explanations or one single theoretical interpretation.[12] Örnebring has pointed out that the dynamic between news work and technology in newsrooms is never static, involving reskilling, multiskilling, and deskilling. The work of journalists (and thus the work of newsrooms) tends to be driven to a degree by technology, where developments are usually the result of long, interconnected processes.[13] The arrival of rewrite staff proves this point—newsrooms had and still maintain a messy dynamic with technology adoption. Reporters and other news workers are neither Luddites nor always savvy. Instead, they adopted the telephone and car, and later, early mobile-reporting devices like tape recorders, incorporating them into existing routines and building new ones. These brought new norms, such as those associated with remote reporting, and built on old norms like timeliness. But it is important to understand that contemporaries like Neal, and the various voices in this history, were enthusiastic for reasons that cannot be explained away as naivete or publisher-pushed fervor in trade publications. Their memoirs reveal a cautious, realistic optimism about the use of tools. This was conditional, but nonetheless real.

The newsroom of the 1930s onward was also characterized by a halting, never totalizing but still influential organizing movement. Facing dramatically enhanced job uncertainty, news workers overcame their traditional antipathy toward "blue-collar" organizing efforts and adopted unionization in the interests of their white-collar aspirations. "Realizing that he is a factory worker always is a jolt to the new reporter, but it is a most necessary one," noted an observer in 1942.[14] As one of the first creative classes to organize, they realized as never before their collective power vis-à-vis management. In doing so they helped to bring about Hallin's "provisional resolution" that created space for a professionalized workforce mostly free of the worst (not all) excesses of publishers and inspired an unprecedented and sustained season of occupational strength and development.[15]

While this was not entirely due to the ANG, news workers had ample reason to feel better about their status by the early 1960s. In the forty years between 1920 and 1960, reporters and editors moved from a working-class, paycheck-to-paycheck existence to a far more comfortable middle-class socioeconomic status. Though it is a simplistic measure, the improvement in baseline salaries (and the reality of *salaries* at all instead of payment "by space," i.e., per story) shows just how far reporters and editors had come. In 1930 the average experienced reporter made about $2,266 a year, or about $34,184 in 2020 dollars. With few if any benefits, that salary could vary wildly and was subject to reduction without notice.

In 1960 the average experienced reporter made about $7,269 a year, or about $63,999 in 2020.[16] The typical reporter at the end of the era also had health insurance, severance pay, paid time off, annual or semiannual pay raises, pensions in some cases, and more job security than his or her predecessors. News workers could afford a house, a car, and a family. They could look forward to a varied career, with decent chances for advancement. They could leave the field into jobs that rewarded their skills, with the option of returning to journalism if they wished later. That newfound reality shaped how news workers felt about themselves and the newsroom.

### THE BEGINNING OF THE END OF EXCLUSIONARY PRACTICES

A final important transition from the newsrooms of early in the century to the later newsrooms of the Cold War was the gradual integration of the newsroom, at first spearheaded by progressive white editors, but later by organizations such as the ASNE and the Society of Professional Journalists. Both of the latter groups were not perfect, and neither were their initiatives. But even the failure of Goal 2000—the ASNE's ambitious effort to achieve voluntary racial representation that was on par with the rest of American society—was still something that would have been unfathomable in the 1940s or before.[17] Still, there was a very long way to go, even by the end of the century. "Minority journalists accounted for just 11 percent of newsroom employees in 1997 when they made up 26 percent of the total population," as Fred Carroll has noted. And yet, a "significant symbolic turning point" had occurred.[18]

As highlighted earlier in this book, by the 1950s and 1960s courageous and enterprising Black journalists such as Carl Rowan bravely integrated white newsrooms, and others, including Philippa Schuyler, integrated the previously all-white beats, including international reporting. These efforts were successful enough to change the nature of the Black press, which had fostered reporting talent for generations before. But a critical role remained and remains for journalism outlets focused on and owned by African American voices, and an updated, holistic history of the Black newsroom needs to be written.[19] As Gerald Horne and Calvin Hall have discussed in their research on the Black press and the memoirs of African American journalists, respectively, Black news workers juggled competing ideas of objectivity and autonomy, often at odds with their white counterparts, but sometimes expanding notions of both in helpful directions.[20] While he examines African American journalists later in the century, Hall notes that

Black news workers throughout the period faced hypocritical criticism from white colleagues and were held to unfair standards. "The sin of feeling less than perfect" was and is a construct of reduced autonomy in many primarily white newsrooms.[21] By telling the stories of Black journalists in the past, media historians can "offer a challenge to the status quo by illuminating the practices that hinder minority journalists from bringing their perspectives to the journalistic enterprise."[22]

### THE ENDURING LEGACY OF THE INDUSTRIALIZED NEWSROOM

The social history of the newsroom and its workers was not one of triumph and perfection. Indeed, it would be a mistake to claim that news workers fully "professionalized" during the decades between and just after the world wars. As Abbott and others have pointed out, "whether or not" news workers and journalism succeeded at adopting a preset group of traits is not the interesting question.[23] The bigger question is, how did these workers define success and "professional" standing? The answer, it seems, at least for a substantial number, was a measure of economic stability and reasonable protection from too much managerial interference. How this worked out could vary greatly depending on where a news worker lived and if his or her newspaper was part of a chain.[24]

There is an important caveat to these generally improved working conditions in the newsroom: they were available to a relative few. Women and minorities were just starting a long road to inclusion in a still white-male-dominated industry. Women had made inroads, and had already helped to transform an all-male space into a more gender-diverse place, from ownership down through the ranks of reporters. Minority news workers were only just beginning to be hired by the end of the 1950s, in scattered and often publisher-led initiatives.[25] Only later, beginning in the 1970s, would more systematic efforts be made to diversify newsrooms.[26]

Looking at the newsroom as a site of professionalizing discourse, and as a place where practitioners operationalized abstract values into concrete decisions contributes to ongoing discussions important to journalism studies. How journalists organized themselves and their workflows, and how they engaged with and attempted to govern temporal limits—these old problems remain relevant. A social history of the newsroom gives rich context to the work of media ethnographers from the 1970s onward. Knowing how the newsroom formed as an aspirational and relational space in the period from the early to mid-twentieth century is crucial to understanding the nature of the journalism created in that space, and what came after.[27]

Knowing why and how newsroom norms developed—partially as a reaction to changes in technology and to the unionization of the newsroom—also enriches our understanding of this space in the American media system. Newsroom ethnographers found complex communities of workers because they *had already been developing* for a half century or longer. More recently, journalism-studies scholars seeking to apply spatial theory to newsroom production are also encountering the legacy of a richly *relational* space.[28] Journalism enacted in different kinds of spaces would have led to a different kind of journalism.

### THE CONTINUING RELATIONAL LEGACY OF THE AMERICAN NEWSROOM

There have been several kinds of newsrooms, from editor-dominated to reporter-driven.[29] The industrial newsroom that dominated the media landscape for much of the twentieth century was large and intricate. It had to be, in order to process information, house and equip newsgathering *and* news-producing workers, and physically create and distribute the news. The model became so efficient that its association with chains and corporate power was intrinsically linked by the end of the twentieth century.

Newsrooms in the first decades of the twenty-first century are facing vast changes in their size, mission, and culture. They are now part of bigger news ecosystems.[30] News production is much more mobile, distributed, and involves complex information flows back from sources and readers, viewers and listeners. This was true before, but now these interactions have greater influence and involve a range of technologies. Reporters and editors do not have to meet in the same space to assemble and then publish the news. It is no longer a physical process housed in a news factory or "plant," with the newsroom part of a facility that prints and ships newspapers. Newsrooms and their workers now collaborate across space and time. The data-driven journalism of the early twenty-first century has relied on joint efforts, even among rivals.[31] By combining their resources, newsrooms will continue to have an outsized impact. The nature of these spaces will continue to evolve, to the point that their identity may become truly virtual, or become hybrids of small, physical spaces and online collaboration tools, as Mel Bunce, Kate Wright and Martin Scott have explored in their work on Slack.[32] As before, with industrial journalism and its attendant technologies, digital, distributed newsrooms will likely develop their own new norms.[33] Already, many newsrooms are doing just that.

Some form of the newsroom, even if more mobile or temporary or mostly online, is important for journalism's future. New or revamped newsrooms will not reflect older, industrialized, and corporate spaces but will instead remain a gathering point for creative work, even during times of crisis.[34] Like programmers, designers, and other creative workers, journalists enjoy and find inspiration from the presence of peers. Despite some sign that they may move online, even the most sophisticated technology firms normally maintain some kind of physical presence. Like legacy technology companies such as Microsoft and Apple, or now Google, journalism outlets have historically relished the clashing and mixing of ideas, personalities, and roles. Their work, with its ineffable tendencies, defining what is "news" on a daily or hourly basis, demands human company. Newsroom ethnographers have long found that reporters and editors rely on each other to decide and determine what is newsworthy.[35] They will continue to make these spaces a physical reality, as well as a digital one. In both cases, newsrooms and their workers will become nimbler, bringing the newsroom with them or creating newsrooms wherever they gather. "The newsroom" will continue to represent, signal, and call to mind many of the ideals and ideas of journalism. It is an enduring shibboleth.

It would be easy to conclude that the big-city newsrooms of the early to mid-twentieth century represented American journalism's "golden age" and that we will never see their like again. This nostalgic perspective paints the newsroom as an idealized workplace. It was not, for the numerous reasons outlined throughout this study. It was messy and sometimes oppressive. It could liberate the best in its workers or it could force them to eke out a meager existence, one far out of proportion to the effort required to enter and remain in that world. It was not open, or later, not friendly, to women and minorities, not for a long time, at least.

As a media historian, I confess that I do tend to over-romanticize these places. They had problems. I, as a white man, would have fit in just fine in many of them (whether or not I would have been kept on is another question, as my telephone-reporting skills are lacking). But their lack of inclusiveness, their tendency toward toxic masculinity and their lack of care for family-focused workers made them hostile, or at least unwelcoming to people of color and women especially; this atmosphere changed over time, beginning in the 1970s, and newsrooms, painfully, slowly, became more representative and humane.[36] Like many institutions, they evolved slowly.

But these newsrooms were also, somewhat paradoxically, empowering. The very act of working together, in a creative space, helped to solidify journalists' occupational identity, and thus their sense of community. It gave them a reason to organize, to adopt technologies, and to better their working conditions. The newsroom was truly "the soul of the newspaper" and a "weapon for democracy," in the words of Walter Williams.[37] I would add that it was and is part of the soul of American *journalism*. That is why one should hope that there will always be newsrooms, in some shape, form, or fashion.

# Appendix

## Newsroom Salaries

Salary data was collected by newspaper publishers and by the federal government, especially the US Department of Labor and its Bureau of Labor Statistics (BLS), from the 1930s through the 1950s (though the US Census Bureau also tracked some data on news workers prior to this). The ANG, through its *Guild Reporter* and *Editor & Publisher* also collected and published information on salaries. The ANG advocated for higher wages, and *Editor & Publisher* often sought to portray publishers in a more positive light (though on occasion both did attempt more balanced reportage of salaries). Journalism educators and scholars publishing in the *Journalism Quarterly* surveyed current, former, and future news workers for insight on salaries. This became of acute interest to both researchers and industry observers as rival TV and radio newsrooms emerged to compete for journalism grads by the end of the 1950s. Salary data (based on weekly averages from industry and government surveys) is summarized in the graph found in chapter 8, on newsroom unionization.[1] The table on the following page is helpful for understanding broad national trends, and for contextualizing the general trend toward better salaries for news workers over time.

Representative Salaries Per Week, ca. 1920–1960

| | 1920s | | | 1930s | | | 1940s | | | 1950s | | |
|---|---|---|---|---|---|---|---|---|---|---|---|---|
| | West | Midwest | East | West | Midwest | East | West | Midwest | East | West | Midwest | East |
| Photographers | | | $20 | $40 | $45 | $43–47 | | $70 | $50–$100 | | $114.70 | $122–157 |
| Copy boys/girls | | | $15 | | | $15–20 | | $33 | | $42.50 | | |
| Rewrite staff | | $40–45 | | $50 | $60–65 | $52.50 | | $83 | $85–110 | | $125.90 | $150–200 |
| Copy editors | No Data | $48–52 | $70 | | $60–65 | $55–60 | No Data | $83 | $50–100 | $108.50 | $101.50–125.90 | |
| Cub reporters | | | $15 | $18 | $25 | $20-25 | | $32.50 | $22.50–25 | | $55 | $50–70 |
| Veteran reporters | | | $40 | $50 | $55 | $45–70 | | $70 | $55–80 | | $50–80 | $80–120 |
| Editorial writers/specialists | | | $30–60 | | | $55–57.50 | | | $72.50–93 | | | $100–200 |

Figure 26. This table shows representative examples of news workers' salaries by region and category of US news workers. Created by the author.[2]

# Notes

### NOTE ON SOURCES

1. Citations for the trade publications, memoirs, textbooks, archival and other material are in the chapter footnotes. What follows is an overview of sources and a brief description of methods used to analyze them, primarily via close reading of representative samples.

2. While the other trade publications and primary-source journals were examined for nearly full runs from 1920 to 1960s, the ASNE's *Bulletin* was only consulted occasionally. For more details on these and other sources, see the bibliographic essay.

3. In the case of *Editor & Publisher*, it had absorbed several other trade publications by the 1920s: the *Journalist* in 1907, *Newspaperdom* and *Advertising* in 1925, and the *Fourth Estate* in 1927. Note also that while the American Society of Newspaper Editors' *Bulletin* was also occasionally consulted, it was not a major source for this study. The publications of the APME and the ANPA covered many of the same topics and were instead used to highlight a pro-management perspective.

4. Interlibrary loans from research libraries around the United States helped to build on the fairly sizable collection of journalism texts held by the UW Libraries, and inherited from the University of Washington's former School of Communications (its journalism school), which merged in 2003 with the former Department of Speech to create the Department of Communication. I should thank Richard Kielbowicz for lending from his extensive private collection, as well as the estate of Donald E. McGaffin, for also permanently lending dozens of texts from its collection.

5. In this case, its microfilm was examined. The other trade publications were examined in bound hard-copy form whenever possible.

6. Will Mari, "An Enduring Ethos," *Journalism Practice* 9, no. 5 (September 2015): 687–703; Joseph Mirando, "Journalism by the Book: An Interpretive Analysis of News Writing and Reporting Textbooks, 1867–1987" (PhD diss., University of Southern Mississippi, 1992); Linda Steiner, *Construction of Gender in Newsreporting Textbooks, 1890–1990* (Columbia, SC: Association for Education in Journalism and Mass Communication, 1992); Chalet Seidel, "Representations of Journalistic Professionalism: 1865–1900" (PhD diss., Case Wesetern Reserve University, 2010).

7. Warren C. Price, *The Literature of Journalism, An Annotated Bibliography* (Minneapolis: University of Minnesota Press, 1959); Warren C. Price and Calder M. Pickett, *An Annotated Journalism Bibliography, 1958–1968* (Minneapolis: University

of Minnesota Press, 1970): Roland Edgar Wolseley, *The Journalist's Bookshelf; An Annotated and Selected Bibliography of United States Journalism* (New York: Chilton, 1961); Roland Edgar Wolseley and Isabel Wolseley, *The Journalist's Bookshelf: An Annotated and Selected Bibliography of United States Print Journalism*, 8th ed. (Indianapolis: R. J. Berg, 1986). An older bibliography (one of the oldest, in fact) that was also helpful: New York Public Library and Carl L. Cannon, *Journalism, A Bibliography* (New York: New York Public Library, 1924).

8. Randal Sumpter, "'Practical Reporting': Late Nineteenth Century Journalistic Standards and Rule Breaking," *American Journalism* 30, no. 1 (April 2013): 47.

9. Sumpter, "'Practical Reporting,'" 48. Here Sumpter is quoting Steiner, "Sex, Lies, and Autobiography: Contributions of Life Study to Journalism History," *American Journalism* 13, no. 2 (1996): 206–11.

10. Calvin L. Hall, *African American Journalists: Autobiography as Memoir and Manifesto* (Lanham, MD: Scarecrow Press, 2009).

11. These are monthly totals based on the Wolseley and Price bibliographies. While not exhaustive, they do give a good idea of just how popular memoir was as a genre (and despite its challenges to the historian as a primary source) among former and current news workers over the period of this study.

12. Will Mari, *A Short History of Disruptive Journalism Technologies* (London: Routledge, 2019).

## INTRODUCTION

1. Hanno Hardt and Bonnie Brennen, "Newswork, History, and Photographic Evidence: A Visual Analysis of a 1930s Newsroom," in *Picturing the Past: Media, History, and Photography*, ed. Brennan and (Urbana: University of Illinois Press, 1999), 11–35.

2. Nikki Usher, "Putting 'Place' in the Center of Journalism Research: A Way Forward to Understand Challenges to Trust and Knowledge in News," *Journalism & Communication Monographs* 21, no. 2 (June 2019): 84–146. Usher is a critical theorizer and assembler of theory about space and place in newsroom settings; her work and that of others who specialize in spatial theory is discussed more below, along with a more meta conception of "the newsroom" and its place in the past. Most descriptions heretofore even in relatively sophisticated journalism studies projects have not attempted to categorize the newsroom beyond its physical manifestation.

3. Daniel C. Hallin, "Commercialism and Professionalism in the American News Media," in *Mass Media and Society*, ed. James Curran and Michael Gurevitch (New York: Oxford University Press, 2000), 242–60.

4. Thomas Hanitzsch, "Deconstructing Journalism Culture: Toward a Universal Theory," *Communication Theory* 17, no. 4 (November 2007): 367–85. Randall Sumpter applies the helpful communities of practice (CoP) theoretical model in his *Before Journalism Schools: How Gilded Age Reporters Learned the Rules* (Columbia: University of Missouri Press, 2018).

5. Pamela J. Shoemaker and Stephen D. Reese, *Mediating the Message in the 21st Century: A Media Sociology Perspective*, 3rd ed.(New York: Routledge, 2014).

6. Pierre Bourdieu, *The Logic of Practice*, trans. Richard Nice (Cambridge, UK: Polity Press, 1990), 57, 58, 60–61. While the concept of *habitus* will not be deployed here, Bourdieu's ideas of a "dialectic between habitus and institutions," including how language is utilized to reinforce supposedly commonsense meanings, has informed my thinking about newsrooms and their spatial anatomies and legacies (along with the *idea* of habitus, even if the theory associated with it is not used in this study). Not to parse Bourdieu too finely or selectively, but a newsroom space, with its focus on language and blue-collar occupational acculturation, reflects some of this dynamic.

7. For a classic theorization of these influences, see Shoemaker and Reese, *Mediating the Message: A Media Sociology Perspective*, 3rd ed. (New York: Routledge, 2014).

8. George Lakoff and Mark Johnson, *Metaphors We Live By* (Chicago: University of Chicago Press, 1980); see also Gitte Gravengaard, "The Metaphors Journalists Live By: Journalists' Conceptualization of Newswork," *Journalism* 13, no. 8 (November 2012): 1064–82, and Will Mari, "'Bright and Inviolate': Editorial-Business Divides in Early Twentieth-Century Journalism Textbooks," *American Journalism* 31, no. 3 (Summer 2014): 378–99.

9. Sumpter's sixth chapter in *Before Journalism Schools* discusses the importance of these imagined newsrooms.

10. Michael Stamm, *Dead Tree Media: Manufacturing the Newspaper in Twentieth-Century North America* (Baltimore: Johns Hopkins University Press, 2018), 9.

11. Kevin Lerner, *Provoking the Press: (MORE) Magazine and the Crisis of Confidence in American Journalism* (Columbia, MO: University of Missouri Press, 2019); Matthew Pressman, *On Press: The Liberal Values That Shaped the News* (Cambridge, MA: Harvard University Press, 2018).

12. Matt Carlson, *Journalistic Authority: Legitimating News in the Digital Era* (New York: Columbia University Press, 2017).

13. Julia Guarneri, *Newsprint Metropolis: City Papers and the Making of Modern Americans* (Chicago: University of Chicago Press, 2017).

14. Barbie Zelizer, "Journalists as Interpretative Communities," *Critical Studies in Mass Communication* 10 (September 1993): 219–37.

15. Meryl Aldridge, "The Tentative Hell-Raisers: Identity and Mythology in Contemporary UK Press Journalism," *Media, Culture & Society* 20, no. 1 (January 1998): 109–27.

16. John Nerone and Kevin G. Barnhurst, "U.S. Newspaper Types, the Newsroom, and the Division of Labor, 1750–2000," *Journalism Studies* 4, no. 4 (November 2003):435–49.

17. C. W. Anderson, "Newsroom Ethnography and Historical Context," 61–79, in *Remaking the News: Essays on the Future of Journalism Scholarship in the Digital Age*, ed. Pablo J. Boczkowski and C. W. Anderson (Cambridge, MA: MIT Press, 2017), 61–79.

18. Richard Edwards, *Contested Terrain: The Transformation of the Workplace in the Twentieth Century* (New York: Basic Books, 1979), 17–18. See also James R. Beniger, *The Control Revolution: Technological and Economic Origins of the Information Society* (Cambridge, MA: Harvard University Press, 1986); Daniel A. Wren, *The History of Management Thought* (Hoboken, NJ: Wiley, 2005); and JoAnne Yates, *Control through Communication: The Rise of System in American Management* (Baltimore: Johns Hopkins University Press, 1989).

19. Alfred D. Chandler, *The Visible Hand: The Managerial Revolution in American Business* (Cambridge, MA: Belknap Press, 1977). For a discussion of Taylorism, see p. 275.

20. Alfred McClung Lee, *The Daily Newspaper in America: The Evolution of a Social Instrument* (New York: Macmillan, 1937), 642, 643, 645.

21. Lee, *Daily Newspaper in America*, 628–31.

22. Aurora Wallace, *Media Capital: Architecture and Communications in New York City* (Urbana: University of Illinois Press), 10.

23. Hanno Hardt and Bonnie Brennen, eds., *Newsworkers: Toward a History of the Rank and File* (Minneapolis: University of Minnesota Press, 1995); Warren Breed, "Social Control in the Newsroom: A Functional Analysis," *Social Forces* 33, no. 4 (May 1955): 326–35; see also his longer, earlier study: "The Newspaperman, News and Society" (PhD diss., Columbia University, 1952). Also Randal A. Beam, *Journalism Professionalism as an Organizational-level Concept* (Columbia, SC: Association for Education in Journalism and Mass Communication, 1990) and Nikki Usher, "Newsroom Moves and the Newspaper Crisis Evaluated: Space, Place, and Cultural Meaning," *Media, Culture & Society* 37, no. 7 (October 2015): 1005–21.

24. Ted Curtis Smythe, "The Reporter, 1880–1900: Working Conditions and Their Influence on the News," *Journalism History* 7, no. 1 (Winter 1980):1–10; Ted Curtis Smythe, *The Gilded Age Press, 1865–1900* (Westport, CT: Praeger, 2003).

25. I should thank my reviewers for their helpful suggestions, including here, in their emphasis on just how much newsrooms shaped modern journalism in the United States (and likely, in their own culturally contingent ways, in other places and times).

26. Karin Wahl-Jorgensen, "News Production, Ethnography, and Power: On the Challenges of Newsroom-Centricity," 21–34, in *The Anthropology of News and Journalism: Global Perspectives*, ed. S. Elizabeth Bird (Bloomington: Indiana University Press, 2010), 21–34.

27. José J. Sánchez-Aranda and Carlos Barrera, "The Birth of Modern Newsrooms in the Spanish Press," *Journalism Studies* 4, no. 4 (November 2003): 489–500; Jürgen Wilke, "The History and Culture of the Newsroom in Germany," *Journalism Studies* 4, no. 4 (November 2003): 465–77. See also Carole O'Reilly and Josie Vine, *Newsroom Design and Journalism Cultures in Australia and the UK: 1850–2010* (London: Routledge, forthcoming).

28. Daniel C. Hallin and Paolo Mancini, *Comparing Media Systems: Three Models of Media and Politics* (Cambridge, UK: Cambridge University Press).

29. Staffan Ericson and Kristina Riegert, eds., *Media Houses: Architecture, Media, and the Production of Centrality* (New York: Peter Lang: 2010).

30. Amber Roessner, Rick Popp, Brian Creech, and Fred Blevens, "'A Measure of Theory'?: Considering the Role of Theory in Media History," *American Journalism* 30, no. 2 (Spring 2013) 260–78; John Nerone, "Does Journalism History Matter?," *American Journalism* 28, no. 4 (Autumn 2011): 7–27; and John Nerone, "Why Journalism History Matters to Journalism Studies," *American Journalism* 30, no. 1 (Winter 2013): 15–28.

31. Pablo Boczkowski, "The Material Turn in the Study of Journalism: Some Hopeful and Cautionary Remarks from an Early Explorer," *Journalism* 16, no. 1 (January 2015): 65–68; Michael Schudson, "What Sorts of Things Are Thingy? And What Sorts of Thinginess Are There? Notes on Stuff and Social Construction," *Journalism* 16, no. 1 (January 2015): 61–64.

32. Kathy Roberts Forde, "Communication and the Civil Sphere: Discovering Civil Society in Journalism Studies," *Journal of Communication Inquiry* 39, no. 2 (April 2015): 113–24; Barbara Friedman, "Editor's Note: Is That a Thing? The Twitching Document and the Talking Object," *American Journalism* 31, no. 3 (July 2014): 307–11.

33. Benjamin Peters, "And Lead Us Not into Thinking the New Is New: A Bibliographic Case for New Media History," *New Media and Society* 11, nos. 1–2 (February/March 2009): 13–30; see also Michael Goddard, "Opening up the Black Boxes: Media Archeology, 'Anarchaeology' and Media Materiality," *New Media and Society* 17, no. 11 (December 2015): 1761–76; Lisa Gitelman, *Paper Knowledge: Toward a Media History of Documents* (Durham, NC: Duke University Press, 2014).

34. Robert W. McChesney and Ben Scott, eds., *Our Unfree Press: 100 Years of Radical Media Criticism* (New York: New Press, 2004); Sam Lebovic, *Free Speech and Unfree News: The Paradox of Press Freedom in America* (Cambridge, MA: Harvard University Press, 2016); Victor Pickard, *America's Battle for Media Democracy: The Triumph of Corporate Libertarianism and the Future of Media Reform* (New York: Cambridge University Press, 2015). For then-contemporary press critics, see Walter Lippmann, *Liberty and the News* (1920; New York: Dover Publications, 2010); Oswald Garrison Villard, *The Disappearing Daily: Chapters in American Newspaper Evolution* (New York: A. A. Knopf, 1944); Will Irwin, *The American Newspaper* (1911; Ames: Iowa State University Press, 1969); A. J. Liebling, *The Press* (New York: Ballantine Books, 1961).

35. There is a great deal of excellent scholarship on the legacy of the Hutchins Commission; for just one example, see Stephen Bates, "Prejudice and the Press Critics: Colonel Robert McCormick's Assault on the Hutchins Commission," *American Journalism* 36, no. 4 (2019): 420–46 and Bates, *An Aristocracy of Critics: Luce, Hutchins, Niebuhr, and the Committee That Redefined Freedom of the Press* (New Haven, CT: Yale University Press, 2020). For an older perspective on the commission's work, see Margaret A. Blanchard, *The Hutchins Commission: The Press and the Responsibility Concept* (Lexington, KY: Association for Education in Journalism, 1977).

36. Kevin Barnhurst, *Mister Pulitzer and the Spider: Modern News from Realism to the Digital* (Urbana: University of Illinois Press, 2016), xiii.

37. Lee, *The Daily Newspaper in America*, 642, quoting from a memoir by George Britt, *Forty Years—Forty Millions: The Career of Frank A. Munsey* (New York: Farrar & Rinehart, 1935) 25.

38. Lee's study synthesized a variety of primary sources, some of which are not easily accessible today.

39. Nerone and Barnhurst, "U.S. Newspaper Types," 438.

40. Nerone and Barnhurst, 440–41.

41. Mari, "'Bright and inviolate,'" 378–99.

42. Usher, "Newsroom Moves and the Newspaper Crisis Evaluated"; Peter Gade, "Newspapers and Organizational Development: Management and Journalist Perceptions of Newsroom Cultural Change," *Journalism & Communication Monographs* 6, no. 1 (March 2004): 3–55; Susan Keith, "Horseshoes, Stylebooks, Wheels, Poles, and Dummies: Objects of Editing Power in 20th-Century Newsrooms," *Journalism* 16, no. 1 (January 2015): 44–60.

43. Sarah Stonbely, "The Social and Intellectual Contexts of the U.S. 'Newsroom Studies,' and the Media Sociology of Today," *Journalism Studies* 16, no. 2 (2015): 259–74; Roger Dickinson, "Accomplishing Journalism: Towards a Revived Sociology of a Media Occupation," *Cultural Sociology* 1, no. 2 (July 2007): 189–208.

44. Peter L. Berger and Thomas Luckmann, *The Social Construction of Reality: A Treatise in the Sociology of Knowledge* (Garden City, NY: Doubleday, 1966); Thomas S. Kuhn, *The Structure of Scientific Revolutions*, 3rd ed.(Chicago, University of Chicago Press, 1996).

45. Breed, "Social Control in the Newsroom."

46. Usher, "Newsroom Moves and the Newspaper Crisis Evaluated," 4. Or as Usher puts it, spaces tend to be fixed, temporally bounded, and then influenced and constructed by people, respectively.

47. Akhteruz Zaman, "Newsroom as Battleground: Journalists' Description of Their Workspaces," *Journalism Studies* 15, no. 6 (2013): 823–24; and Doreen Massey, *For Space* (London: Sage, 2005), 9, 89–90.

48. Zaman, "Newsroom as Battleground," 824.

49. Doreen Massey, *Space, Place, and Gender* (Minneapolis: University of Minnesota Press, 1994), 269.

50. As is elaborated further elsewhere in this study, the physicality of the newsroom space helped to foster this sense of occupational and interpretive community. Henri Lefebvre's *Production of Space*, among other work by spatial theorists, discusses these concepts (though not explicitly applied directly to newsrooms). Another important spatial theorist is David Harvey, whose work is wonderfully explicated by Nikki Usher in the latter's work on newsroom transitions in the early twenty-first century; see Usher, "Newsroom Moves and Newspaper Crisis Evaluated" 1–17; and also David Harvey, *The Condition of Postmodernity: An Enquiry into the Origins of Cultural Change* (Cambridge, MA: Blackwell, 1991) and Harvey, *Spaces of Global Capitalism: Towards a Theory of Uneven Geographical Development* (London: Verso,

2006). As Usher has demonstrated, and I also hope to show, the work of spatial theorists such as Lefebvre and Harvey can be helpfully applied both to journalism studies research, and to a social history of newsroom life in the twentieth-century US. context. Usher's work is particularly helpful, as noted elsewhere (especially in the conclusion), in unpacking theories of relational space as applied to newsrooms.

51. Lefebvre, *The Production of Space*, trans. Donald Nicholson-Smith (Cambridge, MA: Blackwell, 1991); John Urray, "The Sociology of Space and Place," in *The Blackwell Companion to Sociology*, ed. Judith R. Blau (Malden, MA: Blackwell, 2004), 3–15; Harvey, *Spaces of Global Capitalism* . See also Massey, *For Space*.

52. Usher, "Newsroom Moves and the Newspaper Crisis Evaluated," 1005–21; see also her *Making News at The New York Times* (Ann Arbor: University of Michigan Press, 2014); Zaman, "Newsroom as Battleground," 819–34; and Wallace, *Media Capital*.

53. Pablo J. Boczkowski, *News at Work: Imitation in an Age of Information Abundance* (Chicago: University of Chicago Press, 2010); C. W. Anderson, *Rebuilding the News: Metropolitan Journalism in the Digital Age* (Philadelphia: Temple University Press, 2013); David Ryfe, *Can Journalism Survive? An Inside Look at American Newsrooms* (Cambridge, UK: Polity Press, 2012); Wahl-Jorgensen, "News Production, Ethnography, and Power," 21–34.

54. Chris Anderson, Emily Bell, and Clay Shirky, "Post Industrial Journalism: Adapting to the Present," Tow Center for Digital Journalism, 2012, http://towcenter.org/research/post-industrial-journalism-adapting-to-the-present-2/.

55. Shoemaker and Reese, *Mediating the Message*.

56. Ericson and Riegert, *Media Houses*, 5.

57. Ericson and Riegert, 11–12; for Harold Innis, see his classic *Bias of Communication* (Toronto: University of Toronto Press, 2006), originally published in 1951.

58. Stamm, *Dead Tree Media*, 2, 292–93.

59. Nikil Saval, *Cubed: A Secret History of the Workplace* (New York: Doubleday, 2014). More on the position of newsrooms as workplaces vis-à-vis other American places of work and business can be found in chapter 8, on unionization and quality of life in the newsroom. Beyond the scope of this work, Chandler's *Visible Hand* provides rich context, and Harry Braverman's *Labor and Monopoly Capital: The Degradation of Work in the Twentieth Century* (New York: Monthly Review, 1974) provides a further, and vital, critique.

60. Reporters, editors, and various newsroom support personnel could also, arguably, be classified as early members of an information economy.

61. Fred Carroll, *Race News: Black Journalists and the Fight for Racial Justice in the Twentieth Century* (Urbana: University of Illinois Press, 2017), 183.

62. Gwyneth Mellinger, *Chasing Newsroom Diversity: From Jim Crow to Affirmative Action* (Urbana: University of Illinois Press, 2013), 32.

63. Felecia Jones Ross, "Black Press Scholarship: Where We Have Been, Where We Are, and Where We Need to Go," *American Journalism* 37, no. 3 (2020): 301–20.

64. Mary L. Dudziak, *Cold War Civil Rights: Race and the Image of American Democracy* (Princeton, NJ: Princeton University Press, 2000); Thomas Borstelmann, *The*

*Cold War and the Color Line: American Race Relations in the Global Arena* (Cambridge, MA: Harvard University Press, 2001).

65. D'Weston Haywood, *Let Us Make Men: The Twentieth-Century Black Press and a Manly Vision for Racial Advancement* (Chapel Hill: University of North Carolina Press, 2018); Gerald Horne, *The Rise and Fall of the Associated Negro Press: Claude Barnett's Pan-African News and the Jim Crow Paradox* (Urbana: University of Illinois Press, 2017); Jinx C. Broussard, *Giving a Voice to the Voiceless: Four Black Women Journalists: 1890–1950* (London: Routledge, 2003); Carroll, *Race News*; Calvin L. Hall, *African American Journalists: Autobiography as Memoir and Manifesto* (Lanham, MD: Scarecrow Press, 2009); and Mellinger, *Chasing Newsroom Diversity*. See also Gene Roberts and Hank Klibanoff, *The Race Beat: The Press, the Civil Rights Struggle, and the Awakening of a Nation* (New York: Vintage, 2007).

## CHAPTER 2

*Epigraph: Henry B. Lent, "I Work on a Newspaper" (New York: MacMillan), 6. Emphasis in the original.*

1. Michael Schudson in his *Discovering the News: A Social History of American Newspapers* (New York: Basic Books, 1978) discusses some of these issues. Schudson's focus was on the broader formation of an American journalistic culture and on how news workers fit into it. Advancing from that, my work is about how these workers operated more specifically *within* newsrooms.

2. Harry Pence, "The 'Morgue Man' and His Job," *Quill*, April 1919, 1–2; the author describes the early name for a newspaper librarian, the "morgue man," one who was unnecessarily on the bottom of the food chain in a newsroom, subject to the whims of the "lordly reporters," the scoffing of the copy boys, and the object of editors' fury.

3. Thomas E. Jefferson, "Copy Boy," *Guild Reporter*, April 1934, 5.

4. Elias E. Sugarman, *Opportunities in Journalism* (New York: Grosset and Dunlap, 1951), 38.

5. Jefferson, "Copy Boy," 5.

6. Jefferson, 5.

7. Jefferson, 5.

8. Sugarman, *Opportunities in Journalism*, 39.

9. Jefferson, 5.

10. Frederick B. Edwards, "The Road That Leads to New York," *Quill*, October 1925, 6–7.

11. James H. Wright, "Cog vs. Wheel: No, Thanks—I'll Stay in Small City," *Quill*, June 1949, 9–10.

12. Charles C. Clayton, "Photo Journalism," *Quill*, April 1960, 6.

13. Sammy Schulman, *Where's Sammy?*, ed. Bon Considine (New York: Random House), 4–5.

14. Arthur Gelb, *City Room* (New York: Putnam), 6–7.

15. Gelb, *City Room*, 2.

16. Gelb, 15. More on the needed wartime inclusion of women, and what happened after, within newsroom culture, will follow. But it should be noted that unlike World War I, which briefly saw some women enter what had been traditionally male roles only to be forced out after, World War II led to more women who stayed in the field, resisting attempts to oust them. This was the case with the copy "boy" role, as well.

17. Gelb, 27–28.

18. Gelb, 28.

19. Marlen Pew, "Shop Talk at Thirty," *Editor & Publisher*, Dec. 13, 1930, 52.

20. Walter Schneider, "N.Y. News Seeking Jobs for Reporters It Trained," *Editor & Publisher*, Jan. 25, 1941, 34.

21. "5 Girls, 1 Boy in *Binghampton Press* Copy Boy School," *Editor & Publisher*, June 7, 1941, 20.

22. Kenneth E. Olson, "Survey of Daily Newspaper Personnel Shortages," *Journalism Quarterly* 20, no. 1 (1943): 114–15.

23. "Girls Train on Police Beat for N.Y. News," *Editor & Publisher*, Aug. 5, 1944, 30.

24. Helen M. Stratton, "Covers Interests of Women, Also 'Straight News,'" Jan. 6, 1945, 42.

25. "Reconversion Problems of the Press," *Problems of Journalism*, ASNE, April 18–20, 1946, 109–11.

26."Detroit Free Press Tests Editorial Apprentice Plan," *Editor & Publisher*, March 20, 1948. The program was developed in-house by editors George W. Parker and Richard Paulson.

27. "A Fifth Estate—The Copy Boys," *Editor & Publisher*, April 30, 1921, 42.

28. "The Fourth Estate," *Editor & Publisher*, January 15, 1949, 32. This was a recurring series of cartoons in the trade journal that ran off and on from the interwar years into the early Cold War.

29. "Short Takes," *Editor & Publisher*, July 24, 1937, 33.

30. George Kennedy, "Copy Readers Are Young and Copy Boys Are Older," *Editor & Publisher*, August 20, 1960, 60–61.

31. "Journalism School Graduates," *American Editor*, New England Society of Newspaper Editors, April 1960, inside front cover (no page number).

32. Donald Dow Webb, "Letters: In Conference," *Editor & Publisher*, September 5, 1959, 7.

33. Webb, "Letters: In Conference," 7. Capitalized words in the original.

34. "Managing Editors Panel," *Problems of Journalism*, ASNE, April 21–23, 1949, 53.

35. "Managing Editors Panel," 53, 57.

36. "Managing Editors Panel," 53.

37. C. Michael Curtis, "Letters: The Pathetic Exploitation of Copy-Boys," *Editor & Publisher*, September 6, 1958, 7.

38. "Letters: Copy Boys' Chains," *Editor & Publisher*, September 27, 1958.

39. Stanley Walker, *City Editor* (New York: Blue Ribbon Books, 1934), 103.

40. Walker, *City Editor*, 103.

41. Morton Sontheimer, *Newspaperman: A Book about the Business* (New York: McGraw-Hill, 1941), 231.

42. Sontheimer, *Newspaperman*, 231–32.

43. Sontheimer, 233, 240.

44. *Manual of Newspaper Job Classifications* (Washington, DC: United States Department of Labor Wage and House and Public Contracts Divisions, April 1943), 9.

45. *Manual of Newspaper Job Classifications*, 9.

46. Walker, 103, 104–05, 110–11.

47. Walker, 111–12; Erica Fahr Campbell, "The First Photograph of an Execution by Electric Chair," *Time*, April 10, 2014, http://time.com/3808808/first-photo-electric-chair-execution/.

48. Walker, 112–13.

49. "'Smart' Newspaper Work," *Quill*, February 1932, 10.

50. Walker, 114.

51. Sontheimer, 234–35, 243.

52. Sontheimer, 235–36, 239.

53. Sontheimer, 241–42.

54. Norman J. Radder, "Getting the Photograph," *Quill*, April 1920, 7. Note that the older spelling of "employee" (with the one "e") is maintained throughout this study when used in quoted material. Unless otherwise noted, other older spellings are also retained.

55. Radder, "Getting the Photograph," 10.

56. James Melvin Lee, "The Newspaper as an Economic Product," *Editor & Publisher*, May 15, 1926, 8. Lee, the director of NYU's Department of Journalism, was talking specifically about how war correspondents and the photographers working with them faced the same dangers.

57. "Adopts Five-Day Week for Editorial Staff," *Editor & Publisher*, November 8, 1930, 8.

58. "Cameramen Hunt in Packs, Nowadays," *Editor & Publisher*, September 17, 1927, 52.

59. "Our Own World of Letters," *Editor & Publisher*, January 7, 1933, 25.

60. Dale Beronius, "Spoken vs. Written Language," *Editor & Publisher*, April 18, 1936, 86.

61. "Cameraman Makes Good on Tough Assignment," *Editor & Publisher*, November 19, 1932, 38.

62. "Short Takes," *Editor & Publisher*, March 2, 1940, 33.

63. "Editorial: Photos—or Pictures," *Editor & Publisher*, October 13, 1934, 24.

64. "Reporters of Future Will Carry Cameras on Assignments," *Editor & Publisher*, November 5, 1932, 16.

65. Walker, 113–14.

66. Jack Price, "West Virginia Daily Buys Candid Cameras for Local Coverage," *Editor & Publisher*, November 14, 1936, 38. Graflex was the manufacturer of

the ubiquitous "Speed Graphic"; see "Pictures Help Make *Chicago Tribune* a Great Newspaper," *Editor & Publisher*, June 3, 1939, 21.

67. "Daily Buys Cameras for All Reporters," *Editor & Publisher*, March 19, 1938, 30.

68. "Life's Little Tragedies," *Editor & Publisher*, February 25, 1928, 12.

69. Guild Opposing 'Correspondent-Photog' Practice," *Editor & Publisher*, April 20, 1940, 62.

70. "The News and Pictures—Cameras and Reporters," *Problems of Journalism*, ASNE, April 18–20, 1935, 57. Blanchard was commenting on an informal Gannett Newspaper project to train reporters to use smaller, portable cameras.

71. "The News and Pictures—Cameras and Reporters," 58.

72. "N.Y. Police Card Lists Cut, Force Ordered to Respect Credentials," *Editor & Publisher*, March 3, 1934, 53. Mayor Fiorello LaGuardia in 1934 attempted to clamp down on press credentials in order to make them "mean something." Some 2,041 cards were issued, 1,237 of them triangular green press cards allowing their bearers more or less as much access as they wanted, and 804 rectangular red identification press cards that were more restricted; newspaper editors worked with the mayor's office to voluntarily reduce the numbers of cards.

73. "Flood in Upper N.Y. Taxes News Crews," *Editor & Publisher*, July 13, 1935, 20.

74. Jack Price, *News Pictures* (New York, Round Table Press, 1937), 15.

75. "Buys New Camera to Escape Penalty," *Editor & Publisher*, November 10, 1934, 22.

76. "The News and Pictures—Cameras and Reporters," 59–60.

77. Jack Price, "Trade Literature Aid Cameramen," *Editor & Publisher*, December 3, 1938, 39.

78. Gideon Seymour, "Associated Press News Photo Service," *Quill*, January 1936, 10–12.

79. "The Working Press," *Editor & Publisher*, August 23, 1947, 11.

80. W. H. Hornby, "San Francisco News Pattern: Radio-Phone Links Editor and Reporter," *Quill*, February 1947, 9.

81. "*Los Angeles Times'* New $4,000,000 Home Combines Beauty and Efficiency: Magnificent Marble and Limestone Structure Is Air-Conditioned Throughout and Protected Against Earthquake Tremors," *Editor & Publisher*, August 10, 1935, VI.

82. Marlen Pew, "Shop Talk at Thirty," *Editor & Publisher*, September 16, 1933, 48.

83. Pew, "Shop Talk at Thirty."

84. Jack Price, "New Trend in Pictures Means More Work for Cameramen," *Editor & Publisher*, September 12, 1936, 36.

85. Jack Price, "New Picture Magazines Extend Field for News Cameramen," *Editor & Publisher*, November 28, 1936, 28.

86. William Egan, "Akron Staff Attending 'School' Conducted by City Editor," *Editor & Publisher*, September 26, 1936, XXXI.

87. Jack Price, "Baker Pledges His Aid to Move for Photographer Organization," *Editor & Publisher*, October 10, 1936, 42.

88. Jack Price, "New Synchronizing Machines Saves Money in Photo Department," *Editor & Publisher*, December 26, 1936, 36; Jack Price, "Photog Designs Own Developing Tank," *Editor & Publisher*, May 20, 1939, 26. In the latter case, Price was documenting attempts by photographers in Los Angeles to start a national news photographers' network.

89. "Trend to Shorter Hours Shown in Inland Survey of 82 Papers," *Editor & Publisher*, June 12, 1937, 14. Managing editors were among the only other major newsroom group, besides proofreaders (a group not discussed at length because their work fell more on the mechanical side of the paper), to form substantial professional organizations during the period from 1920 to 1960.

90. Jack Price, "Camera Knights," *Editor & Publisher*, July 24, 1937, 30.

91. "News Commandments Adopt Ten 'Self Commandments,'" *Editor & Publisher*, April 16, 1938, 12.

92. Jack Price, "Big City Camera Jobs Are Hard to Get," *Editor & Publisher*, December 17, 1938, 62.

93. "Job Is Hard but Fun, Camera Men Agree," *Editor & Publisher*, February 17, 1940, 28.

94. Louis A. Paige, "Get That Picture," *Editor & Publisher*, April 20, 1940. Paige's drawing shows an enterprising photographer getting into position astride a bathtub (with someone in it), with the caption, "'xcuse me ma'am—I can get a better view of the fire across the street from this window—"; Paige worked for the Utica *Observer-Dispatch* in upstate New York. Walt Munson, "Now—You Take in Reel Life," *Editor & Publisher*, April 20, 1940, 54.

95. Johnny Anderson, "Now Cross Your Legs," *Editor & Publisher*, April 27, 1940, 102.

96. "How Editors Deal with Administrative Problems," *Problems of Journalism*, ASNE, April 19, 1940, 142.

97. Jack Price, "Writer Visit Dallas Photo Departments," *Editor & Publisher*, February 22, 1941, 44; Jack Price, "Oklahoma Dailies Have Modern Equipment," *Editor & Publisher*, February 8, 1941, 29.

98. "How Editors Deal with Administrative Problems," 146.

99. "470 Miles Monthly Set for Reporters in Gas Rationing," *Editor & Publisher*, July 11, 1942; 470 miles was for their "occupational" driving each month, though it is unclear if this applied everywhere or if there were exceptions. Jack Price, "Some Photogs Eligible for 'C' Gas Cards," *Editor & Publisher*, January 23, 1943, 6.

100. "Selective Service Further Clarifies 3-B Status," *Editor & Publisher*, March 27, 1943, 32.

101. Kenneth E. Olson, "Survey of Daily Newspaper Personnel Shortages," 114–15.

102. Ross B. Lehman, "Draft-Drained City Rooms Reach Toward Campus with Welcome Words: Wanted: College-Trained Newspapermen," *Quill*, June 1942, 8–9. Lehman had been editor of the *Daily Collegian* at Pennsylvania State College.

103. Jack Price, "No Present Need for Training Women Photogs," *Editor & Publisher*, July 11, 1942, 16.

104. Jack Price, "More Women Joining News Picture Service," *Editor & Publisher*, September 12, 1942, 20.

105. "From Business Office to Darkroom," *Editor & Publisher*, March 16, 1946, 72. Two examples included Mildred Scruggs and Dorothy Huntsinger, who had been promoted during the war to their positions and had taught themselves, and who worked as photographers for the Spartanburg, South Carolina, *Herald-Journal*.

106. Tom Cameron, "Photography: Red Hair, Perfect 36—Camera Gal, Not Model," *Editor & Publisher*, September 3, 1949, 32.

107. "Photography: Kansas Staff Is Co-Ed Again—With a Bachelor," *Editor & Publisher*, July 12, 1952, 7, 69. The paper was itself an aberration, with an all-women photo staff until the early 1950s.

108. Jack Price, "War Front Photogs Now Getting Credit in Bylines," *Editor & Publisher*, July 10, 1943, 30.

109. Jack Price, "Photo Plants Needs Planning by Photographer," *Editor & Publisher*, March 3, 1945; Jack Price, "Photography: City Staff Ideas Worked Out by Cameramen," *Editor & Publisher*, July 21, 1945, 40.

110. "J-Education: Jobs Becoming More Available for Negro Grads," *Editor & Publisher*, July 2, 1949, 35; 12 percent did not respond.

111. Armistead S. Pride, "'Plain Old-Fashioned Race Prejudice' Bars Jobs to Negroes, Dean Says," April 22, 1955, *Guild Reporter*, 7.

112. "First Negro on Staff," *Editor & Publisher*, March 3, 1956, 50. Forsythe was a "31-year-old Boston native," former freelance writer for the Lynn, Massachusetts, *Telegram News*, a former reporter for the Norfolk, Virginia, *Journal and Guide* and a graduate of the Boston University School of Public Relations in 1950.

113. Carl T. Rowan, *Breaking Barriers: A Memoir* (New York: Little, Brown, 1991); Gwyneth Mellinger, *Chasing Newsroom Diversity: From Jim Crow to Affirmative Action* (Urbana, University of Illinois Press, 2013). More on this issue will be discussed in the chapter on newsroom bosses, and below, throughout.

114. Howard L. Kany and Robert H. Eastabrook, "Experts Eye Pictures, Editorials," *Quill*, April 1947, 8.

115. Kany and Eastabrook, "Experts Eye Pictures, Editorials," 8.

116. James L. Collings, "Editor-Photographer Teamwork Stressed," *Editor & Publisher*, March 26, 1949.

117. James L. Collings, "Photography: Editors Tell How Pic Assignments Are Made," *Editor & Publisher*, January 21, 1950, 39.

118. Ray Erwin, "Newspapers' Color Use Studied at Photo Parley," *Editor & Publisher*, September 26, 1953, 54.

119. James L. Collings, "Photography: Fotog Should Match Reporter: Radosta," *Editor & Publisher*, September 18, 1954, 62.

120. James L. Collings, "Photography: More Regarding Those Picture Assignments," *Editor & Publisher*, January 28, 1950, 24.

121. "Chi. Tribune Has 36 Cars Linked to Radio Relay," *Editor & Publisher*, January 10, 1953.

122. "Along Misery Road," *Editor & Publisher*, September 17, 1960, 12. In this story, for example, seemingly almost reflexively, *Miami Herald* photographer Dan McCoy and reporter Steven Trumbull are shown working together.

123. Willarm C. Haselbush, "Many Newspapers Park Their Misfits with the Night Cty Editor. *The Denver Post* Finds the . . . Nightside Makes a Fine School for Reporters on an Afternoon Daily," *Quill*, August 1953, 6–7.

124. William Kostka Jr., "Big Town Opportunities for the Cub," *Quill*, March 1960, 17–18.

125. James L. Collings, "Photography: Editors Tell Advances Made by Their Papers," *Editor & Publisher*, February 20, 1954, 38.

126. Ray Erwin, "Newspaper' Color Use Studies at Photo Parley," *Editor & Publisher*, September 26, 1953, 9.

127. James L. Collings, "Photography: One Man's Adjustment to Smaller Cameras," *Editor & Publisher*, March 8, 1958, 50.

128. "Technical Progress," *Red Book*, Associated Press Managing Editors, November 12–15, 1958, 40, 43.

129. "What Should a Photographer Do: Take Picture of Tragic Scene or Flee from Irate Onlookers? Asks Arthur W. Geisleman Jr.," *Editor & Publisher*, August 15, 1959, 13.

130. Don Ultang, "News Photography to Photo Journalism," *Quill*, September 1954, 11.

131. "Everything's Under Control," *Editor & Publisher*, February 6, 1960, 36.

132. Eugene S. Pulliam, Jr., "Just Seat 20 Next to Each Other: How to Streamline a Big City Newsroom," *Quill*, February 1950, 8–10.

133. James Colvin, "Photo-Journalism Is Here to Stay," *Quill*, February 1952, 18. Colvin, a public relations director for the Encyclopedia Britannica, had worked as a writer and associate editor for *Popular Mechanics*, as well as a naval officer and historian for the US Navy's Supply Corps.

134. "Queens, Cops, Killers and Tough Competition Beset Chicago Photogs," *Quill*, November 1955, 19. The Chicago Press Photographers Association at the time included "still men, television men, newsroom cameramen, editors, darkroom men and wirephoto technicians."

135. "Newspaper Photography," *Problems of Journalism*, ASNE, April 20, 1956, 165.

136. Walter T. Ridder, "The Decline and Fall of the Press Conference," *Quill*, September 1952, 7. There is evidence that reporters for other new mediums, and the technology required for their coverage, sometimes impeded or at least caused similar tensions at high-profile events like press conferences, but also political conventions and like places where a media-diverse press corps gathered.

137. Bob Warner, "Photography: A Photojournalist Is a Photojournalist," *Editor & Publisher*, July 2, 1960.

138. George S. Bush, "The Men Behind Cameras Make Picture Journalism," *Quill*, July 1957, 9–10.

139. C. William Horrell, "Photojournalism Training Needs More Emphasis," *Quill*, December 1960, 17, 22.

140. Donald Janson, "Everybody in the Act: News Awards for Enterprise," *Quill*, December 1959, 9–10, 18.

141. Clayton, "Photo Journalism," 6. For more on this topic, see scholarship by Stanton Paddock, including "Developing news photography: The post-WWII rise of normative photojournalism instruction in liberal arts journalism education," presented to the Association for Education in Journalism and Mass Communication annual conference, St. Louis, Missouri, 2011.

## CHAPTER 3

1. Or designated as reporters assigned for a time to a rewrite desk, but primarily still thought of as reporters; see "*N.Y. Sun* Grants $100 Minimum for Reporters," *Editor & Publisher*, February 8, 1947, 62. The post–World War II newsroom was a bit of an aberration, because by this point newsrooms in larger cities were highly stratified, both from tradition and necessity. On other papers, GA reporters doubled as rewrite men when needed. Those chosen to serve as backup rewrite staffers were sometimes situated near the rewrite desk, just in case. See Eugene S. Pulliam Jr., "Just Seat 20 Next to Each Other: How to Streamline a Big City Newsroom," *Quill*, February 1950, 8–10.

2. Warren Breed, "Newspaper 'Opinion Leaders' and Processes of Standardization," *Journalism Quarterly* 32, no. 3 (1955): 278. Breed based this paper on his dissertation on the same topic, for which he worked with Paul F. Lazarsfeld and Robert K. Merton at Columbia; Breed was, at the time of this article's publication, an assistant professor of sociology at Tulane. Breed's focus was on the subtle influences unstated "policies" had on news workers, as guided indirectly by publishers and senior management.

3. Here I should thank the book's reviewers for helping parse these positions and their historical evolution.

4. *Manual of Newspaper Job Classifications* (Washington, DC: United States Department of Labor Wage and House and Public Contracts Divisions, April 1943), ii.

5. *Manual of Newspaper Job Classifications*, 8.

6. *Manual of Newspaper Job Classifications*, iii, 8, 18–19.

7. Elias E. Sugarman, *Opportunities in Journalism*, (New York: Grosset & Dunlap, 1951), 47.

8. Sugarman, *Opportunities in Journalism*, 47.

9. Sugarman, 47, 48.

10. Morton Sontheimer, *Newspaperman: A Book about the Business* (New York: McGraw-Hill, 1941), 187, 188.

11. Sontheimer, *Newspaperman*, 187.

12. Sontheimer, 186–87.

13. Arthur Gelb, *City Room* (New York: Putnam, 2003), 215, 228. Gelb notes that a classic example of a book that was, in fact, finished, was Herbert Asbury's *Gangs of New York*, written while Asbury was on the rewrite desk of the *Herald Tribune*, based on clippings from the paper's morgue.

14. Sontheimer, 186–88.

15. Sontheimer, 189.

16. Sontheimer, 189.

17. William D. Ogdon, "Now That I'm a Copy 'Butcher' Myself—Things Appear a Little Different, Says Reporter Who Joined Lords of the Rim," *Quill*, April 1936, 6.

18. Irving Brant, "Where Are the Copy Readers of Tomorrow?" *Editor & Publisher*, June 19, 1920, 5.

19. Carl Kesler, "Readability vs. Writeability," *Quill*, March 1950, 3. Kesler quipped that someday rewrite men might face a mechanical replacement: "The science which now threatens to hydrogen bomb us may come up first with an electronic rewriteman whose mechanical infallibility will need no editor." This gallows humor about being replaced by (analog) machines seems to have prevailed in every department of the newsroom, and, indeed, the whole newspaper (though less whimsically and more seriously on the mechanical side).

20. Arthur Robb, "Shop Talk at Thirty," *Editor & Publisher*, July 1, 1939, 36.

21. "Iced Water, Gum, Cig. Urns Amaze British," *Editor & Publisher*, July 14, 1951, 20.

22. Sontheimer, 190.

23. "Rewrite Man Sorrows for Sins of the Cubs," *Quill*, March 1924, 12.

24. Charles M. Cowden, "Cub Reporter's Ordeal by Wire Comes the First Time He Faces 'Phone and Must Dictate—or Be Damned!" *Quill*, July 1941, 7.

25. Erwin D. Canham, "Shop Talk at Thirty," *Editor & Publisher*, May 6, 1944, 68. Canham was managing editor of the *Christian Science Monitor*.

26. Cowden, "Cub Reporter's Ordeal," 12.

27. "Too Much Writing, No Reporting, Allen Finds in New York Papers," *Editor & Publisher*, June 18, 1921, 13.

28. Marlen Pew, "Shop Talk at Thirty," *Editor & Publisher*, July 13, 1929, 70.

29. "Adopts Five-Day Week for Editorial Staff," *Editor & Publisher*, November 8, 1930, 8.

30. Sontheimer, 190.

31. Gelb, *City Room*, 208. Gelb noted that at the time, being moved to the rewrite desk would normally be considered a reward, specifically for reporters who had the "special ability to turn in smooth copy under deadline pressure." There was also another, less good reason: reporters could be "assigned there to speed up or sharpen their own languid prose." In his own case, he just was not sure, and the editor who reassigned him was mum on the topic. Years later, however, he found out that the city editor, Frank Adams, had been angry that Gelb had not reported to work when Gelb's wife was ill. Their relationship eventually improved, and the incident nearly forgotten.

32. Gelb, 209, 210, 213–14, 217–18, 220, 226.

33. Gelb, 228, 232, 240.

34. Michael Sweeney, *Secrets of Victory: The Office of Censorship and the American Press and Radio in World War II* (Chapel Hill: University of North Carolina Press, 2001), 59.

35. "Sees Small City Newsmen Coming into Their Own," *Editor & Publisher*, August 8, 1942, 11.

36. "15 Women Writers Now with AP, Long a Male Stronghold," *Editor & Publisher*, September 12, 1942, 9.

37. "Situations Wanted: Editorial," *Editor & Publisher*, September 12, 1942, 48.

38. George C. Biggers and Morton Sontheimer, "Should Your Child Be a Newspaperman?" *Quill*, June 1954, 5.

39. Charles Henry Hamilton and J. Q. Mahaffey, "Women in the News Room?" *Red Book*, Associated Press Managing Editors, November 16–19, 1955, 209–12.

40. "New Layout Eases Confabs, Copy Flow," *Editor & Publisher*, February 28, 1948, 10.

41. George Brandenburg, "At Chicago Tribune: News Hole Is Filled by Percentage System," *Editor & Publisher*, January 26, 1952.

42. "*Phila. Inquirer* News Facilities on One Floor," *Editor & Publisher*, September 13, 1952, 13.

43. Willard C. Haselbush, "Many Newspapers Park Their Misfits with the Night City Editor. *The Denver Post* Finds the . . . Nightside Makes a Fine School for Reporters on an Afternoon Daily," *Quill*, August 1953, 6–7.

44. Haselbush, "Many Newspapers Park Their Misfits with the Night City Editor," 6.

45. Roger Simpson, private conversation with author, February 19, 2015.

46. George C. Bastian and Leland D. Case, *Editing the Day's News: An Introduction to Newspaper Copyreading, Headline Writing, Illustration, Makeup, and General Newspaper Methods* (New York: MacMillan, 1932).

47. The incorporation of pre-Internet technologies such as the word processor and microcomputer was explored by Anthony Smith, in his *Goodbye, Gutenberg: The Newspaper Revolution of the 1980s* (New York: Oxford University Press, 1980), but also in the work of some of his peers; see my 2019 book on the topic, too, for Routledge's "Disruptions" series, *A Short History of Disruptive Journalism Technologies: 1960–1990* (London: Routledge, 2019).

48. Sugarman, 49.

49. Sontheimer, 191.

50. Stanley Walker, *City Editor* (New York: Blueribbon Books, 1934), 91–92.

51. Walker, *City Editor*, 92.

52. Sugarman, 49, 51, 52.

53. Sugarman, 50.

54. Sontheimer, 192.

55. Walker, 88.

56. Walker, 93.

57. Sugarman, 50.

58. Sontheimer, 192.

59. These shortened words included "biz," for "business," for example.

60. Sugarman, 50.

61. Sontheimer, 193; Sugarman, 50.

62. Sontheimer, 194.
63. Walker, 94, 96.
64. Sugarman, 51.
65. Walker, 93.
66. Walker, 93.
67. Sontheimer, 191.
68. Walker, 88.
69. Henry Edward Warner, "Songs of the Craft," *Editor & Publisher*, August 15, 1925, 4.
70. "Editorial: Do Women Belong?" *Editor & Publisher*, November 21, 1925, 22.
71. Mildred Philips, "Forum of Female Fraternity of Fourth Estaters," *Editor & Publisher*, May 28, 1921, 301.
72. "Situations Wanted," *Editor & Publisher*, November 10, 1934, 35.
73. Walker, 89.
74. Sontheimer, 194.
75. Walker, 93; also: "Hot-headed young word-painters have been known to fly off the handle when questioned by a copyreader on the facts of a story. This is a great mistake. If the copyreader can't understand it, how can the average reader?"
76. Walker, 93–94; "The results, while not always happy, have produced some exceptionally high-class handlers of copy. The business needs more of them."
77. Walker, 92–93, 95–96.
78. "Our Own World of Letters," *Editor & Publisher*, October 15, 1932.
79. "And That's How Copy Readers Get That Way!" *Editor & Publisher*, June 4, 1927, 12.
80. "Short Takes," *Editor & Publisher*, March 2, 1940, 3.
81. "Short Takes," *Editor & Publisher*, March 27, 1943, 18.
82. "Ray Erwin's Column: Credit the Copyreader," *Editor & Publisher*, February 21, 1959, 4.
83. Arthur Robb, "Shop Talk at Thirty," *Editor & Publisher*, August 16, 1941, 36.
84. Frank Landt Dennis, "City Room 'Short Course' Saves Tempers and Time," *Quill*, August 1942, 5.
85. Ogdon, "Now That I'm a Copy 'Butcher' Myself," 6.
86. Ogdon, 7.
87. Ogdon, 16.
88. Richard Tucker, "Don't Dodge the Desk! That's Where a Young Newspaperman Can Get Real, All-Around Seasoning," *Quill*, February 1940, 13, 19.
89. James H. Wright, "Cog vs. Wheel: No, Thanks—I'll Stay in Small City," *Quill*, June 1949, 9, 10.
90. Hugh S. Baillie, "Headwork behind the Headlines: Initiative and Enthusiasm Help Newsmen Steer Their Course Safely Past Perilous Shoals of Standardization," *Quill*, February 1935, 10. Baillie was executive vice president of United Press (UP). He began working in journalism in 1908 for the *Los Angeles Record*, joining the UP in 1915.

91. Milton Garges, "A.P. News Wires Span 50,000 Miles Operation Costs over $2,500,000," *Editor & Publisher*, August 7, 1919, 17. Garges was "acting chief A.P. traffic department."

92. F. C. Nelson, "Efficient Factory Hidden behind *Hartford Times*' Splendid Facade—Production Departments Arranged That All Work Converges by Shortest Routes on Press Room and Delivery of Finished Papers," *Editor & Publisher*, December 18, 1920, 15.

93. "Finest Newspaper Plant in Southwest Ready," *Editor & Publisher*, May 28, 1921, II; note: "This, with the automatic house telephone system, enables each department to get in touch with each other without a moment's delay. Both systems were installed at great expense."

94. "Finest Newspaper Plant in Southwest Ready," iv.

95. "Human Touch Vitalizes Efficiency in *Washington Star*'s Plant," *Editor & Publisher*, April 22, 1922, 18–19.

96. "*Philadelphia Inquirer* in Palatial Home," *Editor & Publisher*, July 18, 1925, 9.

97. "N.Y. World Adopts Universal Desk," *Editor & Publisher*, May 27, 1922, 36.

98. Samuel Haber, *Efficiency and Uplift: Scientific Management in the Progressive Era, 1890–1920* (Chicago, University of Chicago Press, 1964).

99. Osmore R. Smith, "Controlling Copy Flow Is Secret of Economic Production: *Milwaukee Journal*'s Planning Division Created to Eliminate Costly Edition Time Rush—Search Analysis Revealed Haphazard Methods Prevailing," *Editor & Publisher*, November 17, 1923, 18.

100. Osmore R. Smith, "Inability to Control News Copy Flow Largely a Myth," *Editor & Publisher*, December 1, 1923, 30.

101. Alger Stephen Beane, "Syndicate Copy, Machine Reporting, Producing 'Era of Kiln Dried News,'" *Editor & Publisher*, February 2, 1924, 10.

102. "Editors Exchange Experiences on News Handling," *Editor & Publisher*, May 3, 1924, 14–15.

103. "*Houston Press* Occupies $500,000 Building," *Editor & Publisher*, February 11, 1928, 9.

104. "*Syracuse Herald* in Million-Dollar Plant," *Editor & Publisher*, February 25, 1928, 7.

105. "*Cincinnati Inquirer* in $3,500,000 Building," *Editor & Publisher*, April 14, 1928, 8–9.

106. "*Knoxville News-Sentinel* Publishing from New Modern Building," *Editor & Publisher*, November 10, 1928, 16.

107. "Modern Appointments of Newest Metropolitan Newspaper Building," *Editor & Publisher*, July 13, 1929, 13.

108. "Our Cover—and Other City Rooms," *Quill*, January 1948, 2.

109. "News Room Remodeled," *Editor & Publisher*, May 23, 1931, 16.

110. "*Globe-Democrat* Occupies New Plant," *Editor & Publisher*, November 7, 1931, 13.

111. "Loud-Speaker Device Installed by Daily," *Editor & Publisher*, November 7, 1931, 20.

112. "Dailies Control Copy by Electronic Device," *Editor & Publisher*, August 10, 1935, xxvii.

113. "What Our Readers Say: Copy Desk Veterans," *Editor & Publisher*, November 19, 1932, 35.

114. Marlen Pew, "Shop Talk at Thirty," *Editor & Publisher*, August 5, 1933, 40.

115. Carl Kesler, "'By Guess' Not Good Enough," *Quill*, November 1947, 3.

116. Marlen Pew, "Shop Talk at Thirty," *Editor & Publisher*, January 21, 1933, 32.

117. Marlen Pew, "Shop Talk at Thirty," *Editor & Publisher*, Aug. 5, 1933, 40.

118. Marlen Pew, "Shop Talk at Thirty," Editor & Publisher, Oct. 27, 1934, 40.

119. "Super-Copyreader to Check All Proofs," *Editor & Publisher*, November 5, 1938, 32.

120. "Andrews Speech Cheers Guild in Sixth Annual Convention," *Editor & Publisher*, August 5, 1939, 9.

121. "Sees Small City Newsmen Coming into Their Own," *Editor & Publisher*, August 8, 1942, 11.

122. Francis V. Prugger, "Social Composition and Training of *Milwaukee Journal* News Staff," *Journalism Quarterly* 18, no. 3 (1941): 232. Other estimates from this era guessed that at medium-sized daily papers in cities of two to three hundred thousand, there might be fifty editorial members, of which eight were copy editors; see "How Editors Deal with Administrative Problems,'" American Society of Newspaper Editors, *Problems of Journalism*, April 19, 1940, 142.

123. Kenneth E. Olson, "Survey of Daily Newspaper Personnel Shortages," *Journalism Quarterly* 20, no. 1 (1943): 114–15.

124. "Bright Ideas: Professors on Copydesk," *Editor & Publisher*, May 20, 1944, 22. During peacetime, it was not uncommon for faculty to work over the summer. This tradition continues in a more limited way today, through research and newsroom fellowships.

125. "Chicago *Journal of Commerce* Has All-Girl Copy Desk," *Editor & Publisher*, September 12, 1942, 10.

126. "Copy Gals!" *Editor & Publisher*, January 9, 1943, 10.

127. "Has Two Copy Girls," *Editor & Publisher*, January 23, 1943, 6.

128. Jessica Bird, "What Our Readers Say: Cites 'Slap' at Women Reporters," *Editor & Publisher*, January 23, 1943, 49.

129. "Woman Wields Blue Pencil on *N.Y. Times* Copy," *Editor & Publisher*, January 5, 1946, 63.

130. "E&P Finds Two Other N.Y. Girl Copyreaders," *Editor & Publisher*, March 16, 1946, 65; Barbara Yuncker at the *Post* and Betty Wood at the *Mirror*.

131. William Reed, "Huge Re-Employment Effort Cuts Job Openings in NYC," *Editor & Publisher*, February 16, 1946, 7, 60.

132. "Reconversion Problems of the Press," American Society of Newspaper Editors, *Problems of Journalism*, April 18–20, 1946, 109–11.

133. "*Santa Fe New Mexican* Moves into New Home," *Editor & Publisher*, August 8, 1942, 28.

134. "Tomorrow Is Today at the *Bulletin*," *Editor & Publisher*, May 20, 1944, 15; part of a wartime ad campaign.

135. "*Wall St. Journal* Copy Desk Ends Elbow Knocking," *Editor & Publisher*, September 14, 1946, 52.

136. "New Layout Eases Confabs, Copy Flow," *Editor & Publisher*, February 28, 1948, 10.

137. "New Layout Eases Confabs," 10.

138. "The *New York Times*: 'All the News That's Fit to Print,'" *Editor & Publisher*, March 20, 1948, 4; part of a series of ads the *Times* had taken out in the trade publication showcasing its physical space and work force, often one and the same. An ad from the August 25, 1951 issue of *E&P*, "Why So Many Men Just to Edit Copy?" also showed off the *Times*'s commitment to accuracy.

139. "Octagon-Shape Universal Desk Cuts Congestion," *Editor & Publisher*, January 21, 1950, 27.

140. "Sacramento, Calif., *Bee* Copy Desk," *Editor & Publisher*, July 5, 1952.

141. "*Phila. Inquirer* News Facilities on One Floor," *Editor & Publisher*, September 13, 1952, 13.

142. "Ex-Back Shop Now City Room," *Editor & Publisher*, September 22, 1956, 67.

143. "Efficiency High in Streamlined *Miami News* Plant," *Editor & Publisher*, August 9, 1958, 43–44; "Here Are 'Inside' Stories . . . from New Newspaper Buildings," *Editor & Publisher*, January 3, 1959, 14–15.

144. George Brandenburg, "At *Chicago Tribune*: News Hole Is Filled by Percentage System," *Editor & Publisher*, January 26, 1952.

145. Carl Kesler, "Education for Journalism," *Quill*, May 1951, 3.

146. "*Detroit Free Press* Tests Editorial Apprentice Plan," *Editor & Publisher*, March 20, 1948.

147. Dwight Bentel, "Journalism Education: ACEJ Names Four-Man Advisory Committee," *Editor & Publisher*, March 22, 1952, 34.

148. "Panel on News and Editorial Costs," American Society of Newspaper Editors, *Problems of Journalism*, April 18, 1953, 173. Edward T. Stone, an editor at the *Seattle Post-Intelligencer*, elaborated: "This plan took a lot of doing because our news editor goes on the theory that the local and news desks are separate empires that should never communicate except under the most formal circumstances like exchanging ambassadors or something." The Guild local also did not like the plan and was preparing to oppose it during negotiations, because "any time you monkey with the opportunity for overtime gravy you're headed for trouble."

149. Robert U. Brown, "Shop Talk at Thirty," *Editor & Publisher*, September 13, 1952, 80. Brown added: "We've already eliminated most of the time-honored workers in the newspaper vineyard, as related above. All we need are one or two more automatic devices."

150. "What to Do?" *Quill*, October 1931, 10.

151. G. Norman Collie, "Letters: A Slot Man Talks Back," *Editor & Publisher*, January 4, 1958, 7.

152. Carl Kesler, "A Copyreader Is Also an Editor," *Quill*, August 1950, 3.

153. Merritt L. Johnson, "Memo to Editors: A Good Copyreader Is a Bargain," *Quill*, November 1952, 12. Johnson, a former copy editor for the Chicago *Daily News*, described the still "ancient, beat-up, inefficient, cigarette burned copy desks, and all the old-fashioned, hard, uncomfortable, unadjustable chairs that copy editors are chained to all day," 24.

154. Irving Brant, "Where Are the Copy Readers of Tomorrow?" *Editor & Publisher*, June 19, 1920, 5.

155. "Solving the Problem of Keeping the Copy-Desk in Order," *Editor & Publisher*, April 29, 1922, 62.

156. "Horace in the Slot: Ode to & for Copy Desks," *Editor & Publisher*, July 3, 1953, 4.

157. Richard R. Ryan, "Disillusioned Copy Editor Poses the Question, 'Why Can't Johnny Write?'" *Quill*, July 1957, 15–16. Ryan was a veteran copy editor working for the Corpus Christi *Caller-Times*.

158. Warren Breed, "Newspaper 'Opinion Leaders' and Processes of Standardization," 280–81. Breed noted the newspaper reading, speculating that it might "'look better' to be seen reading than to be merely sitting," and that reading "probably fills certain needs of relaxation and a sense of adequacy."

159. "New Copy Desk Game Invented in Cleveland," *Editor & Publisher*, May 23, 1931, 47.

160. "Short Takes," *Editor & Publisher*, July 13, 1946, 26.

161. Eddie Kitch, "Chicago News Has Its Own Subway: Pneumatic Tubes from Newsroom to Composing Room Are Common. The City Press Newspapers Is Unique," *Quill*, January 1954.

162. "Situations Wanted: Editorial," *Editor & Publisher*, September 12, 1942, 48.

163. "The Fourth Estate," *Editor & Publisher*, March 19, 1955, 46.

164. "The Fourth Estate," *Editor & Publisher*, September 21, 1957, 124.

165. George Kennedy, "Copy Readers Are Young and Copy Boys Are Older," *Editor & Publisher*, August 20, 1960, 60–61. Kennedy, a columnist and writer of "The Rambler" for the *Washington Star*, was thinking back to life in the newsroom ca. the 1920s.

166. Charles C. Clayton, "The Writer's Best Friend," *Quill*, August 1957, 6. Clayton succeeded Carl Kesler as editor of the *Quill*.

167. John Stevens, "J-Grad Discovers Copy Desk Is Not a Dead End Job," *Quill*, February 1959, 15. Stevens was a reporter and former copy editor for the *Indianapolis Star*. He elaborates: "Sometimes the copy desk is viewed as a sort of limbo to which those who couldn't quite make the grade as top reporters are banished. This seldom is the case; most copy readers are there because that is where they prefer. The majority have been reporters, but they are on the copy desk of their own choosing."

168. Charles C. Clayton, "Age of Specialists," *Quill*, September 1959, 7.

169. Donald Janson, "Everybody in the Act: News Awards for Enterprise," *Quill*, December 1959, 9–10; George E. Simmons, "Serendipity of Summer Internships," *Journalism Quarterly* 33, no. 4 (1956): 517–20. A line from Simmons on p. 518 reads,

"The super-copyreader becomes an editor with a title and managerial ability, but not necessarily a managing editor of a newspaper."

170. Carl Rowan, for example, got his start at the *Minneapolis Tribune* as a copy editor.

## CHAPTER 4

1. Robert Darnton, "Writing News and Telling Stories," *Daedalus* 104, no. 2 (Spring 1975): 175–94. While he also discusses the relationships between editors and reporters at some length, his observations on that set of interactions will appear in chapter 6, on supervisors in the newsroom.

2. For a similar account, see David Halberstam's account of his time as a reporter at the *Tennessean*, in Nashville, "The Education of a Journalist," *Columbia Journalism Review* 33, no. 4 (November/December 1994):29–34. Halberstam's interactions with police officers, and some of his discussion of racism on the job, will be discussed below.

3. Darnton, "Writing News," 176–77.

4. Darnton, 177.

5. Darnton, 177, 180.

6. Darnton, 184–85.

7. Darnton, 184–85. For example, "He acquires the tone of the newsroom by listening. Slowly he learns to sound like a New Yorker, to speak more loudly, to use reporter's slant, and to increase the proportion of swear words in his speech. These techniques ease communication with colleagues and with news sources. It is difficult, for example, to get much out of a telephone conversation with a police lieutenant unless you know how to place your mouth close to the receiver and shout obscenities."

8. Darnton, 187.

9. Darnton, 176.

10. Elias E. Sugarman, *Opportunities in Journalism* (New York: Grosset & Dunlap, 1951), 40.

11. Sugarman, *Opportunities in Journalism*, 40.

12. Sugarman, 40.

13. John Dreiske, "Now That I've Lost My Job—Should I Try to Find Work on Another Newspaper or Chuck the Business and Enter Another Field?" *Quill*, October 1932, 5, 9.

14. Sugarman, 41.

15. Sugarman, 41.

16. He references working for this newspaper in his second chapter.

17. Morton Sontheimer, *Newspaperman: A Book About the Business* (New York: McGraw-Hill Book Company, Inc., 1941), 4.

18. Sontheimer, *Newspaperman*, 5.

19. Sontheimer, 8.

20. Sontheimer, 9–10.

21. Sontheimer, 10.

22. Sontheimer, 10–11.

23. Sontheimer, 11.

24. "What to Do?" *Quill*, October 1931, 10. Sometimes a cub was called an "apprentice," at least in older conceptions of the position; see "'St. Louis Plan' May Be Solution of Writers' Discontent," *Editor & Publisher*, September 18, 1919, 74.

25. Thomas P. O'Hara, "The Cub," in Joseph G. Herzberg, *Late City Edition*, ed. Joseph G. Herzberg (New York: Henry Holt and Company, 1947), 14–15, 20–21.

26. O'Hara, "The Cub," 14–15, 20–21.

27. Sontheimer, 14, 16, 17.

28. Sontheimer, 20, 21. "You'll find the men in the other departments a lot of surprisingly good fellows, from the tough-looking mugs in the circulation department to the shyly pleasant ad solicitor, who always makes the sage observation to you, as he walks through the city room when all hell has broken loose, 'lots of excitement today, huh?'"

29. Stanley Walker, *City Editor* (New York: Blue Ribbon Books, 1934), 218.

30. Walker, *City Editor*, 40, 41. Other qualities valued by Walker: "a sound background in history and economics, the ability to translate or even speak two or three foreign languages, a comprehensive knowledge of literature, and sometimes definite expertness in art and music."

31. Walker, 41.

32. Walker, 41.

33. Walker, 43.

34. Roy H. Copperud, *Editor & Publisher*, August 11, 1956, 2. Discussions about the use of bylines as an indication of status, or the rewarding of bylines by editors as a demonstration of their power over reporters, are scattered throughout the trade journals of the time.

35. Sontheimer, 172.

36. Sontheimer, 173–74. Recalling his own first brush with a byline, as a young reporter at the *New York Telegram*, Sontheimer relates how he wrote a colorful obit and was begrudgingly given a byline for it by an editor, only to have it taken away when it was discovered the wrong body had been identified.

37. This can be seen most visibly in the higher and more regularized salaries of the period, as Guild advocacy helped to make the working lives of many reporters better—even for those not in the Guild.

38. Sontheimer, 174.

39. Sontheimer, 175.

40. Sontheimer, 176–77.

41. Walker, 42.

42. Sontheimer, 22, 25.

43. Sontheimer, 23. This was acknowledged as a bit "crude."

44. Sontheimer, 23–27.

45. Sontheimer, 29, 30–31.

46. C. W. Kahles, "Hairbreadth Harry, the Cub Reporter," *Editor & Publisher*, April 17, 1926, 4.

47. "1935 World Almanac: Book of a Million Facts," *Editor & Publisher*, January 12, 1935, 15.

48. "Short Takes," *Editor & Publisher*, November 28, 1936, 16.

49. "News values" is an important topic for journalism studies researchers; see, for example, Tony Harcup and Deirdre O'Neill, "What Is News? Galtung and Ruge Revisited," *Journalism Studies* 2, no. 2 (May 2001): 261–80; or Herbert J. Gans, *Deciding What's News: A Study of CBS Evening News, NBC Nightly News, Newsweek, and Time* (New York: Pantheon Books, 1979).

50. Steuart M. Emery, "The Cub Spirit," *Editor & Publisher*, March 25, 1922, 8.

51. Emery, "Cub Spirit," 8.

52. "Rewrite Man Sorrows for Sins of the Cubs," *Quill*, March 1924, 12.

53. "Training Reporters Schools' Big Task," *Editor & Publisher*, October 1, 1932, 33. This thought is from Kenneth Stewart, a journalism instructor in Stanford's Division of Journalism within its School of Social Sciences.

54. Phillip D. Jordan, "News Room Philosophy," *Quill*, March 1926, 22.

55. Jordan, "News Room Philosophy," 23.

56. Jordan, 22.

57. "Short Takes," *Editor & Publisher*, February 5, 1938, 18. In another typical telling, a young woman cub reporter, described as "A sweet young thing, who knew none of the terms or practices of a city room," was confused by an order to write up an interview "for the bulldog."

58. Philip Schuyler, "Romances of American Journalism: Stories of Success Won by Leaders of the Press," *Editor & Publisher*, October 13, 1928, 10. Part of a recurring series of profiles of well-known/successful figures in the newspaper industry, this article features George B. Parker, editor in chief of Scripps-Howard Newspapers.

59. "Short Takes," *Editor & Publisher*, August 28, 1937, 20.

60. James J. Butler, "Guild Walks Out of Wage Hearing," *Editor & Publisher*, December 8, 1934, 33.

61. "Toledo Guild Schools Trains Cub Reporters," *Editor & Publisher*, July 13, 1935, 41.

62. O. O. McIntyre, "As They View It: In the United States," *Quill*, October 1930, 2.

63. Joseph E. Ray, "Reporters Have Troubles as Army Scribes," *Editor & Publisher*, September 12, 1942, 14. The author was a US Army private assigned to the "Public Relations Section, Quartermaster Replacement Training Center, F[or]t. F. E. Warren, Wyo."

64. William A. Rutledge III, "The Write of Way," *Quill*, February 1942, 13. Rutledge, in what appears to be a recurring column of miscellaneous news about Sigma Delta Chi members, quotes L. D. Hotchkiss, managing editor of the *Los Angeles Times*.

65. John T. Buck, "Woman's Place (So They Say in These Days of World War II) Is in the Home—Edition! 'Ladies of the Press' Take Over," *Quill*, December 1942, 10–11. The article's title was probably a play on the title of a popular (and pioneering) 1936 book about women in journalism, Ishbel Ross' *Ladies of the Press: The Story*

*of Women in Journalism by an Insider* (New York: Harper, 1936). Ross herself had been a reporter at the *New York Herald Tribune.*

66. Buck, "Woman's Place," 10.

67. Buck, 10.

68. Mildred Philips, "Forum of Female Fraternity of Fourth Estaters," *Editor & Publisher*, May 28, 1921, 301.

69. "Declares Organization Is Needed among Editorial Workers," *Editor & Publisher*, June 5, 1919, 20, 37. Carol Bird, a "newswoman and feature writer" with the *Detroit Free Press*, gave a talk called "What Newspaper Work Is a woman Best Fitted For?" In it, she advocated for what she called "regulars," or "the girls who really are news-women," arguing that women could handle certain stories (especially those involving human interest) better than men, that they were observant, and that they could be charming, just like men, calling unfair the fact that men could get away with being "magnetic" while women who were similarly engaging were said to use "sex lure[s]" to get material for their stories.

70. Newsrooms echoed as much as they pushed societal norms.

71. Buck, 11.

72. Margaret Ellington, "Wherein a Feminine Scribe Reports What Happens When through Whims of War: Girl Meets 'Boys' of the City Room!" *Quill*, January 1943, 6.

73. Ellington, "Wherein a Feminine Scribe Reports," 6–7.

74. Ellington, 7.

75. Ellington, "7; "Sees Small City Newsmen Coming into Their Own," *Editor & Publisher*, August 8, 1942, 11.

76. "Short Takes," *Editor & Publisher*, January 6, 1945, 24.

77. "The Fourth Estate," *Editor & Publisher*, February 28, 1948, 38.

78. "The Fourth Estate," *Editor & Publisher*, September 27, 1952, 36; see also "How Do You Think the Guild Will Take It?" *Quill*, July 1956, 27.

79. James H. Wright, "Cog vs. Wheel: No, Thanks—I'll Stay in Small City," *Quill*, June 1949, 9.

80. Wright, "Cog vs. Wheel," 9.

81. "Managing Editors Panel," *Problems of Journalism*, ASNE, April 21, 1949, 56. This opinion was expressed by Russell Wiggins, managing editor of the *Washington Post.*

82. James L. Julian, "Journalism Education: How Does the Talent Perform in the Shop?" *Editor & Publisher*, July 16, 1949, 50.

83. Campbell Watson, "Editors List Moves in Building Papers," *Editor & Publisher*, July 2, 1955, 50.

84. Willard C. Haselbush, "Many Newspapers Park Their Misfits with the Night City Editor. The Denver Post Finds the Nightside Makes a Fine School for Reporters on an Afternoon Daily," *Quill*, August 1953, 6–7.

85. Haselbush, "Many Newspapers Park Their Misfits," 7.

86. "Personnel Training and Recruiting," *Red Book*, Associated Press Managing Editors, November 14–17, 1956, 162.

87. "Personnel Training and Recruiting," 160, 162, 163.

88. Joseph N. Freudenberger, "Gannett Newspapers Devise Program for Training Beginning Staffers," *Quill*, May 1958, 21.

89. "Journalism School Graduates . . .," *American Editor*, New England Society of Newspaper Editors, April 1960, inside front cover (no page number). The NESNE was composed of some of the oldest weeklies and dailies in the country.

90. "Ray Erwin's Column: Credit the Copyreader," *Editor & Publisher*, February 21, 1959, 4.

91. Carl Kesler, "Journalists' Choice," *Quill*, July 1956, 4. As Kesler put it: "Nobody is quicker to discern a promising young newspaperman than the average managing editor, even when he is limited in rewarding such talent."

92. It should be noted that during and after World War II, more women filled that role, even as the nomenclature continued to reflect the position's male-dominated past.

93. Sugarman, 41.

94. Charles M. Cowden, "Cub Reporter's Ordeal by Wire Comes the First Time He Faces 'Phone and Must Dictate—or Be Damned!" *Quill*, July 1941, 7.

95. "Newspaperdom's Great Unsung: The Ultra-Spry New York District Men at Work," *Guild Reporter*, October 1, 1935, 7.

96. Sugarman, 44.

97. Sugarman, 45.

98. Arthur Gelb, *City Room* (New York: Putnam 2003), 152.

99. Gelb, *City Room*, 152.

100. "Personnel Committee," *Red Book*, Associated Press Managing Editors, August 12–15, 1959, 142.

101. Sontheimer, 58–59, 59, 61, 62, 66.

102. Halberstam, "The Education of a Journalist," 30, 34.

103. Halberstam, 34.

104. Sontheimer, 62, 65.

105. Sontheimer, 63–64. In Sontheimer's case, after he reported a case of police brutality—a suspect being beaten by a hose—and his editors were not interested, he "incurred the enmity of the police" and was only saved by "the kindheartedness of the indulgent old veteran who was working the district for an opposition paper." Being adopted by this older reporter ("A big fellow, with dark, oily skin and loose jowls, he had been on this same district for years and never aspired to anything higher," unflappable and chain-smoking) taught Sontheimer how to survive.

106. Sontheimer, 65; as detailed in Fred Fedler's excellent *Lessons from the Past: Journalists' Lives and Work, 1850–1950* (Prospect Heights, IL: Waveland Press, 2000), 163. Sontheimer narrowly escaped getting himself trapped in an ethically suspect relationship with a runner for a lawyer, in which Sontheimer would tip the runner on cases for fifty dollars an accident; the runner did not keep his end of the bargain, and after six such cases, Sontheimer settled for thirty-five dollars and the chance to be free of the arrangement.

107. Sugarman, 40, 41.

108. Sugarman, 42, 43.

109. Sugarman, 42, 43.

110. This theme will be revisited in the chapter on supervisors in the newsroom.

111. Gelb, 153. Gelb, looking back, criticized this policy, calling it a "pitiful waste of first-rate talent" that eventually faded.

112. "Managing Editors Panel," *Problems of Journalism*, ASNE, April 21, 1949, 74–76.

113. "Personnel Training and Recruiting,", 163.

114. "Editorial Workshop: Quirks and Quibbles," *Editor & Publisher*, July 16, 1955, 45.

115. However, this generalization is far too sweeping; for a more nuanced perspective, see Matthew C. Ehrlich and Joe Saltzman, *Heroes and Scoundrels: The Image of the Journalist in Popular Culture* (Urbana: University of Illinois Press).

116. Sontheimer, 185.

117. Sontheimer, 185–86.

118. "Flood in Upper N.Y. Taxes News Crews," *Editor & Publisher*, July 13, 1935, 20.

119. "Evelyn Shuler Runs Job Office for Ledger Staff," *Editor & Publisher*, January 24, 1942, 24.

120. Robert U. Brown, "Shop Talk at Thirty," *Editor & Publisher*, January 20, 1945.

121. "What Makes a Newspaper Great?" *Editor & Publisher*, August 20, 1955, 5. At this early stage of such efforts, it was still a relatively rare phenomenon for a woman or a minority reporter to achieve this kind of status; when it happened, however, ads for their newspapers in trade publications often trumpeted it.

122. For more on the intersections between technology and law enforcement, including public perceptions of both, see Kathleen Battles's excellent *Calling All Cars: Radio Dragnets and the Technology of Policing* (Minneapolis: University of Minnesota Press, 2010).

123. "City Staff Luncheon" and "Discussion," *Problems of Journalism*, ASNE, April 19, 1930, 246.

124. "Copy Desk Luncheon" and "Discussion," *Problems of Journalism*, ASNE, April 19, 1930, 263.

## CHAPTER 5

1. Elias E. Sugarman, *Opportunities in Journalism* (New York: Grosset & Dunlap, 1951), 46.

2. Morton Sontheimer, *Newspaperman: A Book about the Business* (New York: McGraw-Hill, 1941), 66–67.

3. Frank S. Adams, "The Job of the Reporter," in Robert E. Garst, ed., *The Newspaper: Its Making and Its Meaning* (New York: Charles Scribner's Sons, 1945), 115.

4. For an excellent description of this phenomenon, see Randal Sumpter, "'Practical Reporting': Late Nineteenth Century Journalistic Standards and Rule Breaking," *American Journalism* 30, no. 1 (April 2013): 44–64.

5. Peter Kihss, "General Assignment," in *Late City Edition*, ed. Joseph G. Herzberg (New York: Henry Holt, 1947), 44.

6. Leo Rosten, *The Washington Correspondents* (New York: Harcourt Brace, 1937); see Michael Barthel, Ruth Moon, and William Mari, "Who Retweets Who? How Digital and Legacy Journalists Interact on Twitter," Tow Center for Digital Journalism, 2014, http://towcenter.org/research/who-retweets-whom-how-digital-and-legacy-journalists-interact-on-twitter/.

7. Rosten, *Washington Correspondents*, 88–89.

8. Rosten, 88–93.

9. Sontheimer, *Newspaperman*, 71.

10. Sontheimer, 71.

11. Sontheimer, 72.

12. Sontheimer, 72–73.

13. Kihss, "General Assignment," 44.

14. Kihss, 45.

15. Ted Curtis Smythe, "The Reporter, 1880–1900: Working Conditions and Their Influence on the News," *Journalism History* 7, no. 1 (Spring 1980): 1–10.

16. Sontheimer, 73.

17. "Newsmen Cook Own Meals on Police Beat," *Editor & Publisher*, May 6, 1944, 50.

18. Adams, "Job of the Reporter," 122–23.

19. Arthur Gelb, *City Room* (New York: Putnam, 2003), 156. In this smaller, shared space, Gelb had to arrive early to be near the phones to receive his daily orders from his editors, who used wire-service bulletins to develop starting leads for his work; Gelb needed pockets "bulging with nickels" to keep up.

20. Gelb, *City Room*, 151.

21. Gelb, 153.

22. Gelb, 153.

23. Gelb, 154–55, 162.

24. Carl T. Rowan, *Breaking Barriers: A Memoir* (New York: Little, Brown and Company, 1991), 77–78.

25. Rowan, *Breaking Barriers*, 97; see also "Carl Rowan," Tennessee Authors Project, University of Tennessee, 2003, https://web.archive.org/web/20100709003135/http://www.lib.utk.edu/refs/tnauthors/authors/rowan-c.html; "Carl T. Rowan," Landon Lecture Series on Public Issues, Kansas State University, 2018, https://www.k-state.edu/landon/speakers/carl-rowan/.

26. T. Rees Shapiro, "Vivien Rowan, who Battled Racial Discrimination in D.C. Area, Dies at 89," *Washington Post*, April 9, 2011, https://www.washingtonpost.com/local/obituaries/vivien-rowan-who-battled-racial-discrimination-in-dc-area-dies-at-89/2011/03/30/AFOI7U9C_story.html.

27. Rowan, 110–12; the *Tribune* even ran a marketing campaign in the trade press toting Rowan's successes.

28. Fred Carroll, *Race News: Black Journalists and the Fight for Racial Justice in the Twentieth Century* (Urbana: University of Illinois Press, 2017), 181. Of course,

consistent employment and access to opportunities would vary greatly from newsroom to newsroom, and publisher to publisher (or chain to chain), despite a public, national commitment from such groups as the ASNE to push the needle on representation. For an excellent discussion of this issue in the 1950s and 1960s, see Gwyneth Mellinger, *Chasing Newsroom Diversity: From Jim Crow to Affirmative Action* (Urbana: University of Illinois Press, 2013). For more on the Black press, see, among many other excellent scholars, the work of Gerald Horne and Calvin Hall.

29. It should be noted that while a "beat" described an assigned news routine and set of sources, it could also describe a scoop, or the beating of a rival to a story. For the purposes of this chapter, I will be using the former definition unless otherwise noted. For an example of the latter, see "Editorial: W.R.—reporter," *Editor & Publisher*, Oct. 13, 1928, 30, which describes how "chasing a real beat is something to celebrate."

30. "Too Much Writing, No Reporting, Allen Finds in New York Papers," *Editor & Publisher*, June 18, 1921, 13, 35. This assessment by Eric Allen, the chair of the University of Oregon's School of Journalism, was rebuffed by J. E. Hardenbregh, the managing editor of the *New York Evening Post* and the president of the New York City News [service], along with Bruce Bliven, the managing editor of the *New York Globe* (and an author of a textbook on newspaper business practices).

31. Malcolm W. Bingay, "An Editor's Case Against the Guild," *Editor & Publisher*, June 26, 1937, 12. Bingay, the "editorial director" for the *Detroit Free Press*, was an avowed opponent of Guild influence on newsrooms like his own, believing that union membership eroded a reporter's loyalty to the paper.

32. "Girl Edited Seattle Daily," *Editor & Publisher*, December 27, 1930, 34. A managing editor criticized women reporters' coverage for being too "graphic," and they were forced to adopt a softer approach with a "heartbalm" story, truer to what was culturally expected of them in the newsroom. Brittain went on to a long and distinguished career in local advertising. See Vanessa Ho, "Outspoken Pioneer Mari Brattain Made Advertising Women's Work," *Seattle Times*, August 24, 1992, http://community.seattletimes.nwsource.com/archive/?date=19920824&slug=1509194.

33. Stanley Walker, *City Editor* (New York: Blue Ribbon Books, 1934), 256–58, 260–62. As Herrick put it, "Let her strive to write all her news better than as many men as she can. Let her write the way the world says a man writes; not the way a man says a woman writes."

34. Sontheimer, 182.

35. India McIntosh, "Girl Reporter," in Herzberg, *Late City Edition*, 48.

36. McIntosh, "Girl Reporter," 47–48, 49, 50–51.

37. McIntosh, 50–51, 54, 55. McIntosh relates one story of a group of New York-based reporters and photographers dispatched to cover an explosion and fire at a US Navy base in New Jersey. A Navy shore patrolman (military police officer) stopped a truck containing two women reporters, including McIntosh, explaining that no women could pass. A male photographer spoke up: "These aren't women," he explained, "they're reporters." The patrolman, momentarily confused, waved them forward.

38. Bob Frazier, "Timber! Lady Crashes He-Man Forestry Beat," *Editor & Publisher*, September 17, 1949, 26. Majorie Goodwin was a "lady lumber reporter" for the Eugene (Oregon) *Register-Guard.*

39. Richard Brooks, "'Round Their Beats: Gal Reporter Lives Teen Gang Violence," *Editor & Publisher*, September 3, 1955, 12. "Round Their Beats" was a recurring feature in *Editor & Publisher* during the 1950s, showcasing reporters—both men and women—and unique beat experiences.

40. "The Judge Likes a Good Story: Reporter Tells a Cub Where News Is Hidden," *Editor & Publisher*, September 8, 1956.

41. "Why Women Are Superior as Reporters," *Editor & Publisher*, September 14, 1957, 88. According to Gay Pauley, UP women's editor, "We are better endowed psychologically. We can out report any man on a beat because Nature has blessed us with insatiable curiosity. We were born nose-y." It can be surmised from the context—namely, the first meeting of the New Jersey Association of Daily Newspaper Women—that Pauley was speaking more than a little in jest, in the midst of serious advocacy for an enhanced role for women.

42. "Women Want Equal Chance and Pay in Editorial Work: Lack of Opportunity Is Blamed on Men with Bustle-Era Views," *Editor & Publisher*, August 30, 1958, 13, 54.

43. William Reed, "Huge Re-Employment Effort Cuts Job Openings in NYC," *Editor & Publisher*, February 16, 1946, 7, 60.

44. Rick Friedman, "Meet Dan Lehane: On the Job—No. 1: Federal Courthouse," *Editor & Publisher*, July 16, 1960, 60–61.

45. James H. Wright, "Cog vs. Wheel: No, Thanks—I'll Stay in Small City," *Quill*, June 1949, 9.

46. Louis Alexander, "Here's How to Cover 1,578 Square Miles . . . in Texas, of Course," *Quill*, April 1956, 11, 15. Alexander was the county editor and reporter for the *Houston Chronicle.*

47. Eugene S. Pulliam Jr., "Just Seat 20 Next to Each Other: How to Streamline a Big City Newsroom," *Quill*, February 1950, 8–10.

48. Bonnie Brennen, *For the Record: An Oral History of Rochester, New York, Newsworkers* (New York: Fordham University Press, 2001), 32. Brennen's extensive oral history and interviews of eighteen news workers (seventeen of which appear in her study) from the town's two papers is invaluable.

49. J. Russell Wiggins, "Journalism Faces Challenges," *Quill*, November 1950, 13, 86.

50. Vermont Royster, "Journalism Ethics: No Margin for Error in Business Reporting," *Quill*, November 1960, 15, 24.

51. "Continuing Study Report: New Techniques and Technical Progress Committee," *Red Book*, Associated Press Managing Editors, August 12–15, 1959, 136.

52. Arthur Robb, "Shop Talk at Thirty," *Editor & Publisher*, July 1, 1939, 36.

53. Roger Yarrington, "Church Editor Job Offers Professional and Personal Challenge Far from Dull," *Quill*, January 1958, 10.

54. M. Allen Parker, "Scanning the Skies for News Stories," *Quill*, April 1941,

6–7, 12. Some newspapers assigned an aviation "editor" to this beat, though that title, along other, more narrow section titles, could be misleading; see Sontheimer, 181–82.

55. Arthur J. Snider, "A Science Writer Has His Problems, Including the Habits of Scientists," *Quill*, October 1955, 15.

56. Thomas F. Gieryn, "Boundary-Work and the Demarcation of Science from Non-Science: Strains and Interests in Professional Ideologies of Scientists," *American Sociological Review* 48, no. 6 (December 1983): 781–95. While Gieryn is addressing how "boundary-work" is used by scientists toward nonscientists, journalists perform similar discursive work. See also Barbie Zelizer, "Journalists as Interpretative Communities," *Critical Studies in Mass Communication* 10 (September 1993): 219–37. Zelizer discusses how reporters enact boundaries temporally, too, bounding their group in the past as well as the present through the use of historical memory.

57. Snider, "A Science Writer," 15. Snider was a science reporter for the *Chicago Daily News*.

58. Sugarman, 62.

59. Sugarman, 62.

60. Wright, "Cog vs. Wheel," 9–10.

61. Sugarman, 61–79. Some of these highly specialized beats were only offered at the largest newspapers as full-time positions, and at smaller newspapers were sometimes a collateral duty for a regular beat reporter.

62. Sugarman, 60. Three hundred dollars a week was a remarkable sum when the ANG's stated goal by the late 1950s was one hundred and fifty dollars a week for veteran reporters in the biggest cities. See John Barry, "A Modest Wage Goal: $150? Magazines, Radio & TV Already Pay More," September 11, 1953, *Guild Reporter*, 1, 7.

63. "Our Own World of Letters," *Editor & Publisher*, May 20, 1933, 26. Such loftier writers as Robert H. Davis, a former *New York World* reporter, were able through their work to be "removed . . . from the hurly-burley of the city room and the worries of an editor's office."

64. Sontheimer, 178–79. Political "specialists" could be distinguished from those who covered politics as beat reporters by specialists' comparative independence, though differences between the two roles could become hazy and varied by newspaper organization.

65. Because correspondents existed so far out of the newsroom's orbit, they are not a focus of this study. They did tend to bring newsroom norms with them, however.

66. Sontheimer, 180.

67. Sontheimer, 182–85.

68. Marlen Pew, "Shop Talk at Thirty," *Editor & Publisher*, October 13, 1934, 44.

69. John W. Perry, "Helen Rowland Says 'Find a Specialty,'" *Editor & Publisher*, March 22, 1930, 9. She went on: "Hit the same nail over the head year in and year out. Sooner or later your proficiency—if it really is proficiency—will be noticed. When you . . . find your niche, concentrate on quality rather than quantity."

70. Hanson Baldwin, "The Job of the Specialist," in Garst, *The Newspaper*, 151–53.

71. Baldwin, "The Job of the Specialist," 151–53..
72. Baldwin, "Job of the Specialist," 159.
73. Charles C. Clayton, "Age of Specialists," *Quill*, September 1959, 7.
74. Clayton, "Age of Specialists," 7.
75. Sontheimer, 221–22.
76. Sontheimer, 79–81, 221.
77. Sugarman, 81.
78. Sugarman, 82. Though Sugarman does not mention him by name, Duncan Hines (1880–1959), a famous food writer, was one such columnist. Sontheimer cited 1937 US House of Representative Ways and Means Committee data that showed that well-known columnist Walter Winchell was making more than $74,200 a year, Walter Lippmann more than $62,400, and Broun and Pegler $36,200 and $46,200, respectively; see Sontheimer, 222. At one point Broun was known as the "highest paid reporter in the country"; see Philip Schuyler, "Personal Journalism Is Coming Back—Broun," *Editor & Publisher*, March 15, 1924, 7. By 1945 Pegler was making ninety thousand dollars a year; see Luther Huston, "If Columnists Are Giving You Cat Meat for Top Sirloin: Hire Better Reporters!" *Quill*, January–February 1945, 5.
79. Sontheimer, 222.
80. Sugarman, 83.
81. "Shop Talk: Building a City Staff," *Problems of Journalism*, ASNE, April 17, 1931, 163. The editor in question was Henry Justin Smith, the managing editor of the *Chicago Daily News*, who seems to have empathized with his reporters more than some.
82. "Manpower Recruiting, Pay and Turnover: Personnel Panel," *Red Book*, Associated Press Managing Editors, November 15–19, 1960, 75.
83. Sontheimer, 222.
84. Sontheimer, 223.
85. Walter H. Wood, "The Chicago Tribune's New Home Latest in Plant Construction," *Editor & Publisher*, June 5, 1920, 36. "Stars" had their own "private compartments above the local room, which in reality is only a half story or balcony. Among these satellites with special work rooms will be B.L.T. (Burt Leston Taylor), who is nationally known for his 'Line O'Type' column; 'Doc' W. A. Evans . . . health expert; Sidney Smith, creator of 'Dok Yak' and 'Andy Gump' in the cartoon world; Carey Orr, able cartoonist and father of the 'Tiny Trib;' and Frank King, who has immortalized the auto-owning clan through his cartoon strip on 'Gasoline Alley.'"
86. Peter Kihss, "When a Reporter Turns Columnist," *Quill*, January 1936, 9.
87. Rosalie Armistead Higgins, "Her Beaux Started Helen Rowland on Career as 'Solomon's Wife,'" *Editor & Publisher*, April 17, 1920, 8, 58.
88. Mildred E. Phillips, "Forum of Feminine Fraternity of Fourth Estates," *Editor & Publisher*, June 4, 1921, 30–31.
89. "Take It from Beulah, by Beulah Schacht: You've Got to Hand It to Beulah," *Editor & Publisher*, March 14, 1953, 25.
90. James L. Collings, "Syndicates: Oh Marie! Whatta Gal and Whatta Reporter," *Editor & Publisher*, Jan. 7, 1956, 40.

91. "It's an Ill Wind—," *Quill*, January 1932, 10.

92. Huston, "If Columnists Are Giving You Cat Meat," 5. Huston, manager of the Washington Bureau of the *New York Times* and a ranking official in Sigma Delta Chi, said, echoing others, that "except for the comic artists, no other journalistic field open to the man who lives by his typewriter offers such rich rewards."

93. Huston, 5.

94. Erich Brandeis, "It May Be Tough, So What! Thanks, Says Columnist, I'll Take the Big City," *Quill*, October 1949, 9, 13. Broun was known, for example, for his ability to mix it up with the humblest leg man.

95. Sugarman, 55. "Editorial workers," somewhat confusingly, was the term applied occasionally to all of a newspaper's nonmechanical (and nonbusiness staff), though still distinguished from "editorial writer," the term I have used for the sake of clarity in this section.

96. Sugarman, 56, 57. Some editorial writers were generalists, while others focused on state politics, for example, 58.

97. Sugarman, 58.

98. Hugh S. Baillie, "Headwork Behind the Headlines: Initiative and Enthusiasm Help Newsmen Steer Their Course Safely Past Perilous Shoals of Standardization," *Quill*, February 1935, 9–10.

99. Sontheimer, 199.

100. Sontheimer, 199–200.

101. "Small City Daily Best to Start on, Journalism Students Told," *Editor & Publisher*, July 7, 1923, 12.

102. As Marion Marzolf explains, the "objectivity standard" had a long and complex origin (and application) in the US journalism tradition. See *Civilizing Voices: American Press Criticism, 1880–1950* (New York: Longman, 1991), 119–32.

103. Pew, "Shop Talk at Thirty," 44.

104. Philip Schuyler, "Newspaper Makers at Work," *Editor & Publisher*, March 1, 1924, 16. Though it was sometimes written by others, Philip Schuyler was the primary writer of this recurring column through the mid-1920s in *Editor & Publisher* that profiled editors and discussed trends in journalism.

105. "Editorial: Picking a Fight," *Editor & Publisher*, February 22, 1936.

106. "How Editors Deal with Administrative Problems," *Problems of Journalism*, American Society of Newspaper Editors, April 19, 1940, 142. These were from papers of under one hundred thousand circulation, and thus out of the usual range of this study; the numbers make it clear, however, that editorial writers were a proportionally small part of a newspaper's staff.

107. Francis V. Prugger, "Social Composition and Training of Milwaukee Journal News Staff," *Journalism Quarterly* 18, no. 3 (September 1941): 232, 237.

108. "St. Paul Dispatch-Pioneer Press Now Printing in New Plant," *Editor & Publisher*, January 11, 1941, 44.

109. "Ex-Back Shop Now City Room," *Editor & Publisher*, September 22, 1956, 67.

110. Pulliam, "Just Seat 20 Next to Each Other," 8–10.

111. Robb, "Shop Talk at Thirty," 36.

112. Robert Eastabrook, "'Forgotten Men' to Meet: Editorial Writers Form New Newspaper Group," *Quill*, August 1947, 5, 13.

113. Charles C. Clayton, "Defense of the Eggheads," *Quill*, January 1958, 4.

114. Clayton, "Defense of the Eggheads," 4.

115. Gordon A. Sabine, "J-School Surveys All Oregon: Editorial Writers Yearn for 'Another Hour a Day,'" *Quill*, January 1951, 5, 10.

116. "Press Institute Formed for Working Newsmen," *Editor & Publisher*, February 16, 1946, 5, 56.

117. "Publishers and Guild Differ on 'Profession,'" *Editor & Publisher*, January 17, 1948, 15, 60. At least this was the line of reasoning offered by Cranston Williams, general manager of the ANPA; this debate will be analyzed in greater detail in the chapter on supervisors and news workers, as well as in chapter 8, on unionization in the newsroom.

118. "Publishers and Guild Differ on 'Profession,'" 15, 60.

119. "J-Education: Jobs Becoming More Available for Negro Grads," *Editor & Publisher*, July 2, 1949, 35. See also Mellinger, *Chasing Newsroom Diversity*.

120. See Rosten; also Warren Breed, "Social Control in the Newsroom: A Functional Analysis," *Social Forces* 33, no. 4 (Man 1955): 326–35; and Breed, "The Newspaperman, News and Society" (PhD diss., Columbia University, 1952).

121. As noted above, I have put "newsroom-based writers" under a larger umbrella category of "outliers," including specialists, feature writers, columnists, and editorial writers.

122. Philippa Duke Schuyler, *Adventures in Black and White*, 286 (New York: Intercultural Alliance of Artists and Scholars, 2018); Carroll, *Race News*, 184. Carroll discusses how the few prominent Black writers of the 1950s and 1960s wrote mostly for elite northern magazines, such as *Harper's*, *New Republic*, *Nation*, *Commentary*, *Saturday Review*, and *Esquire*. That would change, painfully, by the end of the 1960s and start of the 1970s, in important ways that Carroll, Jinx Broussard, Calvin Hall, D'Weston Haywood, Gerald Horne, and other scholars who study the parallel development of the Black press describe in detail.

123. Zelizer, "Journalists as Interpretative Communities," 219–37.

124. Zelizer, 233.

125. For more on the ideas of "secondary socialization," and social constructionism as a theoretical concept that has some utility (with caveats) for understanding newsrooms and their relational dynamics, see Peter L. Berger and Thomas Luckmann, *The Social Construction of Reality: A Treatise in the Sociology of Knowledge* (Garden City, NY: Doubleday, 1966), especially 138–47. I do not pretend to be an expert on this body of work, but it does influence, even if it is unacknowledged, older newsroom studies within journalism studies. For example, in regard to how Gaye Tuchman (*Making News: A Study in the Construction of Reality* [New York: Free Press, 1978]) used Berger and Luckmann in her research on newsroom life (and also for how I have used their work, though more in passing), see Sarah Stonbely, "The Social and Intellectual Contexts of the U.S. 'Newsroom Studies,' and the Media Sociology of Today," *Journalism Studies* 16, no. 2 (March 2015): 265–67.

## CHAPTER 6

1. Other studies, such as the work of Susan Keith, have pointed out the interesting dynamics of the copydesk, and inform this chapter. See Keith, "Horseshoes, Stylebooks, Wheels, Poles, and Dummies: Objects of Editing Power in 20th-Century Newsrooms," *Journalism* 16, no. 1 (January 2015): 44–60. On the managing editor, see "Baltimore Hearst Papers Sign with Editorial Group," *Editor & Publisher*, April 2, 1939, 26; and Howe V. Morgan, "Entertainment or Enlightenment?" *Quill*, July 1932, 8.

2. Alfred McClung Lee, *The Daily Newspaper in America: The Evolution of a Social Instrument* (New York: Macmillan, 1937), 205.

3. Mildred E. Phillips, "Forum of Feminine Fraternity of Fourth Estates," *Editor & Publisher*, June 4, 1921, 30–31.

4. L. A. Wilke, "As They View It: Those City Editors," *Quill*, November 1931, 2.

5. Richard Edwards, *Contested Terrain: The Transformation of the Workplace in the Twentieth Century*, 18. Edwards is interested in how capitalism in large industrial and then later corporate firms altered relationships between managers and workers.

6. Robert Darnton, "Writing News and Telling Stories," *Daedalus* 104, no. 2 (Spring 1975): 179.

7. Warren Breed, "Social Control in the Newsroom: A Functional Analysis," *Social Forces* 33, no. 4 (May 1955): 326–35; see also his doctoral dissertation, "The Newspaperman, News and Society"(Columbia University, 1952). As noted elsewhere, Breed's work, along with Leo Rosten's, prefigured the classic newsroom ethnographies of the 1960s, 1970s, and 1980s.

8. Breed, "Newspaperman, News and Society," 147, 154–55. This "wiring-in" season, i.e., the period in which reporters passed through their cub stage, is explored elsewhere in this study.

9. "News and Administration: Personnel and Recruiting," *Problems of Journalism*, ASNE, April 21–23, 1955, 171–72. This perspective was from Byron Harless, of the *St. Petersburg Times*, though his precise role is unclear.

10. Stanley Walker, *City Editor* (New York: Blue Ribbon Books, 1934), 18–19. Walker knew much about the temperament and changing norms of city editors, having been one at the *New York Herald Tribune*. He wrote, "The boss of the city room . . . invents strange devices for the torture of reporters, [he is] this mythical agate-eye Torquemada with the paste-pots and scissors. Even his laugh, usually directed at something sacred, is part sneer. His terrible curses cause flowers to wither, as the grass died under the hoofbeats of the horse of Attila the Hun. A chilly, monstrous figure, sleepless, nerveless, and facing with ribald mockery the certain hell which awaits him."

11. Walker, *City Editor*, 1–2.

12. Walker, 4.

13. Marlen Pew, "Shop Talk at Thirty," *Editor & Publisher*, November 24, 1928, 44.

14. Pew, "Shop Talk at Thirty," November 24, 1928, 44. In this case, the fictional newspaper in question had been conducting a campaign advocating for a new

highway "diverting heavy automobile traffic from residential and retail shopping streets to more appropriate thoroughfares."

15. "Ask Ed Moore; They Still Do, He Won't Retire," *Editor & Publisher*, July 1, 1950, 38. This profile of a reporter, on the *Portland Press Herald*, in Portland, Maine, who was also a semiretired state editor of nearly fifty years' experience, emphasizes how he was relied on for his institutional memory.

16. Marlen Pew, "Shop Talk at Thirty," *Editor & Publisher*, January 12, 1929, 48.

17. George A. Brandenburg, "Local Room Training Is Essential to Men on Overseas Assignments," *Editor & Publisher*, November 21, 1931, 20.

18. George E. Simmons, "Serendipity of Summer Internships," *Journalism Quarterly* 33, no. 4 (December 1956): 518.

19. "Romances of American Journalism," *Editor & Publisher*, April 12, 1930, 14. From a profile of Robert P. Holliday, publisher of the *San Francisco Call-Bulletin*.

20. Howard Long, "The Book Beat: Newspaper Novel," *Quill*, October 1960, 21.

21. Carl Kesler, "'[My] Guess' Not Good Enough," *Quill*, November 1947, 3.

22. Daniel J. Leab, *A Union of Individuals: The Formation of the American Newspaper Guild, 1933–1936* (New York: Columbia University Press, 1970), 56.

23. George C. Bastian and Leland D. Case, *Editing the Day's News: An Introduction to Newspaper Copyreading, Headline Writing, Illustration, Makeup, and General Newspaper Methods* (New York: Macmillan, 1932), 38. Bastian had been a copy editor at the *Chicago Daily Tribune* and a lecturer in news editing at the Medill School of Journalism at Northwestern University, while Case had been a staff member of the Paris edition of the *New York Herald Tribune* and an assistant professor at Medill. Their textbook's breakdown of the ideal day was quoted verbatim by Frank Thayer in his text on *Newspaper Management* (New York: D. Appleton-Century, 1938), 46–50.

24. Bastian and Case, *Editing the Day's News*, 48, 50.

25. George Brandenburg, "Malony, *Chicago Tribune* M.E., Tells How He Runs His Job," *Editor & Publisher*, February 22, 1941, 5. Note that this comes from a profile, and thus some of the thoughts of J. Loy Malony, a WWI veteran and M.E. at the *Chicago Tribune*, are paraphrased.

26. "Dear Lauds Women in Journalism," *Editor & Publisher*, July 1, 1944, 45.

27. "Q and A panel," *Editor & Publisher*, July 14, 1956, 7.

28. "New Layout Eases Confabs, Copy Flow," *Editor & Publisher*, February 28, 1948, 10. The effect of these streamlining efforts on the copydesk in particular is discussed further in chapter 3, on copy editors and reporters.

29. "How Editors Deal with Administrative Problems," *Problems of Journalism*, ASNE, April 18–19, 1940, 145–46. Even this innovation, though, was slow in coming. For many years at most newspapers, assigning photos was still under the aegis of the city editor or his (or in some rare cases, her) equivalent. See, for example, "Reporting First Qualification of Picture Editor," *Editor & Publisher*, July 1, 1950, 40.

30. See, for example, Allen M. Widen, "Round Their Beats: Half-Hour Staff Forum Breeds Opinions, Ideas," *Editor & Publisher*, January 7, 1950, 48.

31. George Brandenburg, "At *Chicago Tribune*: News Hole Is Filled by Percentage System," *Editor & Publisher*, January 26, 1952. See also "What Our Readers Say: Hiss and Make-up," *Editor & Publisher*, August 20, 1955, 2, 55.

32. "Bears in the Bull Pen," *Editor & Publisher*, July 16, 1955, 6.

33. Brandenburg, "At *Chicago Tribune*."

34. Robert M. Neal, *News Gathering and News Writing* (New York: Prentice-Hall, 1942), 51–54.

35. "Agness M. Underwood Collection," Special Collections & Archives, California State University Northridge, accessed December 6, 2015, http://library.csun.edu/SCA/Peek-in-the-Stacks/Underwood; Agness Underwood, *Newspaperwoman* (New York: Harper & Brothers, 1949), 279.

36. Underwood, *Newspaperwoman*, 279–80.

37. Underwood, 284, 286–87.

38. Underwood, 292. On reporters calling in from bars: "I don't ask reporters or photographers what saloon they're calling from when they phone the city desk; I ask whether they have the story."

39. Edwin L. James, "The Organization of a Newspaper," in Robert E. Garst, ed., *The Newspaper: Its Making and Its Meaning* (New York: Charles Scribner's Sons, 1945), 13; James Philip MacCarthy, *The Newspaper Worker: A Manual for All Who Write* (New York: Frank-Maurice, 1925), 9.

40. Don C. Seitz, *Training for the Newspaper Trade* (Philadelphia: J. B. Lippincott, 1916), 56.

41. Carl N. Warren, *News Reporting: A Practice Book* (New York: Harper & Brothers, 1929), 4.

42. Bastian and Case, *Editing the Day's News*, 259–61. Chapter 7, on technology adoption in the newsroom, discusses these issues further.

43. Frank W. Rucker and Herbert Lee Williams, *Newspaper Organization and Management* (Ames: Iowa State College Press, 1955), 160, 164, 167.

44. Bastian and Case, *Editing the Day's News*, 261.

45. Donald J. Hornberger and Douglass W. Miller, *Newspaper Organization*, 3–4, 5–7 (Delaware, OH: Ohio Wesleyan University, 1930). Hornberger and Miller were business administration and English faculty members at Ohio Wesleyan. Their work echoes memoirs and "how-to" vocational guides from this era in its emphasis on the informality of most newsroom structures. For more, see Will Mari, "'Bright and Inviolate': Editorial–Business Divides in Early Twentieth-Century Journalism Textbooks," *American Journalism* 31, no.3 (September 2014): 378–99.

46. Hornberger and Miller, *Newspaper Organization*, 9.

47. Rucker and Williams, *Newspaper Organization and Management*, 34.

48. Elias E. Sugarman, *Opportunities in Journalism* (New York: Grosset & Dunlap, 1951), 58–59.

49. Hornberger and Miller, 17–18, 26.

50. For examples of an emerging and rich literature on journalistic concepts of (and debates over) time, see Mike Ananny, "Networked News Time: How Slow—or Fast—Do Publics Need News to Be?" *Digital Journalism* (published online, February

2016): 1–18, https://doi.org/10.1080/21670811.2015.1124728; Richard B. Kielbowicz, "Regulating Timeliness: Technologies, Laws, and the News, 1840–1970," *Journalism & Communication Monographs* 17, no. 1 (February 2015): 5–83; Ford Risley, "Newspapers and Timeliness," *American Journalism* 17, no. 4 (Fall 2000): 97–103. Both media historians and media technology theorists are interested in how ideas of temporal proximity have changed, and why. While this study does not delve too deeply into the question, suffice it to say that the newsroom helped to develop timeliness as we know it in journalism due to its intense time-regulating routines and workflows.

51. Philip Kinsley, "Reporting Must be Improved to Clarify News Stream," *Editor & Publisher*, November 7, 1925, 44.

52. "Editorial: The Mechanical Side," *Editor & Publisher*, October 25, 1930, 56.

53. "Our Own World of Letters," *Editor & Publisher*, October 13, 1934, 34.

54. Edith Bristol, "Get the Story!" *Editor & Publisher*, May 25, 1935, 7.

55. MacCarthy, *Newspaper Worker*, 12. To be fair, as MacCarthy points out, even in the 1920s traditional editors would sometimes be understanding if circumstances were beyond a reporter's control.

56. Carl N. Warren, *Modern News Reporting* (New York: Harper & Brothers, 1951), 450. This edition was revised from its initial 1934 iteration. A version was adopted by the US military for use by media personnel during World War II.

57. Warren, *News Reporting*, 6.

58. Eric W. Allen, "Journalism as a Profession," *Quill*, April 1920, 3.

59. Orien W. Fifer, Jr., "Tales from the Police Beat: Experiences of All Sorts Fall to the Lot of the Reporter at Headquarters," *Quill*, August 1931, 13.

60. Charles C. Clayton, "Is the Bloom Off the Peach?" *Quill*, December 1956, 6.

61. "How Editors Deal with Administrative Problems," 146. See also "I Told You," *Editor & Publisher*, March 17, 1956, 57: an ad for the Teletype Corporation shows a flying city editor, watched by two female staffers, with the caption, "I told you he'd fly into a rage if we misused those trade-marks."

62. Hugh S. Baillie, "Headwork Behind the Headlines: Initiative and Enthusiasm Help Newsmen Steer Their Course Safely Past Perilous Shoals of Standardization," *Quill*, February 1935, 8, 10. Baillie was executive vice president of the United Press. He was reflecting on his first few jobs in daily newspaper journalism, starting with the *Los Angeles Record* in 1908. He observed that newspapers had since become "modern factories, of complete and blanket coverage of all events out [of] the city limits by the press associations, of fixed standards of all sorts."

63. "What About Accuracy? Editors Tell How They Make Reporters Careful," *Quill*, April 1927, 12.

64. "What About Accuracy?", 13.

65. "Now They Can Tell Twins Apart," *Editor & Publisher*, November 10, 1934, 12.

66. "The Shop Talkers," *Editor & Publisher*, June 16, 1923, 40.

67. Eugene S. Pulliam, Jr., "Just Seat 20 Next to Each Other: How to Streamline a Big City Newsroom," *Quill*, February 1950, 8–10.

68. "*N.Y. World* Adopts Universal Desk," *Editor & Publisher*, May 27, 1922, 36.

69. "Equipment Review: *Yakima Republic* and *Herald* Move into New Million Dollar Plant," *Editor & Publisher*, September 8, 1951, 46. In this case, Robert W. Lucas, the executive editor, utilized a "wall facing the newsroom . . . paneled in clear glass."

70. Darnton, "Writing News and Telling Stories," 177. Darnton was, of course, in time a noted historian. His account of newsroom life helps to inform chapters in this book that touch on near peer and peer dynamics in the newsroom.

71. "What About Accuracy?", 14, 22. For more on bulletin boards, which were classic sites or at least expressions of newsroom control and tension, see also Donald Janson, "Everybody in the Act: News Awards for Enterprise," *Quill*, December 1959, 9–10, 18.

72. Steuart M. Emery, "The Cub Spirit," *Editor & Publisher*, March 25, 1922, 8.

73. "Newspaper Makers at Work," *Editor & Publisher*, March 29, 1919, 12.

74. "Newspaper Makers at Work," *Editor & Publisher*, April 5, 1924, 14. In this case, Victor F. Watson is profiled; Watson was the assistant publisher and managing editor of Hearst's *New York American*, known for his "littered desk in a cubby hole on the 7th floor."

75. Mildred Philips, "Forum of Female Fraternity of Fourth Estaters," *Editor & Publisher*, May 28, 1921, 301. Philips is remarkably frank for her era, at least for a trade-journal columnist, and addresses sexism by editors, as well as the challenges of being a woman in a male-centric newsroom environment, foreshadowing the work of other women. Philips notes that editors had a particularly hard time accepting women in more traditionally male-dominated positions, including that of crime reporter.

76. Pew, "Shop Talk at Thirty," January 1929, 48.

77. "City Staff Luncheon" and "Discussion," *Problems of Journalism*, ASNE, April 17–19, 1930, 246.

78. "City Staff Luncheon" and "Discussion," *Problems of Journalism*, 246.

79. "City Staff Luncheon" and "Discussion," 246. This thought was from A. R. Holcombe, managing editor of the *New York Herald-Tribune*.

80. Seitz, *Training for the Newspaper Trade*, 57.

81. Chester B. Bahn, "I Am the Post," *Editor & Publisher*, April 8, 1922, 5.

82. Philip Schuyler, "Romances of American Journalism: Stories of Success Won by Leaders of the Press," *Editor & Publisher*, October 13, 1928, 10.

83. "Shop Talk: Building a City Staff," *Problems of Journalism*, ASNE, April 16–18, 1931, 162. This story was recounted by Henry Justin Smith, the managing editor of the *Chicago Daily News*.

84. "Short Takes," *Editor & Publisher*, April 6, 1940, 14.

85. "Short Takes," *Editor & Publisher*, August 28, 1937, 20.

86. Darnton, "Writing News," 178.

87. Darnton, "Writing News," 178–79.

88. Darnton, "Writing News," 179.

89. Darnton, "Writing News," 179.

90. "How to Get a Job," *Editor & Publisher*, May 1, 1926, 49.

91. Harry Pence, "The 'Morgue Man' and His Job," *Quill*, April 1919, 1.

92. James S. Pope, "A Managing Editor Discusses Need for Higher Standards," *Journalism Quarterly* 24, no. 1 (March 1947): 30.

93. "How Editors Deal with Administrative Problems," 143. This was from a discussion facilitated by J. R. Wiggins, managing editor of the *St. Paul Dispatch and Pioneer Press*, during a panel on newsroom-management issues.

94. "How Editors Deal with Administrative Problems," 145.

95. "How Editors Deal with Administrative Problems," 143.

96. "Editorial: Unanswerable," *Editor & Publisher*, October 27, 1934, 22.

97. "Editorial: Which Way?" *Editor & Publisher*, November 28, 1936, 24. See also, "Editorial: Guild Legalism," *Editor & Publisher*, May 8, 1937, 30.

98. L. E. Claypool, "Cutting the Editorial 'Turnover,'" *Editor & Publisher*, February 12, 1921, 18.

99. Claypool, "Cutting the Editorial 'Turnover,'" 18.

100. Samuel Haber, *Efficiency and Uplift: Scientific Management in the Progressive Era, 1890–1920* (Chicago: University of Chicago Press, 1964). See also Milton J. Nadworny, *Scientific Management and the Unions, 1900–1932: A Historical Analysis* (Cambridge, MA: Harvard University Press, 1955). For larger trends in management theory, see Daniel A. Wren, *The History of Management Thought* (Hoboken, NJ: Wiley, 2005). For a critical perspective on the use of labor in a free market during this era, see Harry Braverman, *Labor and Monopoly Capital: The Degradation of Work in the Twentieth Century.*

101. John W. Moffett, "What Does He Mean—Myth? Lyle Webster's Article about the Country Weekly Field Draws a Spirited Reply," *Quill*, January 1931, 7, 15. Moffett was coeditor of the *Eldora* (Iowa) *Herald-Ledger.*

102. L. A. Wilke, "As They View It," 2. Wilke was city editor of the *Fort Worth Press.*

103. "As They View It: Editors or Floor-Walkers?" *Quill*, September 1934, 14. From a letter to the editor by J. N. Heiskell, editor of the *Arkansas Gazette.*

104. Marlen Pew, "Shop Talk at Thirty," *Editor & Publisher*, Nov. 10, 1928, 44.

105. James E. Pollard, "Who's a Journalist? Writers No Longer Have Sole Claim to Title Many Have Scorned in Past," *Quill*, November 1937, 9. Pollard was the author of *Principles of Newspaper Management* (New York: McGraw-Hill, 1937).

106. Arthur Gelb, *City Room* (New York: Putnam, 2003), 66. The euphoria of seeing one's byline as a reporter, and its importance as a shared experience among reporters, is discussed in chapters 4 and 5, on peer-to-peer dynamics.

107. Zvi Reich, "Constrained Authors: Bylines and Authorship in News Reporting," *Journalism* 11, no. 6 (December 2010): 707–25.

108. "The Paths of Glory," *Editor & Publisher*, April 21, 1934, 17.

109. Eugune H. Gutenkunst, "An Answer to Editor Poe: In Which the Writer Makes Reply to the Question, 'Where Are the Good Reporters,'" *Quill*, March 1931, 8, 15. This was part of an ongoing discussion, in the midst of the early part of the Depression, over the "living wage."

110. "Higher Pay for Reporters Urged to Raise News Writing Standard," *Editor & Publisher*, July 16, 1927, 12. This is part of a summary of an editorial by Olin W. Kennedy, managing editor of the *Miami Herald*, written for the ASNE's *Bulletin*, and titled, "A recipe for better reporting." The highest pay brackets, he argued, should still be reserved for editors.

111. "L.A. Salary Increases," *Editor & Publisher*, September 26, 1936, 20.

112. The work of Marc Linder is especially helpful to understanding this topic. See his *"Time and a Half's the American Way": A History of the Exclusion of White-Collar Workers from Overtime Regulation, 1868–2004* (Iowa City, IA: Fănpìhuà Press, 2004), and his other, comprehensive, studies. Much more on this topic is also explored in chapter 8, on unionization in the newsroom.

113. This topic is elaborated further in this chapter's conclusion and elsewhere.

114. "Publishers and Guild Differ on 'Profession,'" *Editor & Publisher*, January 17, 1948, 60.

115. "Publishers and Guild Differ on 'Profession,'" 60.

116. Kesler, "'[My] Guess' Not Good Enough," 3.

117. Carl Kesler, "Journalists' Choice," *Quill*, July 1956, 4.

118. Louis Alexander, "What Shall We Tell the High School Senior?" *Quill*, September 1959, 18.

119. "Scientific Hiring," *Red Book*, Associated Press Managing Editors, November 16–19, 1955, 194. In this case, Tom C. Harris, probably an editor at the *St. Petersburg Times*, and Byron Harless, a psychologist and personnel director for the paper, led a discussion on "scientific methods of testing, hiring and training personnel." HR departments' role in shaping newsroom life, especially after World War II, is explored further in chapter 8, on unionization.

120. "News and Administration: Personnel and Recruiting," *Problems of Journalism*, ASNE, April 21–23, 1955, 161. The editor was Lee Hills, affiliated with the *Detroit Free Press* and the *Miami Herald*, though his exact role is unclear.

121. "News and Administration: Personnel and Recruiting," 169. In this case, the speaker was Ralph Casey of the University of Minnesota.

122. "News and Administration: Personnel and Recruiting," 167–68.

123. "News and Administration: Personnel and Recruiting," 167.

124. "Are We Getting the Cream of the Crop?," *Problems of Journalism*, ASNE, April 15–17, 1954, 71, 72. Jenkin Lloyd Jones, of the *Tulsa Tribune*, noted that this was partially an issue of perception, as pay for entry-level reporters had improved: "Our newspaper's average reporter and deskman weekly salary is right at $100. We'll put a freshly bediapered college tyro to work for $65 a week for the first three months with raises or dismissal guaranteed. The bottle-fed, ink-stained wretches of tradition, with their Bohemian bachelorhoods, their shiny blue serges, and their unfinished novels, are figments of the past."

125. Philip Schuyler, "Newspaper Makers at Work," *Editor & Publisher*, May 3, 1924, 34.

126. Philip Schuyler, "Newspaper Makers at Work," *Editor & Publisher*, January 19, 1924, 16.

127. James Melvin Lee, "Our Own World of Letters," *Editor & Publisher*, April 14, 1928, 46; Lee was commenting on McIntyre, a writer for *Cosmopolitan*.

128. "The Fourth Estate," *Editor & Publisher*, September 19, 1959, 68; Philip Schuyler, "Newspaper Makers at Work," *Editor & Publisher*, March 15, 1924, 12. Joseph J. Early, managing editor of the *Brooklyn Standard Union*, was profiled here.

129. "Folks Worth Knowing," *Editor & Publisher*, May 17, 1924, 23. The profile here was of Aaron G. Benesch.

130. Seitz, 58.

131. Lucile Brian Gilmore, "Newspaper Makers at Work," *Editor & Publisher*, February 16, 1924, 14.

132. "Newspaper Makers at Work," *Editor & Publisher*, June 26, 1919, 11. This was William "Bill" Curley. For another example, see "Newspaper Makers at Work," *Editor & Publisher*, July 24, 1919, 17.

133. "Remodeling Plant," *Editor & Publisher*, March 20, 1926, 54. In this case, the *Chicago Daily News* had private offices for its managing editor, the assistant managing editor, and news editor. See also "*Syracuse Herald* in Million Dollar Plant," *Editor & Publisher*, February 25, 1928, 7, though it should be noted in this latter case that it was the "sporting" and managing editors who "alone" had their own offices. See also "*Los Angeles Times* New $4,000,000 Home Combines Beauty and Efficiency: Magnificent Marble and Limestone Structure Is Air-Conditioned Throughout and Protected against Earthquake Tremors," *Editor & Publisher*, August 10, 1935, II–VIII, XII–XIII, XVII, XX–XIV (from a special section detailing newsroom technology and architecture).

134. "Iced Water, Gum, Cig. Urns Amaze British," *Editor & Publisher*, July 14, 1951, 20. This organizational form contrasted severely to the much more hierarchal and private system of offices and routines that governed British national newspapers at the time. The work of Carole O'Reilly at Salford University in the United Kingdom addresses newsrooms in the British Commonwealth, and is important to note here. It should be noted, too, that British newsrooms made use of "telephone reporters" (their term for rewrite staffer) and often contained a somewhat open floor plan. For more, see C. Denis Hamilton, "The Making of a Newspaper," 3–37, in *The Kemsley Manual of Journalism* (Ipswich, UK: Cassell, 1950). Also see Carole O'Reilly and Josie Vine, *Newsroom Design and Journalism Cultures in Australia and the UK: 1850–2010* (London: Routledge, forthcoming).

135. "Newspaper Makers at Work," *Editor & Publisher*, August 15, 1925, 20. This particular column profiled James W. Irwin, the managing editor of the *Wisconsin State Journal*.

136. Arthur Robb, "Shop Talk at Thirty," *Editor & Publisher*, December 17, 1938, 76. Much more on this general theme can be found in chapter 8, on unionization.

137. Arthur Robb, "Shop Talk at Thirty," *Editor & Publisher*, Jan. 1, 1938, 36. See "Selective Service Further Clarifies 3-B Status," *Editor & Publisher*, March 27, 1943, 32; Arthur Robb, "Shop Talk at Thirty," *Editor & Publisher*, February 13, 1943, 48; "Knickerbocker News, Guild Sign Contract," *Editor & Publisher*, February 13, 1943, 20.

138. Tom Wallace, "Editors in Shirtsleeves: The 1930 Kind Are Less Colorful but More Independent Than the Giants of the Nineteenth Century," *Quill*, September 1930, 7. For another example of the "short-sleeve" metaphor for the idealized editor, see Marlen Pew, "Shop Talk at Thirty," *Editor & Publisher*, June 8, 1935, 40. See also "What Do They Do? (The M.E.'s That Is)," *Editor & Publisher*, August 8, 1953, 10, and James Collings, "What Do They Do? (The M.E.'s That Is)," Aug. 15, 1953, 53.

139. O. O. McIntyre, "As They View It: In the United States," *Quill*, October 1930, 2.

140. "The Fourth Estate," *Editor & Publisher*, August 7, 1954, 36. See also "What Readers Say: 'Realism' in Movies," *Editor & Publisher*, August 22, 1953, 2, 56.

141. Gelb, *City Room*, 23.

142. Neal, *News Gathering and News Writing*, 37. Neal was the news editor of the *Wisconsin State Journal*, former assistant professor at the University of Wisconsin's School of Journalism, and author of journalism textbooks.

143. Gelb, 36–37.

144. Neal, 38.

145. Neal, 40–44.

146. Victor Green and Edmund C. Arnold, "What Makes a Good Editor," *Quill*, May 1959, 22. *The Quill* ran a "Good Editor" contest that sought examples of exemplary editors.

147. "Shop Talk: Building a City Staff," *Problems of Journalism*, 165; this was Henry Justin Smith, managing editor of the *Daily News*.

148. Bryan Putman, "The Marines Have Landed," *Quill*, September–October 1944, 9. Putman was a sergeant in the US Marine Corps.

149. A. T. Newberry, "Reporter on 'Spite' Assignment Wrote Model Christmas Story," *Editor & Reporter*, December 27, 1930, 18.

150. "5-Day Week for Staff," *Editor & Publisher*, September 14, 1935, 38. See also "*Indianapolis Star* Starts New Wage, Hour Schedule," *Editor & Publisher*, July 10, 1937, 16, and "Ray Erwin's Clippings Column: Editor's Memo to Staff," *Editor & Publisher*, July 17, 1954, 4.

151. "Short Takes," *Editor & Publisher*, August 2, 1941, 14.

152. George A. Brandenburg, "Imagine My Embarrassment: In Which a Writer Reveals How He Felt When He Summoned the Fire Department by Mistake," *Quill*, November 1930, 7.

153. William A. Rutledge III, "The Write of Way," *Quill*, February 1942, 13.

154. Margaret Ellington, "Wherein a Feminine Scribe Reports What Happens When Through Whims of War: Girl Meets 'Boys' of the City Room!" *Quill*, Jan. 1943, 6–7.

155. "Personnel," *Red Book*, Associated Press Managing Editors, November 12–15, 1958, 152. The senior staffer quoted here is I. William Hill, chairman of the APME Personnel Committee c. 1959.

156. "Manpower Today and Tomorrow: Personnel Panel," *Red Book*, Associated Press Managing Editors, August 12–15, 1959, 52.

157. "Continuing Study Report: Personnel Committee," *Red Book*, Associated Press Managing Editors, November 15–19, 1960, 143.

158. "Policies of the 'Little Twinkler' Live," *Quill*, March 1926, 3–5.

159. "Managing Editors Panel," *Problems of Journalism*, ASNE, April 21–23, 1949, 54; Nikil Saval, *Cubed: A Secret History of the Workplace* (New York: Doubleday, 2014). See also "Good Editors Must Anticipate News Trends, Says Harry Grant," *Editor & Publisher*, July 10, 1937, 14.

160. Donald J. Wood, *Newspaper Personnel Relations* (Oakland, CA: Newspaper Research Bureau, 1952), 42.

161. "Reporters Find Friend in Col. Geo. McCain," *Quill*, Oct. 1923, 11.

162. Dan Albrecht, "Editors Shouldn't Be Hermits!" *Quill*, Feb. 1937, 3, 16.

163. "The Book Beat: Inside Picture," *Quill*, June 1940, 15. Published by Harcourt, Brace and Co., it was authored by Neil MacNeil, a former assistant managing editor at the *New York Times*, and whose expressed intent was to bust myths about newsrooms.

164. For more on the relationship newspapers had with their readers, see Thomas C. Leonard, *News for All: America's Coming-of-Age with the Press* (New York: Oxford University Press, 1995).

165. Walter J. Pfister, "This Word-Weary, Long Suffering City Editor Prints a Catechism for Cubs," *Quill*, November 1940, 10, 12.

166. Marlen Pew, "Shop Talk at Thirty," *Editor & Publisher*, December 8, 1934, 36.

167. George Robert Harris, "But the Old Spirit Lives on," *Editor & Publisher*, February 5, 1920, 5, 8.

168. "Shadow of Tragedy Filled News Room," *Editor & Publisher*, December 22, 1928, 42. In this case, the newsroom at the *Long Beach* (California) *Press-Telegram* mourned their "chief," who died in a plane crash.

169. "Editorial: John Anthony Malloy," *Editor & Publisher*, March 27, 1943, 22.

170. "Editorial: Vacations," *Editor & Publisher*, July 24, 1948, 40.

171. "Heart-Breaking Job, Being a City Editor," *Editor & Publisher*, August 25, 1956, 53.

172. Both editors and reporters often found that their closest friends were their fellow practitioners. At the same time, though, some felt that for routine to be effective, it had to be more impersonal. See William T. Ellis, "J. K. Ohl, the Man and the Editor," *Editor & Publisher*, July 3, 1920, 10. Ohl was a former *New York Herald* editor and foreign correspondent.

173. Wood, *Newspaper Personnel Relations*.

174. See Robert H. Giles, *Newsroom Management: A Guide to Theory and Practice* (Indianapolis: R. J. Berg, 1987). These issues are explored thoroughly—and at the time, concurrently, in Doug Underwood's *When MBAs Ruled the Newsroom: How the Marketers and Managers Are Reshaping Today's Media* (New York: Columbia University Press, 1993).

175. Wood, *Newspaper Personnel Relations*, 1.

176. Wood, 24.

177. Wood, 2.

178. Wood, 3, 18.
179. Wood, 22.
180. Wood, 26–27.
181. Wood, 27, 29. He follows with a detailed description of a "personnel training" program, including chapters on "actual training," "methods of training," how to build a training manual, how to evaluate a training program, and how to find and train new executives. While he refrains from specific recommendations for workshops, Wood does encourage newspaper management to run training that is "practical and interesting" and to "sell the program continuously" to workers, with more experienced workers encouraged to participate. See 27, 30.
182. Wood, 32, 34.
183. Wood, 37, 38, 66; they should also be held in the mornings, and kept closer to forty-five minutes, since any later or longer would result in staff members probably becoming "restless and disinterested."
184. Wood, 59.
185. Wood, 40–42, 43, 45; Wood, in turn, is quoting from Franklin D. Schurz, who appeared in the March 25, 1950 issue of *Editor & Publisher*, 18.
186. Wood, 45–46. 47.
187. Wood, 51, 54. For examples of then-current HR literature that Wood cites, see Vernon G. Schaefer and Willis Wissler, *Industrial Supervision—Controls* (New York: McGraw-Hill, 1941); Dale Yoder, *Personnel Management and Industrial Relations* (New York: Prentice-Hall, 1942); and Burleigh B. Gardner and David G. Moore, *Human Relations in Industry* (Chicago: Richard D. Irwin, 1950).
188. Wood, 56.
189. Wood, 6, 57, 58. His own guide was intended to encourage adoption of management and training programs under the loose umbrella of "human relations" (though also called industrial or labor relations, or as he describes, "personnel programs").
190. Hanno Hardt and Bonnie Brennen, eds., *Newsworkers: Toward a History of the Rank and File* (Minneapolis: University of Minnesota Press, 1995).
191. Kevin Lerner, *Provoking the Press: (MORE) Magazine and the Crisis of Confidence in American Journalism* (Colombia: University of Missouri Press, 2019).
192. For more on this, see Gwyneth Mellinger, *Chasing Newsroom Diversity* (Urbana: University of Illinois Press, 2013); but also Fred Carroll, *Race News: Black Journalists and the Fight for Racial Justice in the Twentieth Century* (Urbana: University of Illinois Press, 2017); and the work of D'Weston Haywood, Gerald Horne, and Calvin Hall.
193. Robert U. Brown, "Shop Talk at Thirty," January 20, 1945. Brown, the editor of *Editor & Publisher*, predicted "a network of 'walkie-talkies' linking the star reporters of a newspaper all over town" that would also connect them back to the desk.

## CHAPTER 7

1. Published by Sigma Delta Chi, later the Society of Professional Journalists, the *Quill* evolved from a college fraternity publication when it was launched in 1919

to a more alumni-centered organization and then finally a professional group. See Charles C. Clayton, *Fifty Years for Freedom: The Story of Sigma Delta Chi's Service to American Journalism, 1909–1959* (Carbondale: Southern Illinois University Press, 1959), 35.

2. Charles M. Cowden, "Cub Reporter's Ordeal by Wire Comes the First Time He Faces 'Phone and Must Dictate—or Be Damned!" *Quill*, July 1941, 7.

3. A. M. Lee believed that the growth in the use of the telegraph by the end of the 1800s paved the way for the use of the telephone early in the century, by increasing the expectation and ability to handle higher and higher daily word counts, first via telegraph and human operators working with typewriters, then with more automated systems, in the form of teletypewriters. He estimated that by 1920, the AP had a 100 such machines, but by 1935, it had 3,000, which had the effect, however, of reducing the number of human telegraphers from some 1,096 in 1920 to just about 500 in 1934, before the position was eliminated by the AP in November 1935. However, between twelve hundred and thirteen hundred operators were needed for the machines' "operation and upkeep." The estimated average daily number of words transmitted by the AP went from fifteen thousand in 1900 to seventy-five thousand in 1920, before steadying at around sixty thousand or so in 1935. See Alfred McClung Lee, *The Daily Newspaper in America: The Evolution of a Social Instrument* (New York: Macmillan, 1937), 527–52.

4. Some of the material in the following section has appeared in Will Mari, "Technology in the Newsroom," *Journalism Studies* 19, no. 9 (July 2018): 1366–89, and is reprinted here with permission.

5. Robert MacDougall, *The People's Network: The Political Economy of the Telephone in the Gilded Age* (Philadelphia: University of Pennsylvania Press, 2014), 6–7.

6. JoAnne Yates, *Control through Communication: The Rise of System in American Management* (Baltimore: Johns Hopkins University Press, 1989); Carolyn Marvin, *When Old Technologies Were New: Thinking about Electric Communication in the Late Nineteenth Century* (New York: Oxford University Press); Richard White, *Railroaded: The Transcontinentals and the Making of Modern America* (New York: W.W. Norton, 2011).

7. Nikki Usher, "Putting 'Place' in the Center of Journalism Research: A Way Forward to Understand Challenges to Trust and Knowledge in News" *Journalism & Communication Monographs* 21, no. 2 (June 2019): 84–146; Kevin Barnhurst, *Mister Pulitzer and the Spider: Modern News from Realism to the Digital* (Urbana: University of Illinois Press, 2016); Richard B. Kielbowicz, "Regulating Timeliness: Technologies, Laws, and the News, 1840–1970," *Journalism & Communication Monographs* 17, no. 1 (February 2015): 5–83.

8. Richard Edwards, *Contested Terrain: The Transformation of the Workplace in the Twentieth Century* (New York: Basic Books, 1979), 17.

9. C. W. Anderson and Juliette De Maeyer, "Objects of Journalism and the News," *Journalism* 16, no. 1 (August 2014): 6.

10. Bruno Latour, *Reassembling the Social: An Introduction to Actor-Network-Theory* (Oxford: Oxford University Press, 2007); Amy Schmitz Weiss and David Domingo,

"Innovation Processes in Online Newsrooms as Actor-Networks and Communities of Practice," *New Media & Society* 12, no. 7 (May 2010): 1156–71.

11. Morton Sontheimer, *Newspaperman: A Book about the Business* (New York: McGraw Hill, 1941), 190.

12. Susan Keith, "Horseshoes, Stylebooks, Wheels, Poles, and Dummies: Objects of Editing Power in 20th-Century Newsrooms," *Journalism* 16, no. 1 (January 2015): 44–60.

13. Keith, "Horseshoes, Stylebooks, Wheels, Poles, and Dummies," 5, 8–10.

14. Andrew Abbott, *The System of Professions: An Essay on the Division of Expert Labor* (Chicago: University of Chicago Press, 1988).

15. Henrik Örnebring, "Technology and Journalism-as-Labor: Historical Perspectives," *Journalism* 11, no. 57 (February 2010): 57–74. Note that he describes "deskilling" in particular with technology's use in increasing productivity and the gradual erosion of skills from various forms of work, 59, 60.

16. Örnebring, "Technology and Journalism-as-Labor," 60–61, 66–67.

17. Örnebring, 68.

18. Marianne Salcetti, "The Emergence of the Reporter: Mechanization and the Devaluation of Editorial Workers," in *Newsworkers: Toward a History of the Rank and File*, ed. Hanno Hardt and Bonnie Brennen (Minneapolis: University of Minnesota Press, 1995), 67.

19. Morton Sontheimer points this out in his autobiographical how-to for young news workers, *Newspaperman*. By the end of the 1930s, "salaries went up and hours went down, and heedless firings began to drop off when each one meant several hundred dollars in dismissal pay," 325. This topic is explored thoroughly in chapter 8, on newsroom unionization.

20. I thank my colleague Matt Bellinger for helping to inspire some of the ideas contained here.

21. "Reporting in a Storm," *Fourth Estate*, July 6, 1901, 10.

22. "News by Telephone," *Fourth Estate*, February 24, 1900, 4; "Gathering the News by Aid of Telephone," *Fourth Estate*, August 29, 1903, 15.

23. "Telephone and Newspaper Office Combined," *Fourth Estate*, February 23, 1901, 15.

24. H. L. Mencken, *Newspaper Days 1899–1906* (New York: Alfred A. Knopf, 1955), 18.

25. Thomas Harrison Baker, *The Memphis Commercial Appeal: The History of a Southern Newspaper* (Baton Rouge: Louisiana University Press, 1971), 217. Note the presence of an early parallel communication technology, a telegraph sounder, in use by a reporter in the bowler hat on the right.

26. By the 1940s these ambitious claims had been tempered as the rewrite desk's function matured and its staff members were expected to be more creative, as noted earlier in this study.

27. "The Telephone in News Service," *Telegraph and Telephone Age*, February 16, 1914, 110. "Special" or "specials" were dispatches by a newspaper's own correspondents, in contrast to wire-service stories, which were provided by a third-party service.

28. Kielbowicz, "Regulating Timeliness," 5–83.

29. George Saint-Amour, "Veteran Morse Men on 'Block' as 'Mux' Chases Them from Jobs: Automatic Printers Have Telegraphers on the Run—Some Learn to Be Chiropractors; Others Study Law—Appeal to Editors for a Chance," *Editor & Publisher*, March 10, 1928, 22.

30. Saint-Amour, "Veteran Morse Men on 'Block,'" 22.

31. "Telegrapher Commits suicide," *Editor & Publisher*, April 14, 1928, 40.

32. The focus of this chapter is on news-*gathering* technology, not on news-*producing* technology, such as the above-mentioned telegraph machines, but the latter's adoption shows some of the complexities for news workers who fit somewhere between the editorial and mechanical sides of a newspaper.

33. Saint-Amour, 22.

34. "News by Telephone Direct to the Type-Setter," *Telegraph and Telephone Age*, December 16, 1913, 735.

35. These were sometimes called "pony reports."

36. "Associated Press Telephone Service," *Telegraph and Telephone Age*, May 1, 1911, 322.

37. "Space-Saving Table for Crowded Local Room," *Editor & Publisher*, August 7, 1919, 19.

38. "Looking Ahead in Construction of Newspaper Homes," *Editor & Publisher*, January 29, 1921, 11.

39. "Human Touch Vitalizes Efficiency in *Washington Star*'s Plant," *Editor & Publisher*, April 18, 1922, 18.

40. "*Scranton Republican* in New Home," *Editor & Publisher*, October 13, 1928, 38. "Every desk in the business department is equipped with a telephone."

41. A helpful working definition of "coordination," inspired by Richard Edwards, is the production of goods by individual workers operating as a unit, as achieved by tradition, established routines, and/or the mutually beneficial distribution of power among these workers in a production process. See Edwards, *Contested Terrain*, 17.

42. I thank my reviewers for this important distinction.

43. "Newspapers Get Biggest 'Beats' Over Telephone," *Telegraph and Telephone Age*, July 16, 1923, 352.

44. Louis M. Lyons, *Newspaper Story: One Hundred Years of The Boston Globe* (Cambridge, MA: Belknap, 1971), 261.

45. "Newspapers Get Biggest 'Beats' Over Telephone."

46. John Wilds, *Afternoon Story: A Century of the New Orleans States-Item* (Baton Rouge: Louisiana State University Press, 1976).

47. Paul D. Augsburg, "The Dog-Watch Poet," *Editor & Publisher*, February 26, 1921, 12.

48. "Rewrite Man Sorrows for Sins of the Cubs," *Quill*, March 1924, 12.

49. Philip Schuyler, "Newspaper Makers at Work," *Editor & Publisher*, October 17, 1925, 20.

50. Stewart Emery, "Gathered at Random: 'Big News,'" *Editor & Publisher*, April 17, 1929, 47.

51. Louis Flood, "Among Those Present in [the] Social Dept.: Pix or People Perhaps, but Penguins—Phooey!" *Editor & Publisher*, January 5, 1946, 56.
52. "The High Priest of the Craft," *Editor & Publisher*, April 22, 1922, 56.
53. J. Charles Poe, "Where Are the Good Reporters? Inexperienced Boys or Broken Down Veterans and Incompetents Apply at This Editor's Door," *Quill*, January 1931, 10.
54. Arthur J. Sinnott, *Problems of Journalism*, American Society of Newspaper Editors, April 17, 1931, 172–73.
55. Sontheimer, 190.
56. "How a Reporter Should Spend His Time," *Editor & Publisher*, February 23, 1957, 71.
57. Mitchell Charnley, "City Room Cynics Unmasked," *Quill*, April 1932, 4.
58. Orien W. Fifer Jr., "Tales from the Police Beat: Experiences of All Sorts Fall to the Lot of the Reporter at Headquarters," *Quill*, August 1931, 13.
59. "*Los Angeles Times'* New $4,000,000 Home Combines Beauty and Efficiency: Magnificent Marble and Limestone Structure is Air-Conditioned throughout and Protected against Earthquake Tremors," *Editor & Publisher*, August 10, 1935, II, VI.
60. Marion May Dilts, *The Telephone in a Changing World* (New York: Longmans, Green, 1941), 75.
61. Gelb, *City Room* (New York: Putnam, 2003), 209.
62. "*Toledo News-Bee* Rrenovates Plant," *Editor & Publisher*, August 14, 1937, IV.
63. Cowden, "Cub Reporter's Ordeal," 6.
64. "Canton Repository Now Printing from High-Speed Plant," *Editor & Publisher*, April 28, 1928, 140.
65. "On Convention Program at Dallas," *Quill*, November 1949, cover photo.
66. "Dailies' News Plants Rise All across the U.S.," *Editor & Publisher*, August 14, 1948, 59.
67. "The Fourth Estate," *Editor & Publisher*, January 10, 1953, 40.
68. "Here Are 'Inside' Stories . . . from New Newspaper Buildings," *Editor & Publisher*, January 3, 1959, 14–15.
69. Private conversation with author, February 19, 2015.
70. Frank Landt Dennis, "City Room 'Short Course' Saves Tempers and Time," *Quill*, August 1942, 5.
71. Dennis, "City Room 'Short Course'," 8.
72. James H. Wright, "Cog vs. Wheel: No, Thanks—I'll Stay in Small City," *Quill*, June 1949, 9.
73. Sontheimer, 229.
74. Will Mari, *A Short History of Disruptive Journalism Technologies* (London: Routledge, 2019).
75. Cowden, 7, 12.
76. Sam Justice, "Grab That Phone! But Heaven Help You If You Find You've Drawn a Gagster or a Nut," *Quill*, November 1939, 12.
77. "Daily Posts Model Rules of Conduct," *Editor & Publisher*, July 10, 1937, 29.
78. Dennis, 5.

79. Yandell C. Cline, "Reporters' Questions Often Suggest 'No' Answer When They Want 'Yes,'" *Editor & Publisher*, June 18, 1927, 43.

80. Bill Cunningham, "Demands Press Box for Football Writers," *Editor & Publisher*, November 10, 1928, 26.

81. "Special Telephone Equipment Speeds Work of Rewrite Battery," *Editor & Publisher*, February 2, 1924, 20.

82. "*Buffalo Courier-Express* in New Plant," *Editor & Publisher*, December 13, 1930, 19, 78.

83. Sontheimer, 119.

84. Sontheimer, 120.

85. Jack Price, *News Pictures* (New York: Round Table Press, 1937), 192.

86. William W. Lutz, *The News of Detroit: How a Newspaper and a City Grew Together* (Boston: Little, Brown, 1973), 101.

87. Gelb, *City Room*, 161.

88. Gelb, 162.

89. Sontheimer, 121.

90. Sontheimer, 122, 123.

91. Sontheimer, 123–24.

92. George Brandenburg, "City Desk Secretary: Quiet Miss Whitesides Directs News Traffic," *Editor & Publisher*, September 5, 1959, 10.

93. Eugene S. Pulliam Jr., "Just Seat 20 Next to Each Other: How to Streamline a Big City Newsroom," *Quill*, February 1950, 8–10.

94. Gelb, 211.

95. "Photo Trailers Speed Coverage: Several Newspapers Using Portable Darkroom—Picture Transmitters, Phones, Short Wave Radio Aid Photographers," *Editor & Publisher*, January 11, 1941, 41, 45.

96. "Mobile Photo Unit," *Editor & Publisher*, September 14, 1946, 54. See Bureau of Labor Statistics, US Dept. of Labor, "CPI Inflation Calculator," at https://www.bls.gov/data/inflation_calculator.htm, accessed June 14, 2020; please note that figures were updated to 2020 equivalents as needed.

97. For much more on facsimile technology from this era, see Charles R. Jones, *Facsimile* (New York: Reinhart Books, 1949).

98. "Mobilphones Due," *Editor & Publisher*, July 13, 1946, 73. Reviews and previews of proposed or recently installed newsgathering gear could often be found in *Editor & Publisher*'s "Equipment Review Section," a monthly installment covering developments in newsroom and mechanical-plant technology.

99. Dilts, *Telephone in a Changing World*, 76.

100. "In Reverse," *Editor & Publisher*, September 14, 1946, 81.

101. "*Boston Traveler* Uses Radio-Phone," *Editor & Publisher*, September 28, 1946, 50.

102. "Assignment En Route," *Editor & Publisher*, September 14, 1946, 54.

103. W. H. Hornby, "*San Francisco News* Pattern: Radio-Phone Links Editor and Reporter," *Quill*, February 1947, 8–10.

104. Hornby, "*San Francisco News* Pattern," 8.

105. Hornby, 9.

106. Hornby, 9.

107. Hornby, 10.

108. "Pictures and Stories 'Phoned on-the-Spot," *Editor & Publisher*, January 4, 1947, 28.

109. "For On-Spot Pictures with Story," *Editor & Publisher*, January 11, 1947, 59.

110. "Equipment Review: *Denver Post*'s Mobile Photo Unit Described; Model of Compactness," *Editor & Publisher*, July 10, 1948, 50.

111. "55 Dailies Join Pleas for Mobilphone Service," *Editor & Publisher*, October 9, 1948, 6.

112. James L. Collings, "Photography: More Regarding Those Picture Assignments," *Editor & Publisher*, January 28, 1950, 24.

113. "The Fourth Estate," *Editor & Publisher*, September 16, 1950, 42.

114. "The Fourth Estate," *Editor & Publisher*, February 18, 1956, 47.

115. "*Chi. Tribune* Has 36 Cars Linked to Radio Relay," *Editor & Publisher*, January 10, 1953, 58.

116. "Car-Radio System Has 35-Mile Range," *Editor & Publisher*, August 25, 1956, 42.

117. "'Not Like Old Days' with Mobile Telephone," *Editor & Publisher*, March 28, 1953, 57.

118. Reidy spoke at the Rochester Photo Conference in upstate New York, which was attended by representatives from newspapers, as well as from the camera and film industry.

119. John J. Reidy, "Mobile Radio Improves Reporting Techniques," *Editor & Publisher*, September 26, 1953, 38.

120. "Iced Water, Gum, Cig. Urns Amaze British," *Editor & Publisher*, July 14, 1951, 20.

121. Reidy, "Mobile Radio Improves Reporting Techniques," 38.

122. Reidy, 38.

123. Anthony Smith, *Goodbye Gutenberg: The Newspaper Revolution of the 1980's* (New York: Oxford University Press, 1980).

124. Dilts, 150.

125. Robert U. Brown, "Shop Talk at Thirty," *Editor & Publisher*, January 20, 1945, 72.

126. Brown, "Shop Talk at Thirty," 72.

127. "Walkie-Talkie for Winnie's Welcome," *Editor & Publisher*, January 12, 1952, 71.

128. "Radio-Phone Used to Get Story in Air," *Editor & Publisher*, January 25, 1947, 10; "Radiophones Added," *Editor & Publisher*, February 23, 1953, 40.

129. "The Working Press," *Editor & Publisher*, August 23, 1947, 11.

130. "The Fourth Estate," *Editor & Publisher*, September 19, 1953, 40.

131. "The Last Word," *Editor & Publisher*, August 11, 1956, 13.

132. "Tiny Recorder Helps Moley in Reporting," *Editor & Publisher*, August 9, 1958, 14.

133. "Reporter's Dream?—May Be," *Editor & Publisher*, September 18, 1954, 66.

134. Harvey L. Katz, "Wire Recorded: Inaccurate? Play That Quote Back!" *Quill*, October 1948, 11–12.

135. "Tape Recorder Used at Education Parley," *Editor & Publisher*, March 5, 1955, 36.

136. "Oregonian Pursues Explore of Rackets," *Editor & Publisher*, July 14, 1956, 10.

137. Bureau of Labor Statistics, US Dept. of Labor, "CPI Inflation Calculator," April 22, 2015, http://www.bls.gov/data/inflation_calculator.htm.

138. "New Layout Eases Confabs, Copy Flow," *Editor & Publisher*, February 28, 1948, 10.

139. Robert Brown, "Shop Talk at Thirty," *Editor & Publisher*, Sept. 13, 1952, 80. Brown added: "We've already eliminated most of the time-honored workers in the newspaper vineyard, as related above. All we need are one or two more automatic devices."

140. Briefly defined, an affordance is "the type of action or a characteristic of actions that a technology enables through its design." See Jennifer Earl and Katrina Kimport, *Digitally Enabled Social Change: Activism in the Internet Age* (Cambridge, MA: MIT Press, 2011), 10.

141. Price, *News Pictures*, 14. Price went on: "Wire flashes have been converted into paragraphs and the papers put on the street within two minutes of the time they were received. The telegraph, telephone, teletype, cable and radio are the instruments that flash world news to the 'desk,' whose high interpreter is the city editor."

142. Benjamin Peters, "And Lead Us Not into Thinking the New Is New: A Bibliographic Case for New," in *New Media & Society* 11, no. 13 (February 2009): 13–30.

143. Keith, 44–60.

144. See Mari, *A Short History*.

## CHAPTER 8

1. Carl Ackerman, "A New Deal Newspaper Salaries," *Quill*, May 1934, 4.

2. Philip M. Glende, "Labor Makes the News: Newspapers, Journalism, and Organized Labor, 1933–1955" (Ph.D. diss., University of Wisconsin, 2010), 10. Glende's research is especially important for looking at the *perception* by other journalists of the ANG's activities and mission. See Glende, "Labor Makes the News: Newspapers, Journalism, and Organized Labor, 1933–1955," *Enterprise & Society* 13, no. 1 (March 2012): 39–52 and "Labor Reporting and Its Critics in the CIO Years," *Journalism & Communication Monographs* 22, no. 1 (March 2020): 4–75.

3. Among several excellent other examples: Glende, "Labor Makes the News"; Daniel J. Leab, *A Union of Individuals: The Formation of the American Newspaper Guild, 1933–1936* (New York: Columbia University Press, 1970); and Marc Linder, *"Time and a Half's the American Way": A History of the Exclusion of White-Collar Workers from Overtime Regulation, 1868–2004* (Iowa City: Fănpìhuà Press, 2004). See also Marianne Salcetti, "Competing for Control of Newsworkers: Definitional

Battles between the Newspaper Guild and the American Newspaper Publishers Association, 1937–1938" (Ph.D. diss., University of Iowa, 1992) and Sam Kuczun, "History of the American Newspaper Guild" (Ph.D. diss., University of Minnesota, 1970), as well as the scholarship of Dale Benjamin Scott.

4. Bonnie Brennen, "Newsworkers during the Interwar Era: A Critique of Traditional Media History," *Communication Quarterly* 43, no. 2 (Spring 1995): 197–209.

5. "Anti-CIO Guildsmen form AFL Union in Chicago for Newsmen Only," *Editor & Publisher*, July 24, 1937, 5, 13, 32. Fears of radicalization drove some of these departures, and they sometimes resulted in odd situations where groups of differently unionized news workers in the same newsroom would find themselves on opposing sides of a picket line, due to differing union policies. See also "*N.Y. Sun* News Staff Forms Own Union to Deal with Management," *Editor & Publisher*, July 24, 1937, 5; the Sun Editorial Employees Union, not connected to the ANG, was formed by members of the *Sun* in New York as an alternative to the ANG. See also "Duluth Papers Forced to Suspend by Strike," *Editor & Publisher*, April 16, 1938, 8. In one instance, a suit was filed by the Portland, Oregon, Guild local over an alleged attempt by publishers and management at the Guy P. Gannett chain paper there to form a "company union." Typically, in these disputes, the NLRB would be notified, a representative sent to ascertain the facts, report back to the NLRB, after which either an initial ruling would be issued or the NLRB would send more representatives to facilitate an election of the news workers there.

6. Alfred McClung Lee, *The Daily Newspaper in America: The Evolution of a Social Instrument* (New York: Macmillan, 1937). See his table XXXII, "Newswriters' unions under the jurisdiction of the American Federation of Labor: 1923–1936," 753.

7. "White collar" as a label for workers, and as an economic and social status, can be complex and rife with hidden assumptions. For our purposes, "white collar" will refer to an aspirational middle-class status. See Mark McColloch, in *White Collar Workers in Transition: The Boom Years, 1940–1970* (Westport, CT: Greenwood Press, 1983). For other classic studies of these workers, see C. Wright Mills, *White Collar: The American Middle Class* (New York: Oxford University Press, 1951) and Harry Braverman, *Labor and Monopoly Capital: The Degradation of Work in the Twentieth Century* (New York: Monthly Review Press, 1974).

8. Some of the material in the following section has appeared in Will Mari, "Unionization in the American Newsroom, 1930 to 1960," *Journal of Historical Sociology* 31, no. 3 (September 2018): 265–81, and is reprinted here with permission.

9. Beside the excellent work of Leab, see also Bonnie Brennen, "Work in Progress: Labor and the Press in 1908," in *Journalism 1908: Birth of a Profession*, ed. Betty Houchin Winfield (Columbia: University of Missouri Press, 2008), 147–61.

10. Leab, *Union of Individuals*, 13.

11. Leab, 14, 16.

12. Walter Williams, "Barbed Entanglements of the Press," *Quill*, July 1919, 6.

13. "Editorial: Trend Toward Organization," *Editor & Publisher*, September 11, 1919, 32. See also "Editorial: Craft Organization," *Editor & Publisher*, October 9,

1919, 22. In another officially voiced *Editor & Publisher* response to the then-recent spate of early unionization attempts and demands for better wages by journalists, we read, "It is folly to assume that editors and reporters are the one class that is immune and exempt under the present reign of high costs of living. . . . the movement for normal salaries for news writers under present conditions has made rapid strides lately and this is due to a recognition by publishers of the principle of a fair wage for everyone who has a part in the making of a newspaper."

14. "Detroit Is against Writer' Unions," *Editor & Publisher*, November 20, 1919, 24. See also "No Union at Portland," *Editor & Publisher*, August 28, 1919, 12.

15. "Dailies in Four Cities Oppose News Writers' Union," *Editor & Publisher*, September 4, 1919, 10.

16. "Plan to Form Union of N.Y. Writers," *Editor & Publisher*, July 17, 1919, 12.

17. Leab, 16–21.

18. Joseph Loftus, "Unions in the City Rooms? 'Never,' Declares This Newspaperman in Telling the Story of the Scranton Scribes' Organization," *Quill*, November 1932, 3–4. This particular ITU chapter was sometimes also referred to as "Scranton Newswriters Union No. 3."

19. "Why Writers' Union Died in Rochester," *Editor & Publisher*, October 23, 1919, 24.

20. Leab, 20–22, 26. See also "Period of Labor Unrest: Methods of Enforcing Wage Demand Draws Rebuke from I.T.U—406 New Contracts in 1920—Writers Organize," *Editor & Publisher*, January 15, 1920, 22. Other cities where writers reportedly organized included Baltimore; Bridgeport, CT; Brockton, MA; Butte, MT; Chicago; Evansville, IN; Fresno, CA; Hartford, CT; Louisville, KY; Lynn, MA; Manchester, NH; Montreal, Quebec; New Haven, CT; Omaha, NE; Pittsburgh, PA; Portland, OR; Rochester, NY; Salt Lake City; San Francisco; San Diego; Springfield, MA; Toronto, Ontario; Syracuse, NY; Waterbury, CT; Wheeling, WV; and Worcester, MA. Most of the strikes and other organizing efforts in these cities soon petered out.

21. "N.Y. German Press Workers Plan Labor Union," *Editor & Publisher*, July 3, 1919, 20. See also "Now Propose Labor Union of Chicago News Writers," *Editor & Publisher*, September 11, 1919, 24.

22. "American Journalists Association Forms as Editorial Workers National Body," *Editor & Publisher*, October 16, 1919, 5, 20. See also "'St. Louis Plan' May Be Solution of Writers' Discontent," *Editor & Publisher*, September 18, 1919, 74.

23. Richard L. Stokes, "The American Journalists' Forum: Salutatory," *Editor & Publisher*, June 5, 1920, 19. James W. Brown, *Editor & Publisher*'s publisher, donated a weekly column's worth of space to the American Journalists Association, "a growing professional and non-union organization of editors, reporters and newspaper writers and artists, together with instructors and students of schools of journalism."

24. Leab, 22.

25. Leab, 20, 22. See also "Writers Seek Way Out of I.T.U," *Editor & Publisher*, May 6, 1922, 6. In the latter case, the ITU was frustrated that the Newspaper Writers' Union No. 1 of Boston was not paying its dues, a common problem with these

early, abortive ITU chapters made up of reporters and editors. See also "Writers Ask A.F. of L. Aid," *Editor & Publisher*, May 27, 1922, 24.

26. Sam G. Riley, *Biographical Dictionary of American Newspaper Columnists* (Westport, CT: Greenwood Press, 1995), 42–43. See also "New York Reporters Ask Union Chapter," *Editor & Publisher*, November 24, 1923, 16. In Broun's words, part of his motivation was that "newspaper work is unduly precarious. In all large cities there is a disposition to discharge certain members of staffs to encourage others." See also "Reporters' Union Marks Time," *Editor & Publisher*, December 15, 1923, 4. While Leab downplays Broun's role in these early efforts (he writes that Broun did "little more . . . than serve as a name on a letterhead" (see Leab, 44), Broun *did* use his popularity to attract attention to the nascent cause. It is true that it was only later that he threw himself more into the proverbial breach. His was a unique personality that would lead disparate groups of reporters and editors into unionization, but not quite yet.

27. Ted Curtis Smythe, "The Reporter, 1880–1900: Working Conditions and Their Influence on the News," *Journalism History* 7, no. 1 (March 1980): 1–10; Smythe, *The Gilded Age Press, 1865–1900* (Westport, CT: Praeger, 2003). See also the chapter on newsroom working conditions in Glende, "Labor Makes the News."

28. Daniel C. Hallin, "Commercialism and Professionalism in the American News Media," in *Mass Media and Society*, ed. James Curran and Michael Gurevitch (New York: Oxford University Press), 242–60. Hallin calls this the "provisional resolution."

29. Moe Raiser, "20 Years Later 'Mau-rice' Still Remembers," *Guild Reporter*, October 8, 1954, 7.

30. Charles A. Perlik Jr., "Newspaper Guild Now in 26th Year," *Quill*, November 1959, 80.

31. J. Charles Poe, "Where Are the Good Reporters? Inexperienced Boys or Broken Down Veterans and Incompetents Apply at This Editor's Door," *Quill*, January 1931, 10.

32. Poe, "Where Are the Good Reporters?" 10–11.

33. "Managing Editors Panel," *Problems of Journalism*, ASNE, April 21–23, 1949, 51–52.

34. The National Industrial Recovery Act was signed into law in June 1933. The FDR administration created the National Recovery Administration to draft and administer codes for separate industries. Eventually, the NIRA was struck down as unconstitutional in May 1935 (it had been set to expire that June). "National Industrial Recovery Act (1933)," National Archives and Records Administration, http://www.ourdocuments.gov/doc.php?flash=true&doc=66?, accessed January 30, 2016, "An Act to encourage national industrial recovery, to foster fair competition, and to provide for the construction of certain useful public works, and for other purposes, June 16, 1933." It is important to note that the Wagner Labor Relations Act, otherwise known as the National Labor Relations Act, passed later in July 1935, guaranteed the right to form, join, and negotiate as a union and created the NLRB, with its regional system of facilitators and arbiters. "National Labor Relations Act (1935)," National Archives and Records Administration, http://www.ourdocuments.gov/doc.php?doc=67, accessed January 30, 2016.

35. Marlen Pew, "Shop Talk at Thirty," *Editor & Publisher*, September 16, 1933, 48. He adds, "The first essential of the journalist is a decent regard for his fellows. Petty tyrants do not surround themselves with talent. And unless a light of decency and fairness burns in a newspaper office the publisher may well turn the key in the lock, for [he] has no mission." As noted, Pew and the other editors and commenters at *Editor & Publisher* (and generally those who represented groups like the ASNE, ANPA, or even the APME) would later take on a far more oppositional perspective toward unions, unionization, and the Guild in particular, before reaching a détente of their own by the late 1950s. Pew also quotes an anonymous "young reporter," who says that low pay is not as much of a concern for him, since the "romance of newspaper life is compensatory," as is "this business of being fired without notice, or even any reason beyond the whim of some duffer who doesn't like the cut of my job or slashes the payroll by checking off every other name on the list. Newspapermen yield unbounded loyalty and deserve some."

36. "Editorial: Editorial Pay," *Editor & Publisher*, October 13, 1934, 24.

37. "Marlen Pew Is Dead; Held Post at Columbia," *Columbia Daily Spectator*, October 19, 1936.

38. Glende, "Labor Makes the News," 251.

39. Arthur Robb, "Shop Talk at Thirty," *Editor & Publisher*, August 16, 1941, 36. Robb wrote, "Their interests are not those of circulation solicitors or route men, nor of advertising salesmen, nor of accountants, stenographers, clerks, office boys or copy boys. The primary function of reporters, desk men, make-up editors, editorial writers, and writing specialists is the production of material which will interest the public and keep the paper sold to the public."

40. Robb, "Shop Talk at Thirty," August 16, 1941, 36.

41. Norman Isaacs, "A Newspaperman's Job Is Also a High Calling," *Quill*, June 1956, 7.

42. Carl R. Kesler, "The Case of the Old Pro," *Quill*, June 1956, 3.

43. "The Guild and the Labor Situation," *Problems of Journalism*, ASNE, April 21–22, 1944, 28, 29. The ANPA reported that as of January 1, 1944, there were 141 newspapers with contracts with the Guild (at least from their membership), of which some 69 included both news and business departments, 56 for news, and 16 just for business; this included high-profile New York-based newspapers such as the *New York Herald Tribune*, as well as the *Chicago Tribune*; the Guild's own accounting varied slightly, with 173 contracts, covering more than "200 editorial shops," 129 of which were with 165 daily or Sunday newspapers, a total of about 9 percent of the daily and newspaper field. It is important to remember that newspapers with Guild units would remain in the minority.

44. "Editorial: No Closed Shop," *Editor & Publisher*, June 26, 1937, 30.

45. "NLRB Saturated with Anti-Press Feeling," *Editor & Publisher*, January 4, 1941, 6. See also "Editorial: Signed Labor Pacts," *Editor & Publisher*, January 11, 1941, 62.

46. "Editorial: Rights of Management," *Editor & Publisher*, May 20, 1944, 34. Publishers also accused unions of leftist tendencies, including infiltration by

communists. Since the history of the Guild and the Communist party could be the basis of its own study, I will avoid delving too deeply into an analysis of the ANG's internal politics except for where it bears directly on the unionization of the newsroom. See Morton Sontheimer, *Newspaperman: A Book About the Business*, 325.

47. "Arbitration Voted for Guild's Own Staff," *Editor & Publisher*, July 14, 1956, 15, 74. See also George A. Brandenburg, "Big City Guilds Strives Anew to Block Wire Service Local: Issue Flares at 24th Convention; New England Publishers Warned," *Editor & Publisher*, July 13, 1957, 14, 73.

48. Leab, 44.

49. "Writers to Oppose Newspaper Code," *Editor & Publisher*, September 16, 1933, 9. See also Leab, 60.

50. Leab, 51.

51. Edwin Emery, *History of the American Newspaper Publishers Association*, 225 (Minneapolis: University of Minnesota Press, 1950).

52. Leab, 40, 67–70, 71, 75–77, 79.

53. Emery, *History of the American Newspaper Publishers Association*, 225. While it might be easy to dismiss this perspective, the open and unabashed antagonism between FDR and many conservative publishers helped to create and sustain a climate of hostility and suspicion by both sides that was not aided when the ANG took a more unionist stance from mid-1934 onward.

54. Leab, 84.

55. Dale Benjamin Scott, "Labor's New Deal for Journalism—The Newspaper Guild in the 1930s" (Ph.D. diss., University of Illinois at Urbana–Champaign, 2009).

56. "Guild Defeated on Quincy Daily," *Editor & Publisher*, February 16, 1946, 14.

57. "Office Guild Formed for N.Y. Dailies," *Editor & Publisher*, May 22, 1937, 16.

58. Walter Galenson, *The CIO Challenge to the AFL: A History of the American Labor Movement, 1935–1941* (Cambridge, MA: Harvard University Press, 1960), 559.

59. Linda Steiner, "Gender at Work: Early Accounts by Women Journalists," *Journalism History* 12, no. 1 (Spring 1997): 2–12, specifically table 1, "number of male and female editors and reporters in the newspaper and magazine industry, 1890–1950, and U.S. population increase over precious census #," on p. 4. Steiner notes the total population of the united States over this same period, from 106 million in 1920 to 151 million in 1950; the number of working men and women in the field was 33,773 in 1920. Steiner uses data from the US Department of Commerce and Labor.

60. Elias E. Sugarman, *Opportunities in Journalism* (New York: Grosset & Dunlap, 1951), 92.

61. Galenson, *The CIO Challenge to the AFL*, 560. He goes on to note that in an ANPA survey in 1939, of the 266 cities with ANPA members, the ANG had locals in 79. That meant that there were Guild elements of various sizes in 88 percent of cities with a population of more than 200,000, in 39 percent of cities between 100,000 and 200,000 people, and in just 10 percent of cities with a population level below that (see 560). Granted, this number probably did not encompass in-house unions and some newspapers which had Guild units but no contracts (lingering

verbal agreements). See "Editorial: Pressure by Writers," *Editor & Publisher*, February 8, 1936, 26. *E&P*'s editors derided the ANG's early membership, saying the latter only had four thousand out of a possible forty thousand members. This would change, of course, but the cultural barriers (not to mention the economic ones) were high to total unionization.

62. Emery, 238. Emery went as far as to describe them as "quite normal."

63. Robb, "Shop Talk at Thirty," *Editor & Publisher*, January 1, 1938, 36.

64. "*Toledo Blade* Bans Reporters' Outside Jobs," *Editor & Publisher*, July 26, 1947, 61. A Toledo *Blade* reporter, Eleanor Coakley (president of the local ANG chapter), was transferred to the "newspaper's reference library" after she was elected to the position of recording secretary for the Toledo Industrial Union Council, the primary organizer of union activity in the city. The guild filed a petition to the NLRB, even as the paper's management insisted that Coakley's salary would be the same, and that her transfer was necessary for maintaining the appearance of neutrality in news reporting.

65. Leab outlines the influential early case of Dean Jennings in his ANG history, pp. 182–88. Taking place over 1934–1935, it showed the limits of early federal industry codes. The ANPA resisted attempts by the NLRB to intervene, creating a chilling effect on unionization and on the ANG that nearly led to the movement stalling completely. The Wagner Act and a more militant ANG after 1935 helped to embolden news workers enough for it to continue—long enough, at least, for World War II and postwar prosperity to intervene. The immediate effect in the Bay Area was to slow down the ANG's efforts there, however, and it led to intimidation like the example mentioned here: "The circumstances of Jennings' resignation greatly affected the other employees. Many of them, professing fear for their jobs, resigned from the Guild." See "RG 25: Records of the National Labor Relations Board; Administrative and Other Records of the Regional Offices of the National Labor Relations Board, ca. 1934. Seattle Administrative Files, Miscellaneous Correspondence, District 17, Decisions-Elections, Box No. 1," folder labeled "Decisions, Mr. Smith's File," box 1, NLRB report on Jennings' dismissal, 5–7, located at the National Archives-Pacific Northwest Region, Seattle. This particular report indicates that testimony with a transcript had been sent from the regional board to the national board. The report appears to be a copy possibly requested by Charles W. Hope, who directed District 17 (which covered Washington and Oregon) from the Federal Office Building in Seattle. Hope, incidentally, made an annual salary of $3,400. He may have been interested in comparable cases because the Hearst paper in Seattle would soon strike. For more on that confrontation, see William E. Ames and Roger A. Simpson, *Unionism or Hearst: The Seattle Post-Intelligencer Strike of 1936* (Seattle: Pacific Northwest Labor History Association, 1978).

66. Sontheimer, *Newspaperman*, 325.

67. "Editorial: Cross-Currents," *Editor & Publisher*, July 10, 1937, 24; Glende, "Labor Makes the News," 28.

68. Robb, "Shop Talk at Thirty," *Editor & Publisher*, December 17, 1938, 76.

69. For an extended and classic discussion of this process, see Alfred D. Chandler

Jr., *The Visible Hand: The Managerial Revolution in American Business* (Cambridge, MA: Belknap, 1977).

70. "Editorial: Two Speeches," *Editor & Publisher*, September 18, 1954, 38. The editorial cited M. Flynn, president and general manager of the *New York News*: "Management changes from something you work for and are loyal to, to the antagonist on the other side of the bargaining table. . . . The natural pride in the paper one represents changes to a sense of [a] division of interests."

71. "*L.A. News* Staff Participates in Advisory Council," *Editor & Publisher*, July 11, 1942, 27.

72. Joseph Dragonetti, "Phila. Paper Expands Personnel Activities," *Editor & Publisher*, August 6, 1949, 30. In 1948 there were 11,300 job applications to the *Inquirer*, with 3,780 interviews and 501 placements, meaning a one in eight applicant-to-job ratio.

73. Frank W. Rucker and Herbert Lee Williams, *Newspaper Organization and Management* (Ames: Iowa State College Press, 1955), 498.

74. Robert C. Bassett, "'Kiss and Tell' Doctrine Impractical and Indecent: NLRB Urged to Review Rulings and Be More Realistic and Moral," *Editor & Publisher*, February 5, 1955, 52. Bassett was the publisher of the *Milwaukee Sentinel.*

75. "Financial Report Enough for Union," *Editor & Publisher*, August 25, 1958, 10.

76. "Publishers and Guild Differ on 'Profession,'" *Editor & Publisher*, January 17, 1948, 15, 60. This is from one of several crucial hearings during the decades from 1930 to 1950 in which the federal government established a working definition of a "professional" news worker. The ANPA was represented by Cranston Williams, its general counsel, in this instance, and the Guild by Sam B. Eubanks, its executive vice president.

77. "Newspapers Seek Exemption from Wage-Hour Provisions: Brief Submitted to Administrator Asserts Journalism Is a Profession, Not Manufacturing Process . . . Business Preponderantly Intrastate," *Editor & Publisher*, October 15, 1938, 3, 29, 30, 33. See also "Hearings Loom on Wage-Hour Press Exemption," *Editor & Publisher*, October 22, 1938, 4. The federal government's test at the time for a "professional" included the following criteria: "'A professional' is any employee:

(a) Who is customarily and regularly employed in work

(1) Predominantly intellectual and varied in character as opposed to routine mental, manual, mechanical or physical work, and

(2) Requiring the consistent exercise of discretion and judgment both as to the manner and time of performance as opposed to work subject to active direction and supervision, and

(3) Of such a character that the output produced or result accomplished cannot be standardized in relation to a given period of time, and

(4) Based upon educational training in a specially organized body of knowledge, as distinguished from a general academic education and from an apprenticeship, and from training in the performance of routine mental, manual, mechanical or physical processes in accordance with a previously indicated or standardized formula, plan or procedure, and

(b) Who does no substantial amount of work of the same nature as that performed by non-exempt employees of the employer."

78. "Hearings Loom on Wage-Hour Press Exemption," *Editor & Publisher*, October 22, 1938, 4.

79. "Editorial: Let Reason Rule," *Editor & Publisher*, November 5, 1938, 20. Part of the publishers' argument went: "The service that newspapers render through the expert and conscientious work of people whose job keeps them alert for 24 hours a day over a long period should not be jeopardized by making those services cost more than they are worth either to the newspapers or the people who buy newspapers."

80. "Andrews Speech Cheers Guild in Sixth Annual Convention," *Editor & Publisher*, August 5, 1939, 9, 34.

81. See, for example, Andrew Abbott, *The System of Professions: An Essay on the Division of Expert Labor* (Chicago: University of Chicago Press, 1988).

82. For more on national trends with newsroom salaries, see the table in the appendix.

83. Galenson, *The CIO Challenge to the AFL*, 564.

84. Based on surveys of self-reported "actual" salary data as collected in *Journalism Quarterly*, the *Quill*, *Editor & Publisher*, APME *Red Book*, the *Guild Reporter*, and other primary, contemporary sources. These estimates are for reporters who were "veterans" (three to six years into a career), vs. cubs or beginners, working for larger daily newspapers of one hundred thousand circulation or more, as distributed nationally as possible, but possibly partially inflated due to the presence of New York City in some of the survey results (which almost always, along with certain other cities such as Chicago and San Francisco, had an effect on the total average). Note that "editors" are middle-grade news or assistant managing editors, copy editors, and rewrite staff, sometimes referred to as "desk men" or "desk workers." Note also that other variations in salary data could be influenced by the requirement in the post–World War II era by two-year, compulsory military service. Note finally that specific data for white-collar obligations was not routinely tracked by the BLS until later in the century. Data for manufacturing/production workers, however, is more readily available, and there are scattered hints as to the weekly salaries of white-collar workers, broadly defined. For example, McColloch, in *White Collar Workers in Transition*, estimated that bank clerks made about thirty dollars a week in 1940. Leab, in his *Union of Individuals*, believed most office clerks made about the same in 1929.

85. "Salaries and Working Conditions of Newspaper Editorial Employees," *Monthly Labor Review*, published by the United States Bureau of Labor Statistics, May 1935, 1142.

86. "Thomas Firm against Guild Shop," *Editor & Publisher*, February 22, 1941, 45.

87. Henry J. Allen and Irving Brant, "This Conflict between the Publishers and the Guild," *Quill*, December 1937, 12, 14, 16. Allen was editor of the *State Journal* and Brant was editor of the *Star-Times*.

88. "Editorial: Maintenance Provision," *Editor & Publisher*, July 15, 1944, 34. *Editor & Publisher*'s editorial board felt this was yet another sign of the Guild's radicalization: "The guild is no longer a professional organization as it was first intended. It

is a trade union committed to the CIO and taking sides on all political issues." See also "Sacramento Publisher Protests Guild Clause," *Editor & Publisher*, March 3, 1945, 67. The publisher of the *Sacramento Union*, William H. Dodge, protested the membership clause that was part of a recent contract with the *Union* and its ANG unit; the contract was being accepted "under protest and because the nation is at war." The NLRB had recently ruled that the editorial and circulation departments at the paper were to act as a single unit for bargaining purposes.

89. A Guild "chapter" covered a city or region or press association/syndicate, while a "local" was the unit at the organizational or newspaper level (and locals were sometimes referred to, slightly confusingly, as "units.")

90. Campbell Watson, "Guild Debate Flares up over Local Autonomy: Powers Sought by ANG Officers Termed Too Broad; Aid for Tacoma," *Editor & Publisher*, July 12, 1952, 11, 70. It is unclear from Guild claims at this point, however, how close the majority of its members were to its hundred-dollars-a-week goal.

91. "S.F. Conducts Arbitration on Pay and Hours," *Editor & Publisher*, August 9, 1952, 63. See also "Awards in S.F. Bow to N.Y. for Top Guild Pay," *Editor & Publisher*, August 23, 1952, 13.

92. "Commentator Hits Reporters' Low Pay," *Editor & Publisher*, February 18, 1956, 60.

93. George C. Biggers and Morton Sontheimer, "Should Your Child Be a Newspaperman?" *Quill*, June 1954, 4–5.

94. Rucker and Williams, *Newspaper Organization and Management*, 497–98.

95. Emery, 185. The ANPA's data was from thirty-six cities, based on day wages and a six-day workweek.

96. US Bureau of the Census, *Historical Statistics of the United States, 1789–1945* (Washington, DC: US Bureau of the Census, 1949), 69. See chapter titled "Series D 152–163, Hours and Wage Rates, Indexes of Union Hourly Wage Rates and Weekly Hours, Building and Printing Trades, 1907–1945."

97. Susan B. Carter, "Table Ba4440–4483, Hourly and Weekly Earnings of Production Workers in Manufacturing, by Industry: 1947–1999," in *Historical Statistics of the United States*, Millennial Edition Online, ed. Susan B. Carter et al. (Cambridge, UK: Cambridge University Press, 2006). Data based on US Bureau of Labor Statistics (BLS), "Nonfarm Payroll Statistics from the Current Employment Statistics: National Employment, Hours, and Earnings," retrieved from BLS Internet site, https://www.bls.gov/, August 18, 2000. Data from the BLS does make it clear that these numbers are for *production* workers, not office or editorial workers, so as long as that distinction is apparent, there does appear to be evidence that mechanical workers continued to be the better paid kind of news worker through the decade. A final caveat: the BLS data also includes non-newspaper publishing, which may depress the figures slightly—ITU-contracted printers probably made more than other mechanical workers in publishing, which would resonate with the $92.48 amount. See also Robert A. Margo, "Table Ba4320–4334, Annual Earnings in Selected Industries and Occupations: 1890–1926," in Carter et al., *Historical Statistics of the United States*. Data based on Paul H. Douglas, *Real Wages in the United States, 1890–1926*

(Boston: Houghton Mifflin, 1930). As a final note, "mechanical" was the most common adjective (followed by "typographical") used to describe those newspaper workers or staff who produced, but did not write, edit, or take photographs. In my case, I will follow this convention, but sometimes also refer to these staff members as "production workers."

98. "Manpower Today and Tomorrow: Personnel Panel," *Red Book*, APME, August 12–15, 1959. A couple of caveats: The sample size of the survey was relatively small (some 185 former journalism students), and the actual number of newsroom workers was even smaller, at 33. In addition, the experiences of one program and its graduates may be idiosyncratic. But this data does seem consistent with other news workers' experiences throughout the country during the mid-decade. It is true that in New York, San Francisco, Chicago, and other major media centers, editorial workers were approaching parity with their mechanical-worker comrades.

99. "Six-Day Week Resumed," *Editor & Publisher*, March 3, 1934, 51.

100. "Salaries and Working Conditions of Newspaper Editorial Employees," *Monthly Labor Review*, May 1935, 1144.

101. "Guild Opposing 'Correspondent-Photog' Practice," *Editor & Publisher*, April 20, 1940, 62.

102. "Court Upsets NLRB Order to Reinstate Agnes Fahy: Board's Function Is to Help Set Up Agreements, Not Enforce Them, U.S. Ruling Holds. . . . Guild Demands That NLRB Appeal," *Editor & Publisher*, February 8, 1941, 7, 49.

103. "Discharged Guildsman Gets 30 Weeks' Salary," *Editor & Publisher*, July 13, 1946, 81.

104. "Employees Buy Stock," *Editor & Publisher*, April 5, 1924, 30.

105. L. E. Claypool, "Cutting the Editorial 'Turnover,'" *Editor & Publisher*, February 12, 1921, 18.

106. "Curtis Gives Free Insurance to All Employees," *Editor & Publisher*, October 30, 1919, 30.

107. "Sickness Insurance for Phila. Guild," *Editor & Publisher*, May 25, 1935, 39. See also "*Butte Miner* Insures Employees," *Editor & Publisher*, May 1, 1920, 26.

108. "Hall Announces New Benefits for Employees," *Editor & Publisher*, July 27, 1946, 32. In this case, on the Anderson, South Carolina, *Independent* and *Daily Mail*, as well as the affiliated radio station WAIM.

109. Doris Willens, "Health-Welfare Programs Increase—Along with Cost: Fringe Benefits for Newspaper Workers Spiral in Range," *Editor & Publisher*, July 30, 1955, 11, 53. New contracts sometimes included semiannual increases in health benefits. See "Job Transfer Options Given in Guild Pact," *Editor & Publisher*, March 17, 1956, 14.

110. Perlik, "Newspaper Guild Now in 26th Year," 80.

111. "Bright Ideas: Employee Insurance," *Editor & Publisher*, January 1, 1944, 14. This plan also covered a radio station, WNBH, also owned by these papers' publishers; the two areas are geographically adjacent, which may explain the same name for the two newspapers.

112. "Wolfe Papers Provide Insurance for 820," *Editor & Publisher*, September 14, 1946, 20. In this case, these plans could be found at the *Columbus Dispatch*, *Ohio State Journal*, and *Columbus Star*.

113. For much more this topic, see Matthew C. Ehrlich and Joe Saltzman, *Heroes and Scoundrels: The Image of the Journalist in Popular Culture* (Urbana: University of Illinois Press, 2015).

114. Dorothy Ducas, "These Newspapermen!" *Quill*, April 1932, 6.

115. Ducas, "These Newspapermen!" 6. Emphasis added.

116. Ducas, 6–7. "There are quite a few married women reporters, and in general they get along better with the men because they are married."

117. "Woman's Work," *Editor & Publisher*, February 17, 1951, 26.

118. "Tribune Underwrites Honeymoon," *Editor & Publisher*, March 1, 1924, 12.

119. George A. Brandenburg, "Until 'Thirty' Do Us Part: 6 Husband-Wife Teams Toil on Daily's Editorial Staff," *Editor & Publisher*, February 6, 1960, 15, 65.

120. "Oregon U. Journalism Graduates Traced," *Editor & Publisher*, February 25, 1928, 26.

121. "City Room Romance Ends with Newshawks Covering Own Wedding," *Guild Reporter*, October 1, 1943, 9.

122. "Strike Can't Faze Him," *Guild Reporter*, December 1, 1936, 5. Forrest Williams and Lois Read, a Seattle reporter and artist, respectively, got married in the wake of the Hearst strike there.

123. "Ding Dong! Ding Dong!" *Guild Reporter*, April 4, 1938, 1. In this case, in Newark, New Jersey, there was a supposed spike in marriages and children due to the Guild presence on the city's newspapers.

124. "Shop Talk: Building a City Staff," *Problems of Journalism*, ASNE, April 16–18, 1931, 165. See also Patterson's *I Like People: The Autobiography of Grove Patterson, Editor In Chief of the Toledo Blade* (New York: Random House, 1954).

125. "Situations Wanted," *Editor & Publisher*, October 1, 1932, 33.

126. "5 Girls, 1 Boy in Binghamton Press Copy Boy School," *Editor & Publisher*, June 7, 1941. Part of a short feature on an in-house training program at the Binghamton, NY, *Press*, a "two-year beginners school to train workers in the editorial department."

127. "Women in the News Room?" *Red Book*, Associated Press Managing Editors, November 16–19, 1955, 210.

128. "Short Takes," *Editor & Publisher*, March 27, 1943, 18.

129. "'Unwritten Law' No Sub for Pay," *Guild Reporter*, December 15, 1941.

130. "Report and Rulings of the Commission" in regard to the case of the Allentown, Pennsylvania, Morning Call Publishing Company and The Chronicle and News Publishing Co. vs. the Lehigh Valley chapter of the ANG; from "Records of the National War Labor Board (World War Two): Records of the Daily Newspaper Printing and Publishing Commission: Records Relating to Newspaper Guild Cases, 1943–45," folder "Report & Rulings A-----G, box 2553, finding aid PI-78, entry 333, stack 530, row 52, compartment 30, shelf 2, located at the National Archives at College Park, MD. Note that this was a smaller newspaper than those normally

considered by this study. The *Morning Call* had a daily circulation of 52,058 and a Sunday circulation of 43,655, and the *News* a circulation of 18,205.

131. Steiner, "Gender at Work," 2–12.

132. Women were often expected to take an early retirement, or as has been explored above, informally and unfairly quit their jobs soon after marriage or at least the arrival of children. But enough resisted these norms, or returned to work in newsrooms, to create a special class of worker that pioneered a new norm among white-collar women.

133. "New Guild Contract," *Editor & Publisher*, August 5, 1944, 28.

134. "Guild Moves to Organize Negro Papers," *Editor & Publisher*, August 4, 194, 22.

135. Milburn P. Akers and Fletcher Martin, "How Integration Worked on One Newspaper Staff," *Guild Reporter*, June 22, 1955. See also Peter Nieman Martin Sr., "Nieman Moments: Fletcher P. Martin, NF '47," *Nieman Reports*, Summer–Fall 2013, https://niemanreports.org/articles/fletcher-p-martin-nf-47-2/.

136. "Dailies' Cooperation Asked in Solving Negro Problem," *Editor & Publisher*, August 4, 1945, 7, 60–61, 67.

137. "Number of U.S. Daily Newspapers, 5-Year Increments," Pew Research Center, March 12, 2007, https://www.journalism.org/numbers/number-of-u-s-daily-newspapers-5-year-increments/.

138. Perlik, 80. Note that the number of newspapers covered by Guild contracts was still in the minority: there were some 1,763 daily newspapers in the United States in 1960. "Number of U.S. Daily Newspapers, 5-Year Increments," Pew Research Center, March 12, 2007, http://www.journalism.org/numbers/number-of-u-s-daily-newspapers-5-year-increments/.

139. Sugarman, *Opportunities in Journalism*, 92.

140. In 1955 the two organizations would reunite as the AFL-CIO. See Joseph W. Bloch, "Founding convention of the AFL-CIO," *Monthly Labor Review*, published by the United States Bureau of Labor Statistics, February 1956, 141–49.

141. Sontheimer, 325.

142. Louis Alexander, "What Shall We Tell the High School Senior?" *Quill*, September 1959, 17–18. Alexander, who worked for the Houston *Chronicle*, was a freelancer and a part-time journalism lecturer at the University of Houston, responded to a list of twelve questions asked by a University of South Dakota senior. He also reported that "most large newspapers maintain a forty-hour week, and either pay for overtime or don't permit it. Most small ones expect the reporter to work almost as hard as the editor or publisher, and *he* doesn't wind his wrist watch."

143. A close reading of dozens of journalists' memoirs from the era, of course, often reflects on their own generation's time as superior to that of the then-present. The romantic nature of news workers and their self-perceptions certainly fueled this tendency. Thus I use it with some caution. But most of the memoirs published through the end of the midcentury, commenting on working conditions of their younger colleagues, concede (and in some cases, even insist) that times had changed for the better, even if this meant a less romantic, and more modern, era had arrived. For

some concrete numbers, please also see the appendix on newsroom salaries, to see the potential overall impact of unionization and the ANG's advocacy for better pay.

144. "'Good-Old' Days Had Color, But So Did Kerosene Lamp," *Guild Reporter*, October 28, 1955, 7.

## CONCLUSION

1. Aurora Wallace, *Media Capital Architecture and Communications in New York City* (Urbana: University of Illinois Press, 2012); Akhteruz Zaman, "Newsroom as Battleground: Journalists' Description of Their Workspaces," *Journalism Studies* 15, no. 6 (2013): 819–34. Wallace examined newsroom exteriors, and Zaman was focused on news workers' metaphors for their newsroom spaces. This study borrows from both but is focused on the interiors of newsrooms and how the social lives and work culture of news workers developed therein. Where it does lightly borrow from spatial theory, it relies on the work of such theorists as Henri Lefebvre and his *Production of Space,* trans. Donald Nicholson-Smith (Cambridge, MA: Blackwell, 1991)and David Harvey and his *Spaces of Global Capitalism: Towards a Theory of Uneven Geographical Development* (London: Verso, 2006). I have relied on Nikki Usher's helpful interpretation of these theories; see her "Newsroom Moves and the Newspaper Crisis Evaluated: Space, Place, and Cultural Meaning," *Media, Culture & Society* 37, no. 7 (June 2015): 1005–21.

2. I should thank Michael Stamm for inspiring some of this analysis, with his *Dead Tree Media: Manufacturing the Newspaper in Twentieth-Century North America* (Baltimore: Johns Hopkins University Press, 2018), along with the members and organizers of the Paperology Reading and Activity Group, including Juliette De Maeyer, Aleksandra Kaminska, Ghislain Thibault, and Alysse Kushinski; the group is associated with the Artefact Lab, in the Department of Communication at the Université de Montréal.

3. Doreen Massey, *Space, Place, and Gender* (Minneapolis: University of Minnesota Press, 1994), 264–65; Massey specifically identifies the "industrial corporation," which the newsroom of the mid-twentieth century most certainly was, as a specific example of a space-as-social.

4. David T. Z. Mindich, *Just the Facts: How "Objectivity" Came to Define American Journalism* (New York: NYU Press, 1998); Henrik Örnebring and Michael Karlsson, "Journalistic Autonomy," in *The Oxford Research Encyclopedia of Communication* (New York: Oxford University Press, 2019), 762–78. See also Örnebring's forthcoming book on the topic.

5. Pamela J. Shoemaker and Stephen D. Reese, *Mediating the Message in the 21st Century: A Media Sociology Perspective*, 3rd ed. (New York: Routledge, 2014). In an update of their classic work of media sociology, Shoemaker and Reese's original model of five layers gets a revamping, so now in addition to describing the original three inner layers of influence (individual, routine practices, media organizations), they also describe social institutions and social systems (in place of the older "extraorganizational" and "ideological level of influence").

6. Robert Darnton, "Writing News and Telling Stories," *Daedalus* 104, no. 2 (Spring 1975): 175–94.

7. Andrew Abbott, *The System of Professions: An Essay on the Division of Expert Labor* (Chicago: University of Chicago Press, 1988), 7–9, 18.

8. Abbott, *System of Professions*, 34, 40–44, 48–52.

9. Patricia L. Dooley, *Taking Their Political Place: Journalists and the Making of an Occupation* (Westport, CT: Greenwood Press, 1997), 25–26, 126.

10. Alfred McClung Lee makes a critical point in *The Daily Newspaper in America: The Evolution of a Social Instrument* (New York: Macmillan, 1937); it was not so much the telephone itself but the systematization brought by the switchboards early in the twentieth century, and the development of devoted rewrite staff and leg men, that helped the phone reach its full potential as an instrument of news collection (628–29, 642–43).

11. Robert M. Neal, *News Gathering and News Writing* (New York: Prentice-Hall, 1942), 16.

12. Peter L. Berger and Thomas Luckmann, *The Social Construction of Reality: A Treatise in the Sociology of Knowledge* (Garden City, NY: Doubleday, 1966). While elegant and influential, Berger and Luckmann's theory (and its further development by Michel Foucault) is not easily applied to the multifaceted institution that is the newsroom.

13. Henrik Örnebring, "Technology and Journalism-as-Labor: Historical Perspectives," *Journalism* 11, no. 57 (February 2010): 57–74.

14. Neal, *News Gathering and News Writing*, 16.

15. Daniel C. Hallin, "Commercialism and Professionalism in the American News Media," in *Mass Media and Society*, ed. James Curran and Michael Gurevitch (London: Arnold, 2000), 242–60.

16. Determined from Bureau of Labor Statistics (http://www.bls.gov/) inflation calculator (http://www.bls.gov/data/#calculators), and rounded up to the nearest dollar, using 1930 and 1960 as reference points. By comparison, the median annual salary for all US-based reporters in 2014 was $36,000. Note that BLS data may not account for experience level (which previous data tended to do) and reflects starting salaries and also work in all mediums of journalism, not just print. Granted, the salary data from the 1920 to 1960 period used in this study reflects larger daily newspapers, which tended and still tend to pay better than smaller daily or weekly newspapers. See "Reporters, correspondents, and broadcast news analysts," Occupational Outlook Handbook, Bureau of Labor Statistics, http://www.bls.gov/ooh/media-and-communication/reporters-correspondents-and-broadcast-news-analysts.htm#tab-5, accessed February 15, 2016. Note that estimates were revised for the BLS calculator in 2020 where needed.

17. For a thorough discussion of the successes and failures of this program, see Gwyneth Mellinger, *Chasing Newsroom Diversity: From Jim Crow to Affirmative Action* (Urbana: University of Illinois Press, 2013).

18. Fred Carroll, *Race News: Black Journalists and the Fight for Racial Justice in the Twentieth Century* (Urbana: University of Illinois Press, 2017), 206.

19. Carroll, *Race News*, 206.

20. Gerald Horne, *The Rise and Fall of the Associated Negro Press: Claude Barnett's Pan-African News and the Jim Crow Paradox* (Urbana: University of Illinois Press, 2017); Calvin L. Hall, *African American Journalists: Autobiography as Memoir and Manifesto* (Lanham, MD: Scarecrow Press, 2009).

21. Hall, *African American Journalists*, 74.

22. Hall, 98.

23. Abbott. Abbott's "jurisdictional approach" remains current for scholars of the sociology of occupations and work. For a more extended discussion of the concept of "professionalization" in the newsroom, see Silvio Waisbord's *Reinventing Professionalism: Journalism and News in Global Perspective* (Cambridge, UK: Polity Press, 2013), 80–93. Randal Beam's *Journalism Professionalism as an Organizational-Level Concept* (Columbia, SC: Association for Education in Journalism and Mass Communication, 1990) also remains relevant and useful for understanding how power dynamics worked out in the newsroom.

24. Bonnie Brennen, *For the Record: An Oral History of Rochester, New York, Newsworkers* (New York: Fordham University Press, 2001).

25. Mellinger, *Chasing Newsroom Diversity.*

26. For good examples, see Beth Kaszuba, "'Mob Sisters': Women Reporting on Crime in Prohibition-era Chicago" (PhD diss., Pennsylvania State University, 2013) and Hall.

27. Dooley, *Taking Their Political Place*, 25–26, 126.

28. Usher, "Newsroom Moves," 1005–21.

29. John Nerone and Kevin G. Barnhurst, "U.S. Newspaper Types, the Newsroom, and the Division of Labor, 1750–2000," *Journalism Studies* 4, no. 4 (November 2003): 435–49.

30. As just a few examples of journalism-studies scholarship indicate, newsrooms continue to fascinate researchers: Nikki Usher, *Making News at The New York Times* (Ann Arbor: University of Michigan Press, 2014); David Ryfe, *Can Journalism Survive? An Inside Look at American Newsrooms* (Cambridge, UK: Polity Press, 2012); C. W. Anderson, *Rebuilding the News: Metropolitan Journalism in the Digital Age* (Philadelphia: Temple University Press, 2013); Pablo J. Boczkowski, *News at Work: Imitation in an Age of Information Abundance* (Chicago: University of Chicago Press, 2010). Other recent studies that touch on newsroom culture and its relevance for the changing journalism landscape in the United States include: Stamm, *Dead Tree Media*; Kevin Lerner, *Provoking the Press: (MORE) Magazine and the Crisis of Confidence in American Journalism* (Columbia: University of Missouri Press, 2019); Matthew Pressman, *On Press: The Liberal Values That Shaped the News* (Cambridge, MA: Harvard University Press, 2018); Matt Carlson, *Journalistic Authority: Legitimating News in the Digital Era* (New York: Columbia University Press, 2017); Julia Guarneri, *Newsprint Metropolis: City Papers and the Making of Modern Americans* (Chicago: University of Chicago Press, 2017).

31. On the Media, "Behind the Panama papers," WNYC, April 6, 2016, http://www.wnyc.org/story/behind-panama-papers/, accessed April 26, 2016.

32. Mel Bunce, Kate Wright, and Martin Scott, "'Our Newsroom in the Cloud': Slack, Virtual Newsrooms and Journalistic Practice," *New Media & Society* 20, no. 9 (September 2018): 3381–99.

33. Mel Bunce, "Management and Resistance in the Digital Newsroom," *Journalism* 20, no. 7 (February 2017): 890–905.

34. Hanaa' Tameez, "Six McClatchy Newspapers and Its DC Bureau Will Vacate Their Offices, Leaving Journalists Working Remotely Until at Least 2021," *Nieman Lab*, June 10, 2020, https://www.niemanlab.org/2020/06/six-mcclatchy-newspapers-and-its-dc-bureau-will-vacate-their-offices-leaving-journalists-working-remotely-until-at-least-2021/; a number of news stories throughout the 2020–21 coronavirus pandemic focused on the closing of physical newsrooms as cost-saving measures, but there are a number of newsrooms that—despite pressure to the contrary—have kept these newsrooms open, or have reopened them.

35. Herbert J. Gans, *Deciding What's News: A Study of CBS Evening News, NBC Nightly News, Newsweek, and Time*, 2nd ed.(Evanston, IL: Northwestern University Press, 2004); Gaye Tuchman, *Making News: A Study in the Construction of Reality* (New York: Free Press, 1978). There are other, later examples of solid ethnographic work into the 1980s and beyond. For a summary of this literature, see Sarah Stonbely, "The Social and Intellectual Contexts of the U.S. 'Newsroom Studies,' and the Media Sociology of Today," *Journalism Studies* 16; no. 2 (March 2015): 259–74.

36. Mellinger.

37. Robert A. Willier, "Dean Williams' Last Class Lecture Described by Former Student," *Editor & Publisher*, August 10, 1935, 12.

**APPENDIX**

1. Sources: "Earnings in Journalism," *Journalism Bulletin* 2, no. 4 (January 1926): 29–33; "Journalism Is Broad Road to Fame but Wealth Lies Outside: Young Reporters Must Become Fiction Writers, Executive or Owner or Be Content with a Top Salary of $3,000 at 45, Journalism Teachers' Committee Reports," *Editor & Publisher*, February 6, 1926, 20; "News Workers among Highest Paid on Newspapers, A.N.P.A. Tells NRA," *Editor & Publisher*, December 8, 1934, 5, 31; "Survey by N.Y. Guild Shows Average Pay," *Editor & Publisher*, May 5, 1934, 6; "A.N.P.A. Survey Shows Editorial Wages," *Editor & Publisher*, May 5, 1934, 10, 37; "Editorial: Editorial Pay," *Editor & Publisher*, October 13, 1934, 24; "Salaries and Working Conditions of Newspaper Editorial Employees," *Monthly Labor Review*, published by the US Bureau of Labor Statistics, May 1935, 1137–48; C. E. Shuford, "Do Newspapers Pay? Three Studies Show the $30 Cub Only a Myth: A Newsroom May Not Be a Royal Road to Riches, but It Has Been Maligned, Texas Surveys Indicate," *Quill*, May 1955, 11; Charles T. Duncan, "Slight Drop in Demand for Journalism Graduates," *Journalism Quarterly* 35, no. 4 (December 1958): 469–71; Charles T. Duncan, "Newspapers Slipping as No. 1 Outlet for Journalism Graduates," *Journalism Quarterly* 36, no. 4 (December 1959): 476–78; "Manpower Today and Tomorrow: Personnel Panel," *Red Book*, APME, August 12–15, 1959, 47–55; Charles A. Perlik Jr., "Newspaper Guild Now in 26th Year," *Quill*, November 1959,

70, 81–82; "Manpower Recruiting, Pay and Turnover: Personnel Panel," *Red Book*, APME, November 15–19, 1960, 46. Note that this data is for 1926 white-collar business workers, and so see Robert A. Margo, "Table B 4320–4334, Annual Earnings in Selected Industries and Occupations: 1890–1926," in *Historical Statistics of the United States*, Millennial Edition Online, ed. Susan B. Carter et al. (Cambridge, UK: Cambridge University Press, 2006). Data based on Paul H. Douglas, *Real Wages in the United States, 1890–1926* (Boston: Houghton Mifflin, 1930).

2. Salary data was generally gathered from later in the decade whenever possible to reflect change over time. Where possible, comparable cases were used. There may be slight inflation due to the fact that many figures were from ANG-negotiated contracts; specific examples are used where possible. The "Midwest" is defined as parts of the Southwest, and "non-NYC East" included big cities (with newspapers with one hundred thousand circulation or more) outside of New York (i.e., cities such as Baltimore and Philadelphia). Bolded numbers are estimated. Data is incomplete for some years and categories.

Sources: Marlen Pew, "Shop Talk at Thirty," *Editor & Publisher*, July 13, 1929, 70; "Capitol Guild, Daily Reach Agreement," *Editor & Publisher*, January 11, 1936, 30; "Baltimore Hearst Papers Sign with Editorial Group," *Editor & Publisher*, April 2, 1939, 26; "*Detroit Times* Giving $62,000 in Pay Raises," *Editor & Publisher*, September 28, 1946, 48; Schulman, *Where's Sammy?*, 6; "Bargaining Policy up at Guild Meet," *Editor & Publisher*, April 7, 1934, 11, 38; "Survey by N.Y. Guild Shows Average Pay," *Editor & Publisher*, May 5, 1934, 6; "Ten Metropolitan Dailies Post Minimum Wages, Hours Notices," *Editor & Publisher*, December 12, 1936, 8; "*Indianapolis Star* Starts New Wage, Hour Schedule," *Editor & Publisher*, July 10, 1937, 16; "News Workers among Highest Paid on Newspapers, A.N.P.A. Tells NRA," *Editor & Publisher*, December 8, 1934, 5, 31; "*Boston Herald-Traveler* Signs Guild Contract," *Editor & Publisher*, February 19, 1938, 45; "*Buffalo News* Signs Contract with Guild," *Editor & Publisher*, July 15, 1944, 40; "N.Y. Sun Grants $100 minimum for Reporters," *Editor & Publisher*, February 8, 1947, 62; "$3–$6 Raises Given on 2 Detroit Papers," *Editor & Publisher*, February 23, 1952, 10; Charles A. Perlik Jr., "Newspaper Guild Now in 26th Year," *Quill*, November 1959, 80; Irving Brant, "Where Are the Copy Readers of Tomorrow?" *Editor & Publisher*, June 19, 1920, 5; "Phila. Ledger Signs Guild Shop Contract," *Editor & Publisher*, August 5, 1939; "*San Francisco News* Sets Minimum Wage Levels; Guild Is 'Gratified,'" *Editor & Publisher*, November 14, 1936, 10; "*Baltimore Sun* Signs Its First Guild Contract," *Editor & Publisher*, September 3, 1949, 9; "Guild Starts Talks with *N.Y. Times*," *Editor & Publisher*, August 20, 1960, 62; "Raise for Scranton Newswriters," *Editor & Publisher*, August 20, 1921, 11; "Scranton News Writers Get New Wage Scale," *Editor & Publisher*, August 18, 1923, 10; "Two Hearst Dailies Post Minimums," *Editor & Publisher*, December 26, 1936, 4; "New Orleans Item Signs Guild Contract," *Editor & Publisher*, March 28, 1953, 44; "Feeling the Pulse of a Dying Daily," *Editor & Publisher*, September 3, 1927, 11; "Three Tacoma Papers Post Wage Supplements," *Editor & Publisher*, May 8, 1937, 45; "One-Year Contract Signed with Guild in Milwaukee," *Editor & Publisher*, July 10, 1937, 43; "No *World-Telegram* Guild

Contract," *Editor & Publisher*, October 27, 1934, 5; "$70 Scale for 5-year Reporters in Knoxville," *Editor & Publisher*, February 22, 1947, 38; "Guild Contracts Signed by *N.Y. Mirror*, U.P.," *Editor & Publisher*, May 24, 1941, 14; C. E. Shuford, "Do Newspapers Pay? Three Studies Show the $30 Cub Only a Myth: A Newsroom May Not Be a Royal Road to Riches, but It Has Been Maligned, Texas Surveys Indicate," *Quill*, May 1955, 11; "*Boston Herald-Traveler* Signs Guild Contract," *Editor & Publisher*, February 19, 1938, 45; "Report and Rulings of the Commission" in the case of the *Buffalo Evening News* and the Buffalo Newspaper Guild, 9; Elias E. Sugarman, *Opportunities in Journalism* (New York: Grosset & Dunlap, 1951), 58.

# Bibliography


#### TRADE PUBLICATIONS AND OTHER PRIMARY SOURCE JOURNALS

*Bulletin* (ASNE)
*Editor & Publisher* (adsorbed the *Journalist* in 1907, *Newspaperdom* and *Advertising* in 1925, and the *Fourth Estate* in 1927)
*Guild Reporter* (ANG)
*Journalism Quarterly* (*JQ*)
*Nieman Reports* (Nieman Foundation at Harvard)
*Problems of Journalism* (ASNE)
*Red Book* (APME)
*Quill* (Sigma Delta Chi, i.e., the Society of Professional Journalists, or SDC, i.e., SPJ)

#### ARCHIVES AND SPECIAL COLLECTIONS CONSULTED

DePauw University Archives and Special Collections, Greencastle, Indiana
National Archives at College Park, Maryland.
National Archives-Pacific Northwest Region, Seattle, Washington
University of Oregon Knight Library, Eugene, Oregon
University of Washington Special Collections, Seattle

#### MEMOIRS CONSULTED

This list is built from a larger collated list based on several journalism bibliographies. The memoirs on this list have been closely read to corroborate other primary and secondary sources. See "Note on Sources" for more details.

Gelb, Arthur. *City Room*. New York: Putnam, 2003.
McIntosh, India. "Girl Reporter." In *Late City Edition*, edited by Joseph G. Herzberg, 47–55. New York: Henry Holt and Company, 1947.
Mencken, H. L. *Newspaper Days 1899–1906*. New York: Alfred A. Knopf, 1955.
Patterson, Grove. *I Like People: The Autobiography of Grove Patterson*. New York: Random House, 1954.
Rowan, Carl T. *Breaking Barriers: A Memoir*. New York: Little, Brown, 1991.
Schulman, Sammy. *Where's Sammy?* Edited by Robert Considine. New York: Random House, 1943.

Schuyler, Philippa Duke. *Adventures in Black and White*. Edited by Tara Betts. New York: Intercultural Alliance of Artists and Scholars, 2018. First published 1960 by Robert Speller & Sons (New York).

Sontheimer, Morton. *Newspaperman: A Book about the Business*. New York: McGraw-Hill, 1941.

Underwood, Agness. *Newspaperwoman*. New York: Harper & Brothers, 1949.

Walker, Stanley. *City Editor*. New York: Frederick A. Stokes Company, 1934.

## SECONDARY SOURCES

Abbott, Andrew. *The System of Professions: An Essay on the Division of Expert Labor*. Chicago: University of Chicago Press, 1988.

Adams, Frank S. "The Job of the Reporter." In Garst, *The Newspaper*, 109–24.

Aldridge, Meryl. "The Tentative Hell-Raisers: Identity and Mythology in Contemporary UK Press Journalism." *Media, Culture & Society* 20, no. 1 (January 1998): 109–27.

Ames, William E., and Roger Simpson. *Unionism or Hearst: The Seattle Post-Intelligencer Strike of 1936*. Seattle: Pacific Northwest Labor History Association, 1978.

Ananny, Mike. "Networked News Time: How Slow—or Fast—Do Publics Need News to Be?" *Digital Journalism*. Published online, February 2016: 1–18. https://doi.org/10.1080/21670811.2015.1124728.

Anderson, C. W. "Newsroom Ethnography and Historical Context." In *Remaking the News: Essays on the Future of Journalism Scholarship in the Digital Age*, edited by Pablo J. Boczkowski and C. W. Anderson, 61–79. Cambridge, MA: MIT Press, 2017.

———. *Rebuilding the News: Metropolitan Journalism in the Digital Age*. Philadelphia: Temple University Press, 2013.

Anderson, C. W., and Juliette De Maeyer, "Objects of Journalism and the News." *Journalism* 16, no. 1 (August 2014): 3–9.

Anderson, Chris, Emily Bell, and Clay Shirky. "Post Industrial Journalism: Adapting to the Present." Tow Center for Digital Journalism, 2012. http://towcenter.org/research/post-industrial-journalism-adapting-to-the-present-2/.

Baker, Thomas Harrison. *The Memphis Commercial Appeal: The History of a Southern Newspaper*. Baton Rouge: Louisiana State University Press, 1971.

Baldwin, Hanson. "The Job of the Specialist." In Garst, *The Newspaper*, 146–61.

Barnhurst, Kevin G. *Mister Pulitzer and the Spider: Modern News from Realism to the Digital*. Urbana: University of Illinois Press, 2016.

Barthel, Michael, Ruth Moon, and William Mari. "Who Retweets Who? How Digital and Legacy Journalists Interact on Twitter." Tow Center for Digital Journalism. Accessed Feb. 1, 2014. http://towcenter.org/research/who-retweets-whom-how-digital-and-legacy-journalists-interact-on-twitter/.

Bastian, George C., and Leland D. Case. *Editing the Day's News: An Introduction to Newspaper Copyreading, Headline Writing, Illustration, Makeup, and General Newspaper Methods*. New York: Macmillan, 1932.

Bates, Stephen. *An Aristocracy of Critics: Luce, Hutchins, Niebuhr, and the Committee That Redefined Freedom of the Press*. New Haven, CT: Yale University Press, 2020.

———. "Prejudice and the Press Critics: Colonel Robert McCormick's Assault on the Hutchins Commission." *American Journalism* 36, no. 4 (November 2019): 420–46.

Battles, Kathleen. *Calling All Cars: Radio Dragnets and the Technology of Policing*. Minneapolis: University of Minnesota Press, 2010.

Beam, Randal A. *Journalism Professionalism as an Organizational-Level Concept*. Columbia, SC: Association for Education in Journalism and Mass Communication, 1990.

Beniger, James R. *The Control Revolution: Technological and Economic Origins of the Information Society*. Cambridge, MA: Harvard University Press, 1986.

Berger, Peter L., and Thomas Luckmann. *The Social Construction of Reality: A Treatise in the Sociology of Knowledge*. Garden City, NY: Doubleday, 1966.

Blanchard, Margaret A. *The Hutchins Commission: The Press and the Responsibility Concept*. Lexington, KY: Association for Education in Journalism, 1977.

Boczkowski, Pablo J. "The Material Turn in the Study of Journalism: Some Hopeful and Cautionary Remarks from an Early Explorer." *Journalism* 16, no. 1 (January 2015): 65–68.

———. *News at Work: Imitation in an Age of Information Abundance*. Chicago: University of Chicago Press, 2010.

Borstelmann, Thomas. *The Cold War and the Color Line: American Race Relations in the Global Arena*. Cambridge, MA: Harvard University Press, 2001.

Bourdieu, Pierre. *The Logic of Practice*. Translated by Richard Nice. Cambridge, UK: Polity Press, 1990.

Braverman, Harry. *Labor and Monopoly Capital: The Degradation of Work in the Twentieth Century*. New York: Monthly Review, 1974.

Breed, Warren. "The Newspaperman, News and Society." PhD diss., Columbia University, 1952.

———. "Social Control in the Newsroom: A Functional Analysis." *Social Forces* 33, no. 4 (May 1955): 326–35.

Brennen, Bonnie. *For the Record: An Oral History of Rochester, New York, Newsworkers*. New York: Fordham University Press, 2001.

———. "Newsworkers During the Interwar Era: A Critique of Traditional Media History." *Communication Quarterly* 43, no. 2 (Spring 1995): 197–209.

———. "Work in Progress: Labor and the Press in 1908." In *Journalism, 1908: Birth of a Profession*, edited by Betty H. Winfield, 147–61. Columbia: University of Missouri Press, 2008.

Britt, George. *Forty Years—Forty Millions: The Career of Frank A. Munsey*. New York: Farrar & Rinehart, 1935.

Broussard, Jinx C. *Giving a Voice to the Voiceless: Four Black Women Journalists, 1890–1950*. London: Routledge, 2003.

Bunce, Mel. "Management and Resistance in the Digital Newsroom." *Journalism* 20, no. 7 (February 2017): 890–905.

Bunce, Mel, Kate Wright, and Martin Scott. "'Our Newsroom in the Cloud': Slack, Virtual Newsrooms and Journalistic Practice." *New Media & Society* 20, no. 9 (September 2018): 3381–99.

Bureau of Labor Statistics, US Department of Labor. "CPI Inflation Calculator." Accessed March 3, 2020. http://www.bls.gov/data/inflation_calculator.htm.

Campbell, Erica Fahr. "The First Photograph of an Execution by Electric Chair." *Time*, April 10, 2014. http://time.com/3808808/first-photo-electric-chair-execution/.

Carlson, Matt. *Journalistic Authority: Legitimating News in the Digital Era*. New York: Columbia University Press, 2017.

Carroll, Fred. *Race News: Black Journalists and the Fight for Racial Justice in the Twentieth Century*. Urbana: University of Illinois Press, 2017.

Carter, Susan B. "Table Ba4440–4483, Hourly and Weekly Earnings of Production Workers in Manufacturing, by Industry: 1947–1999," in Carter et al., *Historical Statistics* (online, no page numbers).

Carter, Susan, et al., eds., *Historical Statistics of the United States*, Millennial Edition Online. Cambridge, UK: Cambridge University Press, 2006. https://hsus.cambridge.org/HSUSWeb/HSUSEntryServlet.

Chandler, Alfred D., Jr. *The Visible Hand: The Managerial Revolution in American Business.* Cambridge, MA: Belknap, 1977.

Clayton, Charles C. *Fifty Years for Freedom: The Story of Sigma Delta Chi's Service to American Journalism, 1909–1959*. Carbondale: Southern Illinois University Press, 1959.

Darnton, Robert. "Writing News and Telling Stories." *Daedalus* 104, no. 2 (Spring 1975): 175–94.

Dickinson, Roger. "Accomplishing Journalism: Towards a Revived Sociology of a Media Occupation." *Cultural Sociology* 1, no. 2 (July 2007): 189–208.

Dilts, Marion May. *The Telephone in a Changing World*. New York: Longmans, Green, 1941.

Dooley, Patricia L. *Taking Their Political Place: Journalists and the Making of an Occupation*. Westport, CT: Greenwood Press, 1997.

Dudziak, Mary L. *Cold War Civil Rights: Race and the Image of American Democracy*. Princeton, NJ: Princeton University Press, 2000.

Earl, Jennifer, and Katrina Kimport. *Digitally Enabled Social Change: Activism in the Internet Age*. Cambridge, MA: MIT Press, 2011.

Edwards, Richard. *Contested Terrain: The Transformation of the Workplace in the Twentieth Century*. New York: Basic Books, 1979.

Ehrlich, Matthew C., and Joe Saltzman. *Heroes and Scoundrels: The Image of the Journalist in Popular Culture*. Urbana: University of Illinois Press, 2015.

Emery, Edwin. *History of the American Newspaper Publishers Association*. Minneapolis: University of Minnesota Press, 1950.

Ericson, Staffan, and Kristina Riegert, eds. *Media Houses: Architecture, Media, and the Production of Centrality*. New York: Peter Lang, 2010.

Fedler, Fred. *Lessons from the Past: Journalists' Lives and Work, 1850–1950*. Prospect Heights, IL: Waveland Press, 2000.

Forde, Kathy Roberts. "Communication and the Civil Sphere: Discovering Civil Society in Journalism Studies." *Journal of Communication Inquiry* 39, no. 2 (April 2015): 113–24.

Friedman, Barbara. "Editor's Note: Is That a Thing? The Twitching Document and the Talking Object." *American Journalism* 31, no. 3 (September 2014): 307–11.

Gade, Peter. "Newspapers and Organizational Development: Management and Journalist Perceptions of Newsroom Cultural Change." *Journalism & Communication Monographs* 6, no. 1 (March 2004): 3–55.

Galenson, Walter. *The CIO Challenge to the AFL: A History of the American Labor Movement, 1935–1941*. Cambridge, MA: Harvard University Press, 1960.

Gans, Herbert J. *Deciding What's News: A Study of CBS Evening News, NBC Nightly News, Newsweek, and Time*. 2nd ed. Evanston, IL: Northwestern University Press, 2004.

Gardner, Burleigh B., and David G. Moore. *Human Relations in Industry*. Chicago: Richard D. Irwin, 1950.

Garst, Robert E. *The Newspaper: Its Making and Its Meaning*. New York: Charles Scribner's Sons, 1945.

Gieryn, Thomas F. "Boundary-Work and the Demarcation of Science from Non-science: Strains and Interests in Professional Ideologies of Scientists." *American Sociological Review* 48, no. 6 (December 1983): 781–95.

Giles, Robert H. *Newsroom Management: A Guide to Theory and Practice*. Indianapolis: R. J. Berg, 1987.

Gitelman, Lisa. *Paper Knowledge: Toward a Media History of Documents*. Durham, NC: Duke University Press, 2014.

Glende, Philip M. "Labor Makes the News: Newspapers, Journalism, and Organized Labor, 1933–1955." PhD diss., University of Wisconsin, 2010.

———. "Labor Makes the News: Newspapers, Journalism, and Organized Labor, 1933–1955." *Enterprise & Society* 13, no. 1 (March 2012): 39–52.

———. "Labor Reporting and Its Critics in the CIO Years." *Journalism & Communication Monographs* 22, no. 1 (March 2020): 4–75.

Goddard, Michael. "Opening up the Black Boxes: Media Archeology, Anarchaeology and Media Materiality." *New Media & Society* 17, no. 11 (2015): 1761–76.

Gravengaard, Gitte. "The Metaphors Journalists Live By: Journalists' Conceptualization of Newswork." *Journalism* 13, no. 8 (November 2012): 1064–82.

Guarneri, Julia. *Newsprint Metropolis: City Papers and the Making of Modern Americans*. Chicago: University of Chicago Press, 2017.

Haber, Samuel. *Efficiency and Uplift: Scientific Management in the Progressive Era, 1890–1920*. Chicago: University of Chicago Press, 1964.

Halberstam, David. "The Education of a Journalist." *Columbia Journalism Review* 33, no. 4 (Nov.–Dec. 1994): 29–34.

Hall, Calvin L. *African American Journalists: Autobiography as Memoir and Manifesto*. Lanham, MD: Scarecrow Press, 2009.

Hallin, Daniel C. "Commercialism and Professionalism in the American News Media." In *Mass Media and Society*, edited by James Curran and Michael Gurevitch, 242–60. London: Arnold, 2000.

Hallin, Daniel C., and Paolo Mancini. *Comparing Media Systems: Three Models of Media and Politics*. Cambridge, UK: Cambridge University Press, 2004.
Hamilton, C. Denis. "The Making of a Newspaper." In *The Kemsley Manual of Journalism*, 3–37. Ipswich, UK: Cassell, 1950.
Hanitzsch, Thomas. "Deconstructing Journalism Culture: Toward a Universal Theory." *Communication Theory* 17, no. 4 (November 2007): 367–85.
Harcup, Tony, and Deirdre O'Neill. "What Is News? Galtung and Ruge Revisited." *Journalism Studies* 2, no. 2 (May 2001): 261–80.
Hardt, Hanno, and Bonnie Brennen. "Newswork, History, and Photographic Evidence: A Visual Analysis of a 1930s Newsroom." In *Picturing the Past: Media, History, and Photography*, edited by Bonnie Brennan and Hanno Hardt, 11–35. Urbana: University of Illinois Press, 1999.
———, eds. *Newsworkers: Toward a History of the Rank and File*. Minneapolis: University of Minnesota Press, 1995.
Harvey, David. *The Condition of Postmodernity: An Enquiry into the Origins of Cultural Change*. Cambridge, MA: Blackwell, 1991, 1992.
———. *Spaces of Global Capitalism: Towards a Theory of Uneven Geographical Development*. London: Verso, 2006.
Haywood, D'Weston. *Let Us Make Men: The Twentieth-Century Black Press and a Manly Vision for Racial Advancement*. Chapel Hill: University of North Carolina Press, 2018.
Herzberg, Joseph G., ed. *Late City Edition*. New York: Henry Holt, 1947.
Hornberger, Donald J., and Douglass W. Miller. *Newspaper Organization*. Delaware, OH: Bureau of Business Service, Ohio Wesleyan University, 1930.
Horne, Gerald. *The Rise and Fall of the Associated Negro Press: Claude Barnett's Pan-African News and the Jim Crow Paradox*. Urbana: University of Illinois Press, 2017.
Innis, Harold. *The Bias of Communication*. Toronto: University of Toronto Press, 1951, 2006.
Irwin, Will. *The American Newspaper*. Ames: Iowa State University Press, 1911, 1969.
James, Edwin L. "The Organization of a Newspaper." In Garst, *The Newspaper*, 3–21.
Jones, Charles R. *Facsimile*. New York: Rinehart Books, 1949.
"Journalism School Graduates." *American Editor*, New England Society of Newspaper Editors, April 1960. Inside front cover (no page number).
Kaszuba, Beth. "'Mob Sisters': Women Reporting on Crime in Prohibition-Era Chicago." PhD diss., Pennsylvania State University, 2013.
Keith, Susan. "Horseshoes, Stylebooks, Wheels, Poles, and Dummies: Objects of Editing Power in 20th-Century Newsrooms." *Journalism* 16, no. 1 (January 2015): 44–60.
Kielbowicz, Richard B. "Regulating Timeliness: Technologies, Laws, and the News, 1840–1970." *Journalism & Communication Monographs* 17, no. 1 (February 2015): 5–83.

Kihss, Peter. "General Assignment." In Herzberg, *Late City Edition*, 36–55.
Kuczun, Sam. "History of the American Newspaper Guild." PhD diss., University of Minnesota, 1970.
Kuhn, Thomas S. *The Structure of Scientific Revolutions*. 3rd ed. Chicago: University of Chicago Press, 1996.
Lakoff, George, and Mark Johnson, *Metaphors We Live By*. Chicago: University of Chicago Press, 1980.
Latour, Bruno. *Reassembling the Social: An Introduction to Actor-Network-Theory*. Oxford: Oxford University Press, 2007.
Leab, Daniel J. *A Union of Individuals: The Formation of the American Newspaper Guild, 1933–1936*. New York: Columbia University Press, 1970.
Lebovic, Sam. *Free Speech and Unfree News: The Paradox of Press Freedom in America*. Cambridge, MA: Harvard University Press, 2016.
Lee, Alfred McClung. *The Daily Newspaper in America: The Evolution of a Social Instrument*. New York: Macmillan, 1937.
Lefebvre, Henri. *The Production of Space*. Translated by Donald Nicholson-Smith. Cambridge, MA: Blackwell, 1991.
Lent, Henry B. *I Work on a Newspaper*. New York: MacMillan, 1948.
Leonard, Thomas C. *News for All: America's Coming-of-Age with the Press*. New York: Oxford University Press, 1995.
Lerner, Kevin. *Provoking the Press: (MORE) Magazine and the Crisis of Confidence in American Journalism*. Columbia: University of Missouri Press, 2019.
Liebling, A. J. *The Press*. New York: Ballantine, 1961.
Linder, Marc. *"Time and a Half's the American Way": A History of the Exclusion of White-Collar Workers from Overtime Regulation, 1868–2004*. Iowa City: Fănpìhuà Press, 2004.
Lippmann, Walter. *Liberty and the News*. 1920. New York: Dover, 2010.
Lutz, William W. *The News of Detroit: How a Newspaper and a City Grew Together*. Boston: Little, Brown, 1973.
Lyons, Louis M. *Newspaper Story: One Hundred Years of The Boston Globe*. Cambridge, MA: Belknap, 1971.
MacCarthy, James Philip. *The Newspaper Worker: A Manual for All Who Write*. New York: Frank-Maurice, 1925.
MacDougall, Robert, *The People's Network: The Political Economy of the Telephone in the Gilded Age*. Philadelphia: University of Pennsylvania Press, 2014.
*Manual of Newspaper Job Classifications*. Washington, DC: United States Department of Labor Wage and House and Public Contracts Divisions, April 1943.
Margo, Robert A. "Table Ba4320–4334, Annual Earnings in Selected Industries and Occupations: 1890–1926," in Carter et al., *Historical Statistics of the United States*.
Mari, Will. "'Bright and Inviolate': Editorial-Business Divides in Early Twentieth-Century Journalism Textbooks." *American Journalism* 31, no. 3 (September 2014): 378–99.
———. "An Enduring Ethos." *Journalism Practice* 9, no. 5 (September 2015): 687–703.

———. *A Short History of Disruptive Journalism Technologies*. London: Routledge, 2019.

———. "Technology in the Newsroom." *Journalism Studies* 19, no. 9 (July 2018): 1366–89.

———. "Unionization in the American Newsroom, 1930 to 1960." *Journal of Historical Sociology* 31, no. 3 (September 2018): 265–81.

Marvin, Carolyn. *When Old Technologies Were New: Thinking about Electric Communication in the Late Nineteenth Century*. New York: Oxford University Press, 1990.

Marzolf, Marion. *Civilizing Voices: American Press Criticism, 1880–1950*. New York: Longman, 1991.

Massey, Doreen. *For Space*. London: Sage, 2005.

———. *Space, Place, and Gender*. Minneapolis: University of Minnesota Press, 1994.

McChesney, Robert W., and Ben Scott, eds. *Our Unfree Press: 100 Years of Radical Media Criticism*. New York: New Press, 2004.

McColloch, Mark. *White Collar Workers in Transition: The Boom Years, 1940–1970*. Westport, CT: Greenwood Press, 1983.

Mellinger, Gwyneth. *Chasing Newsroom Diversity: From Jim Crow to Affirmative Action*. Urbana: University of Illinois Press, 2013.

Mills, C. Wright. *White Collar: The American Middle Class*. New York: Oxford University Press, 1951.

Mindich, David T. Z. *Just the Facts: How "Objectivity" Came to Define American Journalism*. New York: New York University Press, 1998.

Mirando, Joseph. "Journalism by the Book: An Interpretive Analysis of News Writing and Reporting Textbooks, 1867–1987." PhD diss., University of Southern Mississippi, 1992.

Nadworny, Milton J. *Scientific Management and the Unions, 1900–1932: A Historical Analysis*. Cambridge, MA: Harvard University Press, 1955.

Neal, Robert M. *News Gathering and News Writing*. New York: Prentice-Hall, 1942.

Nerone, John. "Does Journalism History Matter?" *American Journalism* 28, no. 4 (Summer 2011): 7–27.

———. "Why Journalism History Matters to Journalism Studies." *American Journalism* 30, no. 1 (April 2013): 15–28.

Nerone, John, and Kevin G. Barnhurst. "U.S. Newspaper Types, the Newsroom, and the Division of Labor, 1750–2000." *Journalism Studies* 4, no. 4 (November 2003): 435–49.

New York Public Library and Carl L. Cannon. *Journalism, A Bibliography*. New York: New York Public Library, 1924.

O'Hara, Thomas P. "The Cub." In Herzberg, *Late City Edition*, 14–15, 20–21.

O'Reilly, Carole, and Josie Vine. *Newsroom Design and Journalism Cultures in Australia and the UK: 1850–2010*. London: Routledge, forthcoming.

Örnebring, Henrik. "Technology and Journalism-as-Labor: Historical Perspectives." *Journalism* 11, no. 57 (February 2010): 57–74.

Örnebring, Henrik, and Michael Karlsson. "Journalistic Autonomy." In *The Oxford Research Encyclopedia of Communication*, edited by Henrik Örnebring, 762–78. New York: Oxford University Press, 2019.

Peters, Benjamin. "And Lead Us Not into Thinking the New Is New: A Bibliographic Case for New." *New Media and Society* 11, nos. 1–2 (February/March 2009): 13–30.

Pickard, Victor. *America's Battle for Media Democracy: The Triumph of Corporate Libertarianism and the Future of Media Reform*. New York: Cambridge University Press, 2015.

Pollard, James E. *Principles of Newspaper Management*. New York: McGraw-Hill, 1937.

Pressman, Matthew. *On Press: The Liberal Values That Shaped the News*. Harvard University Press, 2018.

Price, Jack. *News Pictures*. New York: Round Table Press, 1937.

Price, Warren C. *The Literature of Journalism, An Annotated Bibliography*. Minneapolis: University of Minnesota Press, 1959.

Price, Warren C., and Calder M. Pickett. *An Annotated Journalism Bibliography, 1958–1968*. Minneapolis: University of Minnesota Press, 1970.

Reich, Zvi. "Constrained Authors: Bylines and Authorship in News Reporting." *Journalism* 11, no. 6 (December 2010): 707–25.

Riley, Sam G. *Biographical Dictionary of American Newspaper Columnists*. Westport, CT: Greenwood Press, 1995.

Risley, Ford. "Newspapers and Timeliness." *American Journalism* 17, no. 4 (January 2000): 97–103.

Roberts, Gene, and Hank Klibanoff. *The Race Beat: The Press, the Civil Rights Struggle, and the Awakening of a Nation*. New York: Vintage, 2007.

Roessner, Amber, Rick Popp, Brian Creech, and Fred Blevens. "'A Measure of Theory?': Considering the Role of Theory in Media History." *American Journalism* 30, no. 2 (June 2013): 260–78.

Ross, Felecia Jones. "Black Press Scholarship: Where We Have Been, Where We Are, and Where We Need to Go." *American Journalism* 37, 3 (September 2020): 301–20.

Ross, Ishbel. *Ladies of the Press: The Story of Women in Journalism by an Insider*. New York: Harper, 1936.

Rosten, Leo. *The Washington Correspondents*. New York: Harcourt, Brace, 1937.

Rowan, Carl T. *Breaking Barriers: A Memoir*. New York: Little, Brown, 1991.

Rucker, Frank W., and Herbert Lee Williams. *Newspaper Organization and Management*. Ames: Iowa State College Press, 1955.

Ryfe, David. *Can Journalism Survive? An Inside Look at American Newsrooms*. Cambridge, UK: Polity Press, 2012.

Salcetti, Marianne. "Competing for Control of Newsworkers: Definitional Battles between the Newspaper Guild and the American Newspaper Publishers Association, 1937–1938." PhD diss., University of Iowa, 1992.

———. "The Emergence of the Reporter: Mechanization and the Devaluation of Editorial Workers." In Hardt and Brennen, *Newsworkers*, 48–74.

Sánchez-Aranda, José J., and Carlos Barrera. "The Birth of Modern Newsrooms in the Spanish Press." *Journalism Studies* 4, no. 4 (November 2003): 489–500.

Saval, Nikil. *Cubed: A Secret History of the Workplace*. New York: Doubleday, 2014.

Schaefer, Vernon G., and Willis Wissler. *Industrial Supervision—Controls*. New York: McGraw-Hill, 1941.

Schudson, Michael. *Discovering the News: A Social History of American Newspapers*. New York: Basic Books, 1978.

———. "What Sorts of Things Are Thingy? And What Sorts of Thinginess Are There? Notes on Stuff and Social Construction." *Journalism* 16, no. 1 (January 2015): 61–64.

Scott, Dale Benjamin. "Labor's New Deal for Journalism—The Newspaper Guild in the 1930s." PhD diss., University of Illinois at Urbana–Champaign, 2009.

Seidel, Chalet. "Representations of Journalistic Professionalism: 1865–1900." PhD diss., Case Western Reserve University, 2010.

Seitz, Don C. *Training for the Newspaper Trade*. Philadelphia: J. B. Lippincott, 1916.

Shoemaker, Pamela J., and Stephen D. Reese. *Mediating the Message in the 21st Century: A Media Sociology Perspective.* 3rd ed. New York: Routledge, 2014.

Smith, Anthony. *Goodbye, Gutenberg: The Newspaper Revolution of the 1980s*. New York: Oxford University Press, 1980.

Smythe, Ted Curtis. *The Gilded Age Press, 1865–1900*. Westport, CT: Praeger, 2003.

———. "The Reporter, 1880–1900: Working Conditions and Their Influence on the News." *Journalism History* 7, no. 1 (Spring 1980): 1–10.

Stamm, Michael. *Dead Tree Media: Manufacturing the Newspaper in Twentieth-Century North America*. Baltimore: Johns Hopkins University Press, 2018.

Steiner, Linda. *Construction of Gender in Newsreporting Textbooks, 1890–1990.* Columbia, SC: Association for Education in Journalism and Mass Communication, 1992.

———. "Gender at Work: Early Accounts by Women Journalists." *Journalism History* 12, no. 1 (Spring 1997): 2–12.

Stonbely, Sarah. "The Social and Intellectual Contexts of the U.S. 'Newsroom Studies,' and the Media Sociology of Today." *Journalism Studies* 16, no. 2 (March 2015): 259–74.

Sugarman, Elias E. *Opportunities in Journalism*. New York: Grosset & Dunlap, 1951.

Sumpter, Randall. *Before Journalism Schools: How Gilded Age Reporters Learned the Rules*. Columbia: University of Missouri Press, 2018.

———. "'Practical Reporting': Late Nineteenth Century Journalistic Standards and Rule Breaking." *American Journalism* 30, no. 1 (April 2013): 44–64.

Sweeney, Michael. *Secrets of Victory: The Office of Censorship and the American Press and Radio in World War II*. Chapel Hill: University of North Carolina Press, 2001.

Tameez, Hanaa'. "Six McClatchy Newspapers and Its DC Bureau Will Vacate Their Offices, Leaving Journalists Working Remotely until at Least 2021." *Nieman Lab*, June 10, 2020. https://www.niemanlab.org/2020/06/six-mcclatchy-newspapers-and-its-dc-bureau-will-vacate-their-offices-leaving-journalists-working-remotely-until-at-least-2021/.

Thayer, Frank. *Newspaper Management*. New York: D. Appleton-Century, 1938.

Tuchman, Gaye. *Making News: A Study in the Construction of Reality*. New York: Free Press, 1978.

Underwood, Doug. *When MBAs Ruled the Newsroom: How the Marketers and Managers Are Reshaping Today's Media*. New York: Columbia University Press, 1993.

Urray, John. "The Sociology of Space and Place." In *The Blackwell Companion to Sociology*, edited by Judith R. Blau, 3–15. Malden, MA: Blackwell, 2004.

Usher, Nikki. *Making News at The New York Times*. Ann Arbor: University of Michigan Press, 2014.

———. "Newsroom Moves and the Newspaper Crisis Evaluated: Space, Place, and Cultural Meaning." *Media, Culture & Society* 37, no. 7 (June 2015): 1005–21.

———. "Putting 'Place' in the Center of Journalism Research: A Way Forward to Understand Challenges to Trust and Knowledge in News." *Journalism & Communication Monographs* 21, no. 2 (June 2019): 84–146.

Villard, Oswald Garrison. *The Disappearing Daily: Chapters in American Newspaper Evolution*. New York: A.A. Knopf, 1944.

Wahl-Jorgensen, Karin. "News Production, Ethnography, and Power: On the Challenges of Newsroom-Centricity." In *The Anthropology of News and Journalism: Global Perspectives*, edited by S. Elizabeth Bird, 21–34. Bloomington: Indiana University Press, 2010.

Waisbord, Silvio. *Reinventing Professionalism: Journalism and News in Global Perspective*. Cambridge, UK: Polity Press, 2013.

Walker, Stanley. *City Editor*. New York: Blue Ribbon Books, 1934.

Wallace, Aurora. *Media Capital: Architecture and Communications in New York City*. Urbana: University of Illinois Press, 2012.

Warren, Carl N. *Modern News Reporting*. New York: Harper & Brothers, 1951.

———. *News Reporting: A Practice Book*. Harper & Brothers, 1929.

Weiss, Amy Schmitz, and David Domingo. "Innovation Processes in Online Newsrooms as Actor-Networks and Communities of Practice." *New Media & Society* 12, no. 7 (May 2010): 1156–71.

White, Richard. *Railroaded: The Transcontinentals and the Making of Modern America*. New York: W.W. Norton, 2011.

Wilds, John. *Afternoon Story: A Century of the New Orleans States-Item*. Baton Rouge: Louisiana State University Press, 1976.

Wilke, Jürgen. "The History and Culture of the Newsroom in Germany," *Journalism Studies* 4, no. 4 (November 2003): 465–77.

Wolseley, Roland Edgar. *The Journalist's Bookshelf; An Annotated and Selected Bibliography of United States Journalism*. New York: Chilton, 1961.

Wolseley, Roland Edgar, and Wolseley, Isabel. *The Journalist's Bookshelf: An Annotated and Selected Bibliography of United States Print Journalism*. 8th ed. Indianapolis: R. J. Berg, 1986.

Wood, Donald J. *Newspaper Personnel Relations*. Oakland, CA: Newspaper Research Bureau, 1952.

Wren, Daniel A. *The History of Management Thought*. Hoboken, NJ: Wiley, 2005.

Yates, JoAnne. *Control through Communication: The Rise of System in American Management*. Baltimore: Johns Hopkins University Press, 1989.

Yoder, Dale. *Personnel Management and Industrial Relations*. New York: Prentice-Hall, 1942.

Zaman, Akhteruz. "Newsroom as Battleground: Journalists' Description of Their Workspaces." *Journalism Studies* 15, no. 6 (March 2013): 819–34.

Zelizer, Barbie. "Journalists as Interpretative Communities." *Critical Studies in Mass Communication* 10 (September 1993): 219–37.

# Index

# About the Author

Will Mari is Assistant Professor of Media Law & History at the Manship School of Mass Communication at Louisiana State University. He is author of *A Short History of Disruptive Journalism Technologies: 1960–1990*, and *Newsrooms and the Disruption of the Internet: A Short History of Disruptive Technologies, 1990–2010*. He lives in Baton Rouge, Louisiana.